Olorgesailie

PREHISTORIC ARCHEOLOGY AND ECOLOGY

A Series Edited by Karl W. Butzer and Leslie G. Freeman

Olorgesailie
Archeological Studies of a Middle Pleistocene Lake Basin in Kenya

Glynn Ll. Isaac Assisted by Barbara Isaac

The view from the Ngong Hills westward into the Rift Valley. Mount Olorgesailie is the low dome in the distance.

The University of Chicago Press

Chicago and London

For my parents, Frances and Edwyn, who implanted

in me curiosity about history and natural history

GLYNN LL. ISAAC is professor of anthropology at the University of California. He served as deputy director at the Centre for Prehistory and Palaeontology in Nairobi from 1962-65 and has been working with Richard Leakey since 1970 as coleader of the Koobi Fora Research Project. Isaac is coeditor of *Human Origins: Louis Leakey and the East African Evidence; After the Australopithecines;* and *Earliest Man and Environments in the Lake Rudolf Basin.*

The University of Chicago Press, Chicago 60637
The University of Chicago Press, Ltd., London

©1977 by The University of Chicago
All rights reserved. Published 1977
Printed in the United States of America
81 80 79 78 77 987654321

Library of Congress Cataloging in Publication Data

Isaac, Glynn L 1937-
   Olorgesailie.

   (Prehistoric archeology and ecology)
   Bibliography: p.
   Includes index.
   1. Acheulian culture--Kenya--Olorgesailie National
Park. 2. Olorgesailie National Park, Kenya--Antiquities.
3. Kenya--Antiquities. I. Isaac, Barbara, joint author.
II. Title. III. Series.
GN772.4.A53I82   967.6'2   76-22962
ISBN 0-226-38483-7
ISBN 0-226-38484-5 pbk.

CONTENTS

ILLUSTRATIONS

Frontispiece   The view from the Ngong Hills westward

Plates
Following p. 96

Following p. 272

Figures

TABLES

SERIES EDITORS' FOREWORD

The 1960s saw great strides in the exacting excavation of a number of important mid-Pleistocene archeological residues. These include key Acheulean sites such as Kalambo Falls, Latamne, Terra Amata, Torralba and Ambrona, Amanzi Springs, and Olorgesailie. The last is a site cluster that provides a unique example of spatial archeology in this particular time-range. Originally produced in 1969 as Glynn Isaac's doctoral dissertation, the Olorgesailie study was long sought out by professionals and students alike in university microfilm archives or through borrowing of some of the rare bound copies. It is, therefore, a splendid service to all concerned that Isaac has revised and tailored the voluminous original to fit the scope and space limitations of the Prehistoric Archeology and Ecology Series.

The great majority of Acheulean sites represent open-air occupations, and almost all such sites pose serious problems of context. The majority were apparently situated in stream channels or are, at least, preserved in moderate to high-energy fluvial deposits. The Olorgesailie site complex is no exception, and the problem of context is, of course, critical in the final analysis. Isaac recognizes that several of the Olorgesailie occurrences have been reshuffled by "kinematic wave" action, so that they are not strictly in primary, undisturbed context. In several instances, he points out that reorientation and redistribution of the archeological materials by such fluvial sorting processes make it impossible to use the size or the nature of particular distributions as a guide to prehistoric population estimates or other sophisticated interpretations.

Given this fundamental problem, by no means unique to Olorgesailie, it is difficult to determine what activities were carried on at the various localities or where in the landscape the people lived. For example, if campsites were located on top of a river bank, which was subsequently undercut by stream erosion, the eroded materials might be redeposited like the pebbles of gravel bars along a mainly sandy streambed by the kinematic wave process. In such a case, the heavier archeological residues could potentially be aggregated at intervals along the streambed, with bare areas between aggregations; under such circumstances, the assumption that people were especially attracted to living on sandy channels would be misleading. Fortunately, such instances of problematical interpretation appear to be rare in the Olorgesailie basin. Nonetheless, the matter of disturbed associations, with mixing of discrete temporal aggregates, or spatial "jumbling" of contemporaneous materials, or both, remains a persistent problem in all fluvial sites. A "semi-primary"

xiii

context, with basic preservation of relative associations and only limited lateral movement or reorientation, can only be demonstrated by systematic study of the size classes, orientation, and inclination of all site macro-components.

Olorgesailie: Archeological Studies of a Middle Pleistocene Lake Basin in Kenya provides a wealth of information on mid-Pleistocene human activities and illustrates many of the problems faced in analyzing the materials and striving for reasonable conclusions. Isaac is to be congratulated for the finely balanced level of detail, the sober discussions of procedure, and the range of generalizations he offers. His careful documentation of this important site complex will be greatly appreciated by a broad spectrum of readers. In the years to come, *Olorgesailie* will surely be recognized as a milestone in the study of mid-Pleistocene archeological sites.

Karl W. Butzer
Leslie G. Freeman

ACKNOWLEDGMENTS

The research reported here was initiated by Drs. Louis and Mary Leakey, who discovered the archeological wealth of Olorgesailie and carried out the first investigation
there between 1942 and 1945. My continuation of the research was made possible by my appointment to a succession of research posts under the direction of the late Dr. Louis
Leakey.

I wish to acknowledge Dr. Leakey's generosity in offering so magnificent a research
opportunity to a young graduate student. Furthermore, I would like to express my appreciation of Dr. Leakey's forbearance in allowing me to take over and use my own initiative in
the development of a research program. Without the support, help, and encouragement of
both Louis and Mary Leakey, this investigation could not have been carried out. We regret
that Louis did not live to see this report published.

Throughout the research and the preparation of this report, my wife, Anne Barbara
Isaac, has shared the burden of work. Her contribution has been indispensable. She has
surveyed, drafted, edited, advised, typed, catered, and given encouragement. Without her
skill and tireless effort at the drawing board the illustrations could not have been so
thorough. She ought to be a joint author, but will not accept her dues.

R. M. Shackleton generously made available his geological maps and sections, and
these provided an invaluable and time-saving basis for my own stratigraphic work. B. H.
Baker, the late W. W. Bishop, R. L. Hay, R. W. Hey, and R. M. Shackleton have all given
valuable geological advice on field problems and on the preparation of reports.

The experiment in quantitative methods was partly inspired by C. B. M. McBurney, who
also, as the supervisor of my thesis research, gave me advice on aspects of method and
presentation. D. McClaren of the Cambridge University Department of Statistics gave me
useful advice on concepts and methods at an early stage of analysis. J. Tucker wrote a
program for reduction of data with the Titan computer in Cambridge.

Before the research in East Africa, D. A. Roe and I worked together on some pilot
studies of Acheulean material. The system of measurements which Roe (1964) proceeded to
elaborate has been of considerable value.

Conversations, in the field and elsewhere, with a number of scholars have proved a
valuable source of ideas. Among these scholars I include Grahame Clark, J. Desmond Clark,
the late D. L. Clarke, G. Cole, L. R. Freeman, M. R. Haldemann-Kleindienst, F. Clark Howell,
C. M. Keller, D. Pilbeam, D. A. Roe, and many others.

Financial support for field work came from the Boise Fund, Oxford; the Wenner-Gren Foundation, New York; and the British Institute of History and Archaeology in East Africa. The British Academy gave a small grant toward laboratory and writing-up expenses, and the Wenner-Gren Foundation furnished a stipend for a year I spent preparing the dissertation and the present publication.

In recognition of Louis Leakey's role as instigator of the Olorgesailie research, the L. S. B. Leakey Foundation of Pasadena has generously made a grant towards the cost of preparing this volume for publication. This help is gratefully acknowledged.

I received help from numerous persons and institutions in Kenya, including my parents, Dr. and Mrs. W. E. Isaac, the late Mrs. R. Savage (Shirley Coryndon), R. J. Clarke and the staff of the Centre for Prehistory and Palaeontology.

Mrs. Grace Buzaljko has helped patiently with the editorial aspects of converting this monograph from its original form as a thesis.

Further details of the background to my researches at Olorgesailie are set out in Appendix A, "A Brief History of Research at Olorgesailie."

While this volume was in press, death took three of those associated with the work: Shirley Coryndon, Bill Bishop and David Clarke. They were part of a goodly company whose enthusiasm and humour have sustained us. They will be sorely missed.

We shared the work of digging at Olorgesailie and all its vicissitudes with a crew of Kenyans under the foremanship of Kanyugi Ikenywa and Kanunga Mangea. We learned much from them.

Asante sana

1. BACKGROUND

This study of a complex of Acheulean sites at Olorgesailie was conducted as an experiment in the application of various concepts and techniques that are relatively new to
the investigation of Lower Paleolithic culture. Olorgesailie was suitable as a testing
ground because artifacts could be recovered from fine-grained sediments that had preserved
detailed evidences of archeological associations. These could be related to stratigraphy
and to features of the original environment. This preservation was in marked contrast to
the sites that have yielded most of the evidence on which the classic interpretations of
Middle Pleistocene culture had previously depended. Until recently, most hand axes found
in Africa, Asia, and Europe had been recovered from relatively coarse alluvial or littoral
deposits. Even those that were extracted from more promising contexts generally had provenance records concerning only position in a generalized vertical stratigraphic sequence.
Before 1960, we lacked almost entirely any published body of data relating to elementary
archeological features, such as the size, arrangement, or exact contents of a series of
Lower Paleolithic campsites. Hence it has been impossible to determine the degree to
which the contents of near contemporary associations resemble, or differ, from one another.
Clearly if we are ever to have any firmly based knowledge of human life in Lower and
Middle Pleistocene times, or if we are ever to place on a firm basis our classification of
early culture through the evidence of stone artifacts, then these gaps must be filled by
extensive systematic excavation. Preservation at Olorgesailie is not perfect, and some of
the material has been rearranged in varying degrees since its discard by prehistoric communities. However, the resolution is such that inquiries into some of the foregoing
topics could usefully be attempted.

One can conveniently distinguish two facets to research in Paleolithic prehistory.
The first type of study involves the recognition of specific stone-craft traditions. By
tracing sequential development in artifacts and changing geographic patterning, a version
of culture-history can be established which does not require knowledge of the economic
patterns on which the cultures depended. In contrast, the second type of study takes as
its focus of investigation the total ecological, economic, and sociological content of
prehistoric behavior. Artifacts are studied mainly in relation to their function in particular activities. In this type of study, the evidence from food refuse and settlement
patterns is just as important as the evidence from artifacts.

The two lines of inquiry are ultimately complementary, but the emphasis in studies

1

of the Paleolithic has hitherto been heavily culture-historical. Since the Olorgesailie research involved both types of investigation, a brief review of the state of knowledge in each field will help to define the objectives of the studies reported in this monograph.

Middle Pleistocene Culture-History: Assumptions and Problems

During the development of Lower Paleolithic studies, certain assumptions came to underlie many interpretations. These premises deserve consideration as guideposts to some fundamental problems that require investigation. The assumptions are seldom explicitly stated and have been subjected to very little critical examination (Isaac 1972b).

Investigation of Lower Paleolithic artifacts began effectively with Boucher de Perthes' paper of 1846 (Daniel 1950), but the science did not gain impetus or real significance until the advent of an acceptable evolutionary theory in 1859. Darwin's major work, published in that year, implied the existence of a transitionary period during which one or more species evolved physically in the direction of *Homo sapiens* and concurrently developed from possession of zero material culture to the achievement of the varied material culture universally associated with mankind in historic times. Simple stone artifacts of Pleistocene age were an important verification of this corollary hypothesis and were of great interest not only to archeologists but to paleontologists and geologists as well. In consequence, much of the development of the study has been influenced by paleontological concepts and assumptions, rather than by anthropological and archeological ones. In particular, there has grown up the conviction that stone artifacts, at every level of sophistication, constitute a sufficient basis for identifying cultural taxa, just as fossilized hard parts of organisms are used in the recognition of extinct biological taxa.

Moreover, a further assumption has tended to creep into paleolithic archeology. It has tacitly been supposed that there is a direct correspondence between distinctive stone artifact assemblages, or even single types, and distinct cultural taxa. This is a dubious proposition, but lack of adequate contemporary or historical data bearing on the actual relationship between artifact assemblages and cultural entities has made it impossible to investigate the assumption directly.

The idea that single types of stone tools (*fossiles directeurs*) or even specific percentage patterns of combinations of types as expressed, for example, in *graphiques cumulatives* are exclusively diagnostic for correspondingly defined paleocultural entities has often led to the interpretation of prehistory in terms of parallel, coexisting phyla. This type of hypothesis arises when a broad range of variant aggregates is found in each of a series of stratigraphic zones. If the analogy of genetic continuity is borrowed from paleontology, then each of the recurrent variants appears as a cultural lineage. However, unless the data include evidence for geographic or chronological segregation, anthropologists now tend to look on such parallel lineage constructs with skepticism.

A classic two-phyla theory of European culture in the middle and early Upper Pleistocene was formulated by Breuil (1932). Breuil's hypothesis, though in need of further testing, is anthropologically credible, as the two phyla appear to be appropriate to distinct geographic provinces (McBurney 1950). In Africa, an analogous cultural dichotomy has been postulated (Jones 1929) and considered by various authors (Alimen 1957; J. D. Clark 1950). The two proposed cultures were known as Acheulean ("Stellenbosch") and the Hope Fountain; but Hope Fountain industries are now generally, though not universally, regarded as distinctive activity facies of the Acheulean cultural entity (Clark 1959, 1970; Kleindienst 1961). The label Developed Oldowan (M. D. Leakey 1971) now seems to be replacing Hope Fountain.

In a critique of Breuil's two-phyla interpretation of European Middle Pleistocene prehistory called *l'évolution buissonnante*, Bordes (1950a) makes sound comment on the complexity of variation in industries of the period but later suggests an elaborate reticulate pattern of evolution and classification, which supposes that each observed variant assemblage fairly represents a cultural totality. Such elaborate exegesis of what is a small sample of sites widely scattered in space and time seems to me to have uncertain validity and it may obscure important features of the primary data.

Conceptual problems such as these have led me to question the existing taxonomy and nomenclature of Middle Pleistocene archeological materials. The difficulties stem first from the huge scale of the space-time continuum, from which very few good samples are available and secondly from uncertainty over the nature of the variants that are to be classified. Suffice it to say here that the concern of paleoanthropologists is turning away from technical questions of assemblage taxonomy and toward issues of cultural process and economic function.

The preservation at Olorgesailie of a number of artifact occurrences from a single locality and a restricted time span provides the opportunity for testing some of the most important assumptions which have hitherto underlain much research and interpretation. The studies of artifact assemblages reported in this volume are largely directed at clarifying the nature of variation and at exploring some possible lines of socioeconomic explanation for assemblage diversity.

Subsistence and Behavior during the Middle Pleistocene

Following the discoveries of Boucher de Perthes in the 1840s, the attention of archeologists was directed primarily to the history and classification of artifacts. However, an initial period of more catholic curiosity and speculative inquiry is evident in the writings of pioneers such as Sir John Lubbock (1865), Sir John Evans (1897), and G. de Mortillet (1883:248-52).

The meager conclusions reached concerning man's way of life during the Lower Paleolithic or River Drift period can be represented by a quotation from Sir John Evans (1897; 656-57), " . . . living, as in all probability man must have done, by the chase, his numbers must necessarily have been small as compared with those of the animals on which he subsisted . . . . The evidence seems to justify us in regarding these River Drift or Cave Folk as hunters and probably nomads." De Mortillet (1883:248) and other writers suggested that brutality, general economic deprivation, and an absence of articulate speech were features of Chellean life.

Studies during the first half of the twentieth century added little to the knowledge of the economy, ecology, and demography of human life in Middle Pleistocene times. The abundant Acheulean material from alluvial deposits does not readily sustain reconstructions of behavior other than stone-craft practices, and little effort was made to seek out and excavate sites where circumstances were more favorable. The textbooks of the early 1900s either entirely ignore aspects of Middle Pleistocene culture other than artifact morphology and geography (Burkitt 1933) or include a few brief remarks which differ little from the speculative conclusions of the previous century (cf. Osborn 1916:150; MacCurdy 1924:109-29; Peake and Fleure 1927:129-30; Davison 1934:52-57; and L. S. B. Leakey 1934:71-78, 88-99).

Studies of two individual sites constitute important exceptions to this generalization: Torralba in Spain (Cerralbo 1913; MacCurdy 1924; Obermaier 1925) and Choukoutien in

China (Black 1933; Breuil 1939; Movius 1948). Although these sites were not excavated in a way which would now be considered appropriate, they did demonstrate the possibility of direct documentation of the behavior and hunting practices of early man. However, systematic pursuit of such evidence was long delayed, and eventually it was in Africa that a movement in this direction began.

The excavations made by M. D. and L. S. B. Leakey at Olorgasailie in the years 1943-47 were formative in regenerating interest in the investigation of Acheulean ways of life. The exhibition excavations established at Olorgesailie were visited by the delegates to the 1947 Pan-African Congress and by numerous prehistorians in subsequent years. Thereafter other sites in Africa began to be excavated in a comparable fashion; for example, Olduvai Gorge (L. S. B. Leakey 1957; M. D. Leakey 1967, 1971), Kalambo Falls (J. D. Clark 1954, 1969b), Isimila (Howell et al. 1962), Cave of Hearths (Mason 1962), Montagu Cave (Keller 1973), Amanzi (H. Deacon 1970), and Melka Kunturé (Chavaillon 1974). More sites are shown in figure 1.

The first scholars to extend this research endeavor beyond Africa were those who had previously worked in Africa. Examples are the Torralba and Ambrona excavations in Spain from 1961 to 1966 (Howell 1966) and the Latamne excavations in Syria in 1962 and 1964 (J. D. Clark 1966). However, related research objectives have developed independently in other places: at Vértésszöllös in Hungary (Kretzoi and Vertes 1965), 'Ubeidiya in Israel (Stekelis 1966; Stekelis et al. 1969), and Terra Amata in France (de Lumley 1969, 1975).

Investigations into early Pleistocene culture in East Africa have also received considerable stimulus from the recent spate of discoveries of fossil hominids in the region and from the intensification of research into primate behavior. Both of these independent lines of inquiry have posed for the archeologist, challenging questions about the nature of early human behavior (cf. DeVore and Washburn 1963; Washburn 1965; Fox 1967; Isaac 1968, 1969, 1971, 1972a and b).

The archeological potential of carefully selected sites in East Africa and elsewhere is such that we can be confident that these questions can be answered from an accumulation of factual data. As will become apparent in the ensuing exposition of the Olorgesailie evidence, there are many aspects of the evidence from single sites or localized site complexes that cannot be immediately interpreted. The recurrence of similar features in other sites should lead to recognition of the behavior patterns represented.

The Plan of the Book

This report was first compiled as a rather lengthy thesis, which is available as a source of specific information and of discourse on methods (Isaac 1968). In the conversion from the dissertation to this book, I have made every effort to streamline the presentation, since I believe that our science will be best served by developing a tradition of publishing concise monographic reports, supported by archival depositions of highly specific information on sites.

Chapter 2 deals with geology, stratigraphy, dating, and what is known of the paleo-environmental circumstances under which the Middle Pleistocene peoples lived. Chapter 3, intended as a reference section, presents as succinct a summary as possible of the characteristics of each of the Olorgesailie excavated sites. Chapter 4 offers a summary of my interpretations of the sites in behavioral and ecological terms. I regard this as the single most interesting part of the study.

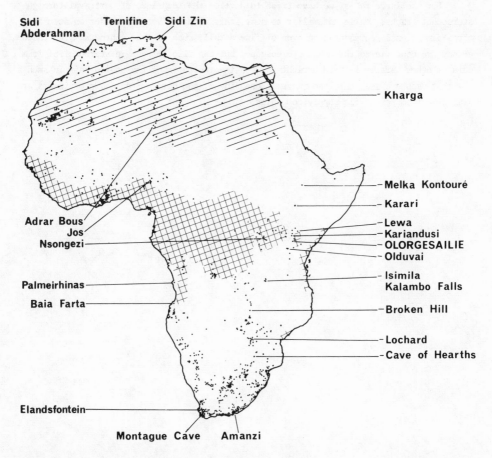

Figure 1. Map of Africa showing major Acheulean sites.

The next four chapters summarize the results of laboratory studies of the artifacts. Chapter 5 deals with general issues and with the comparative study of assemblage composition, and each of chapters 6, 7, and 8 deals with a major artifact class: bifaces and other large tools, small tools, and debitage (flakes and cores). Each of these chapters treats successively the internal differentiation of the class, the differences among Olorgesailie assemblages, and finally comparisons with data from other relevant sites.

The final chapter offers a commentary on the contribution of Olorgesailie to the resolution of general problems in Middle Pleistocene archeology.

There are six appendixes that provide a brief history of researches at Olorgesailie, technical reports, definitions of terminology, and additional technical data of various sorts.

I have tried to provide adequate graphic representation of sites and artifacts without inflating the bulk and cost of the book. Figures of the artifacts have been restricted to the role of facilitating the translation of attributes into a graphic sense of the morphology because I am confident that the numerical data provide clear information on assemblage characteristics.

For the large tools, we have tried to develop the technique of portrayal through stereophotographs. While unfamiliar to some, this method gives the reader an accurate three-dimensional representation even of fine detail, such as scar contours. The photographs are best viewed through a stereoscope, but can also be seen in stereorelief if a card or other barrier is held upright between the two parts of the stereo pair in such a way that each eye sees only the image on one side of the card. Stereoscopic viewers are available from scientific supply companies.

2. THE SETTING OF THE ARCHEOLOGICAL EVIDENCE
TOPOGRAPHY, GEOLOGY, AND ENVIRONMENTS

East Africa has extraordinarily favorable circumstances for preserving archeological evidence dating from the Lower and Middle Pleistocene. These circumstances are associated with the development of the Rift Valleys. Intermittent local subsidence of the earth's crust has repeatedly created lake basins and other traps for sediment. Volcanic vents within the Rift and along its margins have erupted alkaline and calcium-rich tuffs that have formed layered deposits favorable to the preservation of bone. Periodic earth movements have resulted in physiographic changes that shifted the areas of deposition and raised buried sediments and their fossil contents up into zones of erosion. As a result of these processes, sediments and volcanic formations ranging from Miocene to Holocene are exposed at different points along the course of the Rift.

The Olorgesailie sedimentary basin has been formed in this way. It is situated within the Eastern or Gregory Rift Valley at the southern end of that portion which traverses the Kenya highlands. Figures 2 and 3 show that the physiography and vegetation of the surrounding area are extremely diversified. Within a 40-mile radius of the sites, local precipitation varies from 380 mm to more than 1300 mm yearly. The valley is bounded by variable escarpments and has a rugged terrain with a jumble of lava ridges, small plains, and volcanic massifs (frontispiece). The floor of the Rift slopes up from its lowest point at Lake Magadi (altitude 604 m) to its highest point at Gilgil, 130 km north of Olorgesailie, where it attains an altitude of 2070 m. The Olorgesailie sites are at altitudes ranging from 940 m to 1040 m. The escarpment crests bounding this sector of the Rift slope from 1800 m above sea level at the latitude of Magadi to 3000 m or more at the latitude of Nakuru.

Most of the country carries some variety of *Acacia* savannah as its natural climax vegetation, though the plains to the east of the valley support grasslands, which have perhaps been extended by burning (Trump 1967). The escarpment crests carry dense woodland vegetation, which merges into extensive montane forests on the well-watered highlands. The floor of the Rift at the latitude of Olorgesailie can be characterized as semiarid. Evaporation far exceeds precipitation, and permanent water bodies such as Lake Magadi are strongly saline. Trump has classified the vegetation as "mixed acacia bushland," a variant of the widespread *Commiphora-Acacia* bushland characteristic of the arid parts of East Africa. Undergrowth is generally dense on the rock ridges and mountains. On the alluvial flats the nonarboreal vegetation fluctuates, and the grasses and annuals have great surges of growth during wet years (fig. 3).

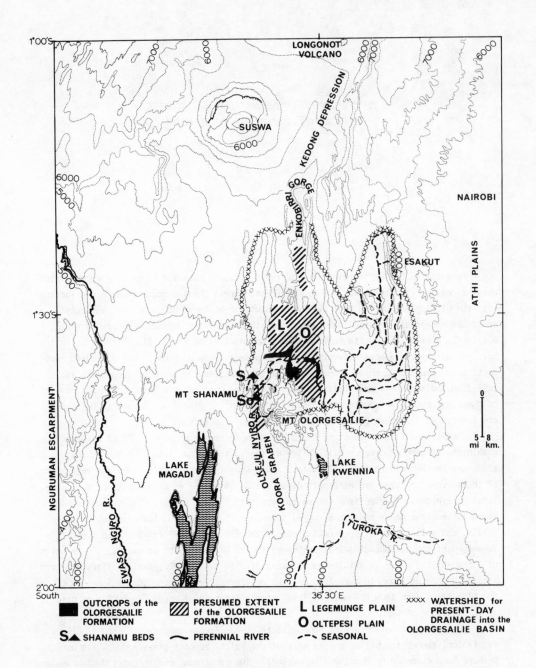

Figure 2. The topography of the Olorgesailie area.

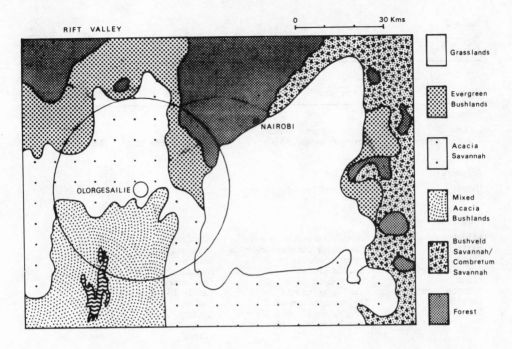

Figure 3. Vegetation zones in the Olorgesailie area (based on Trump 1967).

Perennial streams and rivers traverse the plains on either side of the Rift Valley. Some descend the western escarpment and flow within the Rift to enter Lake Natron. However, over most of the valley floor in the Olorgesailie area, fresh surface water occurs only seasonally or in ephemeral playa lakes such as the Kwennia, which come into being during a run of wet years (pl. 1). The geological and paleobotanical evidence from the Pleistocene sediments at Olorgesailie make it quite clear that for prolonged periods there was a stable freshwater lake in the area. The nearest equivalent body of water at the present time is Lake Naivasha. Whether the former lake at Olorgesailie was made possible by a different climatic regime or by different drainage conditions has not yet been ascertained.

The regional fauna includes a wide range of large mammals, as shown in table 1. Early travelers' accounts of the area (Thomson 1885) stress the abundance of game, especially of the gregarious species on the Athi plains: zebra, wildebeest, hartebeest, and gazelle. Smaller herds of these grazing animals occur in the Rift, wandering in response to changes in the availability of vegetation and surface water. Browsing animals, such as rhinoceros and gerenuk (Waller's gazelle), are more permanent inhabitants of the thickets (Stewart 1967).

A comparable diversity of environmental conditions certainly prevailed in the area throughout the Pleistocene, although the position and relative size of the zones may have varied considerably.

Regional Geology

Detailed study of the Olorgesailie sedimentary formations was a prerequisite of the archeological research, and therefore I undertook to extend the earlier studies made by

Table 1

Selected List of Game Animals in the Olorgesailie Area and the Adjoining Plain (partly after Stewart 1967)

Common Name	Latin Name	Relative Abundance	Seen at Olorgesailie 1961-65
Primates			
Baboon	*Papio doguera neumanni*	Common	Yes
Vervet monkey	*Cercopithecus aethiops*	Wooded parts only	No
Lagomorphs			
Hares	*Lepus* and *Pronolagus* spp.	Common	Yes
Gregarious ungulates			
Wildebeest	*Connochaetes taurinus*	Abundant	No
Hartebeest	*Alcelaphus buselaphus cokii*	Abundant	Yes
Zebra	*Equus burchelli*	Abundant	Yes
Grant's gazelle	*Gazella granti*	Abundant	Yes
Eland	*Taurotragus oryx*	Less common	Yes
Thomson's gazelle	*Gazella thomsonii*	Mainly high plains	No
Impala	*Aepyceros melampus*	Common	Yes
Giraffe	*Giraffa camelopardalis*	Common	Yes
Oryx	*Oryx beisa callotis*	Rift floor only; rare	Yes
Other ungulates			
Gerenuk	*Litocranius walleri*	Rift floor only	Yes
Dik-dik	*Rhynchotragus kirkii*	Common	Yes
Waterbuck	*Kobus ellipsiprymnus*	Escarpment and rivers only	No
Warthog	*Phacochoerus aethiopicus*	Common	Yes
Rhinoceros	*Diceros bicornis*	Present	Yes
Elephant	*Loxodonta africana*	Transitory	Yes
Hippopotamus	*Hippopotamus amphibius*	Athi River only	No
Large carnivores			
Lion	*Panthera leo*	Common	Yes
Leopard	*Panthera pardus*	Common	Yes
Cheetah	*Acinonyx jubatus*	Present	Yes
Cape hunting dog	*Lycaon pictus*	Intermittent	Yes
Spotted hyena	*Crocuta crocuta*	Common	Yes
Striped hyena	*Hyaena hyaena*	Present	Yes

In addition jackals, bat-eared foxes, servals, genets, civets, and mongooses have been observed.

R. M. Shackleton (1955, and unpublished) and by B. H. Baker (1958). New stratigraphic observations made it possible to determine the relationships between sites in the Formation, and also permitted partial reconstruction of the environmental context of the sites.

The principal process initiating and controlling sedimentation in the Olorgesailie basin has been tectonic deformation of the Rift Valley floor (Baker and Mitchell, 1976. Deposition took place in an irregular depression created by faulting and subsidence. Fault movement continued during the accumulation of the Olorgesailie Formation; and finally, tilting and fault movement together changed the local base levels to such an

extent that deposition in the Olorgesailie area largely ceased, and erosion of the deposits commenced in some localities.

The maps in figures 2, 4, and 5 indicate clearly the general form and topographic
context of the Olorgesailie basin. The displacement on a series of closely spaced fault
lines has combined to effect the relative subsidence of an irregular, subrectangular area
immediately to the north of the eroded Tertiary volcano, Mount Olorgesailie. This rec-
tangular segment of the basin is divided into eastern and western halves, the Legemunge
and Oltepesi plains. From the southwest corner of the Legemunge Plain, a narrow graben,
the Koora, cuts through the Mount Olorgesailie volcanics and extends southward for more
than 40 kms. For details of the complex regional geology the reader is referred to Baker
1958; McCall et al. 1967; Williams 1967; and Baker et al. 1972. While this monograph was
in press, a detailed comprehensive new report on recent studies was prepared by Baker and
Mitchell 1976.

The entire floor of the complex graben system has been mantled with sediments, but
natural exposures of the sedimentary strata are limited to the southern margins of the
Legemunge and Oltepesi plains. A variety of sedimentary formations, of which the earliest
is the thickest and most widespread, crop out in this area (see pl. 2). This unit has
been defined as the *Olorgesailie Formation* (Isaac, in press; Shackleton, in press), and
more detailed accounts are given in these papers than can be offered here (see fig. 6).

The Formation consists of a series of well-stratified diatomites, pale yellowish volcanic siltstones, and claystones, and subordinate quantities of brown siltstones and volcanic sands. It attains a maximum thickness of about 55 m. The sum of the maximum thicknesses of the individual members is about 76 m. Shackleton (1955, and unpublished) referred to these beds as the Kamasian Beds, and Baker (1958) used the label Olorgesailie
Lake Beds. Baker and Mitchell (in press) use the name Legemunge Beds. It is proposed
that these names be superseded by the formal name Olorgesailie Formation. All the archeological evidence treated in this report was derived from this stratigraphic unit.

The Olorgesailie Formation

The map in figure 5 presents a plan of exposures of the Formation and its members,
based on survey work by R. M. Shackleton in 1943-46. His map is being published in color
at a scale of 1:10,000 (Shackleton, in press). The localities at which I made measured
records of the stratigraphy are marked. These measured sections are spaced along exposures with approximately west-east (A-V) and north-south (a-1) alignments. By projecting
each group of measured sections onto a plane with the appropriate orientation, I was able
to compile composite transect diagrams (figs. 7-10) that provide a useful method of documenting the stratigraphic and paleoenvironmental settings of the archeological sites.
Table 2 provides a condensed summary of the thicknesses and characteristics of the Members
of the Formation.

Figure 7 shows the whole west-east composite section drawn with the base of Member 12
as a horizontal section datum. As can be clearly seen, it is not possible to plot the
strata as continuous bands across the section. Field studies and analysis of the record
showed conclusively that faulting and deformation took place during deposition. The section shows the dislocation of beds by faults and the thickening of beds in localities
where subsidence was actively taking place. In order to reduce the stratigraphic confusion
of such a diagram, the section has been divided into upper and lower halves, which were
replotted with different correlation planes (figs. 8 and 9). It is clear that the

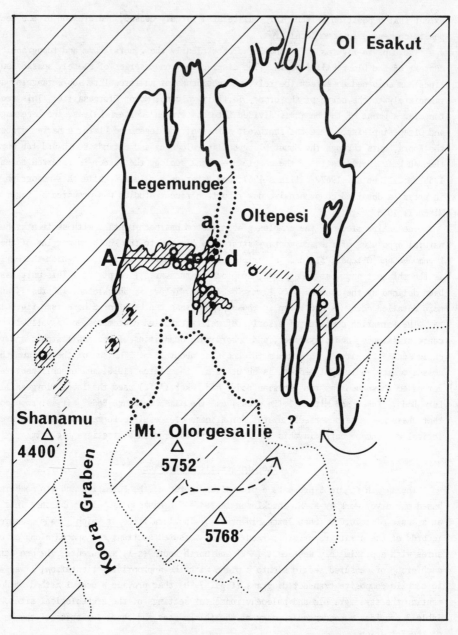

Figure 4. Plan of the Olorgesailie sedimentary basin.

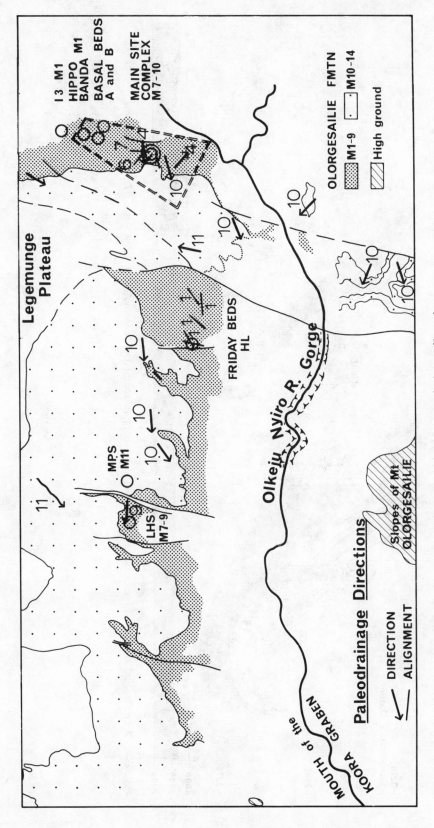

Figure 5. Plan of the outcrops of the Olorgesailie Formation showing paleodrainage directions. Numbers refer to Members in which paleochannel was observed.

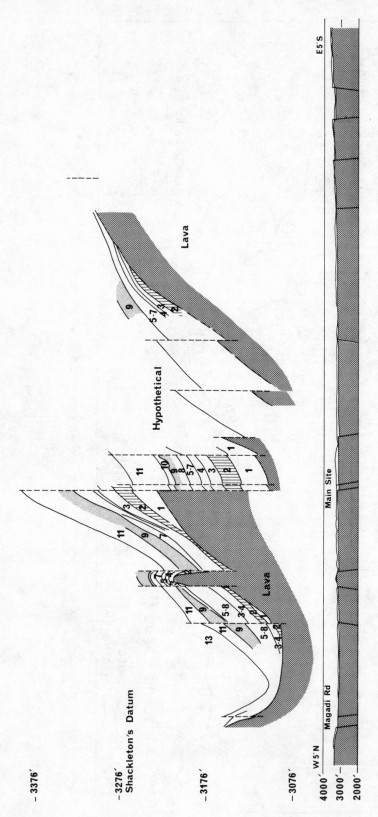

Figure 6. A cross section of the basin showing the present-day configuration of beds and faults, K8 = M8, etc. (from Shackleton).

Table 2

Summary of the Characteristics of the Members of the Olorgesailie Formation

	Measured observed thickness
Member 14 Pale diatomaceous siltstones, redeposited siltstones, and porous limestones. Outcrops are known only in the western sector of the Legemunge plain.	3m
Member 13 (Poorly exposed) Brown claystones, diatomaceous silts, and diatomites. Numerous root channels.	12m
Member 12 Vitric tuff with pumice lapillae, volcanic sand, redeposited sediment particles, diatomites. Locally vivid RED.	2m
Member 11 Over most of its distribution, the following sequence of lithologies can be distinguished: Brown siltstones and silty clays comparable to silts accumulating in the area today. (2 - 4m) Diatomites, volcanic silts, cemented by calcium carbonate (1 - 4.5m) Brown silts, clays, and fine sands (0 - 4m) Varied pale yellow volcanic silts, clays, and diatomaceous silts with hard RED bands (2 - 5m)	18m
Member 10 Coarse volcanic sands and pumice gravels, and subordinate quantities of lava granule gravel. Shows a facies change in the west (locs. O-D) with silts and redeposited diatomite predominating over sand.	3m

Widespread disconformity

Member 9 Upper diatomites (1 - 2m) Upper volcanic sand (0 - 0.6m) A *main diatomite* bed with an ash fall horizon (2 - 4m) "*Basal bed*" of volcanic glass, sand, and derived sediment rubble (0 - 2m) The diatomites show facies change from pure diatomite in the west to diatomaceous volcanic silts in the east.	7.5m

Widespread disconformity

Member 8* Pale grey brown tuffaceous shales ("marls") with beds of hard volcanic siltstones which may be bright RED.	3.4m
Member 7 Pale yellow volcanic silts, diatomaceous silts, plus a paleosol horizon with partial alteration of underlying sediments to green clay. "Cut and fill" bedding evident in excavations. Fine subdivisions have been defined at the Main Site.	4.5m
Member 6 Greenish silty volcanic sandstone	1m
Member 5 Massive root marked greyish yellow volcanic silts. Weathered and altered during deposition.	2m
Member 4 Coarse volcanic sandstones and pumice granule gravels with finer grained sand and sandy silt facies in the west.	3.4m

Widespread minor disconformity

Member 3 Grey silt, volcanic sandstone. Angular glass sherds of fine to medium grain size predominate, becoming coarser upward.	3.7m
Member 2 Diatomites, grading into fine silty volcanic sand.	5m
Member 1 Volcanic siltstones, diatomites, and brown clays with root channeling and paleosol horizons.	9m

*Members 5 - 8 are distinguishable only in the vicinity of the Main Site.

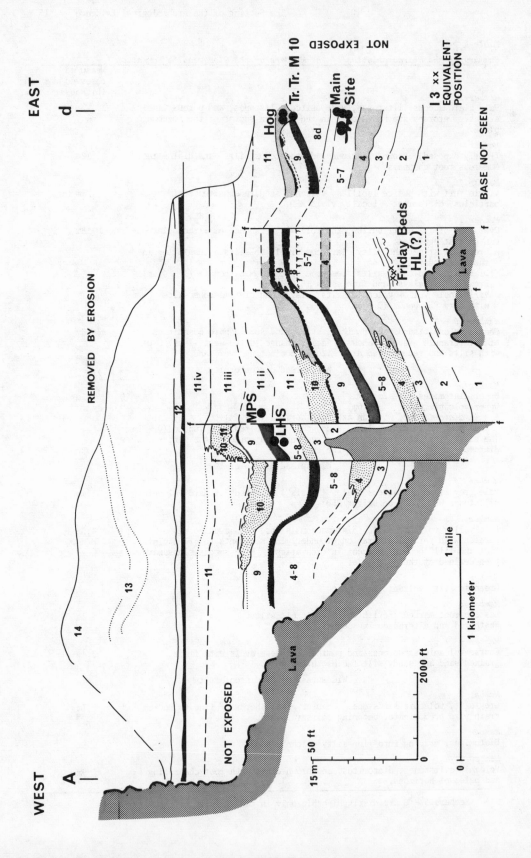

Figure 7. A diagrammatic west to east cross section through the Olorgesailie Formation from the western bounding scarp to the Main Site. The section has been compiled to eliminate post-Olorgesailie Formation deformation: the base of Member 12 was used as an arbitrary datum plane and all boundaries are scaled in terms of the thickness of the sediments between them and the datum plane. Since no single line of sections provides sufficient information, measurements from all sections along the southern margin of the Legemunge plain have been projected on the map in figure 5. There is clear evidence of extensive tectonic deformation during the deposition of the Formation.

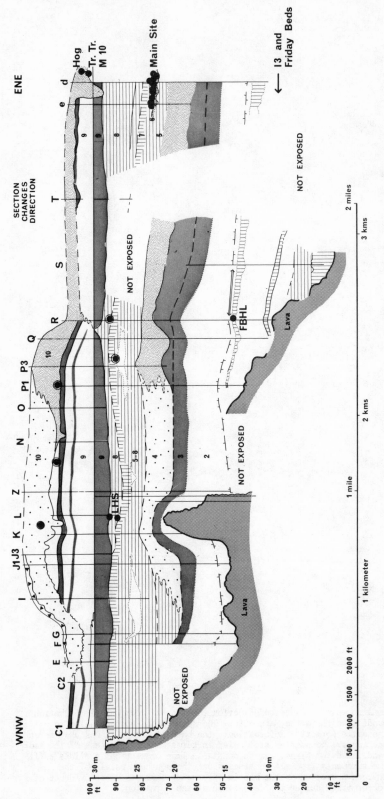

Figure 8. Shows in greater detail Members 1 through 10 correlated to a bedding plane in Member 9, so as to eliminate the disruption of these members.

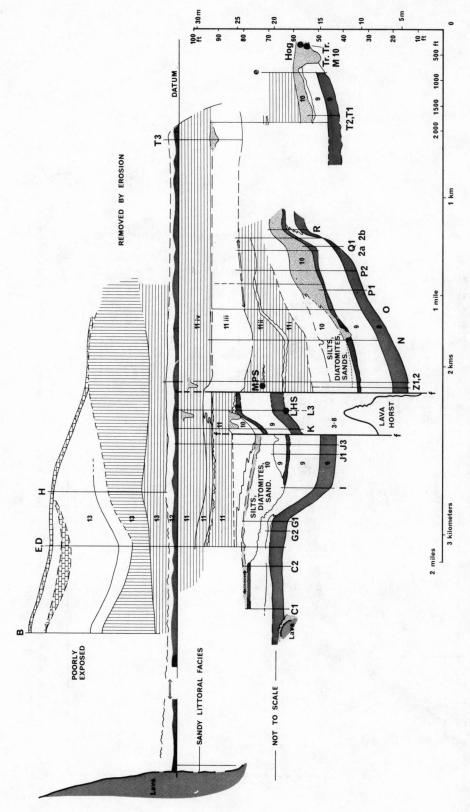

Figure 9. Provides details for Members 10 through 13 drawn with Member 12 as the datum plane.

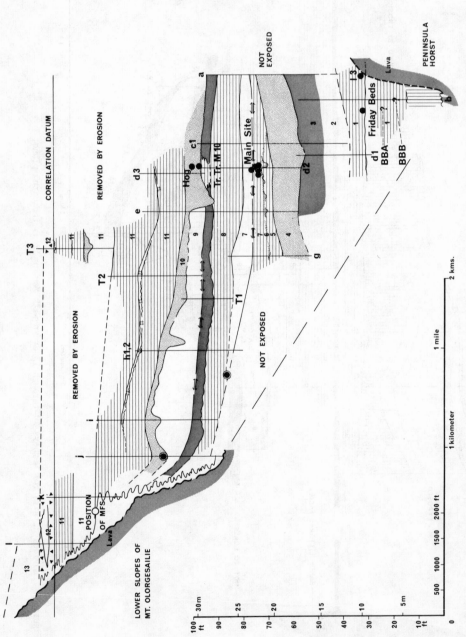

Figure 10. A section constructed with Member 12 as the datum plane for the south-north line of measurable sections between the foot of the mountain and the peninsula.

principal deformation took place during the deposition of Members 10 and 11.

Figure 7 shows the composite section based on the north-south alignment of exposures. This transect is parallel to the regional trend of fault lines and consequently does not show the same degree of deformation. The members overlapped each other as they buried the volcanic rocks forming the lower slopes of Mount Olorgesailie.

Several members show significant facies differentiation that provided important paleo-graphical evidence. In general, where a difference is observed, the finer-grained and more diatomaceous facies occur in the west around the mouth of the Koora, and the coarser or less diatomaceous facies occur in the easterly exposures away from the Koora (see, for example, Members 4, 9, and 10). This difference suggests that the segment of the basin at the mouth of the Koora was flooded during times when the area immediately to the northeast was exposed. The evidence of drainage channels and crossbedding corroborates this inference (fig. 5). Most channels and flow directions are oriented toward the mouth of the Koora (Isaac, in press).

From this evidence it can be tentatively concluded that during deposition of the Olorgesailie Formation, the lowest point in the basin, and hence the deepest water, usually lay within the Koora graben. It appears that the Legemunge and Oltepesi segments of the basin constituted a kind of atrium to the Koora and were flooded only at times of rela-tively high water. However, it is possible that during the deposition of Members 1 through 3, the lowest point in the basin lay within the eastern or Oltepesi sector. Exposures are virtually confined to a fluctuating zone of transition between lacustrine, deltaic, and alluvial environments of deposition. The archeological materials are concentrated in floodplain deposits that were generally at least a kilometer distant from stable lake waters (see table 6, chap. 4).

The diatom fossils (J. L. Richardson, pers. comm.) indicate fresh to slightly brackish water conditions throughout deposition. The flora includes both planktonic and epiphytic species.

The freshwater conditions of the former Lake Olorgesailie contrasted markedly with the highly saline water conditions of neighboring Lakes Natron and Magadi and their pre-cursors throughout much of the Pleistocene (Baker 1958; Isaac 1967a; Hay 1965). Lakes Magadi and Natron lie at the lowest points of the Rift Valley floor (604m and 607m above sea level, respectively) and have no drainage exits. The length of time during which the lake waters existed in the Olorgesailie basin without becoming very saline gives clear evidence that a salt-regulating mechanism must have been present. Whether this was an outlet through a surface overflow channel, such as exists for the freshwater lakes of the Western Rift Valley, or a subterranean leak, as is believed by some to exist for modern Lake Naivasha, or whether salts were bonded in the sediments cannot at present be deter-mined.

The normal history of sedimentation in a freshwater lake with a surface outlet in-volves progressive reduction in average water depth because sedimentation raises the floor level and channel erosion lowers the overflow. Since the Olorgesailie Formation gives evidence of oscillations among deep water, shallow water, and floodplain deposition through the accumulation of 55m or more of sediments, it seems unlikely that a surface out-let could have occupied a fixed altimetric relationship to the rock floor of the basin. It is known that certain fault blocks within the basin were subsiding relative to fault blocks forming the margins, and this mechanism may have served to maintain a more or less constant height difference between the outlet and the floor. However, an hypothesis

involving an underground exit would explain the observed situation just as well and perhaps more simply. At the present time, moderately large volumes of water are delivered
into the basin by the Olkeju Ngiro River and dispersed by seepage and evaporation. The
fact that water does not accumulate at the surface even in times of heavy spates may indicate the existence of a sizable subterranean outlet.

A reconnaissance visit to the southern end of the Koora graben resulted in the discovery of traces of a fairly recent pool of water there which had eventually flowed out
into the Magadi basin, cutting a spectacular gorge in the process. The traces are suspected to pertain to a small, early Holocene, pluvial lake, rather than to the Middle
Pleistocene lake (Marsden, pers. comm.).

The fresh waters of Lake Olorgesailie may have been an important attraction for prehistoric man. The floodplains surrounding the saline Middle Pleistocene precursor of Lake
Natron were apparently much less visited by Acheulean man (see Isaac 1967a:250;1972c). At
Olduvai the Acheulean sites tend to lie along the former stream channels away from the
playa lakes (Hay 1967a, 1976).

Sedimentation Rates

Without internal dating evidence or varves, it is not possible to make any reliable
estimate of the rate at which the various members of the Olorgesailie Formation were deposited. Banding in some members has been observed, but it is unlikely that the bands are
rhythmically seasonal. However, some comparative data indicating the range of values
within which the Olorgesailie rates probably fall are available.

Data from a core taken from beneath Lake Naivasha by Livingstone and coworkers provide
sedimentation rates for diatomaceous earth in the Eastern Rift Valley (Richardson 1966;
Richardson and Richardson 1972). During the phase from about 9200 B.P. to 5650 B.P., the
"Gamblian high stand," when the lake was probably 60m or more deep, the average rate was
0.116 gm of inorganic sediment per cm^2 per year. During the subsequent period when the
lake was smaller, the average rate dropped to 0.049 gm per cm^2 per year. I determined
that the specific gravities of relatively pure diatomaceous earths at Olorgesailie varied
from 0.48 to 0.69, and computations of rates using the Naivasha data show corresponding
variations. The more rapid Naivasha sedimentation rate would lead to an estimate of 400
to 600 years per meter; the slower rate suggests 1000 to 1300 years per meter. The presence of epiphytic forms in most Olorgesailie diatomites suggests that its sedimentation
rate was closer to that of the shallower phase, and therefore to the slower rate of deposition, in Lake Naivasha.

Bonadonna (1965) reported, on the basis of apparent varves, that Middle Pleistocene
diatomites accumulated in the Val dell'Inferno, Italy, at an average rate of 575 years per
meter. Livingstone (1965) reported a rate of 0.108 gm per cm^2 per year for diatomaceous
earths in part of Lake Tanganyika. This figure needs to be reduced by 10% to allow for
combustible organic component. The rate is intermediate between the two values from Lake
Naivasha. Rates of marine diatomite accumulation in various localities in the Gulf of
California span these estimates (Calvert 1966). Calvert's values (1966:table 3) would
give a range of rates from 280 years per meter to 80,000 years per meter for consolidated
diatomites with the specific gravity of the Olorgesailie examples. The lake basins in the
semiarid parts of western North America are of interest because of a degree of comparability in climate and hydrology with the Eastern Rift and because numerous C-14-dated cores
there have been studied. It appears that these lakes commonly accumulate clastic sediments

at a rate of approximately 1 meter per 3000 years (1 foot per 1000 years), for example, Searles Lake muds, 4100 years per meter (Flint and Gale, 1958:706); Teals Marsh, 2000 years per meter (Hay, 1966).

In summary the following can be said.

1. It seems unlikely that sedimentation at Olorgesailie was faster than the most rapid accumulation at Lake Naivasha. Since the cumulative thickness of diatomite beds in the Olorgesailie Formation is about 18 m, these beds must represent a time span of 7000 to 10,000 years. The remaining two-thirds of the Formation must involve at least as much time, suggesting a figure of 14,000 to 20,000 years as the absolute minimum for the whole Formation.

2. If the rate for the better-fitting Naivasha sedimentation pattern is used, the Olorgesailie figures must be more than doubled: i.e. 30,000 to 50,000 years.

3. Data from Olduvai and certain non-African lake basins show that the Olorgesailie Formation could conceivably represent a time span of 100,000 to 200,000 years.

Paleoclimate

Satisfactory direct indicators of paleoclimatic conditions have not yet been discerned in the Olorgesailie Formation. An attempt to recover a pollen record was largely unsuccessful (D. A. Livingstone, pers. comm.). The sediments themselves give ample evidence of hydrological conditions that differ markedly from those of the present, and the existence of a once-stable freshwater lake in the now semiarid Rift floor has been taken as evidence documenting pluvial conditions (cf. Leakey 1951; S. Cole 1963; Flint 1959a,b). However, the former existence of a lake is in fact only evidence of a different state of balance between water influx and water loss. This balance is affected by (1) topography and the size of the catchment areas of inflowing streams; (2) the form of the basin center and the extent to which the water is spread out or confined to a deep pool; (3) the outlet mechanism; and (4) climate, especially the overall evaporation-precipitation balance. In an area in which extensive tectonic deformation is known to have gone on throughout the Pleistocene, it is very difficult to evaluate the degree to which climatic variation may also have been an important determinant of hydrological changes.

Lake Naivasha is an example of a large freshwater lake situated in a part of the Rift where the precipitation on the floor is less than 50 mm yearly, but where perennial rivers descend from the heavy rainfall areas on either side to sustain the lake. The Olorgesailie area is not flanked by comparable highlands and there are no perennial streams in the area today, so that it does seem likely that climatic conditions were somewhat wetter during the deposition of the Olorgesailie Formation. However, other possibilities cannot be eliminated. The catchment area for the Olorgesailie basin may formerly have included large adjoining areas, such as the Kedong basin and the Turoka River catchment area. The additional influx provided by these sources might have been sufficient to sustain a more or less stable lake even under climatic conditions comparable with those of the present.

Initiation of lacustrine deposition in the Olorgesailie area and its cessation were clearly controlled by tectonic processes, so that the beginning and end of the wetter climatic episode, if it existed, are not in evidence. The water-level fluctuations documented within the Formation can probably be attributed to a combination of tectonic modifications and climatic oscillations of the kind recorded for East Africa in late Quaternary and even in historic times (Richardson 1966; Thompson and Sansom 1967: fig. ii; Butzer et

al. 1972). It should be clear that vague paleoclimatic evidence of the kind presently
available at Olorgesailie is of no value whatsoever for stratigraphic correlation.

Later deformation of the Olorgesailie Formation has been such that the former lake
basin could not hold water unless the southern end of the Koora graben was raised 300 m
to be level with the Legemunge plain. It seems certain that deposition of the Olorgesailie
Formation was terminated by the tilting and faulting that brought about the lowering of the
southern margin of the basin. Comparable large displacements are known to have affected
early Pleistocene formations in the region, for example, the Peninj Group (Isaac 1965,
1967a) and the Olduvai Group (Leakey 1951; Hay, 1976).

The Age of the Olorgesailie Formation

There are three principal lines of evidence that can be used for estimating the age
of the Olorgesailie Formation:

1. Measurements of isotopic ratios
2. Correlation of contained fossils
    a. Fauna
    b. Artifacts
3. Estimates of the time span implied by depth of sediments and extent of
    geomorphic change.

None of these methods has yet provided an age estimate that is as precise and definite as
one would wish.

Potassium-argon measurements have been made on volcanic materials from several Formations in the Magadi regional sequence (Baker and Mitchell, in press) and from two members
of the Olorgesailie Formation. The results for the latter are shown in table 3. The
Olorgesailie Formation unconformably overlies the Magadi Plateau trachytes, for which
Baker and Mitchell (1976) give an age range of 0.63 to 1.25 m.y., based on a combination
of potassium-argon dates and paleomagnetic evidence.

Pumice from Members 4 and 10 has been dated by Evernden and Curtis (1965), and pumice
from Member 10 by J. A. Miller (1967). The scatter of values suggests that the material
dated may have derived from reworked deposits of various ages, but there is a distinct
possibility that the two lowest values of 0.425 and 0.486 million potassium-argon years
are valid estimates. The pumice from Member 10 dated by Miller appeared to be very fresh.
However, one or two potassium-argon dates, especially when selected from a scatter of
values, cannot be relied upon in the absence of other checks on their reliability. All
that can be said is that there is no specific dating evidence in East Africa or elsewhere
which *precludes* an age of 400,000 years for the fossil and artifact contents of the
Olorgesailie Formation. In fact other results obtained elsewhere in recent years make
this age estimate seem very reasonable (Isaac 1972a; Isaac and Curtis 1974).

Paleomagnetic determinations have been made by Dr. A. Brock on five samples collected
from Member 1 of the Formation. All these showed weak normal polarity, which is consistent
with an age of less than 700,000 years. F. Brown of the University of Utah, has confirmed
these results with further tests (pers. comm.).

Paleontological Correlations

The taxonomic composition of the Olorgesailie sample of mammalian fossils is listed
in table 4. From comparative studies, it is clear that the Olorgesailie fauna is closely

Table 3

Potassium-Argon Ages for Samples from the Olorgesailie Formation Shown in Relation to the Regional Sequence

A. Dating samples taken from the *Olorgesailie Formation*

Member 10	Cambridge 834	0.425 ± .009	Pumice
Member 4	Berkeley 413	0.486	Anorthoclase
Member 10	Berkeley 925	1.45	Anorthoclase
Member 4	Berkeley 923	1.64	Anorthoclase
Member 4	Berkeley 435	2.9	Rerun of 413

Samples from the basal units of the Formation show normal paleomagnetic polarity (Brock, pers. comm.).

B. The *Regional Sequence* of dated units (from Baker and Mitchell, 1976)

Suswa Volcanics	no dates yet available
Olorgesaile Formation	0.42, 0.49 m.y.
Ol Doinyo Nyukie Volcanics	0.66 m.y.
(Magadi) Plateau Trachytes	0.63-1.25 m.y.
Ol Tepesi basalts	1.4-1.6 m.y.
Ol Keju Nero basalts	
Limuru Trachytes	1.9 m.y.
Mt. Olorgesailie volcanics	2.2-2.8 m.y.
Singaraini basalts	2.3 m.y.
Ol Esayeti volcanics	3.6-6.7 m.y.

Table 4

A List of Fossil Mammal Taxa Identified from the Olorgesailie Formation

Taxon	Synonyms	Authority (see key below)
*Theropithecus oswaldi mariae	Simopithecus	3, 5
*Elephas recki (advanced stage)	Archidiskodon	1, 6
*Stylohipparion albertense		4
Equus aff. grevi		4
*Equus oldowayensis		1, 4
Ceratotherium simum		1, 4
*Metridiochoerus meadowsi	Tapinochoerus	2, 4
*Hippopotamus gorgops		1, 4
Giraffa camelopardis		4
*Giraffa gracilis (?)		7
*Sivatherium olduvaiensis	Libytherium	1, 4
Strepsiceros sp.		7
Tragelaphus sp.		7
Taurotragus sp.		7
*Homoioceros sp. ?		7
Kobus sp.		7
Redunea sp.		7
*Gorgon sp.		7
*Phenacotragus sp. ?		7
Aepyceros sp.		7

Key to authorities:

1. MacInnes, in Leakey 1951
2. Leakey 1958
3. Leakey and Whitworth 1958
4. Cooke 1963

5. M. G. and R. E. F. Leakey 1973
6. Coppens, pers. comm.
7. Gentry, pers. comm.

*
Denotes extinct taxa.

allied to other faunal samples which are regarded as being of Middle Pleistocene age
(McInnes, in Leakey 1951; Cooke 1963; Meave G. Leakey and R. E. Leakey 1973).

Subdivisions of the Middle Pleistocene faunal stratigraphy are not firmly established.
The small sample from Olorgesailie can be matched with the faunas from the upper part of
Olduvai Bed II or from Bed IV. The lower boundary of this faunal zone has commonly been
taken at the Lemuta Member (eolian tuff) of Bed II at Olduvai. An age estimate of 1.65
m.y. for this member is based on potassium-argon dates and paleomagnetic evidence (R. L.
Hay, in press). The upper time limit of the zone is unknown, and the time span during
which the numerous extinct elements of the Middle Pleistocene fauna died out is not yet
documented in any rock-stratigraphic sequence in eastern or southern Africa.

Later Pleistocene faunal samples from the Gamblian beds of the Nakuru-Naivasha area
lack most of the extinct forms characteristic of the Olorgesailie and other mid-Pleistocene
faunas. In southern Africa an equivalent disappearance of taxa occurred between the Vaal-
Cornelia and the Florisbad-Vlakkraal faunal span (Bishop, in J. D. Clark, compiler 1967;
H. B. S. Cooke 1967).

Archeological Correlations

Comparative studies indicate that the Olorgesailie assemblages are later in the East
African technological and typological sequence than are the Lower Acheulian assemblages
from Olduvai Bed II (M. D. Leakey 1967) or from the Humbu Formation in the Natron area.
The Humbu Formation assemblage is probably 1.5 to 1.3 million years old (Isaac and Curtis
1974).

All the Olorgesailie assemblages appear to be somewhat less refined than the Acheulean
tools from Kalambo Falls, for which a minimum C-14 age determination of 61,700 ± 1,300
years (GRN-4986) supersedes earlier estimates (Vogel and Waterbolk 1967). Amino acid
racemization measurements on wood from Kalambo imply an age two or three times greater
than this 61,000 year minimum (J. D. Clark, pers. comm.). However, the significance of
morphological seriation is reduced by the fact that the terminal Acheulean assemblage at
Nsongezi (G. H. Cole 1967, and personal impressions) appear to show a degree of archaism
indistinguishable from that of the Olorgesailie samples. Lack of refinement, therefore,
is not an entirely reliable chronological indicator.

No assemblage with definite Middle Stone Age or Sangoan technical or typological features is known from the Olorgesailie Formation, though an industry including Levallois
cores and flakes is known from the Koora beds which unconformably overlie the Formation.
The predominance of First Intermediate and Middle Stone Age industries in eastern and
southern Africa after about 60,000 B.P. (see Deacon 1966:77; Beaumont and Vogel 1972;
Sampson 1974) suggests that this figure is a *terminus ad quem* for the Formation.

The Magnitude of Post-Olorgesailie Formation Geological Change

All the above lines of stratigraphic and chronological evidence leave the upper limit
of the age of the Olorgesailie Formation poorly defined. The vague indications are merely
that the faunas and artifacts are at least 60,000 years old. The magnitude of the geomorphological changes that have occurred since the cessation of deposition in the Legemunge
sector of the basin suggests that the Formation is much older than the minimum estimate.
Major changes in the basin include the following:

1. Tilting and faulting have produced a downward displacement of the southern margin of the basin which amounts to at least 300 m, relative to the Legemunge plain.
2. Because of the tilting, the Formation has been totally eroded from an area at least 1.5 km wide and 5 km long.
3. Subsequent to dissection of the Formation, a gorge 3 km long and up to 30 m deep has been cut by the Olkeju Ngiro River into the Olkeju Ngiro basalts at the foot of Mount Olorgesailie.

Too little is known of rates of deformation or erosion in East Africa to make a reliable estimate of the time span represented by these changes, but a period of not less than 100,000 years seems likely, particularly for the cumulative tectonic deformation.

In summary, then, it appears that the cultural events and hominid behavior patterns documented in the Olorgesailie Formation must date between 700,000 and 60,000 years ago. The potassium-argon age determinations of approximately 400,000 years are consistent with biostratigraphical correlations and with geochronometric data at other localities. For representation of the probable time relations of Olorgesailie to other East African Middle Pleistocene Formations, readers are referred to Isaac (1975).

3. SITES AND EXCAVATIONS

It is a commonplace that prehistory consists of inferences about human behavior in the past, based on evidence that derives from no more than a minute fraction of the sum of prehistoric human acts. Whether or not an archeologist is using the methods of statistics, his information about the totality of prehistory stems from samples, and many aspects of his interpretation can be placed on a sound footing only if he pays careful attention to the nature of the sample involved.

The decision to focus attention on a complex of sites in the deposits of a single lake basin amounts to a sampling decision. The Olorgesailie sites are of interest because it is supposed that the behavior documented in their features represents in some way patterns of behavior that existed over a wider area than the basin, but clearly the geographic and chronological extent of these patterns of behavior must be determined from other samples.

Furthermore, even when samples of traces of Middle Pleistocene behavior are taken from a restricted area and from a limited time span, it cannot be supposed that the available evidence is a random sample of all material culture even in that area. The formation of an archeological record of the activities of human societies is subject to bias at every stage between the behavioral acts themselves and the moment of archeological interpretation. Most aspects of behavior do not leave direct physical traces, and even potential indicators are subject to great differences in their durability through time and in their visibility to the archeologist. The following is a short list of the bias, or uncertainty of relations, that the available Olorgesailie samples are known to show.

1. Only behavior within the circumlacustrine zone of deposition is available for investigation. No traces of artifacts or activities have been discovered on the hills, mountains, and ravines that dominate the physiography of the region. This is a common bias in samples of early cultural material (Isaac 1972c).

2. Even within the basin, sites are available for study only along areas exposed by erosion; these are confined to the southern corner of the basin, and the extent of exposure of any depositional surface constitutes much less than 1% of the total area over which deposition occurred.

3. In general, only loci of activities made conspicuous by a concentration of stone artifacts have been investigated. In excavating one such concentration, H/9, we encountered a horizon littered with unmodified stones. These stones had probably been introduced by man, but under most circumstances they would be invisible.

28

4. All vestiges of plant foods or of material culture made from wood or fiber are lacking from the Olorgesailie sites.

5. The contents and configuration of sites has in varying degrees been influenced by the mechanical and chemical effects of nonhuman agencies, such as stream currents or weathering.

In summary, the surviving evidence at even the best sites consists only of partially patterned associations of (a) stone artifacts, (b) bone refuse, and (c) the paleogeographical context of artifact concentration. Since structural features, such as pits, banks, or stone arrangements could have been preserved if they had existed, the fact that substantial traces of them have not been recognized may be significant.

Error and bias arise also from the uneven character of the units we are obliged to use in analysis. In this study the minimal unit is termed an *archeological occurrence*, a label used to denote materials in their field context (Bishop and Clark 1967:868-69, 893). The term is applied to associated sets of artifacts, food refuse, and other finds that form a sufficiently restricted spatial and stratigraphic cluster, enabling such a set to be judged as a legitimate and indivisible entity for inclusion in comparative studies. Maximum precision of behavioral and culture-taxonomic inference will be achieved if each occurrence used in an analysis represents the patterned traces of a single occupation episode or of a series of exactly superimposed occupations that are effectively homogeneous with regard to their characteristics. This ideal probably holds for only a small proportion of occurrences. In practice it is difficult to distinguish undisturbed unitary occupation sites from composite sites or from partially disturbed sites.

These uncertainties work together to place severe restrictions on the extent to which reconstruction of activities can be attempted, and progress in this area will depend on a great enlargement of the number of excavated samples, so that recurrent patterns can be sought. Both culture-historical and functional interpretation are handicapped because some samples may have been mechanically distorted and others may have had a compound origin. However, the current usefulness of the samples remains relatively great because they are much more tightly defined segments of the space-time continuum of culture than are most of the aggregates on which most of the classic interpretations of the Lower Paleolithic have been based. Analysis of variation among them will certainly contribute to the development of a more realistic exposition of cultural patterns in the Pleistocene. For this reason, in the artifact morphology sections, each sample has been given equal weight, despite the fact that heterogeneity of context exists.

Spatial and Stratigraphic Relationships

The distribution of the archeological occurrences within the basin is shown in figures 5 and 7 (chap. 2), and figure 11 provides a diagrammatic summary of both spatial and stratigraphic relationships. It can be seen that the sites tend to occur as clusters in certain areas and at certain stratigraphic levels. These clusters seem to be associated with particular paleotopographic features, such as the apex of a rocky peninsula or ridge or a braided complex of stream channels. However, I will defer generalization and interpretations until the next chapter.

The stratigraphic configuration of the occurrences is such that it is convenient to recognize three correlated groups, or stratigraphic sets. Figure 11 shows that each set has the property whereby all of its constituent occurrences are closer to each other in time, as expressed by cumulative sedimentation, than they are to any occurrence in another

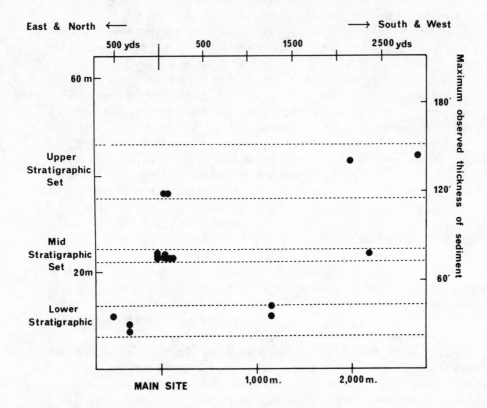

East & North ⟵   ⟶ South & West

Figure 11.   The provenance of site samples shown in relation to cumulative sedimentation
(time) and to their radial distance from Site DE/89 of the Main Site. An intrinsic pattern
of clustering allows the recognition of three stratigraphic sets.

set. The sets have been used as higher order entities in the comparative studies of the
artifacts (see chap. 5). In the next section of this chapter, the occurrences of each set
are briefly described.

Descriptions of Sites and Occurrences

In this monograph it has been necessary for me to reduce to a minimum the quantity of
circumstantial information presented on the numerous sites and occurrences. The general
features of each stratigraphic set and of each site cluster are briefly reported, followed
by a summary of the salient features of each occurrence. In order to compress a large
amount of information into as small a space as possible, I am not attempting a verbal
description; plans and sections serve to transmit much crucial data. Other information is
provided by terse entries keyed into this standard series of items:

1. Alternative site designations
2. Investigator carrying out the excavations, and the date
3. Size of the excavation (given as originally laid out in feet, with approximate
    metric equivalent in parenthesis)

4. Quantity of archeological material recovered
5. Notes on the site location
6. Notes on the stratigraphic context
7. Notes on the disposition of material within the occurrence
8. Assessment of evidence of disturbance
9. Associated faunal and floral remains
10. Notes on specific features of the paleoenvironmental context
11. Comments on the occupation from a paleoanthropological standpoint.

Details of the artifact inventories are presented in table 9 (chap. 5) and comparative treatment, including metrical data, is reserved for the appropriate chapter dealing with the artifacts (chaps. 6-8).

As explained in chapter 1, excavations at Olorgesailie have been carried out by several workers at different times. The data available for the summary descriptions is inevitably of rather uneven character. Understandably, I have the most detailed information on my own fieldwork.

Notes on the Site Designations

There has been no uniform system for labeling the sites at Olorgesailie. I have been tempted to impose one after the fact, but have decided that it would not be sensible to introduce a set of referents that differ from the actual labels on specimens and the entries in notebooks. I am therefore presenting the original idiosyncratic labels. Table 5 provides a list and some information, when known, on the rationale of the label. It will be seen that Louis Leakey used three different principles in labeling:

1. Nicknames, such as Friday Beds, Hog, Meng, and Mid.
2. Trench references, such as Tr. Tr. (Trial Trench)
3. Stratigraphic references, such as Basal Beds A and Land Surface 10.

I also used three different principles:

1. Serial numbers, such as I 3 (Isaac Site 3)
2. Grid reference ciphers on the Main Site, such as H/9
3. Three-letter abbreviations of the type used at Olduvai, such as MFS (Mountain Foot Site).

The Lower Stratigraphic Set of Occurrences

The six excavated sites are all in Member 1, and all but one of them are clustered around the tip of the rocky lava ridge that divides the northern part of the sedimentary basin into eastern and western halves (figs. 12 and 14). Because the apex of the peninsula was subsequently buried by the deposition of Members 2 and 3, it ceased to be as important in determining site location.

Figure 14 shows the stratigraphic section for the area, with the approximate position of the archeological horizons marked; but it should be noted that there is some uncertainty regarding the exact levels of the sites excavated by L. S. B. Leakey.

The occurrences are all stratified in fine-grained diatomaceous volcanic silts and sands belonging to the upper part of Member 1. These deposits show cut-and-fill bedding and some minor weathering and soil formation horizons; they also include diatomite beds. I interpret them as the deposits of a lake margin floodplain that was predominantly subject to low energy fluvial sedimentation but was also flooded periodically during temporary

Table 5
The Designation of Excavated Sites

Abbreviation	Full Designation	Synonyms	Excavations
Members 10 and 11 - Upper Stratigraphic Set			
MFS	Mountain Foot Site	--	
MPS	Merrick Posnansky Site	"Hope Fountain Site"	1957 Posnansky (1959)
Hog	Main Site, "Hog" trenches	Land Surface 11	1943 M. D. and L. S. B. Leakey
Tr. Tr. M10	Main Site, Trial Trench, Member 10	Land Surface 10	1943 M. D. and L. S. B. Leakey
Member 7 - Middle Stratigraphic Set			
LHS	Lava Hump Site		1965 Isaac
Meng	Main Site, Menengetti Trench	Land Surface 8	1943 M. D. and L. S. B. Leakey
H/9 A	Main Site, Grid sq. H/9, Horizon A	--	1962-65 Isaac
H/9 AM	Main Site, Grid sq. H/9, Horizon AM	--	1962-65 Isaac
Mid	Main Site, Mid Trench	Land Surface 9	1943 M. D. and L. S. B. Leakey
H/6 A	Main Site, Grid sq. H/6, Horizon A	--	1963-65 Isaac
DE/89 C	Main Site, Grid sq. D-E/8-9, Horizon C	--	1962-65 Isaac
DE/89 B	Main Site, Grid sq. D-E/8-9, Horizon C	Land Surface 7, Tr. Tr. B 4	1943 M. D. and L. S. B. Leakey and 1962-65 Isaac
DE/89 A	Main Site, Grid sq. D-E/8-9, Horizon C	Land Surface 6, Tr. Tr. B 2	
Member 1 - Lower Stratigraphic Set			
I 3	Isaac Site 3	--	1961-62 Isaac
FB HL	Friday Beds, H. Lambert Site	Land Surface 4	L. S. B. Leakey
FB	Friday Beds	Land Surface 3	L. S. B. Leakey
BBA	Basal Bed A, Locus 1 and 2	Land Surface 2	L. S. B. Leakey
HBS	Hippo Banda Site	?Land Surface 2	L. S. B. Leakey
BBB	Basal Bed B	Land Surface 1	L. S. B. Leakey

fluctuations of the lake (see chap. 2). The area in question subsequently became deeply submerged under stable lake waters from which the pure diatomites of Member 2 were deposited, and it is this lacustrine transgression that creates the stratigraphic gap between the archeological record of the Lower Stratigraphic Set of occurrences and the Middle Stratigraphic Set.

One of the sites, Friday Beds H L, is situated away from the others, about 1 km to the southwest of the Prehistoric Site enclosure. It is associated with a sandstone bed that covers and fills channels in a thin clay horizon that may be a weak paleosol. This unit contains scattered artifacts and fossils along its entire outcrop, a strip some 300 m long. Member 1 otherwise contains very little artifactual material.

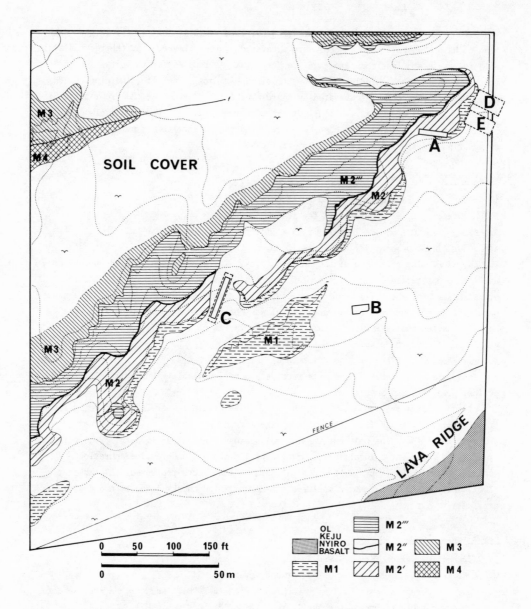

Figure 12. Contoured geological map of the north end of the Prehistoric Site enclosure showing the location of trenches (from a map made by R. M. Shackleton). A = presumed part of BBA; B and C = presumed BBB; D = Hippo Banda; E = exhibit banda with elephant humerus.

I dug one of the six excavated occurrences, I 3, myself. This is the largest excavation to have been undertaken. Four were excavated by Louis Leakey, and the records available for these are less complete than are Mary Leakey's records for the sites she and Louis excavated in the Middle and Upper Stratigraphic Sets. One site, the Hippo Banda Site (HBS), was reportedly excavated by Andrews, the first warden of the Prehistoric Site. I have no records of his excavation, but the occurrence is preserved as a field exhibit, and a brief description is included here, even though the site is not part of the comparative series treated in the chapters on artifacts.

Basal Bed B

1. *Alternative designations.* Land Surface 1.
2. *Excavator.* L. S. B. Leakey in the 1940s.
3. *Size of Excavation.* A 10 x 10 ft (3 x 3m) trench.
4. *Material Recovered.* 488 artifacts (L. S. B. Leakey, in MS).
5. *Location.* The north end of the enclosed area. The site is not labeled on any maps, and I have not relocated it with complete certainty.
6. *Stratigraphy.* Member 1, but the precise horizon and context are uncertain. A nonsequence at an appropriate stratigraphic level was observed in a gully adjacent to the Land Surface 2 sites and is indicated in the section diagram of figure 14b with a query.
7. *Disposition of Material.* No data are available.
8. *Evidence of Disturbance.* No evidence of abrasion.
9. *Associated Faunal Remains.* Exact records are not available. Museum labels report equids, giraffes, and antelopes.
10. *Paleoenvironmental Context.* Silt and clay flats within 100 or 200m of a rocky ridge or peninsula. Distance from contemporary lake margins not known.
11. *Interpretation.* The paleoanthropological status is not clear in detail; the site is presumed to represent a localized occupation of limited but undetermined duration. A manuscript draft report by Leakey records that 488 items were recovered. Kleindienst (1961) analyzed 428. I omitted analysis of the chips and chunks category and analyzed 272 artifacts.

Basal Bed A, Locus 1 and Locus 2

1. *Alternative Designations.* Land Surface 2.
2. *Excavator.* L. S. B. Leakey in August and November 1944.
3. *Size of Excavation.* Locus 1, a trench 20 x 6 ft (6 x 2m). Locus 2, no precise data, but "a considerable richness in a small area" (L. S. B. Leakey, in MS).
4. *Archeological Material Recovered.* Locus 1, 318 artifacts; Locus 2, 247 items.
5. *Location.* The north end of the enclosure, but precise data are not available. Leakey (in MS) reported that Locus 1 was adjacent to the Elephant Humerus exhibition. Locus 2 is said to be 140 m away, but two collapsed trenches occur at approximately this distance.
6. *Stratigraphy.* Member 1, reputedly at the same horizon as the two exhibition sites, Hippo Banda (fig. 13), and Elephant Humerus. These exhibitions are trenches cut into pale yellowish volcanic silts, showing cut-and-fill bedding features and including locally conglomeratic lenses with cobbles derived from the adjacent rocky peninsula. These sites are overlain by thin bedded diatomites with some minor ash fall bands.
7. *Disposition of Material.* At Locus 1, there was apparently a concentration of material in the trench, with a thin scatter in the adjoining area, which was interpreted as a con-

temporary midden (Leakey, in MS). The artifacts in the thin scatter were left in place as
an exhibition.

8. *Evidence of Disturbance.* The proportion of partially rounded specimens seemed somewhat
higher than usual, but appeared also to be related to the deep chemical alteration and
therefore provided no evidence for or against transport and rearrangement.

9. *Associated Faunal Remains.* The fragmentary bones of a hippopotamus carcass, which are
on exhibition in a roofed excavation (see fig. 15), and a nearby elephant humerus are
alleged to be associated (L. S. B. Leakey, in MS), but are treated as separate occurrences
in this report.

10. *Paleoenvironmental Context.* Channeled silt and alluvial flats adjacent to a rocky
peninsula.

11. *Interpretation.* When working with the material initially, I did not know that two localities at the same horizon were involved in the Basal Bed A materials. Kleindienst (1961)
also treated the material collectively. It has not been possible to unscramble the records,
so that this sample, now known to be compound, is of diminished value for comparative purposes. Since the number of specimens analyzed by Kleindienst and myself is less than that
reported in Leakey's notes, other specimens were presumably discarded or stored away from
the main collections. Clearly, little weight should be given to the data presently available on this artifact sample until it has been reanalyzed with the proper distinctions.

Friday Beds

1. *Alternative Designations.* Land Surface 3.
2. *Excavator.* L. S. B. Leakey in August 1944.
3. *Size of Excavations.* A trench 8 x 10 ft (2.4 x 3m) exposing part of a campsite (L. S.
B. Leakey, in MS).
4. *Archeological Material Recovered.* 333 artifacts.
5. *Location.* North end of the enclosure, probably at the site of a trench still visible
at the top of Member 1.
6. *Stratigraphy.* Member 1. If I have correctly identified this site, then the occurrence
is associated with a soil horizon that unconformably overlies stratified diatomites and is
covered by marls that form the top of Member 1. This horizon is well developed and can be
traced as far west as the HL site. Fossils and flakes occur at intervals along its length.
7. *Disposition of Material.* Data are not available.
8. *Evidence of Disturbance.* Because the material is moderately heavily weathered, degrees
of abrasion cannot be distinguished.
9. *Associated Faunal Remains.* No records available.
10. *Paleoenvironmental Context.* On relatively well-drained flats where sediments were
weathering and being redeposited. Adjacent to the rocky peninsula and at least 2 km from
any stable body of lake water.
11. *Interpretation.* A localized sample of an occurrence representing occupation(s) of unknown but limited duration. Localized concentration may or may not imply a discrete occupation episode.

Friday Beds HL (H. Lambert Site)

1. *Alternative Designations.* Land Surface 4.
2. *Excavator.* L. S. B. Leakey in the 1940s.

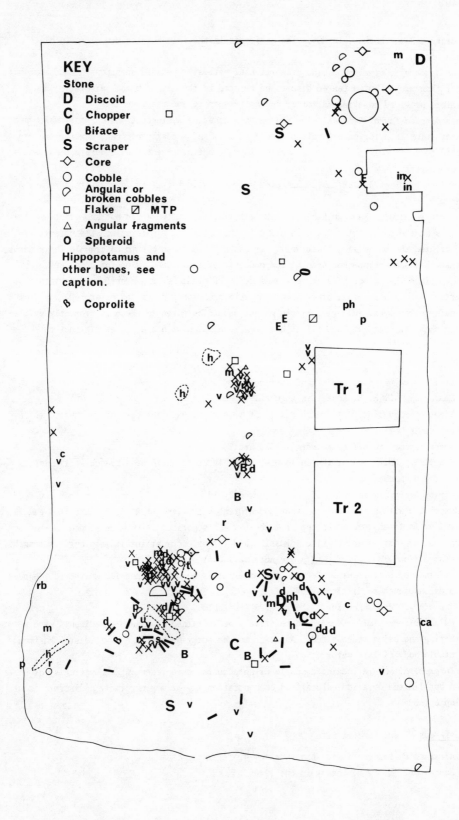

KEY
Stone
D   Discoid
C   Chopper
0   Biface
S   Scraper
◇   Core
○   Cobble
◗   Angular or
    broken cobbles
□   Flake   ▨ MTP
△   Angular fragments
O   Spheroid
Hippopotamus and
other bones, see
caption.

ᖰ   Coprolite

Figure 13. A plot of the distribution of stones and bones at the "Hippo Banda Site" in Member 1 at Olorgesailie. The floor is now a public exhibit. It was excavated in 1948 by the then Warden, Mr. Andrews. No excavation notes or plans are available from the time of excavation and this plan records the positions of the specimens as of September 1976. It is certain that the detailed disposition of material has been affected by 28 years of sweeping, but the overall pattern probably still has archeological significance as an instance of association of a modest number of artifacts with a large part of a skeleton of a large animal--in this case a hippo. (For the location of the site see fig. 12.)

Tr 1 and Tr 2 are two cuttings through the floor made by R. V. Wright in 1960. The underlying pale volcanic silts proved sterile except for a few scattered cobbles which had rolled off the nearby peninsular. BLK 1 is a small upstanding baulk preserving some equid bones at a higher level than the Hippo floor.

The exposed surface with the hippo bones slopes up from west to east with a gradient of 1 in 12. The Hippo bones are effectively confined to the western half of the exposed area. In the southeast corner of the "floor" there is a cluster of lava cobbles and boulders which derive from the adjoining "peninsular" ridge. These were probably introduced by natural agencies.

The following inventory of stones on the floor was made by G. Isaac assisted by L. Laporte, September 1976:

Bifaces	2	Flakes and Flake Fragments	7
Scrapers	4	Angular Waste	4
Choppers	2		
Discoids	2	Cobbles and Pebbles	16
Cores/Core-tools	6	Broken and Angular Cobbles	11
Spheroid	1		
Miscellaneous trimmed	1		

The following inventory of bone preserved in the exhibition was made by A. Hill, R. Foley, and V. Morse in September 1976.

Hippo bones and bone frags.

Cranial frags.	2	Humerus	1 + 3 frags.	Calcaneum	1
Teeth/frags.	12	Radius	5 frags.	Other podials	4
Vertebrae/frags.	44	Ulna	1	Metapodials	4
Ribs/frags.	32	Femur	1	Phalanges	2
Innominate	2	Tibia	1	Sesamoids	1
Long bone frags.	14				
Indeterminable frags.	58				

In addition there are 4 determinable bovid bones and 5 fragments of equid atlas vertebrae, plus some other indeterminable, non-hippo bones. Not all small fragments are individually plotted.

All of the hippopotamus skeletal material could well come from a single individual, except for one unfused humerus epiphysis, which, if it is a hippo bone, must come from a different individual. The hippo is not identical with the modern hippo and is assumed to be *Hippopotamus gorgops*.

Key to the letters used to designate different body parts of the Hippo:

Cranial fragment	c	Tooth	d
Vertebra	v	Rib Shaft	/
Rib: proximal fragment	rb	Innominate	in
Humerus	h	Radius	r
Ulna	u	Femur	f
Tibia	t	Calcaneum	ca
Metapodial	m	Phalange	ph
Other podial	p	Sesamoid	s
Indeterminate fragment	x		
Bovid bone/tooth	B	Equid bone/tooth	E

3. *Size of Excavation.* A trench 5 x 5 ft (~1.5 x 1.5m). Surface traces at the site indicate a concentration with a diameter of less than 45m.

4. *Archeological Material Recovered.* 63 artifacts.

5. *Location.* Precise data is not available, but the site is said to be outside the enclosure and presumed to be along the western line of outcrops of this stratigraphic horizon. A surface concentration and the traces of a trench were located at the point shown in figure 6 (chap. 2). This is presumed to be the site.

6. *Stratigraphy.* The uppermost part of Member 1. The material appears to derive from a complex of units involving a clay (? paleosol) and a volcanic sand that covers it and locally fills small channels that are eroded through it. This complex is overlain by the pure diatomites of Member 2.

7. *Disposition of Material.* No details available.

8. *Evidence of Disturbance.* The material is partially rounded, but abrasion is not distinguishable from weathering.

9. *Associated Faunal Remains.* Fossil bone fragments are relatively common in the supposed vicinity of the site. No record of finds in the excavation is available.

10. *Paleoenvironmental Context.* Silt flats with clay/silt substratum at least 1 km from the rocky slopes of Mount Olorgesailie, and 1 to 2 km from the tip of the peninsula. The artifact horizon is immediately overlain by clay and pure diatomite, indicating that the lake may have been encroaching during the time the site was occupied.

11. *Interpretation.* A small sample of an apparently localized occurrence, probably representing a short duration. Degree of bias relative to total artifact content unknown. Leakey reported 121 specimens (in MS). My analysis included only 63, and I did not become aware of the discrepancy until after leaving Nairobi. The data must therefore be treated as incomplete.

I 3 (Isaac Site 3)(pls. 3, 4).

1. *Alternative designations.* None.

2. *Excavators.* Glynn and Barbara Isaac from 1961 to 1962.

3. *Size of Excavation.* A trench system adjacent to the rock ridge or peninsula, as shown in figure 14 was dug to uncover approximately 130 m^2 (1400 ft^2) of the main artifact-bearing horizon (disconformity). The total extent of the occurrence is judged from surface traces to have been at least 900 m^2.

4. *Archeological Material Recovered.* 5001 artifacts.

5. *Location.* About 100 m outside the northern boundary of the Prehistoric Site enclosure, at a point where erosion is just stripping off silts that formerly covered the southern end of the rocky lava ridge in the Olorgesailie Formation. (see fig. 14).

6. *Stratigraphy.* A series of units near the upper limit of Member 1. Artifacts are scattered through the beds, but the principal occurrence is associated with an irregular, gently eroded surface (disconformity) developed on a small thickness of laminated diatomite. The horizon is covered with massive, root-marked, reworked diatomaceous silts that appear to be low energy alluvial and colluvial deposits. The sediments have been tilted by renewed uplift of the lava ridge, which is actually a narrow horst.

7. *Disposition of Material.* Archeological material occurred in three parts of the profile (see fig. 15): (1) dispersed through silts underlying the unconformity and the diatomite (zone L); (2) concentrated on the erosion surface of the unconformity and in the 15-20 cm of silt immediately overlying it (zone M); and (3) dispersed through the silts overlying

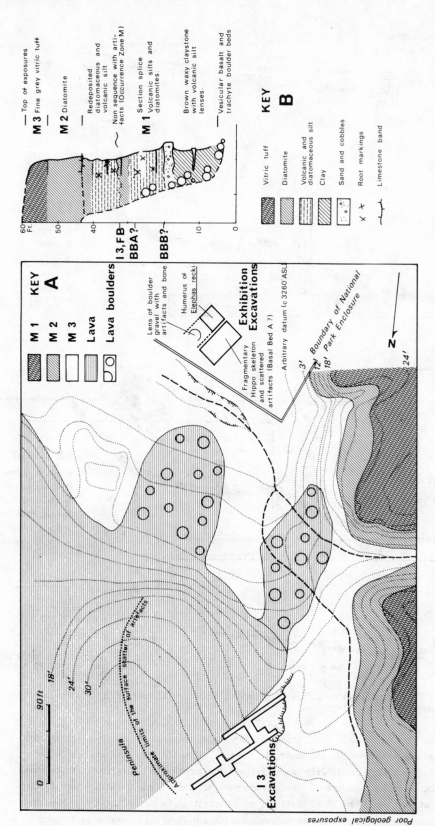

Figure 14. (A) Contoured geological map of Site I 3. Surveyed by N. Iberall and G. Isaac; (B) Composite section illustrating stratigraphy in the vicinity.

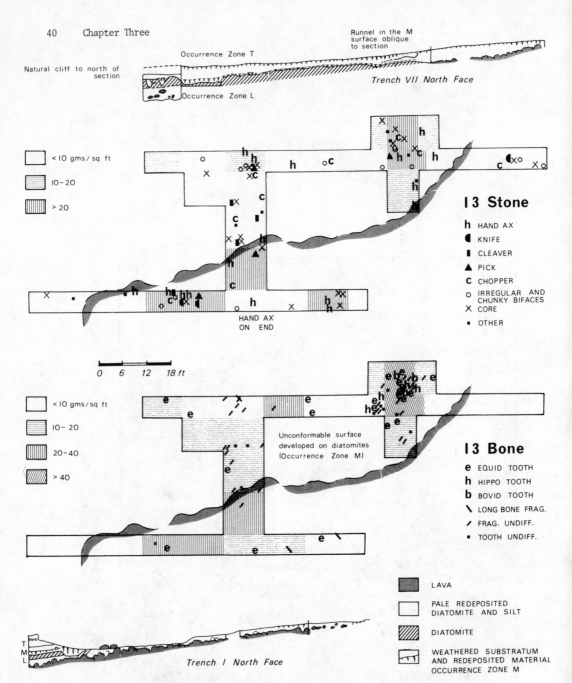

Figure 15.   Plan of excavations of Site I 3 showing densities of material recovered and the location of selected categories.

zone M (zone T). Against the rock surface of the ridge, these three zones were telescoped, making them indistinguishable, and material from this segment of the site was designated zone 0. Tests for significant differences between the zone 0 and M material indicate that these can be treated as samples of the same assemblage. Zones L and T yielded very little material, but what was found shows little or no important differences. As can be seen on the plans, density of finds on the unconformity surface M shows considerable variation, with pieces tending to be concentrated at the junction of the rock slope and silt flats, where a shallow runnel developed locally. One hand ax was found standing on its tip in a manner suggesting that it had been placed in its position by man (see Isaac 1966b).

8. *Evidence of Disturbance*. Erosive processes continued after the accumulation of at least some of the occupation debris, as concentrations were found in the base of erosion runnels. A large proportion of the bone showed signs of weathering and abrasion. The lava specimens were too heavily altered for an independent assessment of abrasion. Experiments (Isaac 1967b:40) indicate that the bone cannot have been exposed for more than a decade or so.

9. *Associated Faunal Remains*. Of the 19.2 kg of bone waste that was recovered, most was finely comminuted. Identifiable remains include fragments of *Equus oldowayensis*, *Stylohipparion albertense*, rhinoceros, hippopotamus, a warthog, various bovids ranging from buffalo size to impala size, and a very few fragments of bird, frog, and fish bones, the last three not being associated with the occupation.

Fine root channels in the redeposited sediments and penetrating into the underlying diatomite indicate a grass/herb vegetation. It is likely that there were trees on the rock ridge. What appears to have been a fossil termitary penetrates from Horizon M.

10. *Paleoenvironmental Context*. A well-drained area on the gentle west slope of the tip of the rocky peninsula surrounded by more swampy alluvial flats that were temporarily subject to erosion and weathering. Stable lake waters were at least 2.5 km away.

11. *Interpretation*. A sample, about 14% or less, of a large scatter of material probably representing a palimpsest of discontinuous occupations with slightly shifting foci. The time span represented might be guessed to lie in the range of 100 to 1000 years. Inspection of surface material does not suggest any pronounced bias of the sample. Consumption of a variety of game meats is one well-documented activity.

The Middle Stratigraphic Set of Occurrences

Following the deposition of Member 1 and the Lower Stratigraphic Set of sites that it contains, there was a major expansion of stable lake waters that submerged the entire area in which natural exposures of Members 1 and 2 now occur. Some 4m of relatively pure diatomite (Member 2) and about 3m of tuffaceous diatomite were laid down. Both these units are archeologically sterile. Member 4 is a relatively thin series of sandstones and pumice granule gravels that probably represents a regressional beach. Members 5 through 8 are the fine-grained deposits of a lake margin floodplain. Member 7 in particular shows gentle cut-and-fill bedding associated with the development of shallow, presumably ephemeral stream channels that traversed the floodplain. It is with outcrops of this group of beds and with Member 7 especially that the major concentrations of artifacts at Olorgesailie are associated. A persistent scatter of artifacts and occasionally more concentrated patches (sites) occur all along the outcrops of Members 5 to 8, but in one locality there is a singular cluster. This area, which has come to be known as the Main Site, is situated on an east-facing erosion scarp that bisects the sedimentary basin. The Prehistoric Site boundaries were fixed to enclose this cluster in the center of the archeological reserve. The area in question is only 115 m from north to south and 65 m from east to west, and yet at least seven distinct artifact occurrences have been found within it. These include several of the spectacular concentrations of large artifacts that helped to make Olorgesailie famous. Aerial views (pls. 5, 6), a plan (fig. 16), and a leveled profile illustrate the modern topographic and structural features of the locality. Plates 7 through 15 illustrate

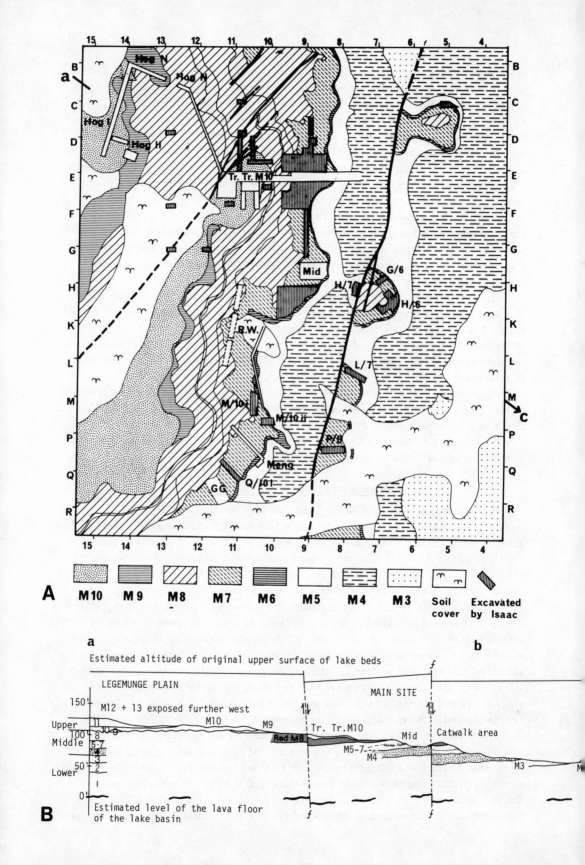

A

M10   M9   M8   M7   M6   M5   M4   M3   Soil cover   Excavated by Isaac

B

a   b

Estimated altitude of original upper surface of lake beds

LEGEMUNGE PLAIN   MAIN SITE

M12 + 13 exposed further west

Upper   Middle   Lower

Estimated level of the lava floor of the lake basin

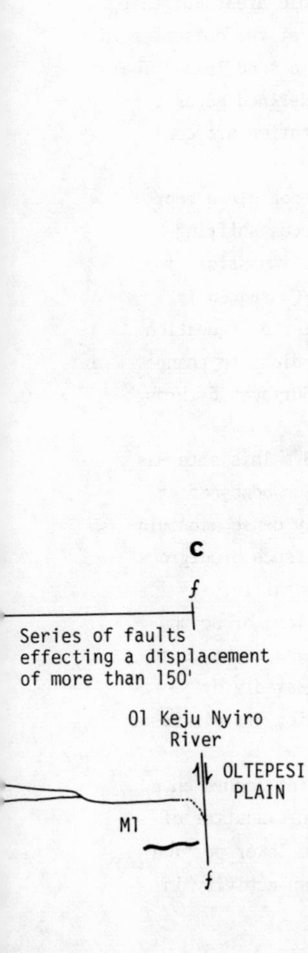

Figure 16. (A) Geological map of the Main Site showing the reference grid (B - R/4 - 15) and the excavations. (Based on R. M. Shackleton with additions); (B) A diagrammatic west to east section down the erosion scarp at the latitude of the Main Site.

c

f

Series of faults
effecting a displacement
of more than 150'

Ol Keju Nyiro
River

OLTEPESI
PLAIN

M1

f

some of the spectacular artifact concentrations that make up the Main Site. It can be seen
that the Olorgesailie Formation is cut by north-south tending faults with differential
movement, establishing a gentle scarp. The sites are being exposed by erosion along one
part of the scarp. Minor faults interact with a gentle westerly dip to induce a doubling
of some of the Member 4 to 8 outcrops (see fig. 16).

The sample of artifact occurrences available for investigation is restricted to a
narrow zone at the erosion front, which is a strip no more than 50-100 m wide. Within this
strip, some sites have been cut extensively by erosion and are represented by a lag concentrate of large pieces lying on the slopes below the position of their source horizon (pls.
7, 8, 18); others are only partly dissected, and the undisturbed portion could be located
in the outcrop and excavated. The location and character of sites further to the east or
west of the outcrop strip are entirely unknown, since these have either been destroyed by
denudation or are deeply buried in the hillside.

Within the Main Site area, individual concentrations of occupation debris were marked
by irregular fan-shaped scatters of stone below the outcrops of the source horizon, with
some pieces still seen embedded in the outcrop. The distribution of derived pieces on the
surface showed clearly the existence of foci of greater density, and these were investigated in a series of trenches and soundings dug by Louis and Mary Leakey. Further excavations during the period from 1962 to 1964 showed that in general these foci were not merely
centers of maximum density in a general scatter of pieces covering the whole area, but that
each was a discrete concentration. This finding had not been anticipated at the outset.

The material of each dense occurrence rests on a bedding plane or in a sand lens. The
concentrations vary in diameter from 5 to 20 m and commonly have sharply defined edges,
rather than gradational boundaries. General features and their interpretation are considered in chapter 4.

The various surfaces on which the accumulation of occupation debris took place represent very minor pauses in deposition or localized erosion during a continuous shifting
process of alluvial and colluvial cut-and-fill aggradation. It has proved impossible to
trace most of these minor disconformities laterally over the whole site. Consequently,
while sequences for certain areas of the Main Site can be established, all the occupation
foci cannot be fitted into a single sequence. It has thus been found expedient to change
from Leakey's designation of the occupation foci by serial numbers (Land Surfaces 6 through
10) to a grid reference scheme (fig. 16).

The site which has been most completely excavated is DE/89, Horizon B. This site was
littered with more than a ton of humanly introduced stone, and the broken-up bones of at
least fifty baboons. The Catwalk area (pls. 7, 8, 18) displays a similarly dense accumulation recently cut into by erosion. Outside the confines of the Main Site, such prodigious
accumulations of archeological material have not been encountered at Olorgesailie.

It is quite clear that the conjunction of so many discrete concentrations of occupation debris within the narrow confines of the Main Site cannot be regarded as a chance occurrence in a random scatter of sites. This small locality was chosen repeatedly by
Acheulean man for reasons that remain uncertain, though various possibilities are discussed
in chapter 4.

In each of the seven artifact concentrations, the archeological material occurs on a
bedding plane or in a thin lens of sediment. In addition, there is a diffuse scatter of
pieces throughout the thickness of the containing silts, principally in the lower portion
of Member 7. These dispersed pieces are assumed to document recurrent human activity in

the locality. The known occupation foci may well be only a fraction of a larger series. The continual use of such camps in the neighborhood would have resulted in the sporadic loss or discard of stone objects throughout the area.

The Main Site lies in the middle of the gap between the toe of the peninsula and the foot of Mount Olorgesailie. This gap is estimated to have been about 2.5 km wide during the time the site was occupied, and through it must have passed all drainage links between the eastern and western halves of the basin. The strata containing the sites include numerous small channels, and most of the occupation sites are associated with streambeds These streambeds have the appearance of ephemeral, seasonal features: very shallow, braided grooves with sandy patches along their courses. The largest were perhaps 15 to 20m wide and 50 to 100 cm deep, with very gently sloping banks (see sections of DE/89, fig. 17). Root marks in the silts that covered the terrain outside the watercourses suggest that the surrounding flats may have been covered with a thick grass and shrub vegetation, and lo- cally with larger bushes. It is possible that the larger bushes and trees were concen- trated along the watercourses, as happens in the area today. The cast of a single large root was preserved in the silts of one site (DE/89 C, pl. 17).

Though there may have been seasonal swamp pools in various parts of the basin, the stable lake waters, if they existed during the time of the occupation of the Main Site, were confined to the Koora trough about 3 km away.

Table 2 contains details of the lithology and stratigraphy of Members 4 to 8, which crop out in the Main Site. Several trenches within the Main Site revealed superimposed occurrences. These are designated Horizons A, B, C, and so on, from the base upward. The sites are reported by starting at the north end of the grid and working south.

I also excavated one occurrence at this Horizon, but outside the Main Site. This was the site of LHS, which was chosen because of its contrast with the Main Site series. About 2 km to the west, a paleosol clay within Member 7 was observed to contain a significant but relatively low density scatter of material. Our excavation uncovered fairly large areas of the horizon and recovered a sample of the material. More such excavations away from the spectacular concentrations will be necessary in order to ascertain whether the latter are distinctive in ways other than their high densities.

Main Site DE/89 (pl. 9)

This is the largest excavation undertaken at Olorgesailie. Figure 17 presents a block diagram of the system of trenches and cuttings, and shows the stratigraphic units involved.

The site was first investigated in 1943 by the excavation of the lowermost steps of Louis and Mary Leakey's "Trial Trench." They recognized two rich archeological horizons, which they labeled B1 (upper) and B2 (lower); these were later referred to as Land Surfaces 7 and 6, respectively. The Leakeys left parts of the highly concentrated archeological material of Land Surface 7 in place under a thatched roof as a public exhibition. These exhibition areas are marked XA and XB on the figure.

In 1962, when I assumed responsibility for completing the research, I decided simply to investigate the margins of the concentrated patch of material the Leakeys had discovered. I expected that densities would fall off in a gradational manner; however, cutting E/89 on the south side of the exhibition shed produced virtually no finds, nor did cutting C/8i on the north side. It was then clear that the occurrence was a highly localized concentration, and I was obliged to demolish the museum-on-the-spot and excavate the block surrounding the Leakey's trial trench and exhibition areas. This is shown in the figure as the central

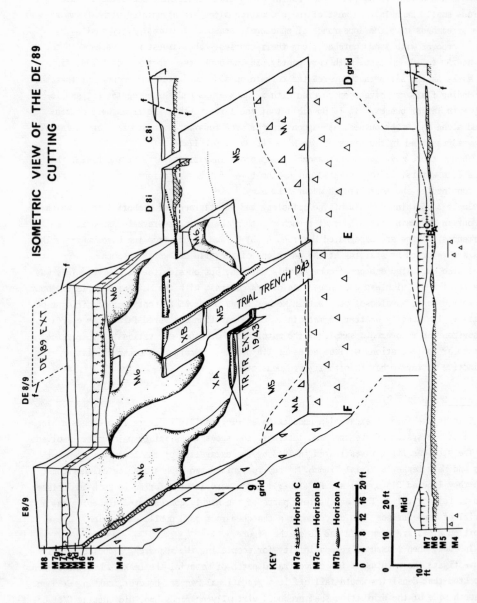

Figure 17. An isometric diagram showing the stratigraphy in Site DE/89 in relation to the layout of trenches. A true scale cross section is shown below.

DE/89 cutting. It became apparent that above the two horizons recognized by the Leakeys there was a third one. I have relabeled these Horizons A, B, and C (bottom to top). It also emerged that all three occurrences are associated with a small paleowatercourse that trends diagonally from southeast to northwest across the site.

The channel was gently incised during the deposition of Member 7, which is a complex layer comprised of fine-grained cut-and-fill fluviatile and floodplain deposits. The channel bed was eroded through Member 6 into the top of Member 5. Initially it had a width of approximately 6m (20 ft). To the northeast, preexisting silts (Member 7a) formed a gentle bank rising at least 60 cm (2 ft) above the channel bed. On the southwest the margin may well have been part of an ill-defined braided complex that merged gently into the floodplain. Horizon A is associated with the very base of the channel cut and shows clear signs of fluvial transport or rearrangement. The watercourse then began to be filled with sediment, and at the same time the floodplain was probably aggrading. A bed of silty sand (Member 7b) some 25 cm thick covered Horizon A and was itself capped by a sheet of somewhat coarser sand (Member 7c) that also spread out to the southwest of the deepest part of the incised bed. As the stippled areas of figure 17 show, elevated banks formed by the sands of Member 6 projected up through these later sands. Spectacularly high densities of artifacts and broken bones occur at the top surface of the Member 7c sands, and it is these that comprise Horizon B (pls. 13, 14, 15). If figures 17 and 18 are compared, it can be seen that the distribution of the archeological material is more or less restricted to the irregular area over which the sands were emplaced. I am inclined to think that the sand and the artifacts were swept in together. However, it seems unlikely that the archeological material comes from very far away. I suspect that this extraordinarily high density of artifacts and bone refuse represents the concentration, brought about by current action, of material formerly scattered along a short stretch of the streambed. Specific evidence is summarized in the section below dealing with Horizon B, and interpretation is discussed in chapter 4.

As the channel continued to be filled with sediment, Horizon B was gently covered with a bed of slightly sandy root-marked silts (Member 7d). Horizon C represents a pause in the process of siltation. A patch of artifacts only 5 or 6 m in diameter occurs with a very minor silty sand lens in the bed of what was by now an indistinct channel which probably sustained only very weak flow. It is likely that the principal stream had shifted and that its former channel was active only at flood stage. It is not clear whether or not the material of Horizon C has been rearranged by current action, but it certainly cannot have been moved far.

The last traces of the channel were filled in by a bed of pale, root-marked silt (Member 7e), which formed part of a more or less level floodplain surface. This surface was evidently stable enough for a soil to develop (Member 7f). Greenish clay was formed or deposited on the upper part of Member 7e, and clay-filled cracks penetrate the underlying units (Members 7e and d). I am indebted to I. W. Cornwall for a report on samples from this paleosol profile.

Over the level floodplain surface that is marked by the Member 7f clays, the fine diatomaceous silts of Member 7g were deposited. These appear to represent swamp and pond deposits that were probably associated with subsidence along the fault planes in this area. The outcrop sections of the site are capped by the hard, reddened sediments of Member 8.

The site closest to DE/89 is the Mid and H/9 complex some 34 m south of it. As the profile in figure 17 shows, the lateral relations could not be determined in detail. The

DE/89 channel deposits merge into the silts of Member 7 when traced in a southerly direction, and then at a certain point beyond that, the northern edge of the Mid-H/9 complex is
encountered at a level within Member 7 that is very close to the one from which the DE/89
channel was incised.

The specifics of each of the three archeological horizons are given below, according
to the standard format being used for site reports.

Main Site DE/89, Horizon A (pls. 10, 11, 12)

1. *Alternative Designations*. Tr. Tr. B2 (L. S. B. Leakey, in MS); Land Surface 6 (L. S.
B. Leakey, in MS; Kleindienst 1961).
2. *Excavator*. L. S. B. Leakey and M. D. Leakey in 1943, and by Isaac from 1962 to 1964.
3. *Size of Excavation*. L. S. B. Leakey (in MS) reports that "only an area 10 x 20 ft
of this particular land surface has so far been excavated." However, the drawn sections
and trench plans indicate an extension (Tr. Tr., ext. 1), making the total area 35 m^2. An
area (XB) of approximately 4.65 m^2 had been left within Trial Trench as an exhibition illustrating Land Surface 7 (Horizon B). This was excavated to the unconformable contacts
with Members 6 and 5, and yielded the sample of Horizon A recovered by Isaac. The large
tools were left in place after measurement and recording.
4. *Archeological Material Recovered*.

Tr. Tr. B2 Leakey (in MS)   675 (103 fresh Acheulean; 20 brown black patina; 552
                                        rolled, derived Tayacian)

      Kleindienst (1961)   740

      Isaac   585 (incomplete record of rubble)

DE/89 A (Isaac 1964-65)   373

5. *Location*. DE/89 grid squares of the Main Site (fig. 16).
6. *Stratigraphy*. The horizon is a local erosion surface where the DE/89 channel has cut
down from a level within the base of Member 7 and incised gently through Member 6, which
is very thin here, and into the top of Member 5. The material occurred within very minor
sand lenses resting on the scoured interface. The horizon was then buried by the emplacement of a lens of silty sand (Member 7b), which was confined to the floor of the channel
itself, and which in fact was localized to scoured-out depressions within the channel,
since it was found to lens out when traced northwest into the DE/89 extension (see fig. 17).
No discernible weathering horizon is associated with this earliest phase of the channel,
and the beds of Member 6 and Member 5 cut by it have proved sterile of artifacts along the
considerable extent of outcrops in which they are exposed. It therefore seems likely that
the time span for the material of this occurrence was restricted to the time span of deposition of Member 7a, from which some of it may derive, and to the period of erosion of the
channel feature.
7. *Disposition of Material*. The artifacts recovered by Isaac were clearly concentrated in
the central runnel of the watercourse, and virtually nothing was found on the banks (pls.
10, 11, 12). Some tendency to preferred orientation transverse to the channel, and also
parallel to it, can be detected.
8. *Evidence of Disturbance*. The stratigraphic context of the pieces concentrated in the
axial gutter of the runnel leaves little doubt that rearrangement has occurred. The large
tools do not, however, show any appreciable degree of rounding from abrasion, perhaps indicating redistribution, rather than prolonged transport in the channel. Many small tools
and flakes show a degree of rounding of arêtes, in excess of the rounding expected from

weathering. It is thus very possible that this aggregate is, as postulated by Leakey
(1952), a compound of more than one site assemblage. However, our understanding of the
mechanics of such processes has advanced very little since Leakey's writing (Isaac 1967b).
9. *Associated Faunal Remains*. Details not available for the 1943 excavation. An equid
cannon bone, a very weathered ?giraffe cannon bone, and a few teeth and phalanges of
Theropithecus sp. (possibly derived from overlying Horizon B before consolidation of intervening sands) were discovered in the 1965 excavations.
10. *Paleoenvironmental Context*. The channel of an ephemeral stream traversing silt flats
surrounding the lake margin. Stable lake waters were probably not less than 5 km away.
The original relationship of the occupation site or sites from which the material is derived is not known, but it is suspected that they must have been in, or immediately adjacent to the watercourse (see chap. 4).
11. *Interpretation*. The artifacts recovered appear to be a sample of an occurrence of
material known to have been disturbed, and in part abraded, subsequent to abandonment.
The occurrence possibly represents the combination of more than one site assemblage; however, the stratigraphic context implies a limited time span for the component source assemblages (if more than one is involved), and derivation from any great distance seems unlikely.

It can be estimated that between 50 and 70% of the surviving occurrence lens was excavated, the extent of the lens prior to erosion cannot be estimated.

Main Site DE/89, Horizon B (pls. 13, 14, 15)

This is the largest individual occurrence exposed by excavation at Olorgesailie, and
one of the largest uncovered anywhere. As already indicated in the introductory discussion
of the DE/89 site as a whole, the occurrence, with a diameter of about 12-15 m is a highly
concentrated patch of artifacts, broken bone, and cobbles. The margins of the patch are
extremely sharply defined, and its distribution is almost exactly coincident with that of
the thin sand lens of Member 7c. Throughout the excavation we debated whether the material
had been dropped by prehistoric humans exactly where we found it, or whether some natural
agency associated with the channel had caused the concentration. Several geologists and
archeologists who visited the site declared themselves unable to envisage how such a
localized concentration could be produced other than by human agencies. However, to us
the close association with a particular sand lens seemed to have contrary indications.
Later, we learned of Luna Leopold's work on the kinematic wave effect in stream transport,
and his theory seemed to provide a possible explanatory mechanism. (This model for interpretation of the site is discussed in chap. 4.) The technical details of information on
the site are set out below using the standard format.
1. *Alternative Designations*. Tr. Tr. B4 (L. S. B. Leakey, in MS). Land Surface 7 (L. S.
B. Leakey 1951; Kleindienst 1961). DE/89, Horizon B (Isaac 1968, and this report).
2. *Excavator*. M. D. and L. S. B. Leakey in 1943 and later (Tr. Tr. B4 and the exhibition
areas XA and XB); Isaac from 1962 to 1965 uncovered the areas surrounding the Leakeys' excavation.
3. *Size of Excavation*. The Trial Trench and extensions of 1943 excavation exposed about
34 m^2 of the occurrence. An additional 12 m^2 were opened up as exhibitions, and these remained available for study in 1963. My excavation of the surrounding areas raised the
total area to about 260 m^2 (see fig. 18). Because the site is in the center of a field
exhibition of the Kenya National Museum, most of the large tools were plotted, recorded,
and measured in place, and preserved as a display.

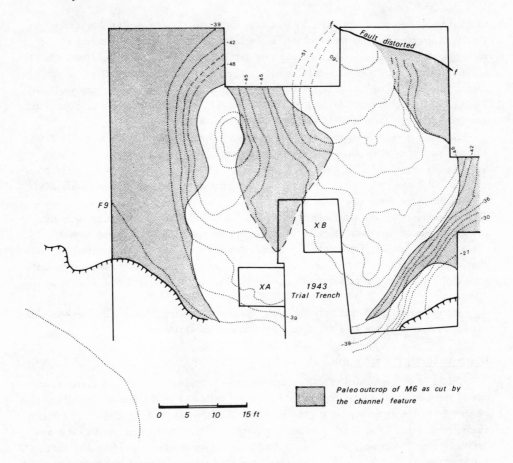

Figure 18. A reconstructed contour plot of the surface termed Horizon B. The effect of post-depositional tectonic deformation has been eliminated by a geometric construction restoring the paleosol, Member 7f, to a horizontal plane. The contour values are computed depths below this plane in inches.

4. *Archeological Material Recovered.*

Recorded by L. S. B. Leakey in MS from Tr. Tr. B4	219	(167 fresh; 52 weathered)
Reported by Kleindienst from Land Surface 7	205	
Recorded by Isaac (table 9) from museum collections and exhibition areas	332	
From the 1962-65 excavations	4429	
Total in this study	4751	

A rough computation of the total weight of material involved in this occurrence produced the following estimates (Isaac 1966b):

Large cutting tools	453 kg
Unmodified boulders and cobbles (?manuports)	422 kg
Debitage and other tools	180 kg
	1055 kg

If the estimate is enlarged to allow for the parts of the site destroyed by erosion, then at least 25 to 50% can be added to these figures. Clearly the occurrence gives evidence that the hominids responsible carried at least one or two tons of stone to this vicinity.

The great majority of the materials are trachytes and other lavas from Mount Olorgesailie (see appendix B1); however, there are smaller quantities of chert, quartz, granite, and gneiss. Of special note is a large granite spheroid weighing 1.7 kg. About two-thirds of the manuports are of the slightly vesicular lavas that crop out on the peninsula a kilometer away. The largest unmodified stones weigh from 4 to 6 kg.

5. *Location*. In the DE/89 grid squares of the Main Site (fig. 16).

6. *Stratigraphy*. On and in a silty sand spread of complex lens representing a phase in the silting of the erosion runnel that contains DE/89 A along its line of deepest incision. The lens is a component of Member 7, with the site designation Member 7c. The underlying Member 7b sandy unit contains relatively few pieces; the material is concentrated in the 8 to 10 cm of the Member 7c sand and especially at its surface. The sand commonly grades upward into silts, Member 7d, the base of which contains many pieces.

7. *Disposition of Material*. The very impressive bulk of material (pls. 13, 14, 15) is almost entirely coincident with the distribution of the Member 7c sandy lens and confined within the limits of the silted channel (about 14 m wide at this point). The plans and photographs show that the material is grouped into irregular clusters with intervening bare patches. In some clusters pieces rest against each other. An analysis of orientation indicates a very slight tendency to alignment transverse and axial to the channel; however, the pattern is not strong enough to achieve significance in an X^2 test (Isaac 1968: pl. III, p. 10).

The distribution of specimens on the floor was mapped on a 1:24 plan. Figures 19 through 23 present plots of the spatial arrangement for the five major categories of items. I have not been able to discern telltale patterns, and the densities of all classes of material seem to be reasonably concordant.

Figure 18 presents a contoured plan of Horizon B. In order to correct for the tectonic tilting that has affected the site, the contours express depth below Member 7f, the clay paleosol that is believed to have formed a more or less level surface after the channel was filled with silt. Comparison of figure 18 with figures 19 through 23 shows the way in which the archeological material is confined to the lower-lying areas and is virtually absent from even the minor topographic highs formed by banks of Member 6 projecting through the sands of Member 7c. Figure 18 also provides a graphic summary of the material scattered on the surface over the area in which erosion has cut back into the horizon.

As the figures show, we extended the excavation in order to ascertain whether the high concentrations continued further along the bed of the paleochannel. We found that the density fell off rapidly in this direction. Plates 13, 14, and 15 show a photograph of the extension and of the downstream margin of the concentrated patch. As can be seen, a minor fault cuts the horizon, displacing it downward to the west. Although it would be possible to excavate further along the paleochannel course, one would need to dig through 5-10 m or more of consolidated overburden to do so.

8. *Evidence of Disturbance*. This occurrence poses complex problems. I favor the interpretation that the prodigious concentration of artifacts represents the telescoping, by stream action involving the kinematic wave effect (see chap. 4), of a series of overlapping occupation scatters. The evidence indicates, but does not prove, that a relatively short time span was involved. The artifacts show a normal range of degree of rounding, but this appears to be closely related to degree of chemical alteration; most coarse trachyte pieces are fresh.

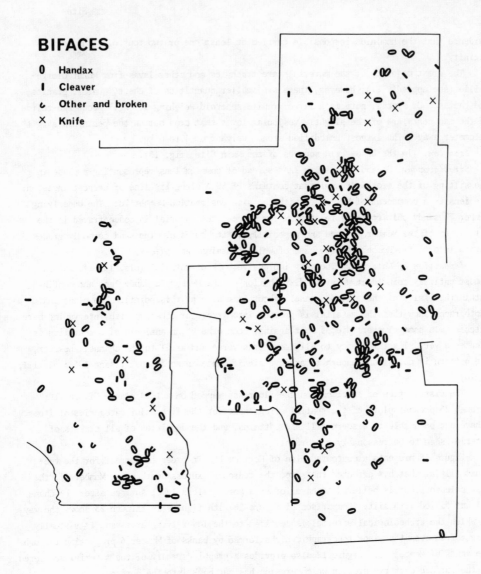

BIFACES

0   Handax

I   Cleaver

ᴄ   Other and broken

✕   Knife

Figures 19 - 23. DE/89, Horizon B. Plans showing the positions of plotted pieces. These plots are based extensively on field excavation records and make apparent the general concordance of the distribution of the various categories of objects with one another and with the areas where the channel feature has cut through the harder green sand of Member 6.

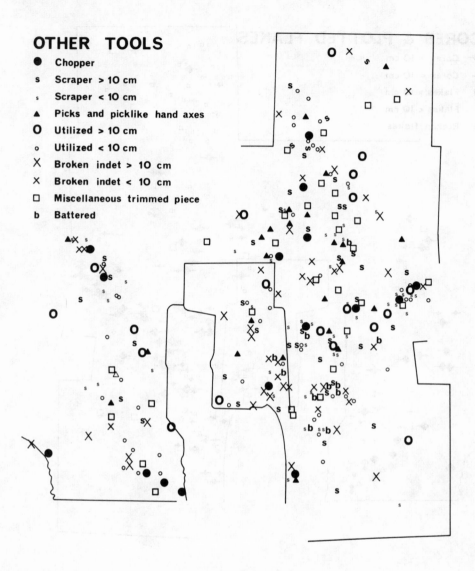

OTHER TOOLS

● Chopper
s Scraper > 10 cm
s Scraper < 10 cm
▲ Picks and picklike hand axes
O Utilized > 10 cm
o Utilized < 10 cm
X Broken indet > 10 cm
X Broken indet < 10 cm
□ Miscellaneous trimmed piece
b Battered

Figure 20.

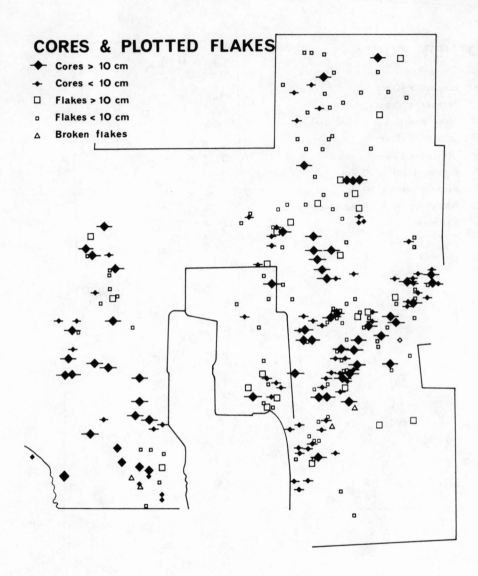

CORES & PLOTTED FLAKES

◆ Cores > 10 cm
◆ Cores < 10 cm
□ Flakes > 10 cm
▫ Flakes < 10 cm
△ Broken flakes

Figure 21.

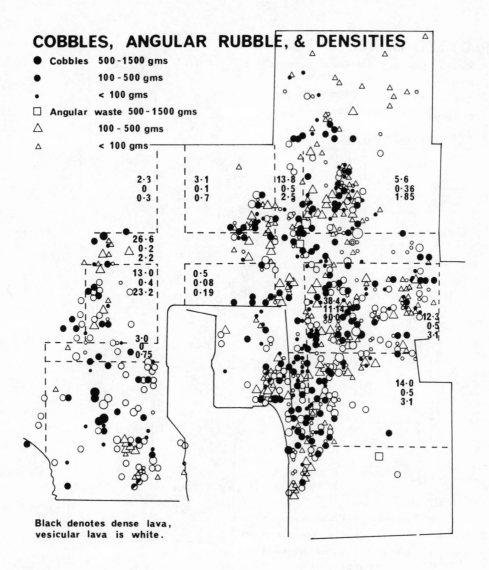

COBBLES, ANGULAR RUBBLE, & DENSITIES

- ● Cobbles 500-1500 gms
- ● 100 - 500 gms
- • < 100 gms
- ☐ Angular waste 500-1500 gms
- △ 100 - 500 gms
- △ < 100 gms

Black denotes dense lava, vesicular lava is white.

Figure 22. During excavation smaller artifacts, mainly small flakes and angular rubble, were collected in sets, "bags," each pertaining to one of the excavation squares shown. The densities of bone splinters in grams per square foot is given in the top number; numbers of flakes per square foot in the middle number; number of angular fragments per square foot in the bottom number.

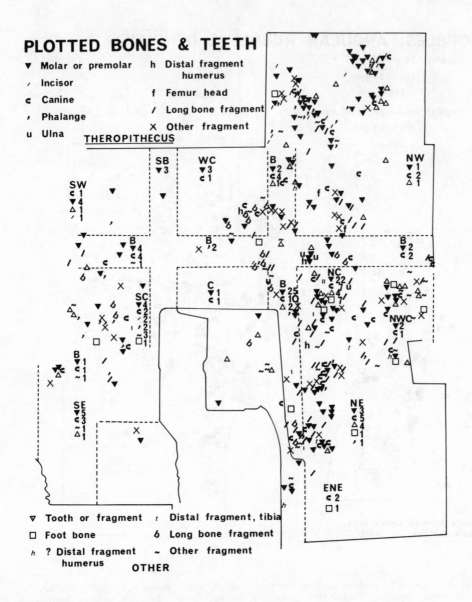

PLOTTED BONES & TEETH

▼ Molar or premolar h Distal fragment humerus
, Incisor   f Femur head
c Canine   / Long bone fragment
, Phalange   X Other fragment
u Ulna

THEROPITHECUS

▽ Tooth or fragment t Distal fragment, tibia
□ Foot bone   b Long bone fragment
h ? Distal fragment ~ Other fragment
  humerus

OTHER

Figure 23. Distribution of bones and teeth with series from small finds bags shown next to the appropriate subarea of the site. The identifications are field identifications.

9. *Associated Faunal Remains*. This occurrence has yielded the largest assemblage of bones recovered from any site at Olorgesailie. The greater part of the material consists of smashed bone splinters, which give every indication of being humanly generated food refuse. The aggregate of unidentifiable bone splinters weighs about 15 kg.

Most of the identifiable specimens belong to the extinct relative of the gelada baboon, *Theropithecus (Simopithecus) oswaldi* (Leakey and Whitworth 1958). There are 1008 complete isolated teeth in the excavated series studied by Meave and Richard Leakey. More can be seen in the portion of the deposit left in place in order to preserve the floor as an exhibit. Of these, 153 of the teeth are deciduous (See appendix B7 by Meave Leakey). This report indicates that the minimum number of adults represented is 44, a figure somewhat lower than that previously given in a letter by L. S. B. Leakey and quoted by Isaac (1968a and b; 1971). Between 6 and 17 individuals appear to be represented by the deciduous teeth. There are also some well-preserved long bones, very numerous phalanges, and some mandibular fragments. Skulls, ribs, and vertebrae have survived in scarcely recognizable form. (See also M. G. and R. E. Leakey 1973.)

Other finds include very fragmentary remains of

> Elephant (*Elephas recki*)
> Hippopotamus
> Rhinoceros
> *Giraffa gracilis* (Gentry, pers. comm.)
> A bovine larger than buffalo or *Pelorovis* (? *Homoioceros* sp.) (Gentry, pers. comm.)
> Various antelope
> Equids
> Suids
> A few small rodent, bird, frog, and fish bones and crocodile teeth, which may
>   not be specifically associated with the occupation.

The bone remains show marked variation in degree of weathering, which suggests that they may have accumulated over a few seasons, rather than at one occupation.

Grass root cavities occur, together with tree and shrub root casts, in the silt adjacent to and within the channel.

10. *Paleoenvironmental Context*. The campsites from which the material derives were probably situated wholly or partly on the sandy floor of the ephemeral drainage channel traversing the silt flats. It is possible that large trees grew along the line of the channel, providing shade for men and roosts for the *Theropithecus* troops. The site was probably not less than 5 km from the stable water of the lake, but the channels may have provided a place where water could be obtained by digging. The rocky peninsula was about 600 m away.

11. *Interpretation*. The material recovered seems to be a sample of a naturally concentrated aggregate that probably represents the compounding of a series of initially more scattered human occupation assemblages. It is believed that the occupation material accumulated during a limited time span, that the material is stylistically homogeneous, and that repeated pursuit of baboons was involved.

Main Site DE/89, Horizon C (pls. 16, 17)

1. *Alternative Designations*. None.
2. *Excavator*. Isaac, from 1962 to 1964.
3. *Size of Excavation*. See figure 18. The occurrence had not been detected in Leakey's 1943 excavation and was not expected. It was discovered during removal of the lower tuffaceous silt portion of Member 7. The slightly elevated southern slope of the old land surface was partially cut into before the feature was observed. Approximately 93 m^2 of the horizon has now been uncovered.

4. *Archeological Material Recovered*. 1154 artifacts, 80 manuports.

5. *Location*. In the DE/89 grid square of the Main Site (fig. 16).

6. *Stratigraphy*. In Member 7, associated with a minor conformity and reincision formed during the silting of the channel that also contains DE/89 A and B. The axis of the channel contains small lenses of sandy silt and derived sediment, pebbles, and crumbs. The entire matrix of the horizon appears to have undergone weathering during the formation of the overlying paleosol, Member 7f, with the development of clay. The artifacts are also very deeply altered.

7. *Disposition of Material*. Most of the collection comes from a cluster of stones, artifacts, rubble, and cobbles in the axis of the runnel (pl. 16). Outside this patch only isolated pieces occur. A complete plot cannot be prepared because of the disturbance of outlying parts of the horizon before its excavation. No significant preferred orientation of pieces or tilting was observed.

8. *Evidence of Disturbance*. The heavy weathering of the stone prevents examination for minor traces of abrasion, but it is clear that the material was not heavily abraded. The concentration was initially interpreted as due to localization of occupation (Isaac 1966b); however, the kinematic wave effect may well account for it, and the site may be a smaller analogue of DE/89 B, which underlies it (see chap. 4).

9. *Associated Faunal Remains*. Small quantities of soft, friable, weathered fossil bone were recovered. Among these only a few equid teeth, a hippopotamus tusk, and a weathered *Theropithecus* tooth were identifiable. A large, ramifying root cast was excavated. Fine white silts appear to have filled a root cavity, and the whole root cast appears to have become somewhat flattened during compaction (pl. 17).

10. *Paleoecological Context*. A channel traversing silt flats at some distance (not less than 5 km) from stable lacustrine conditions. Other circumstances similar to these underlying DE/89 B.

11. *Interpretation*. A sample of a localized occurrence formed by either localized occupation or by rearrangement of material by fluviatile processes.

Main Site Catwalk Surface Aggregate (pls. 7, 8, 18)

The discovery of this dense residual concentration of artifacts on an erosion surface by M. D. Leakey in 1943 led to the locating and excavating of other Main Site concentrations. The material has been left undisturbed on the surface, and a catwalk for visitors has been constructed across the area.

3 and 4. *Size and Composition of the Aggregate*. We laid down a roughly surveyed grid system over the area and made counts of the material. We measured the large tools in alternate grid squares for length, breadth, thickness, and weight, and drew the outlines of a small number of them for a full set of measurements.

5. *Location*. The outcrop of Members 5 through 8 in grid squares HK/67 of the Main Site (fig. 16).

6. *Stratigraphy*. The material is strewn over the modern ground surface, but it is clear that most of the material derives from the lower tuffaceous silts of Member 7. More than one horizon may have contributed. Material from the erosional truncation of occurrence H/6 A (see below) is certainly included in the surface aggregates. However, morphological characteristics indicate that this horizon was not the main source (see chaps. 5 and 6). Some large pieces showing stylistic resemblance to the common forms of the Catwalk aggregate were found on a minor unconformity in the lower Member 7 silts in the H/6 trench (see

pl. 18), and a few more could be seen along the outcrop of this horizon. The aggregate
also shows stylistic similarity with the Mid series, but erosion cut away the intervening
deposits, so that continuity cannot be established.

Trenches H/6 1 and 2, H/7, and K/7 were excavated in order to locate the source horizon of the surface concentration. Trench H/7 proved virtually sterile; trench K/7 revealed
a thin scatter of large tools and some small artifacts. These may constitute one edge of
a source occurrence of the surface aggregate, but too little material was recovered for a
test of morphological consistency.

7. *Disposition of Material.* The surface aggregate is most dense on the northern slope of
the cirque at the head of a minor gully and along the small incised channel. The concentration occupies an area approximately 18 m from east to west, and 15 m from north to
south. The excavations in the adjoining slopes show that the source horizons were no more
extensive than the surface concentration.

It is probable that there has been some selective destruction and erosional removal of
flakes and small tools. All the large tools were of lava, though a few smaller pieces of
quartz and chert were identified. The lava shows a gradation in degree of weathering from
the top (northwest) to the bottom of the site; pieces on the upper slopes near the outcrop
of Members 6 and 7 are relatively fresh and have the pale color characteristic of excavated
specimens. Downslope pieces are progressively darker, taking on a deep red brown colora-
tion, presumably because of the concentration of ferruginous minerals in the altered crust.
Artifacts of coarse trachyte, which are in the majority, tend to exfoliate thin slabs from
their surfaces, while the basaltic and phonolitic lavas simply crumble.

8. *Evidence of Disturbance.* Exposure by recent erosion has destroyed any detailed evidence of the original mode of emplacement of the material.

9. *Associated Faunal Remains.* Not ascertainable.

10. *Paleoenvironmental Context.* Presumably similar to that of the other Main Site occurrences, but details could not be ascertained. Cutting K/7 revealed an abundance of relatively large root casts (up to 1-2 cm diameter) at this general horizon. These might be
indicative of the existence of riverine bush at the time of deposition.

11. *Interpretation.* Apparently a lag concentrate of material from two or more highly localized superimposed horizons. The original situation may well have been very similar to
that exposed in the DE/89 excavations. Clearly, for most purposes, the surface aggregate
is not comparable to the samples from excavations, but the biface tool series has been compared with other biface series. Its distinctive characteristics and internal consistency
(see chap. 6) may imply that most of the aggregate derives from a single idiosyncratic
occurrence.

Main Site H/6, Horizon A (see pl. 18)

This trench was excavated in an attempt to ascertain the archeological context from
which the Catwalk surface aggregate had derived. In order to avoid disturbing the Catwalk
material, which is on public exhibit, we drove the trench in from the side of the hillock
that stands above the Catwalk to get behind the outcrops without disturbing them. Parts
of the H/6 excavations have themselves been made a public exhibit.

1. *Alternative Site Designations.* None.

2. *Excavators.* G. Ll. and A. B. Isaac in 1964.

3. *Size of Excavation.* A trench about 25 x 6 ft (7.6 x 1.8 m) that, with extensions,
gives a total area of 29.3 m^2 (315 ft^2) (see fig. 24).

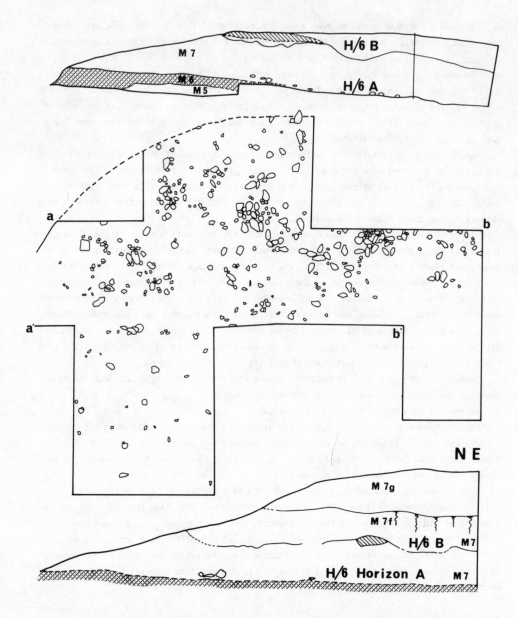

Figure 24. H/6; sections and a plan showing the distribution of larger pieces.

4. *Archeological Material Recovered*. More than 807 artifacts, 72 manuports.

5. *Location*. Main Site grid square H/6, the southeast flank of a residual butte above the Catwalk surface occurrence.

6. *Stratigraphy*. An associated group of artifacts on, in, and lateral to a thin intermittent spread of sand and sandy silts at the base of Member 7. The sands appear to be associated with only weak erosive forces and are not markedly unconformable to the underlying Member 6 green sands. No channel features were observed at this horizon in the trench, but a channel the width of the DE/89 B channel could have escaped detection in the area

available for excavation. The large stones of H/6 A are encased in fine diatomaceous
silts corresponding to the Member 7a unit of DE/89. Scattered artifacts occur throughout
the lower silts of Member 7, and a cut-and-fill feature (Horizon B) yielded a number of
them. Lenses of volcanic ash sand were also found on this horizon. The numbers of specimens in the sediments above Horizon A are too small for inclusion in this analytical study.

7. *Disposition of Material*. The artifacts, rubble, and introduced cobbles lay scattered
over the uneven surface of the sand spread. The density of small pieces was recorded only
by square, but the larger pieces can be seen to form clusters, and at least one of these
was perhaps located in a slight hollow. The density of large pieces diminished markedly
toward the west and southwest, giving the strong impression that the excavation has exposed
the margin of a scatter largely destroyed by erosion. Other cuttings in the hillock con-
firm the absence of material from this horizon further to the west. Various pieces in the
horizon (see pl. 18) are markedly tilted.

8. *Evidence of Disturbance*. The pieces show the degree of weathering normal to the Main
Site, and this prevents any certainty about slight amounts of rounding due to abrasion.
Pieces affected relatively little by weathering appear fresh. Analysis of orientation (X^2
test) does not demonstrate any significant preferred directions. The observed tilts might
be attributed to the action of stream current (Isaac 1967b:37), but the direction of tilting is so variable that this explanation seems unlikely. Trampling could produce such a
random pattern of tilts.

9. *Associated Faunal Remains*. A very small amount of weathered and fragmentary bone lay
scattered among the artifacts. This included a few hippopotamus tooth fragments, a few
fragments of equid teeth, a *Theropithecus* tooth, some long bone fragments and splinters
weighing less than 100 gm, and some small fragments of tortoise, frog, and fish bones.
There is no way of knowing whether these small quantities of bone are occupational refuse.

10. *Paleoenvironmental Context*. Probably an occupation on a sand spread in a broad or ill-
defined braided channel traversing silt flats. Stable lake waters probably at least 5 km
away.

11. *Interpretation*. A part of an artifact scatter of unknown extent. Possibly it was part
of an occupation floor, since there exists no positive evidence for rearrangement or transport and mixing.

Main Site H/9 and Mid

In the center of the Main Site a series of excavations have revealed a very complex
microstratigraphic situation, which has probably not yet been fully resolved. Investigation was begun by the Leakeys, who excavated a trench they called Mid. Part of the horizon
exposed was left in place as an exhibition. In grid square H/9 we excavated a major cutting just to the south of the building that protects the Mid exhibition. It was not feasible to link the two cuttings to discover the exact relations of the horizons. The situation in H/9 proved very complicated, with numerous subsidiary artifact-bearing lenses in
the base of Member 7. On a provisional basis we have divided the H/9 complex into H/9 A
and H/9 AM, under the assumption that H/9 AM is at least in part laterally equivalent to
Mid.

The site complex will be reported as three occurrence units: H/9 A, H/9 AM, and Mid.

Main Site H/9, Horizon A.

1. *Alternative Designations*. None.

2. *Excavators*. G. Ll. and A. B. Isaac from 1962 to 1963.

3. *Size of Excavation*. An open-sided cutting approximately 40 x 40 ft (12.2 x 12.2 m) (fig. 25). Excavation proceeded on a checkerboard basis. Two crossbalks were left until excavation elsewhere in the cutting had been completed. A total area of about 96 m^2 was exposed.

4. *Archeological Material Recovered*. 5923 artifacts, 103 manuports.

5. *Location*. Grid square H/9 of the Main Site (fig. 16).

6. *Stratigraphy*. The principal horizon was found to be a complex of erosion runnels filled with silt and sand lenses. This complex parallels the situation in DE/89, in that the implementiferous deposits rest on an erosion surface cutting through silts forming the base of Member 7. The individual lenses of deposit were given alphabetical designations, and pieces were initially recorded by square and "spit" or unit and were later regrouped according to correlation with the stratigraphic units. A partial sequence of the units was established, from youngest to oldest: (X,Y)/(R,P,K)/V/(S,T).

   Mid Trench is immediately adjacent to H/9, and a sandy lens or lenses resting in the base of Member 7 and cutting into Member 6 yielded abundant artifacts to the Leakeys in 1943. It was not possible to link the sections without demolishing the Mid Site cover. It seems clear that the Mid trench exposed a lens forming part of the same complex of deposits, and probably correlated with lenses X and Y, the uppermost lenses of the H/9 A complex.

   Material from lenses X and Y has been separated as an independent sample, H/9 AM, and not combined with either H/9 A or Mid. The uppermost portions of the Horizon A complex are predominantly silt. Developed on these in the southeast sector of the cutting is a poorly distinguished old land surface strewn with cobbles of vesicular trachyte. This is treated as a separate occurrence, Horizon B, and does not enter into comparative studies of artifacts. The remainder of the section is closely comparable with that in all other Main Site cuttings.

7. *Disposition of Material*. Artifacts, rubble, manuports, and bone fragments were found scattered through the deposits of the complex, but tended to be concentrated along the axes of runnels and in sand lenses (fig. 26). Preferred orientation of specimens was not observed, nor were tilted specimens conspicuous. There are no important discordances between the density patterns of different classes of material. The edges of the scatter were not defined by the cutting, but surface indications and other cuttings including the Mid Trench suggest that the complex has a diameter varying between 18 and 24 m.

8. *Evidence of Disturbance*. Evidence of at least redeposition of material is abundant in the stratigraphic context and the disposition of artifacts. The interaction of rounding by chemical alteration and abrasion makes assessment difficult, but the records indicate a higher incidence of pieces that are probably abraded as well as rounded. The absence of marked preferred orientation and tilting of specimens is anomalous and indicates the need for more extensive experimental work than that reported by me in 1967 (Isaac 1967b).

   The situation disclosed for H/9 A could presumably have arisen in the following three ways, or through some combination of them:

   1. dispersal of a primary concentration of occupation debris by fluvial forces in the braided channel,

   2. fluvial import and deposition of material, picked up from one or more occupation sites along the course of the braided channel,

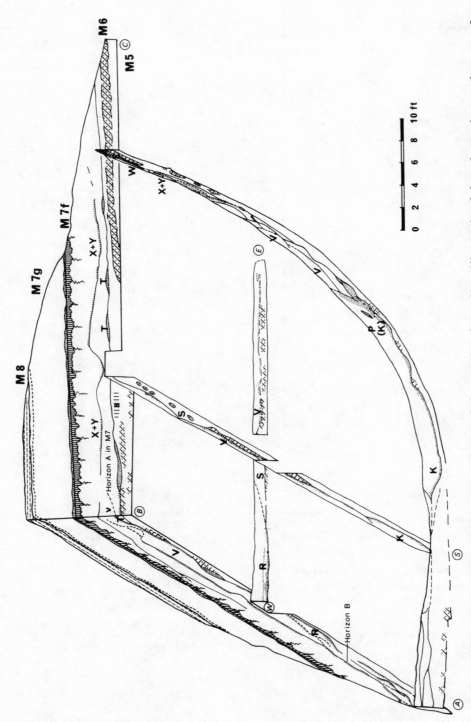

Figure 25. Partly schematic isometric representation of the stratigraphy at Site H/9, as viewed from the southeast. Letters refer to field designations of lenses and other units within the Horizon A complex.

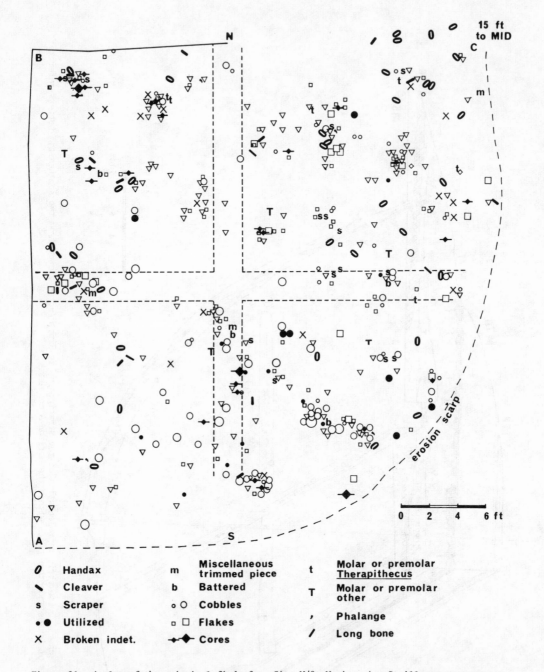

15 ft
to MID

erosion scarp

0	Handax	m	Miscellaneous trimmed piece
↘	Cleaver	b	Battered
s	Scraper	∘ O	Cobbles
•●	Utilized	▫ ▢	Flakes
×	Broken indet.	✦	Cores

t	Molar or premolar *Therapithecus*
T	Molar or premolar other
,	Phalange
/	Long bone

Figure 26. A plan of the principal finds from Site H/9, Horizon A. It illustrates some tendency to elongate clusters that coincide with channel features. H/9 AM material is included in this plot at the northeast edge, closest to the 1943 Mid trench. This plot is based on field catalogues and plot sheets.

3.   redeposition and rearrangement of material discarded during a series of occupations on the channel bed, alternating with fluvial activity.

Certain features of the artifacts favor a compound origin for the aggregate.

9. *Associated Faunal Remains.* More than 2,000 bone fragments were interspersed with the artifacts in the H/9 complex of sands. Most of these fragments were unidentifiable bone splinters with a total weight of 5.02 kg and an average weight of 2.4 g per fragment (cf. I 3, where the average weight per splinter was 1.3 g; and DE/89 B, where it was 0.9 g).

We sorted the fragments into three grades on the basis of extent of weathering, as determined by loss of surface texture, corrosion, and loss of mechanical strength:

"Unweathered" grade	18% by weight	26% by number
Moderate weathering	51%	51%
Extreme weathering	31%	23%

The frequency distribution of weathering grades may imply that material was commonly exposed for several seasons before it was permanently buried.

The rather meager quantity of identifiable scraps of bone and teeth included the following taxa: bovids, such as buffalo, and alcelaphine and reduncine antelope; equids (? *Equus oldowayensis*); suids, mainly warthog; hippopotamus. There were also a possible carnivore long bone; a single *Theropithecus* sp. tooth; and rare rodent, bird, frog and fish bones. None of these rare latter items was necessarily food refuse.

10. *Paleoenvironmental Context.* The source concentrations of the occupation debris were very probably campsites in or adjacent to the sandy-floored channels traversing the silt flats toward the lake some 3 or more km distant.

11. *Interpretation.* A series of samples of derived and rearranged material that is probably compounded from several occupation entities. The time span represented by the compounded series, if that is what it is, is probably very limited in terms of the cultural stratigraphy of the Acheulean; but it may represent a large proportion of the total time span of the sites included in the Middle Stratigraphic Set.

Main Site H/9, Horizon AM

1. *Alternative Designations.* None
2. *Excavators.* G. Ll. and A. B. Isaac from 1962 to 1963.
3. *Size of Excavation.* See H/9 A.
4. *Archeological Material Recovered.* 208 specimens.
5. *Location.* Northeast segment of the H/9 cutting.
6. *Stratigraphy.* Sand lenses in the Member 7 lower silts, spatially contiguous with the Mid Trench artifact concentration and possibly stratigraphically correlated.
7-10. See H/9 A.
11. *Interpretation.* Sample from a complex compound occurrence, which was separated to allow comparison with each of two spatially distinct segments of the same complex. Probably redeposited and disturbed material.

Main Site, Mid Trench

1. *Alternative designations.* Mid in fieldnotes, sections, and artifact labels by M. D. and L. S. B. Leakey. Termed Land Surface 8 in Leakey (1951), and Kleindienst (1961).
2. *Excavator.* M. D. and L. S. B. Leakey in 1943.
3. *Size of Excavation.* A trench 15 x 10 ft (4.5 x 3 m) was cut into the east face of the minor spur (fig. 27). The trench was subsequently extended 10 ft farther to provide an

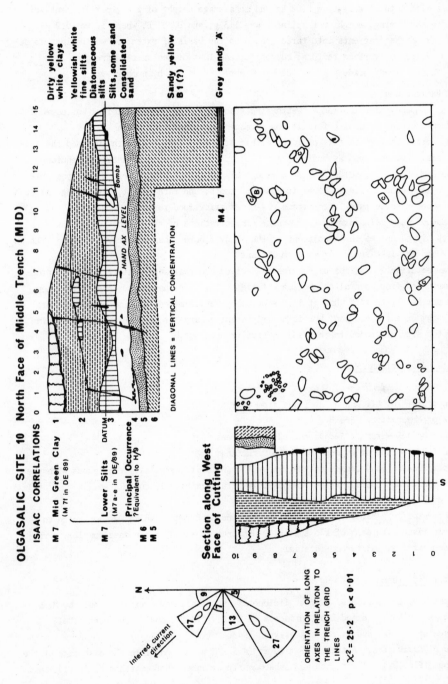

Figure 27. A plan and section of Site Mid, redrawn from field plots by M. D. Leakey, with a graphic analysis of preferred orientation shown adjacent. (The figure is a facsimile of an earlier one and retains the spelling *Olgasailie*, current in 1943.)

exhibition floor, which is still extant.

4. *Archeological Material Recovered*. Records of the totals are as follows:

    Leakey (in MS)   241 (elsewhere, 231)
    Kleindienst 1961   215
    Isaac   212

An additional 109 pieces were reported as having been left in place on the exhibition floor.

5. *Location*. A minor spur in the outcrop of Member 7 in the central portion of the Main Site in grid square G/8 (fig. 16).

6. *Stratigraphy*. Excellent section drawings and sketch plan by M. D. Leakey make the context of the material clear (fig. 27). A concentration of artifacts was found on and in a 13 to 30 cm layer of "silts, some sand" immediately overlying a "consolidated sand" (= Member 6). The correlation of this situation with the closely comparable conformation of deposits in the northern wall of the H/9 cutting makes it very probable that the Mid occurrence is simply a northerly continuation of the complex of cut-and-fill units identified in H/9 A. In particular, Mid probably equates with occurrence units X and Y, which have been treated as a separate unit, H/9 AM.

7. *Disposition of Material*. A plan, reproduced in figure 27, illustrates the conformation of material excavated in 1943. This, in conjunction with the sections, photographs, and the exhibition segment of the floor, shows that the material lay on and in a sandy silt spread that had an uneven surface. Tilting of specimens is not evident in photographs, but preferred orientation is very obvious in the exhibition excavation. An X^2 test on an analysis of orientation in M. D. Leakey's plan of the other part of the floor shows that the pattern has a probability of less than one in a thousand of being random. The preferred alignments are approximately NE-SW, with a minor frequency peak at SE-NW, also at right angles. This indicates current action with a SE-NW axis. The current orientation coincides with the alignment of the channels in the adjoining H/9 A and in DE/89 A.

The relative paucity of flakes and angular rubble in the Mid occurrence might be due to differential transport or to removal by the current (see Isaac 1967b:35-37). Although the extent of the Mid occurrence along the axis of the braided channel complex has not been ascertained, its southern limits are determined in H/9 A and the northern limits in trench F/89. Erosion has truncated any former extension to the southeast that may have occurred along the channel. There is a possibility that the Catwalk surface aggregate, which lies 30 m to the southeast, may incorporate material from a former extension of the occurrence in this direction.

8. *Evidence of Disturbance*. The pronounced orientation of the specimens implies at least rearrangement by hydraulic forces, and the paucity of flakes and waste may be indicative of winnowing action. However, the specimens themselves show no definite evidence of abrasion. Slight degrees of rounding are found to be directly proportional to depth of chemical alteration, and unaltered specimens, large and small, are very sharp and fresh. The existing evidence, coupled with the partial stylistic idiosyncrasy, would seem to favor rearrangement of material deriving from related occupations in the channel at no great distance from the occurrence.

9. *Associated Faunal Remains*. No records available.

10. *Paleoenvironmental Context*. A sandy, ephemeral stream channel traversing silt flats to the lake at least 4 km to the west.

11. *Interpretation*. Sample of an occurrence, possibly a compound of more than one occupation assemblage and certainly subjected to fluvial rearrangement and short-distance transport, therefore probably biased by selective removal of smaller pieces.

Main Site, Meng (Menengetti) Trench

1. *Alternative Designations*. Meng in field notes and museum labels of M. D. and L. S. B. Leakey, presumably in honor of F. Menengetti, who found the site (Leakey 1974:159). Land Surface 8 (Kleindienst 1961). (L. S. B. Leakey's manuscript notes imply that at one stage he equated this occurrence with Land Surface 6, but this opinion was never published.)

2. *Excavators*. M. D. and L. S. B. Leakey in 1943. In addition, G. Della Giustina excavated a small exhibition cutting just to the south on which I have no detailed information, and I excavated subsidiary trenches from which very little archeological material was recovered.

3. *Size of Excavation*. Two trenches, aligned at right angles (fig. 16). The collections appear to have derived mainly from the two extremities of the NNE-SSW trench, designated Meng I, southerly end, and Meng II, northerly end. The right angle trench was evidently designed to expose the stratigraphy, rather than to enlarge the excavated sample of the occurrence.

I excavated Q/10, a trench south of Meng I. This trench cut a sand spread that is probably the same as the one which yielded the Meng collection, but it contained no large tools. The flakes from this trench have not been included in this study.

4. *Archeological Material Recovered*. The following records are available:

      Leakey (in MS)   642
      Kleindienst (1961) 443
      Isaac   426

It is possible that Leakey included material left in an exhibition that later collapsed.

5. *Location*. In grid squares P/9 and P/10 of the Main Site (fig. 16).

6. *Stratigraphy*. Detailed records of the original excavation stratigraphy are not available, but a section by R. M. Shackleton (? after M. D. Leakey) gives basic information, and further investigations were carried out in the vicinity by Isaac in 1963 to 1964.

The artifact concentration comes from the base of Member 7 and is associated with sandy lenses and channel features. These features are for the most part poorly developed, though in one section (Central Trench) the edge of a channel cut 60 cm deep can be seen. The sand lenses grade laterally into the fine yellowish silts that immediately overlie the Member 6 green sand lenses. There is thus some basis for believing that the Meng and H/6 occurrences are the oldest of the Middle Stratigraphic Set of concentrations. All other sand and channel features in Member 7 on the Main Site can be shown to involve cuts through preexisting thicknesses of 30 - 60 cm of Member 7 silts.

A discontinuous sheet of sandy silt can be traced in the base of the Member 7 silts in outcrops trending south and north of the Meng trenches. Cuttings by Isaac revealed low densities of artifacts and bones in these, and it is very likely that the units are laterally equivalent to the Meng occurrence. The small samples recovered do not include bifaces and have not been included in the artifact samples reported here.

7. *Disposition of Material*. No plots or photographs are at present available, but it is apparent that the density must have been very high: approximately 108 pieces and more than 10 bifaces per m^2. The surface indications and the cuttings (Q/10, M/10i and ii, P/8) made in the area by Isaac show that the area of concentration was extremely restricted. The artifacts were probably localized within a weak channel feature.

8. *Evidence of Disturbance*. The association of a high density of pieces within the vicinity of a sand-filled channel is probably indicative of at least rearrangement of the artifacts by fluvial forces. However, the Meng specimens are less deeply altered chemically

than are most Member 7 collections, and it is clear from their fresh and sharp condition (see pls. 53-57) that they have not been subjected to any appreciable amount of abrasion or transport.

9. *Associated Faunal Remains*. No records available.

10. *Paleoenvironmental Context*. Probably on the sandy bed of an ephemeral channel traversing silt flats located at least 5 km from stable lake water.

11. *Interpretation*. A sample of an occurrence probably resulting from a fluvial concentration of a single occupation assemblage. The degree of selective deposition and removal of different size fractions is not known, but the full normal size range is well represented.

The marked idiosyncrasy of the series and its extreme homogeneity definitely seem to indicate that the Meng concentration is the result of occupation on the spot by a single group, or the result of rearrangement and concentration of closely related assemblages along the course of the same channel.

The Upper Stratigraphic Set of Occurrences

Main Site, Trial Trench Member 10 (pl. 21)

1. *Alternative Designations*. Tr. Tr. 110-160 (Leakey, in MS and on museum labels). Land Surface 10 (Leakey, in MS; Kleindienst 1961). The fact that Land Surface 10 occurs within Member 10 as defined by Shackleton is purely coincidental.

2. *Excavators*. M. D. and L. S. B. Leakey in 1943. Additional trenches by G. Ll. and A. B. Isaac from 1962 to 1963.

3. *Size of Excavation*. In 1943 L. S. B. and M. D. Leakey laid out the Trial Trench, which exposed the archeological and sedimentary stratigraphy from the top of Member 4 to Member 10. A plan of the trench and extensions is shown in figure 28. The base of Member 10 was exposed over a total area of about 75 m^2, this area being centered on the axis of a channel feature. In 1962 I excavated further in an attempt to obtain additional artifact samples and information. A series of trenches clarified the stratigraphic character of the occurrence, which had formerly been termed a land surface, and demonstrated that the artifacts were effectively confined to the floor of the channel feature, most of which had either been excavated already or had been destroyed by erosion. A negligible number of artifacts were recovered in 1962.

4. *Archeological Material Recovered*.

Leakey (in MS)	923
Kleindienst (1961)	890
Isaac	850

5. *Location*. In grid squares DE/10,11 of the Main Site. The Tr. Tr. Member 10 occurrence is related to the survival of an erosion residual of the Member 10 volcanic sands and gravels. This residual formed a small knoll, most of which has now been removed by excavation.

6. *Stratigraphy*. The artifacts recovered from the upper portions of the 1943 Trial Trench came almost exclusively from the sands and gravels of Member 10. These deposits overlie earlier beds that can be shown to have been cut by moderately deep erosion channels. In the vicinity of the site, the entire thickness of the upper ash and the main diatomite of Member 9 have been cut out.

One hundred meters to the southwest, a channel with a NE-SW trend can be seen in section. The incised portion of the channel is about 75 m wide and has a maximum depth of 3 m. A thinner and more variable sheet of sands and fine gravels extends as a widespread

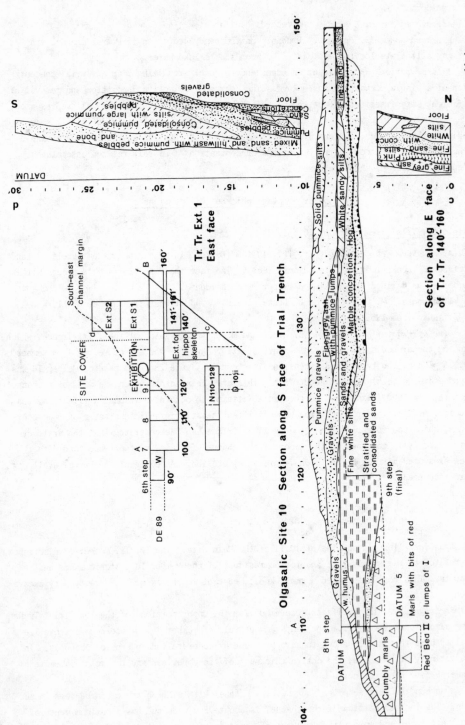

Figure 28. Sections and a plan of Site Tr. Tr. Member 10. A relettered copy of field plots by M. D. Leakey with a plan added.

layer on either side. It is very probable that the channel base sectioned in the Trial
Trench corresponds to that seen in the natural exposures. The deposits consist of variable
volcanic sands and of fine gravels with particles ranging from 2 to 5 mm and a few localized
pockets of slightly coarser material. The granules and pebbles consist of well-rounded
(subspherical) lava particles and of pumice. The occurrence is separated from the adjacent
Main Site occurrences by deposition of about 6 m of silts and clays (Member 7g and Member 8)
and by a diatomite bed that attains a thickness of 3.7 m further to the west.

7. *Disposition of Material.* The sections and notes record that material was found principally at the base of the sands and gravels on an irregular surface or unconformity. There
was a marked concentration of stone in hollows. Three hollows in particular held conspicuously high densities of material. One of these covering an area 1.5 m in diameter, and
with the specimens still embedded in the deposits, has been preserved as a public exhibition (pl. 21). Large bifaces, flakes, and cores lie in and among a fairly tightly packed
group of cobbles. Excavation photographs show that other clusters were similar, but probably larger. It is not known whether the specimens showed a preferred orientation and tilt.

8. *Evidence of Disturbance.* The facts of occurrence on an unconformity within a channel
and of burial by coarse sands and gravels strongly imply a degree of disturbance by fluviatile forces. The concentration into discrete patches has been attributed to human activities, but the elucidation of the kinematic wave effect in channels (see chap. 4) provides a mechanism more in keeping with the other features of the context. The specimens
from this occurrence are much less deeply altered than is usual at Olorgesailie, but show
signs of rounding and polish nonetheless. This effect can safely be attributed to short-
distance transport along the sandy channel bed.

9. *Associated Faunal Remains.* Fragmentary bones, including parts of a hippo carcass and
pig tusks, were recovered. Details of identification are not available.

10. *Paleoenvironmental Context.* The Member 10 sands appear to represent a marked change
from the hydrographic conditions represented by Member 7. It is very likely that they accumulated as the enlarged stable lake represented by the Member 9 diatomites withdrew.
Human occupation may well have occurred in the zone where watercourses discharged onto a
sandy shoreline belt that was still subject to periodic flooding. A stable lake was never
more than 2 km away, and it may frequently have been less.

There seems to have been a fairly intense burst of volcanic activity immediately before the deposition of Member 10. The eruption is documented by the ash bed at the top of
Member 9 and by pumice in Member 10. This latter horizon has yielded one of the two
potassium-argon dates for the Olorgesailie Formation: about 0.4 m.y.

11. *Interpretation.* A sample of artifact material from occupation in the general vicinity
of the occurrence. Part of the sample has been subjected to some transport, and possibly
to some proportional distortion of the representation of various size grades. The context
gives no guarantee that the material derives from a single occupation episode, and the biface morphology may indicate a compound origin.

Main Site, Hog Trench

1. *Alternative Designations.* Hog Trench was a nickname given the cutting by L. S. B.
Leakey (in MS, and on labels). Land Surface 11 (Leakey 1951; Kleindienst 1961).

2. *Excavators.* M. D. and L. S. B. Leakey in 1943.

3. *Size of Excavation.* Four trenches were excavated: Hog I, an open-ended trench about
35 x 5 ft (11 x 1.5 m); Hog II, 20 x 5 ft (6 x 1.5 m); Hog III, 12 x 10 ft (4 x 3 m); Hog N,
15 x 5 ft (4.5 x 1.5 m).

4. *Archeological Material Recovered.*

      Leakey (in MS)   480
      Kleindienst (1961)   434
      Isaac   approx. 221 (rubble recorded by weight only).

5. *Location.* About 50 m west of Tr. Tr. Member 10, a group of excavations were placed in a gentle spur formed by a thick lens of Member 10 sands and gravels. Four trenches, Hog I, Hog II, Hog III, and Hog N (north), sampled a fairly large area of outcrop (see Isaac 1968 for plans and sections).

6. *Stratigraphy.* Material from the several Hog horizons occurred at various levels within the sands and gravels of Member 10. Member 10 attains a maximum thickness of 1.5 m in the trenches, which may imply deposition in a channel, but the margins of the channel (if any) are not defined by the sections.

    The Hog series were characterized as Land Surface 11 in Kleindienst (1961), but given the cut-and-fill characteristics of the Member 10 deposits, correlation by height above the basal unconformity is of uncertain validity.

    The implementiferous deposits are unconsolidated volcanic sands and gravels of pumice and lava granules. The lava clasts range from 2 to 20 mm and the pumice up to 50 mm. The pumice content increases toward the top of the section, where particles range up to 100 m or more in diameter. This pumice appears extremely fresh and provided the material for J. A. Miller's age determination of 426,000 ± 9,000 years old. (See table 3, chap. 2.) Interbedded lenses of relatively fresh vitric tuff and some tuff-silt lenses also occur.

7. *Disposition of Material.* Material is shown on the sections as being dispersed in the gravels and concentrated on bedding planes. Markings on the specimens indicate the following provenance units which can be matched with labeled layers on the sections (the numbers of pieces stated exclude angular waste or rubble):

      Hog I,   layer 3   42 pieces
                  layer 4   37
      Hog II,   layer 2   8
                  layer 3   41
      Hog III,   layer 1   27
      Hog N,   layer 1   118

8. *Evidence of Disturbance.* The character of the deposits strongly suggests that much of the material has undergone at least short-distance transport. The paucity of large tools may relate to differential movement. The material is not markedly abraded, indicating that it probably derives from occupation nearby.

9. *Associated Faunal Material.* No detailed records are available. Portions of one or more hippo carcasses can still be collected from the collapsed trench walls of Hog III. A fine specimen of the mandible of a pig described by L. S. B. Leakey (1958) as *Tapinochoerus meadowsi,* but now put by H. B. S. Cooke into *Metridiochoerus,* was recovered from Member 10 in this area.

10. *Paleoenvironmental Context.* See Tr. Tr. Member 10.

11. *Interpretation.* The sample treated in this report is a compound of the various provenance units, and the context of each of these may imply a compound origin. Nonetheless, the series probably does derive from occupations in the vicinity during a limited time span, and therefore has some limited value as an archeological sample.

Site LHS (Lava Hump Site)

    This locality lies outside the Prehistoric Site enclosure, some 2 km from the Main

Site. However, the main archeological horizons are, as in the Main Site, associated with Member 7. I chose to excavate the site because I had become convinced that archeologists ought not to be entirely mesmerized by spectacular concentrations of artifacts, but should also make a conscious effort to investigate the characteristics of small patches of material and of low-density occurrences. The work done at LHS represents a first step in accordance with this policy, but as one might expect, the returns of information are not dramatic. The value of such investigations will have to be judged after a body of comparative data has been compiled.

1. *Alternative Designations*. None.

2. *Excavator*. Isaac in July and August 1965.

3. *Size of Excavation*. A series of open-sided cuttings were made into the east face of the butte (fig. 29). About 11 m^2 of the unconformity between Member 9 (layer A) and Member 8 (layer B) was exposed, yielding 1 hand ax, 1 irregular core, 3 cobbles, 1 angular block, a hippopotamus tusk, some small crocodile teeth, and fragmentary bone remains. The underlying clay-rich volcanic silts proved virtually sterile, with just over 100 small stone fragments and flakes (wt. about 650 gms) and 300 gms of small bone fragments in 48 m^3 (1700 ft^3) of sediments.

Exposing the paleosol, layer E, was the principal objective of the excavation. About 80 m^2 of this horizon was exposed in the space between the trench walls and the outcrop. This horizon was cleaned, and the medium and large-sized pieces were left in place for plotting. Trenches were subsequently cut into the sterile levels of Member 7 under layer E (fig. 30).

4. *Archeological Material Recovered*. 658 artifacts and 80 manuports from Horizon E.

5. *Location*. About halfway along the south-facing erosion scarp formed by the incision of the Olkeju Ngiro River through the Olorgesailie Formation (figs. 29 and 30). A small horst of lava stands up above the floor of the basin. This tectonic feature largely antedates the sediments which thin out against it and lap over it (fig. 8, chap. 2). The map in figure 29 shows how erosion in modern times is reexposing the lava ridge. Also marked on the map is the distribution of artifacts exposed on the outcrops of Member 7, after the relatively resistant tuff layer of Member 9 has been stripped off. The precise locality selected for excavation was a small butte where a hummock of Members 3 to 8 is protected by a capping of the gray ash of Member 9.

6. *Stratigraphy*. Two principal artifact-bearing horizons, one at the strongly unconformable contact of Member 9 (layer A) with Member 8 (layer B); and the other in layer E, a clay with derived sediment crumbs, which was interpreted as a paleosol, were encountered.

The clay, with derived sediment particles on and in which the LHS layer E artifacts were found, is provisionally correlated with the green clay, which is well developed in all the sections of the Main Site (see, for example, Member 7f in fig. 17). Members 5 through 7 are so drastically reduced in thickness in the westerly outcrop continuation that the individual members cannot be distinguished with complete certainty. It is thus possible that the LHS layer E clay is really laterally equivalent to the Member 8 clays. This possibility is suggested by the presence of red particles. The clay appears to be developed on the underlying beds, rather than deposited on them. The fragments of sediments forming sandy and rubbly patches on layer E at LHS is interpreted to be the result of mechanical disintegration and of sheet wash acting on the old land surface that the horizon represents. In the LHS site there is no evidence of extensive gullying or of any large-scale movement of materials.

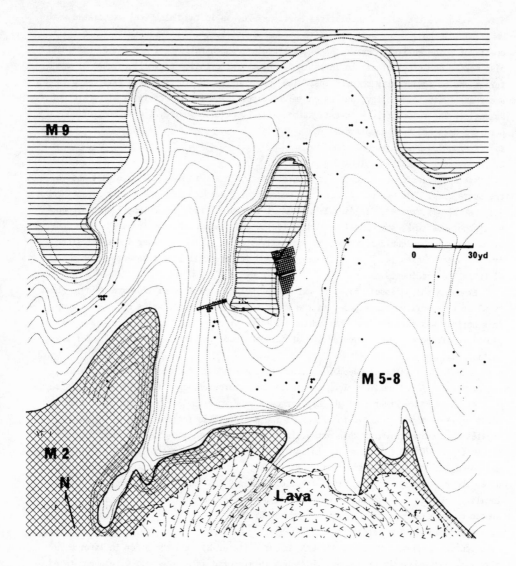

Figure 29. A contoured plan of LHS showing the surface distribution scatter of large bifacial tools. Members 5, 6, 7, and 8 cannot be distinguished with certainty this far west
in the basin. Surveyed by E. Iberall and M. Wynn.

7. *Disposition of Material*. The artifacts and introduced stone lay comparatively widely
scattered on and in the 4 to 6 inch thickness of layer E. Too few of them have axes of
elongation to permit an orientation analysis. No pronounced tilts were observed, and no
specific patterns in the arrangement or grouping of pieces on the sample area of surface
that was examined. The surface indications suggest that this diffuse scatter covers a
fairly wide area, possibly 150 m in diameter (about 6 acres).
8. *Evidence of Disturbance*. As indicated, the stratigraphic context makes it appear unlikely that any very significant disturbance took place subsequent to the discard of the
artifacts by human agencies. The material is relatively deeply altered and, in consequence,

slightly rounded. Rounding by abrasion cannot be distinguished.

9. *Associated Faunal Remains.* Three hundred sixty grams of bone splinters and crumbs
were recovered, comprising approximately 200 fragments. These include an equid tooth and
a crocodile tooth, both in a poor state of preservation.

10. *Paleoenvironmental Context.* The weathered (soil-covered) surface of silt flats adjacent to a lava ridge that might have formed an island or promontory projecting out from
the foot of Mount Olorgesailie. If there was a stable body of lake water at this time, it
must have been in the Koora graben; but as the site is almost opposite the mouth of the
Koora, no minimum distance to lake water can be assigned. It is quite probable that seasonal flooding of the clay soil surface occurred.

11. *Interpretation.* A small local sample (0.1% or less by area) of a large, horizontally
diffuse occurrence probably representing a palimpsest of numerous short-term or casual occupations in the area over a relatively long time span. Distinction of individual occupations was not possible, but might be in a large excavation.

Site MPS (Merrick Posnansky Site)

1. *Alternative Designations.* The Hope Fountain site (Posnansky 1959).

2. *Excavator.* Merrick Posnansky in March and April 1957. This is the only site at Olorgesailie for which a site report has previously been published.

3. *Size of Excavation.* An irregular open-sided cutting exposed 17 m^2 of the two closely
spaced artifact-bearing levels. Additional trenches were cut in order to elucidate the
stratigraphic relationships. See Posnansky (1959) for details.

4. *Archeological Material Recovered.*

M. Posnansky (1959) and M. R. Kleindienst (1961)

Horizon a_1 (upper)	278 artifacts
Horizon a_2 (lower)	88 artifacts
Isaac	292 artifacts

I found material from the site in the store at Olorgesailie, but the packing was dis-
integrating, so that the material was becoming mixed with other collections. I separated
and studied the marked material. Clearly, class analysis data cannot be based on this incomplete surviving collection. However, I took samples of the small tools and flakes from
the collections of the two levels combined, and included them in the measured series.

For the original composition of the samples, see Kleindienst (1961) and Posnansky
(1959).

5. *Location.* A gully erosion exposure in Member 11, about 2 km west of the Main Site
(see fig. 5, chap. 2).

6. *Stratigraphy.* The site is in the middle third of Member 11 in the vicinity of the
maximum thickness (about 18 m) of that member. It is separated at this point by 10 m of
silt and diatomite from the lateral equivalent of the beds containing the next oldest excavated occurrences; Tr. Tr. Member 10 and Hog in Member 10, Main Site. Elsewhere the intervening sediments thin to 4.5 m (fig. 9, chap. 2). The lateral changes in sedimentary
thickness were caused by tectonic subsidence of the block in which MPS is situated. A
considerable though undetermined time interval probably separates the MPS occurrence from
the Member 10 occurrences.

Although Posnansky was correct in assigning the MPS occurrence to a higher stratigraphic position than the Main Site occurrences, designated Land Surfaces 6 through 11 by
Leakey, his stratigraphic correlation was in error. The Red Bed treated by Posnansky

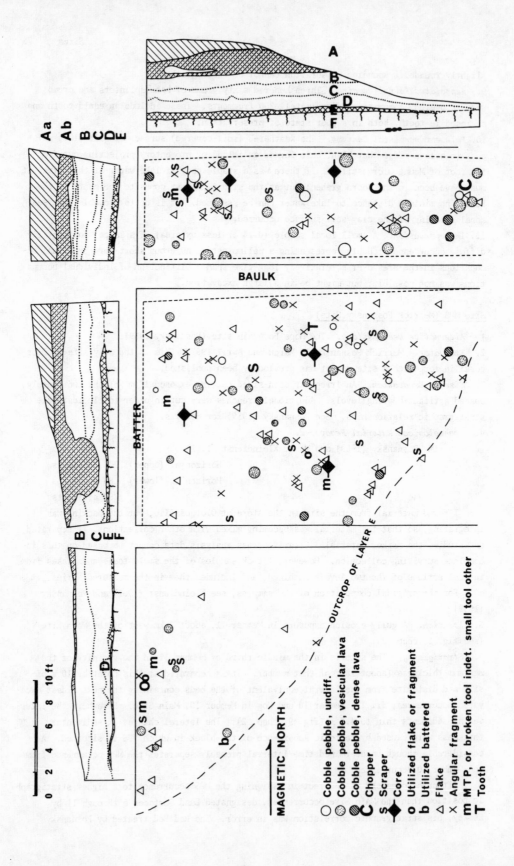

BAULK

BATTER

Aa
Ab
B
C
D
E

A
B
C
D
E
F

B
C
E
F

D

MAGNETIC NORTH

OUTCROP OF LAYER E

0 2 4 6 8 10 ft

○ Cobble pebble, undiff.
◍ Cobble pebble, vesicular lava
⊘ Cobble pebble, dense lava
C Chopper
S Scraper
◆ Core
o Utilized flake or fragment
b Utilized battered
△ Flake
× Angular fragment
m MTP, or broken tool indet. small tool other
T Tooth

Figure 30. A plot of finds in excavation LHS Horizons D, E, and F. (A) Member 9, Pale
gray silty volcanic sand. Disconformity; (B) Members 5-8, Grayish yellow siltstone;
(C) Members 5-8, Yellowish gray silty claystone. Variable gradational contact; (D) Members
5-8, Grayish yellow siltstone with clay. Well-defined bedding plane or disconformity;
(E) Members 5-8, Clay plus redeposited sediment clasts; (F) Altered tuffaceous and diatomaceous siltstone.

equivalent to the Member 8 Red Bed of the Main Site is, in fact, a quite separate red unit
some 14 m higher than Member 8.

7. *Disposition of Material*. It appears from Posnansky's account that the material was
scattered on and in the two variable sand spreads. Posnansky states that the surface indications of artifact concentration extended "some 50 ft along the section." Though I did
not check this in the field, I have the impression that from 75 to 100 ft (20 to 30 m)
might be a truer estimate. The sandy horizon can be traced for some distance to the east,
but contains negligible quantities of stone. It therefore appears that the excavation has
sampled a highly localized occurrence.

8. *Evidence of Disturbance*. Without more detailed information and a larger excavated area,
it is difficult to assess the extent to which the material was deposited by human activity
at the site, or was transported by the fluvial and colluvial agencies that introduced the
sand. There are no clear surface indications of a marked channel feature, so that it
seems probable that the concentration was due to localization of occupation, even though
short-distance stream transport and rearrangement may also have been involved. The possibility of size sorting or of rearrangement of material during stream transport cannot be
eliminated, since large tools are missing from the excavated series. However, the samples
were said to include 8 pebbles larger than 10 cm across, and 5 large cores, the largest
measuring 25 cm in diameter. So the absence of large tools may well have archeological,
rather than hydraulic, significance.

9. *Associated Faunal Remains*. "Though a large number of splinters of bone were found,
little was identifiable. Among the identifiable pieces the following occurred: *Hippopotamus gorgops* Dietrich: tusk; *Equus oldowayensis* Hopwood: molar, proximal end splint bone;
Protopterus." Also there were "unidentifiable remains of a carnivore (? viverid), various
bovids (antelope), fish and frogs, and ostracod crustacean shells. ? *Leptetheriella daday*"
(Posnansky 1959:88).

10. *Paleoenvironmental Context*. Occupation very probably occurred on sand spreads produced
where streams ran out into lake margin flats. The site is opposite the mouth of the Koora
graben, where the sump of the lake basin was situated. The interdigitation of diatomites
and silts in Member 11 suggests that stable lake water may not have been far away. Since
the portion of the basin in which the site is situated was actively subsiding relative to
others, it may have been seasonally flooded and swampy. The layer separating the two occurrences could represent a single flooding.

11. *Interpretation*. Small samples (probably less than 10%) of two similar occurrences.
which were deposited without any appreciable lapse of time.

Site MFS (Mountain Foot Site) (pls. 22 and 23)

1. *Alternative Designations*. None.

2. *Excavator*. G. Ll. Isaac in 1964.

3. *Size of Excavation*. Two small trenches and a number of geological soundings were cut
into the Olorgesailie Formation scarp feature. The main artifact-bearing deposit proved

to be a gray sand complex, of which about 10 m^2 were excavated in Trench I and extension, and about 4.6 m^2 in Trench II. Some artifacts were also recovered from an underlying bed of impure gray green clay.

4. *Archeological Material Recovered.*

Trench I	1411
Trench II	267

1678 specimens (of which 252 are cobbles)

The excavated sample is dominated by flaking debris, cores, and flakes, and includes only a few poorly characterized small scrapers and corelike choppers. Bifaces occur scattered among the debitage and rubble that litter the large erosion bevel that is cut into the site, and several were collected from the outcrops of the artifact horizon. However, none were recovered in the trenches.

5. *Location.* At the foot of Mount Olorgesailie, in the zone where the sediments thin out against the basal slopes, a small northeast-facing scarp of Member 11 sediments stands above a more gently sloping surface. Erosion has uncovered a considerable area of the scree and regolithic deposits that underlie the fine-grained Olorgesailie Formation. This surface is littered with stone rubble, including considerable numbers of artifacts (pls. 22 and 23).

6. *Stratigraphy.* Most of the artifacts on the surface and the samples from the excavation derive from a sandy horizon immediately underlying pale diatomaceous deposits that are laterally equivalent to the main calcified diatomite of Member 11. The equivalent position is marked on the north-south stratigraphic transect (fig. 10, chap. 2). The underlying beds at MFS are clays, passing down into hard yellowish colluvium with scattered small lava gravel particles. Clearly these underlying beds are laterally equivalent to the Olorgesailie Formation, but because they are a distinctive local facies they cannot be correlated with any certainty. It seems very likely that the sandy unit containing the artifacts was deposited as a littoral girdle during the encroachment of the lake, which resulted in the deposition of the overlying diatomites. Stratigraphically, this site is the youngest occurrence investigated in the Olorgesailie Formation.

7. *Disposition of Material.* Stone fragments and artifacts were scattered through the sand and gravel bed. The top of the gray green clay yielded patchy concentrations of flakes and cores jumbled together, with some standing at odd angles (? trampled), but the quantities of these diminished rapidly with excavation downward from the surface. Trench II showed a similar pattern of disposition.

8. *Evidence of Disturbance.* Rearrangement and short-distance movement of these artifacts is a strong possibility. Long-distance transport seems most unlikely, since currents of any strength would surely have introduced quantities of scree material or pebbles from the mountain slopes. The material is relatively fresh.

9. *Associated Faunal Remains.* A few bone splinters were found in the excavation in a moderately good state of preservation. Scattered bone specimens along the outcrop included the symphysis of an equid mandible, a bovid phalange, and the calcaneum of a large ungulate.

10. *Paleoenvironmental Context.* The site lay close to the break in slope between the foot of Mount Olorgesailie and the flats surrounding the former lake. Intermittent occupation appears to have occurred on colluvial deposits and sands at a time when the lake was encroaching. The sand containing most of the artifacts may well have been deposited or reworked as a littoral girdle around the lake margin, indicating that occupation may have been close to the water's edge. Outcrops of trachyte and basalt occur closer to this site

than to any other. The evidence of a lower rate of scree movement on the mountain relative
to that of today may imply that a relatively dense vegetation cover existed in the past.
Even today the adjacent slopes support dense *Acacia* and *Sansevieria* thickets.

11. *Interpretation.* A composite, slightly disturbed sample of a diffuse occurrence at a
locality with distinctive environmental features, including proximity to raw material outcrops. The time span represented by the sample does not appear to be great. Surface observations show that the excavated sample does not represent the full locality range of
forms, since bifaces are present in the surface scatter but not in the excavated samples.

4. RECONSTRUCTING ACTIVITIES AND ECONOMIC PATTERNS

The brief review in chapter 1 has indicated the sparsity of specific information on the economy and behavior of Acheulean groups. Other summaries by Howell and Clark (1963), by Howell (1966), and by Isaac (1971, 1975), have also served to emphasize this deficiency. In this chapter, I will outline the interpretations placed on evidence from Olorgesailie and will review it in the context of information from other sites.

Overall Distribution: Scatters and Patches

Alluvial and colluvial deposits make up approximately two-thirds of the exposed segment of the Olorgesailie Formation. Artifacts are scattered through all these beds, providing good evidence that men were continually present in the area. Though formal measurements have not been taken, it is certain that the average density of worked stone is extremely low. Experience would indicate the occurrence of an introduced stone fragment, flake, or tool every 5 to 30 m along an average line of traverse, the observed strip being 5 to 10 m wide. This suggests occurrence densities between one piece per 15 m^3 and one piece per 150 m^3 of deposit. A human scale for this phenomenon can be indicated by the following figures. A density of one piece per 15 m^3 over 67 km^2 demands an average discard rate of 4 flake fragments and other pieces per day, if 30 cm of sediment accumulates in 1000 years. Clearly we cannot actually make assessment of the rate from the available data. By contrast, about thirty localities with conspicuous concentrations of artifacts have been noted within the basin. The density of stone specimens in excavated occurrences that might be considered occupation sites ranges from about 90 per m^3 at LHS to about 212 per m^3 at DE/89 B. These densities are based on the total excavation yields. The central concentration of the DE/89 B site has a density of about 636 pieces per m^3. The material at both LHS and DE/89 B occurs in approximately 10 cm of matrix associated with an old ground surface. Densities per m^2 are thus one-tenth of the densities per m^3. Despite the spectacular nature of the concentrations, it could well be that there is a greater amount of humanly introduced material outside the areas of concentration than within them.

The relative frequency of tools in relation to waste is probably much lower away from sites. Bifaces occur very rarely in complete isolation. As detailed in chapter 3 and figure 11 (chap. 3), the sites with densities sufficient to justify excavation have a very uneven distribution through the available sections, but the persistent scatter suggests that this is a sampling vagary, since man appears to have been using the basin at all times.

There is no direct evidence concerning the activities that led to the general scatter of artifacts, but they may be presumed to include hunting, foraging, and movement from camp to camp.

Site Location in Relation to Paleogeography

All sites in the sample available for study were stratified in sediments that were deposited in the zone between the lake waters and the hillsides bounding the basin. Within this zone there are recurrent associations with specific minor geomorphic and lithological features.

The area between the lake waters and the margins of the basin was dominated by very gently sloping surfaces composed of fine volcanic and diatomaceous silts. Root-marking patterns attest to widespread grass cover and local patches of bush and trees. Ephemeral streams traversed the flats in shallow, shifting braided channels. The basin floor appears to have been subject to intermittent flooding by these streams and by temporary encroachments of the lake waters. At most times represented in the stratigraphic sample, grass-covered floodplain must have represented 80% or more of the surface available for occupation. However, hardly any of the concentrations of artifacts that have been excavated or observed in outcrop occur on the featureless surfaces within the silts. Most of the sites are clustered in areas where a sandy substratum existed or where a lava ridge projected through the silt flats. The exceptions are a few occurrences on a soil or clay horizon, as at the LHS or Friday Beds HL sites.

The Nature of the Association between Artifact
Concentrations and Sand Deposits

The repeated associations of high concentrations of artifacts with sand lenses could be due either to human behavior patterns involving preference for this kind of substratum, or to hydraulic agencies that deposited the sand. Because very little is known about the specifics of artifact transport by streams, it is not possible at present to make a definitive evaluation of the relative roles of these two alternative mechanisms at Olorgesailie, though it is suspected that both have acted together to produce some of the spectacular artifact concentrations.

The problem was attacked in an experimental program on the shores of Lake Magadi (Isaac 1967b). The discriminants suggested by the Magadi study for the disposition of artifacts affected by stream action are as follows:

1. Upstream tilting of bifaces resting on sand
2. Tendency of bifaces to be arranged transverse to the current
3. Dispersal of initial concentrations, with partial separation of flakes and bifaces.

These distinctive features are very little in evidence at the Olorgesailie sites. Tilting, where recorded (H/6), shows no preferred direction; the alignment of pieces is barely in evidence, except at Mid; material is concentrated, not dispersed; and bifaces commonly occur with large numbers of flakes, except at Mid. As I have said in chapter 3, I believe that the Mid assemblage has been extensively rearranged by transport. Records of tilting and orientation are not available for Tr. Tr. M 10, the other site for which extensive rearrangement is postulated.

According to the conventional criteria invoked in discussions of sites like Kalambo Falls (Clark 1969) or Isimila (Howell et al 1962), it might be supposed that stream action has affected artifact aggregates at Olorgesailie very little (cf. Isaac 1964, 1966b, 1968a). However, this leaves unexplained the coincidence of artifact distribution and sand lens distribution for sites such as DE/89 B. Recent investigations of other aspects of stream transport indicate that under certain circumstances patterns very different from those observed in the experiments at Magadi may develop.

Luna Leopold and his coworkers (Leopold et al 1966; Langbein and Leopold, n.d.) have found that in many streams a kinematic wave effect operates to produce the grouping of coarse particles into gravel bars separated by pools. In ephemeral streams, where the proportion of pebbles and cobbles is low relative to sand and silt, the same effect results in a more or less evenly spaced series of concentrations of stones at intervals along the streambed. The coarse particles tend to come to rest on top of the sand. Unfortunately, the dips and orientations of the stones found in such streambeds have not been measured, but regular alignment was not obvious, and it seems possible that the between-particle interference effects that result in the wave mechanism may also inhibit these other evidences of current action.

Further observations are required, but in the interim I favor the view that some of the Olorgesailie concentrates are the result of kinematic wave effects acting on material already localized in the channel as a direct result of human occupation (fig. 31). However, the balance of evidence weighs against anything more than a secondary role for hydraulic concentrations. This evidence is as follows

1. Known densities on the silty surrounds of the concentrations are so low that source areas representing many miles of channel length would be necessary for the purely mechanical accumulation of artifact aggregates amounting to thousands of pieces (eg., DE/89 B, H/9 A, Meng, Catwalk), and yet the pieces do not show

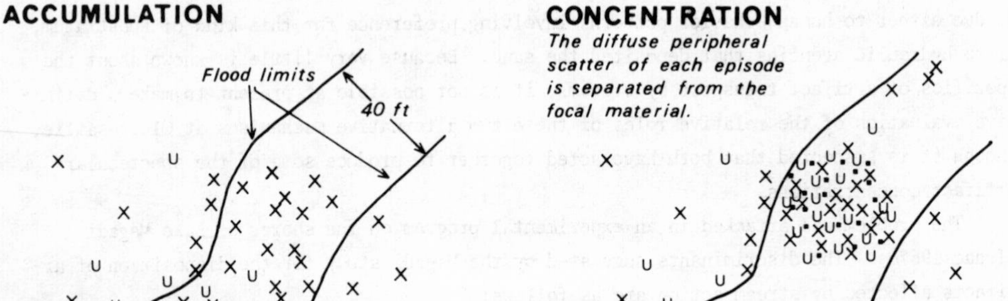

ACCUMULATION

CONCENTRATION
The diffuse peripheral scatter of each episode is separated from the focal material.

Flood limits

40 ft

FLOW

Figure 31. Diagrammatic illustration of an hypothetical mechanism for the concentration of material that accumulated as a scatter along a reach of an ephemeral stream channel. A scatter such as might arise as the result of three partially superimposed occupation episodes. The same area after the passage of one or more floods. Interference between particles causes many to be trapped in a dense group with a mean spacing less than 6 diameters. (See Leopold et al 1966.)

commensurate amounts of abrasion. Specimens collected from the modern riverbed in the Olorgesailie area all show marked rounding by abrasion.

2. The fact that not all sandy channels in the same stratigraphic units and in the same area as the concentrations show artifact content seems incompatible with an hypothesis of concentration from a widespread, diffuse occurrence in the catchment area.

3. The stylistic idiosyncrasy of individual concentrations in the area is totally inexplicable on the basis of mechanical concentration from a large source area.

The generalized model that I have formulated to account for all the principal observed features can be summarized as follows.

1. Sandy channel beds along particular reaches of ephemeral streams were favorite camp spots and were subject to periodic reoccupation by the same hunting band.

2. The kinematic wave effect governing the movement of particles in such channels resulted in the intensive concentration of material from several reoccupations in a patch or series of patches at the downstream end of the occupation zone.

3. The silting of the channels resulted in the periodic burial of aggregates and in changes in the favored location of camp spots.

The artifact aggregates may have been the homogeneous products of one band (Meng; DE/89 A, B, C; H/6 A), or they may have been the relatively heterogeneous products of bands whose workmanship was stylistically distinctive (H/9 A; Tr. Tr. M 10), depending on the duration of the interval during which artifact accumulation occurred. The evidence on artifact style is presented in chapter 6.

This hypothesis has been tailored to fit the facts of the situation at the Main Site. It will have to be tested by further experimental work on the behavior of material in channels and by its applicability to other archeological sites. Many other Acheulean sites are known to be closely associated with stream channels, but for most of these sites the details of artifact disposition are not yet fully reported.

The factors involved in the selection of the braided channels as locations for occupation sites are at present a matter of conjecture, but some possibilities can be listed.

1. Trees and bushes probably grew more densely along the banks of the channels, providing cover and shade and something to climb if predators attacked. The contents of one site, DE/89 B, may imply that baboons used such tree lines as roosting places and that man took advantage of this situation in his hunting practices.

2. The seasonal channels provided a soft, dry substratum in terrain otherwise dominated by tussock grass and clumps of bushes.

3. The slightly sunken levels of the watercourses may have facilitated human movement in the basin with a minimum disturbance of game.

4. Most sites appear to have been remote from the lake waters. It may have been possible to obtain drinking water by scooping pits in the watercourses, though no traces of such pits have yet been found.

Three excavated sites (MPS, Hog, MFS) and a few concentrations known in outcrop are associated with widespread sheets of sands that are not restricted within channels. I have tentatively interpreted these spreads as being due to deltaic deposition and reworking in a littoral girdle subject to periodic encroachment by lake waters. The circumstances of camps in the supposed shore zone may have been similar to those in the silt-flanked watercourses, though tree cover in the shore zone is less likely.

Another cluster of sites is associated with the extremity of a peninsula projecting into the basin. A palimpsest of occupation material on the peninsula and adjacent eroding silt surfaces was exposed in excavation I 3. L. S. B. Leakey had earlier exposed sites (Friday Beds and Basal Beds A and B) on the silts immediately adjacent to this promontory. The lava rock promontory today carries a much more dense cover of *Acacia* and *Commiphora* vegetation than do the surrounding dissected plains. Thus the ridge probably provided a convenient covered access to the basin center, with the added benefit of elevation which could facilitate surveillance of the floodplain. At the site of LHS there may well have been a rocky promontory projecting outward from the foot of Mount Olorgesailie.

In spite of the moderately good exposures of marginal facies of the Olorgesailie Formation, very few sites are in fact associated with portions of the floodplain that abut the hillsides. Of these sites, MFS was the only one sampled by excavation.

Where the relationship of sites to laterally equivalent lacustrine deposits can be traced, the indications are that the sites were a considerable distance from the standing waters (see table 6). There are good reasons for camping some distance from standing fresh water. The mosquitoes are so prodigiously dense that any Masai and Sonjo camps within a mile of the swamps are furnished with sleeping platforms raised 10 to 15 ft, in order to reduce the sleeper's discomfort.

Figure 11 (chap. 3) shows that there are two important spatial and stratigraphic clusters of sites: the Main Site group in Member 7, and the group around the southern tip of the peninsula in Member 1. These two clusters account for eleven of the sixteen excavated occurrences, the remainder being more widely spaced. The clustering is attributed to the optimal conditions these sites offered for camps. Presumably such favorite localities existed at all times during the deposition of the Olorgesailie Formation, but shifted about with changes in the physiography of the basin. Erosion has made available only an incomplete sample.

The Area of Artifact Concentrations and Inferences Regarding Group Numbers

The observed mean diameter of marked concentrations of artifacts at one horizon ranges from 4.5 m (DE/89 C) to 21 m (H/9, and Mid), yielding a range of areas from 66 to 1400 m^2. I thought at one stage in the investigation that the areas of the sites might be used as a basis for estimates of the numerical strength of the occupying groups (Isaac 1968). However, I have since realized that interpretations involving the kinematic wave effect fit the field observations much more closely than my original interpretation of primary occupation patterning; consequently, the population estimates must be abandoned. My initial impression was that there were two modal sizes of site, of which one might correspond to a nuclear family (DE/89 C), and the other to an aggregate of such families (DE/89 B). This impression is potentially verifiable and deserves attention in future studies of site areas that are less distorted than those described here.

The quantities of material at the sites cannot be used in group size estimates, since duration of occupation and frequency of reoccupation are unknown. However, it seems unreasonable to suppose that the 500 hand axes and cleavers, and an aggregate weight of worked stone amounting to considerably more than half a ton, was accumulated in the DE/89 B area entirely by a human group that included only one or two adults. By contrast, it is conceivable that the much smaller Meng aggregate, with its marked stylistic idiosyncrasy, might well have been the work of a group with only one stoneworker. These speculations cannot be defended in detail, but they are presented as constructive lines of thought that can be explored and tested in future work.

Table 6

	BBB	BBA	FB	I 3	FB HL	DE/89 A	DE/89 B	DE/89 C	H/6 A	H/9 A	Mid	Meng	Main Site M75	Main Site Green Clay	LHS	Tr. Tr. M10	Hog	MPS	MFS	Surface observation	Total	%
SUBSTRATUM																						
Eroded channel bed						X										X					2	7%[1]
Sand and fine gravel							X	X	X	X	X	X					X			4	6	22
Silty sand							X	X	X	X	X	X	X				X	X		4	10	37
Silts and clays													X								1	4
Clay and paleosol			X		X									X	X				X	4		
Rocky ground	X	X																X		1	2	7
Uncertain	X	X		X	X									X				X		4	6	22
																					(27)	(27)
TOPOGRAPHY																						
On/near rocky promontory	nr	nr	nr	on											X						5	18%
In/near stream channel					X	X	X	X	?	?	X	X	X	X	X	?	?	?	?	4	10–14	37–52%
Floodplain							X	X	?	?	X	X				?	?	?	?		3	11%
Sand spread (? littoral)												X				?	?	?	?	3	3– 7	11–26%
Piedmont fan																			X	3	4	15%
																					(27)	(27)
Minimum distance (km) from stable lake waters	?	1½	2	1	?	3	3	3	3	3	3	3	3	1								
OCCURRENCE TYPE																						
Vertically concentrated/ horizontally concentrated	X	X	X	X	?	X	X	X	X	X	X	X	X			X		X			12–13	66–72%
Vertically concentrated/ horizontally diffuse														X	X						2	11
Vertically diffuse/ horizontally concentrated														X			X				2	11
Vertically diffuse/ horizontally diffuse													X								1 (18)	6%

[1] 66% associated with sand and/or fine gravel

Comparative Data on Acheulean Site Characteristics

For obvious reasons concerned with preservation, Acheulean sites in Africa and Eurasia commonly occur in alluvial situations or in sedimentary basins. However, the tendency for the concentrations at Olorgesailie to be associated with the channels of ephemeral streams is independent of preservation factors. This kind of preferential association is repeated at other sites, including RHS in the Humbu Formation (Isaac 1967a), the upper Bed II sites at Olduvai (Hay 1967a, 1971; M. D. Leakey 1971, 1975) and the site at Latamne (J. D. Clark 1966a,b). The Isimila sites commonly involved a sandy substratum (Howell et al. 1962; Hansen and Keller 1971), as did the Kalambo occupations (Howell and Clark 1963; J. D. Clark 1969). The possibility thus arises that there were some general patterns of preference for stream channel and sandbar camping places, and this hypothesis deserves scrutiny in future research. It could account for some of the prodigiously large numbers of bifaces recovered from sand and gravel deposits in Europe. It would be extremely interesting to have relative frequency data for Acheulean occurrences in loess or brick earth, and in sands and gravels, in those regions of Europe where contemporaneity between units of each type can be established.

Many localized concentrations of Acheulean artifacts on old ground surfaces are known: Atelier Commont, Sidi Zin, Isimila, and Kalambo. However, plans or plots do not exist for the entire extent of most of the known examples. From the available literature, it appears that details of highly localized patches of artifacts of the kind well represented at Olorgesailie have not often been explicitly recorded. The rich Acheulean site at Latamne (J. D. Clark 1967a,b) is an example of a site that has been studied with care and for which details of the study are available. The less complete descriptions of very high densities of bifaces indicate that the site at the STIC quarry near Casablanca (Biberson 1961:160-61) and the site of Cuxton in the Medway Valley (Roe 1964:251) may have been equally rich. In all the Olorgesailie examples and these other instances, the kinematic wave effect is a possible subsidiary cause of concentration, and the size of resident groups cannot therefore be estimated.

Concerning the area and characteristics of concentration at Isimila and Kalambo, Howell and Clark (1963:524) state that "an average estimate would be approximately an acre, but depending on the circumstances both larger and smaller areas seem to occur . . . . Within most of the living floor sites examined, it is possible to distinguish areas of heavy concentration and others where artifacts are sparse or quite absent." Cook and Heizer (1965) have collected some data on the relationship of settlement size to resident population size for nonagricultural peoples in the Americas. R. Lee (pers. comm.) has observed the relationship among Bushman groups. The regressional relation suggested by this data would indicate a population of 100 ± 30 for a site as large as an acre. Unsatisfactory records for four Paiute villages report approximately an acre for 20 people. The possibility that the Kalambo and Isimila sites are really palimpsests of repeated occupations that were not exactly superimposed requires further investigation. The formation of such palimpsests has been described among the !Kung (Yellen and Harpending 1972). The only concentration at Olorgesailie occupying an area approaching an acre is the I 3 peninsula occurrence, which is believed to be a palimpsest of several occupations. The spatially diffuse patterns, such as that sampled at LHS, have been much less studied because of their low return of material per unit volume excavated. It might be noted that the published accounts of the Torralba and Ambrona occurrences (Howell 1966; Freeman and Butzer 1966) indicate that the artifacts are very sparse and that had it not been for the abundance of bone from butchering refuse, the patterns would not have been determined by excavation. It is possible that diffuse occurrences may prove just as important as concentrations for the full understanding of behavior in the Middle Pleistocene. The localized, vertically dif- fuse occurrence pattern that has been observed at Olorgesailie and Isimila (e.g., Sites K 19, K 12, J 6-J 7, H 9-J 8, Howell et al 1962) can presumably be due either to redeposition of material, as at Hog (?), or to intermittent low-intensity reoccupation of an area, as at MFS (?). Under favorable circumstances, this type of site might yield evidence of cy- clic or seasonal movements.

Tools and Activities

The principal component of all sites is stoneworking waste, which certainly indicates function as ateliers. However, since almost all sites are at least three-quarters of a mile from sources of raw material, stoneworking is unlikely to have been the determinant of their location, and its prominence must be viewed as a consequence of the durability of traces of this craft. The function of the sites as centers of domestic life could best be attested by evidence of sleeping and feeding arrangments. However, there are no traces of bedding and only fragmentary evidence of food consumption. The circumstances make it seem likely that these gaps are due to imperfect preservation, and it seems reasonable to sup- pose that at least some of the artifact concentrations are the durable remnants of the shifting home bases of itinerant bands.

The composition of the artifacts at individual penecontemporary sites varies greatly, but independent evidence of differences in the activities pursued at the different sites is so fragmentary that the choice between hypotheses based on activity differentiation versus those based on cultural differences remains in part a matter of personal predilec- tion (see chap. 9).

At the present stage of research, regrettably little can be said about the economic function of the various artifact forms or about their role in the behavioral adaptation of the groups that made them. If one takes cognizance of ethnographic accounts of stone tool usage, then the range of artifacts at Olorgesailie is sufficient for the performance of any of the economic functions that one might reasonably attribute to Acheulean communities. With these tools, it would have been possible to dismember any carcass; to dress, pierce, and cut up hides; to cut down saplings and small trees; and to shape poles, staves, spears, clubs, and light wooden vessels. The potential of the tool kits is established by the fact that in Australia, stone equipment that is certainly no more elaborate than that found at Olorgesailie permits the performance of all these tasks (D. F. Thompson 1964; Gould 1968). However, in order to ascertain the specific modes of use of the Olorgesailie tool kits, experiments and carefully designed studies of form and damage will be necessary.

Before the relationship of form and function can be properly considered, it is neces- sary to assess the extent to which craftsmen created by conscious design and careful execu- tion standardized varieties of tools. It would be unwise to base elaborate reconstructions of activity differentiation on evidence of variation in tool kit composition as measured either by morphological criteria of forms that are not crucial to function or by typologi- cal categories that do not reflect standardization of form.

Lack of detailed knowledge precludes elaborate interpretations, but certain broad morphological categories can safely be assumed to relate to functional differences. The major categories--large cutting tools, heavy-duty tools, and small scraping tools (Kleindienst 1962)--probably do have such significance. Each of these broad categories covers a wide range of forms, but, as is shown in chapters 6 and 7, these usually prove to be intergrading series and provide little evidence for the existence of numerous distinctive design norms.

The large cutting tools commonly, but not invariably, show a combination of sharp edges, robust edges, and scraping edges, which might support the long-standing suggestion that they were multipurpose tools. The delicacy of many specimens precludes their use for heavy woodworking, and the universal ethnographic evidence for the use of pointed, resilient sticks for digging makes it seem unlikely but not impossible that these stone tools were used for digging. Their utility for skinning animals has been demonstrated by Leakey and others (Howell 1965), though dismemberment and flensing can also be achieved by the use of simple flakes (MacCalman and Grobelaar 1965; Gould 1968, Gould et al 1971).

Binford (1972), following a suggestion by Clark and Haynes (1970), has pointed out that there may be an inverse relation between bifaces and bone refuse: that is to say, sites with abundant bifaces tend to have only small quantities of bone refuse and vice versa. Examination of the available evidence at Olorgesailie shows that with a few notable exceptions, such as DE/89 B, the pattern holds true. Careful consideration needs to be given to the functional implications of this relationship, if further research sustains it.

The small, steeply beveled, and somewhat serrated scraper forms are in general more suitable for whittling and paring staves and wooden objects than for dressing hides (J. D. Clark 1958). The nosed and pointed subform scraper may have served to groove and pierce wood or to pierce hide.

Formalized, trimmed, heavy-duty tools are not conspicuous in the Olorgesailie artifact samples, but the ethnographic data of D. F. Thompson (1964) indicates that the unretouched angular and broken stones that occur in fair numbers may have been serviceable in chopping and hewing activities.

The utilization of the large numbers of flakes and angular fragments that abound on all sites can be safely presumed from ethnographic data, and is partly attested by the chipping and breakage of the edges of many specimens.

Some cores and cobbles show bruising and battering, which may have resulted from their use as hammerstones and pounders. A few such stones appear to have been deliberately reduced to subspherical forms. Interpretation of these as bolas weights or as missile stones is largely conjectural.

Large quantities of unmodified cobbles and subangular blocks occur on most sites. The DE/89 B concentration contains more than a half-ton of cobbles and blocks. The geological circumstances at the Main Site make it certain that this material was carried out into the basin by man. Most of these cobbles are of the vesicular trachyte which outcrops in the peninsula nearby, but which is unsuitable for the manufacture of tools. These cobbles range in weight from less than 100 gm to 7 kg or more. Their function is obscure, but one can speculate that they might have been used as:

1. Hammerstone and anvils
2. Pounding stones for preparing vegetables and for breaking up bones
3. Footings for windbreaks (cf. Kalambo, see Howell and Clark 1963:520; MacCalman and Grobbelaar 1965: pl. 4; M. D. Leakey 1971: pl. 3)
4. Missiles for hunting, or for warding off predators.

One conspicuous pattern of edge damage on cleavers from Olorgesailie has also been observed in specimens from other sites. The delicate transverse edges of numerous specimens (eg., pls. 34, 38, 45, 57) show chipping and breakage. In general the damage consists of fracture scars that have been caused by pressure or impact from the more convex tool face toward the flatter face. This type of damage implies an asymmetrical impact of the edge with the material being worked, that is, a motion akin to adzing.

Obvious examples of this kind of edge damage are illustrated and described in the Sidi Zin report (Gobert 1950). I have seen less obvious examples in collections from Montagu Cave, Isimila, and Kalambo Falls. These observations at least serve to indicate the potential of systematic study of edge damage as a source of information.

Bone Refuse, Hunting Practices, and Diet

Table 7 summarizes the occurrence of bone at the Olorgesailie sites for which records are available. As can be seen, all sites have yielded some bone, though much of it consists only of a small quantity of scraps. The bone is invariably comminuted, a condition provisionally attributed to the process of extracting marrow. There are ethnographic records of hunting groups in Australia eating pounded bone (D. F. Thompson 1964:402, and lecture at Cambridge University, 1966). It is clear that inferences regarding diet and behavior can be made from bone preserved on the sites. However, it is necessary also to consider whether the virtual absence of bone at some sites can be interpreted as indicative of a noncarnivorous diet. Some experimental work has been carried out to elucidate this question. The studies reported in Isaac (1967b) need not be detailed here, and it suffices to say that scavengers and subaerial weathering proved to be extremely powerful dispersive and destructive agencies in the equatorial savannah (see also L. S. B. Leakey 1965a; Washburn 1957; Brain 1967; Yellen, in press). There is thus no reason to suppose that sites with very little bone necessarily imply different dietary patterns from those with abundant bone.

At all sites but three, the preservation of bone is too fragmentary to allow anything more than broad qualitative considerations. The most persistently represented forms of game animals are bovids, hippopotamuses, and equids. These are commonly attested by rather minimal traces: antelope teeth, hippo tusk fragments, and robust equid molars. The durability of teeth and their lack of attraction for scavengers accounts for their ubiquity.

The persistent presence of hippopotamus tusk fragments and some elephant tooth lamellae without any other skeletal parts requires some comment. It is possible that the tusks were used as tools, as some show damaged tips. Thus, their presence may have nothing to do with diet. However, it is equally possible that meat from pachyderm carcasses, whether hunted or scavenged, would have been introduced to home base sites as "fillets." The fragments of hippo bones may thus represent an otherwise undocumented source of meat.

Site I 3, the Exhibition Trench in Basal Bed A, and DE/89 B afforded somewhat more satisfactory economic information than was provided by the other sites. The I 3 excavation sampled less than 15% of an area littered with occupation debris presumed to represent a palimpsest of successive camps. The excavation yielded 19.2 kg of bone, of which 90% or more consists of finely comminuted splinters, with an average weight of 1.3 g per splinter. Correcting this to the specific gravity of unfossilized bone and then extrapolating to take in the whole site area provides a value of 87 kg of bone. If a value of 8% is used for the average bone-to-meat ratio in ungulates, it is possible that at least 1000 kg of meat was consumed at this spot over the period of accumulation. This estimate is based on a series of crude and rather unsatisfactory approximations, but, given the chain of distortions to which the fossil refuse sample was subjected and the uncertainty about occupant group size, it seems that very precise figures would not have any great value. The 7 to 8% value for

Table 7
*Animal Varieties Represented in Samples of Bone Material from Excavations**

| | DE/89 | | | | | | | | |
	I 3	A	B	C	H/6A	H/9A	LHS	MPS[†]	MFS	Notes
Hippopotamus	X		X	X	X	X	X	X		Mainly tusk fragments
Elephant	X		X			X				Mainly tooth fragments
Equids	X	X	X	X	?	X		X	X	
Bovid, large (cf. buffalo, eland)	X		X							
Bovid, medium (cf. hartebeest)	X		X	X		X		?	X	
Bovid, small (cf. Aepyceros)	X		X							
Giraffids		?	X							
Suids	X		X		X					
Baboon (Theropithecus)	?	?	X	?	?	X				Isolated teeth only at sites other than DE/89B
Rhinoceros	X	X		X						
Carnivores						?		X		
Rodents and insectivores			X		X	X				⎫
Birds	X	X	X	X						⎪
Crocodile	?	X	X		X	X	X			⎬ Very small quantities only
Other reptiles					X	X				⎪
Frogs	X	X	X		X	X				⎪
Fish	X	?			X	X				⎭
Weight of bone waste (kg)	19.0	1.0	12.5	1.0	1.0	5.0	0.36	NR	1.0	
Average weight per splinter (gm)	1.3		0.9			2.4	1.8			

* These identifications are presented for their economic rather than taxonomic interest and are therefore listed by vernacular or family names only. The records on which they are based include field notes and laboratory reports by A. W. Gentry and by J. W. Simons. The associations are circumstantial, and the last 5 or 6 items may not be food refuse.

[†]SOURCE: M. Posnansky, 1959.

bone-to-meat ratio is discussed by C. A. Reed (1963:214-15). This estimate can be used only to demonstrate qualitatively the possible economic importance of hunting for the occupying groups, since the relative proportion of meat to other foods remains obscure.

Basal Bed A, an excavation in the silts of Member 1, about 100 yds from the I 3 site, revealed a substantial part of a hippopotamus skeleton, with hand axes and flakes among the bones. No excavation records are available, but the finds have been preserved in situ as an exhibition (see fig. 13, chap. 3). Leakey (in MS) states that the hippopotamus bones, as well as an intact elephant humerus in an adjacent trench, are part of a midden associated with the artifact concentration of Basal Bed A, locality 1 (see chap. 3). Cut-and-fill bedding surfaces have become apparent in the section as a result of differential weathering. Lateral equivalences must therefore be checked by further excavations. Under the circumstances, detailed interpretation would seem inappropriate, but it is quite likely that the site documents a butchery episode, a brief occupation during the dismemberment of a hippopotamus that was killed or found dead here. Some additional hippopotamus bones lay on erosion exposures between the exhibition excavation and the I 3 peninsula. It is possible that the butchery was an extension of activities based at the peninsula site.

From DE/89 B more than 12 kg of bone was recovered (see table 7 and site summary, chap. 3). Most of the material was extremely fragmentary, with an average weight of splinters at 0.9 gm, but a few baboon long bones, many podials, and many teeth remained intact (pl. 14). Most of the bones and teeth are those of *Theropithecus oswaldi* (Andrews), an extinct species of gelada baboon. The taxonomic identification was originally made by L. S. B. Leakey and Whitworth (1958) who assigned the material to *Simopithecus oswaldi*. M. G. Leakey and R. E. F. Leakey (1973), have subsequently done a thorough study of all the material, and they now favor reassignment to the genus *Theropithecus* (M. G. Leakey, pers. comm.)

The *Theropithecus* remains are of special interest, since preservation is good enough for the series to form the basis for tentative inferences regarding hunting practices. Meave Leakey has kindly provided a summary of the osteological material (see appendix B7). It can be seen from this summary that the material represents the remains of at least 44 adult baboons and some 6 to 17 juveniles. Male and female adults are represented in approximately equal proportions. Meave Leakey has also carried out a detailed analysis of the age distribution of the constituent animals, as judged from degree of tooth wear. "The evidence suggests that the age of the individuals hunted was neither very young nor very old, but was mainly juvenile and newly adult. However individuals of all ages also appear to have been sampled." (M. G. and R. E. Leakey 1973:115)

It seems, then, that in seeking suitable models of hunting practices, we need to concentrate on possible methods that would have secured a broad spectrum of age and sex classes, without strong bias. I would not expect such a representative sample to derive from simple, direct, predatory attacks by hominids on baboon or gelada troops during the day.

A killing pattern such as is observed at the site might have been achieved if the baboons had been driven against a hazard or if their waterhole had been poisoned. But driving baboons or geladas against a hazard is almost inconceivable, since the species shows such guile and agility. Poisoning of waterholes, while a possible explanation for the killing pattern, would have resulted in a much broader spectrum of species in the refuse.

An ethnographic analogy provides the inspiration for a plausible if untestable reconstruction. J. Woodburn(1968, and pers. comm.) has described the baboon-hunting technique of the Hadza in Tanzania. The adult hunters normally operate alone, stalking their quarry and killing it with a bow and poisoned arrow. However, they periodically band together for a communal baboon hunt, which takes place at night. They encircle the roosting place of a baboon troop in a grove of trees or on a small rock outcrop. Then they dislodge the baboons by shooting arrows and making a great noise. As the baboons try to break out of the circle, they are clubbed to death with the bow staves. Woodburn reports that six to ten baboons are a normal kill. No data are available for the proportions of ages and sexes of the animals killed, but it seems reasonable to suppose that these proportions might approximate those of the total troop population, perhaps with slight bias against fully mature and experienced individuals being killed. The bow and arrow does not appear to be essential to the hunt, since the arrows are fired blind and serve principally to dislodge and enrage the quarry. Throwing heavy stones and clubbing with wooden staves would seem a possible alternative to the technique used by the Hadza.

The behavior and equipment involved in this model seem well within the range of expectation of Acheulean men, and the evidence at the site, such as it is, fits such an explanation well. If, as is supposed, the seasonal watercourses of the Main Site were partially lined with trees in which *Theropithecus* roosted, as do modern baboons in East Africa (DeVore and Washburn 1963), then the vicinity may have been well suited to periodic baboon hunts. Such a hunting practice would have also given rise to the accumulation in the watercourses of baboon bones and of unmodified missile stones, both of which are prominent in the DE/89 B assemblage. This model is offered as an hypothesis, not as an established fact.

A Brief Review of Comparative Data on Hunting Practices and Subsistence

The assumption that the primeval state of mankind was that of a savage hunter has its origins in thought that lies outside anthropology. The folklore of the classic civilizations and the writings of various postmedieval philosophers have all developed this theme. Since bone is the most durable variety of food refuse, the notion of man as hunter was reinforced by many of the archeological discoveries of the nineteenth century and rapidly came to be regarded as established fact (J. Evans 1897; Lubbock 1865:268-312; de Mortillet 1890:65-70).

I have recently reviewed archeological evidence relating to this question (Isaac 1971, 1975) and will present here only those aspects of the arguments most relevant to interpreting the Olorgesailie evidence.

There is ample evidence that hunting and perhaps scavenging were persistent and widespread practices of Acheulean groups. At a small number of sites, the quantities of flesh implied by the bone refuse may be sufficient to justify the belief that meat was a predominant component of diet. However, in many areas, like Torralba (Butzer 1964:366-72), hunting opportunities may have been intermittent or seasonal. It is possible that other sites with abundant bone represent periodic hunting opportunities, rather than consistent success and a regular meat supply. Scavenging may have been as important as hunting.

At most Acheulean sites we know nothing of the plant components of diet and too little about population size and duration of occupation to estimate the importance of plants from an equation such as: calories from meat + vegetables = population x average daily requirement x number of days (J. G. D. Clark 1954:15; Shawcross 1967). Though the prospects are remote, it is possible that future excavations will unearth sites where the evidence is complete enough for reasonable estimation of several of these factors. At Kalambo Falls the normal condition is reversed, and plant food and bedding, rather than bone, are preserved (Howell and Clark 1963:488; J. D. Clark 1969). The representation is selective and provides qualitative rather than quantitative data.

Data for Bushman (Lee 1968), Hadza (Woodburn 1968), and Pygmies (Turnbull 1962,1968) show that, for all three groups, gathered vegetable foods form the staples of diet, with meat as an essential but smaller component. This dietary pattern appears general among nonagricultural peoples who live away from shorelines and outside the subarctic zone. Very likely it was also the feeding pattern of the Acheulean inhabitants of the Olorgesailie basin. The apparatus required for gathering and preparing plant food is so simple that artifacts afford few clues. Lee reports that the !Kung Bushmen use two natural stones, one flattish and one round, for breaking up the mugongo nuts that form one dietary staple. Woodburn reports that the Hadza use similar unshaped equipment for pounding baobab and other seeds. Humanly introduced stones suitable for such tasks are abundant on the Olorgesailie sites, but their use in preparing vegetable foods is unproven.

Among the Bushmen and Hadza, hunting is the principal economic activity of the adult males, but it may take up less than 20% of their waking time, the remainder being spent in rest, recreation, or the leisurely pursuit of other tasks and crafts. It is also reported that the women who commonly gather vegetable food are usually able to obtain enough for their families in considerably less than half their waking hours (see various contributions to Lee and DeVore, eds., 1968). The widespread notion that early Paleolithic life was filled with deprivation and the need for continuous questing after food is probably erroneous.

The fact that many Olorgesailie sites have yielded little bone may not mean that meat was not consumed at them (Isaac 1967b:39), but it certainly suggests that very large quantities of bone were never present and that dependence on meat for food was, therefore, not necessarily a feature of the life of all Acheulean groups. At Latamne and in the Acheulean layers at the Cave of Hearths, faunal remains have been found in similarly modest quantities (Clark 1966; H. B. S. Cooke in Mason 1962).

While the reconstruction of hunting practices on the basis of the DE/89 B evidence is hypothetical, the site is interesting because it is one of a very small series of sites where any factual basis for reconstruction is available. At two other sites where bone refuse is relatively abundant, there is a high incidence of one species: elephants at Torralba, and *Pelorovis* at Olduvai BK II. These cases may document game drives or the encirclement of herds. Butzer (1964:372) suggests that Torralba was on a seasonal migration route and that hunting success depended on the hampering of the quarry's movements in swampy ground. L. S. B. Leakey (1957) suggested that a *Pelorovis* herd had been driven into a swamp and butchered. Partial corroboration of a hypothesis of this kind is available from the age and sex composition of the Olorgesailie DE/89 B sample, but this information is not yet available for the other sites. Drives and herd encirclement would have involved the cooperation of social groups appreciably larger than nuclear family, and thus the practice has sociological as well as economic interest. Sites such as I 3, Ternifine, Casablanca STIC, and the Cave of Hearths appear to show more generalized bags of game which may have been the result of more opportunistic hunting practices or of individual stalking of the quarry, or the bone remains could have accumulated by scavenging.

Even if men could not regularly kill pachyderms, such as hippopotamuses and elephants, the scavenging of their carcasses may have been an important source of meat. In view of the ineffectiveness of other scavengers in opening and dismembering these carcasses, man may have been able to occupy a partially vacant ecological niche.

Fire

The Olorgesailie sites lack positive traces of the use of fire, in the form of charcoal, visibly burned bone, or obvious hearth structures. At I 3, a hearthlike depression filled with stone and bone was excavated, but no charcoal was detected. Microscopic charcoal particles were found dispersed in some samples of the Member 7 silts overlying the

Main Site occupations (D. A. Livingstone, pers. comm.), but there is no means of distinguishing between humanly induced fire and natural fires, such as those caused by lightning.
Stones have been examined for traces of burning and have been submitted to laboratory scrutiny, both with negative results. Experiments indicate that even if the lavas had been
heated, it would be impossible to detect. However, further testing should be undertaken,
in the hope that thermoluminescence may provide a means of determining if fire was being
used at the sites (Rowlett et al. 1974).

No certain evidence of the use of fire has been found on any Middle Pleistocene sites
in Africa (see Oakley 1956; Howell and Clark 1963:525). Because of otherwise excellent
state of preservation of the sites, it has been widely assumed that human use of fire did
not become general in Africa until the Upper Pleistocene. This assumption rests entirely
on negative evidence that requires careful scrutiny. The underlying basis of the assumption is that charcoal is elemental carbon, and as such is not liable to destruction under
natural conditions. This premise is erroneous in that the form and mechanical strength of
charcoal depends on the partially carbonized framework of organic materials, such as cellu-
lose. These modified organic materials are durable under some conditions, but under the
physicochemical conditions of sediments in equatorial regions, they are not necessarily in-
destructible. This is particularly true where the groundwater is markedly alkaline, as it
is at Olorgesailie. The degradation of the organic framework would convert the charcoal to
an amorphous powder likely to be dispersed by groundwater movement. For equatorial savan-
nas a further factor must be considered. Dead wood is common and is normally so dry that
it undergoes complete combustion, leaving a minimum of charcoal, of which most is so finely
comminuted that it is likely to be dispersed by the wind. Even in cave sites where thick
layers of ash are preserved, there may be little charcoal (C. K. Cooke 1963:80).

When one examines the record of fire in association with Upper Pleistocene cultural
material in Africa, including the record for terminal Acheulean sites, one finds that almost all positive evidence for fire derives from caves. The few First Intermediate and
Middle Stone Age open stations that have been systematically excavated--Kalkbank, Khami
Waterworks, Chaminade, and Prospect Farm--have failed to yield any macroscopic traces of
fire, in spite of the fact that fire was in contemporary use in caves.

Late Acheulean material that occurs in caves (Cave of Hearths) or in open sites that
have been permanently waterlogged (Kalambo Falls) is sometimes associated with traces of
fire. There were no hearth structures at Kalambo, and charcoal provided the sole evidence
for the use of fire (Howell and Clark 1963:525). Burned bone is claimed (Posnansky in
Howell and Clark 1963:525) for the Nyabusoro Late Acheulean/Sangoan site, but is uncon-
firmed. Thus the pattern that appears to emerge is that fire is only documented in African
sites that are older than 10,000 to 20,000 years. Negative evidence from very old or un-
protected sites has little significance, and we are left in ignorance of the time when fire
first came into domestic use in Africa.

Exotic Materials and Territorial Range

The presence on the sites of small quantities of rock types that do not crop out in
the basin attests either to a territorial range that included such outcrops or to trading
contact with adjoining groups. The materials in question are quartz, quartzite, obsidian,
and chert.

Quartz and quartzite occur in the Precambrian metamorphic formations that are exposed
in both Rift Valley walls a little to the south of Olorgesailie. The nearest outcrop to

the east is 43 km from the Main Site; that to the west is 48 km away. The extremely small size and worked-out nature of almost all pieces of this material, save for a few battered cobbles (bolas) and a single biface reported from Meng (L. S. B. Leakey, in MS) and now apparently lost by theft, implies great economy in its use. The paucity of quartz might imply that travel in the direction of the outcrops was infrequent or that direct access to the material was not available and that barter was involved.

Obsidian was also used sparingly. Most of it is found in small chips, though a total of three bifaces of obsidian have been recovered from two sites. The nearest obsidian source, Oldoinyo Nyegi, is just outside the southern end of the basin, 26 km from the Main Site.

A few small fragments and flakes of chert occur at all the sites; small chert scrapers and borers occur more rarely. The material is diverse, including a range of brownish cherts and dark, opaque green cherts. The sources of these are not known. Translucent white chert, which is abundant in the adjacent Magadi and Natron basins (Baker 1958; Isaac 1967a), 26 km and 77 km away, respectively, is not present at any Acheulean site, though it occurs in the post-Olorgesailie Formation Middle and Later Stone Age materials. Either there was no movement or contact in the direction of chert sources or, as seems more likely from the geological evidence (chap. 2), the Magadi chert series had not yet been exposed by grid faulting.

Taken together, the evidence suggests that, compared to the local lavas, these exotic materials were highly prized. It can be argued that the labor of portage may not have been the only factor limiting the available quantities of exotic raw materials. For a site such as DE/89 B, the ratio of distances between quartz outcrops and lava outcrops is about 100 to 7; the ratio by weight of lava to quartz at the site is 100 to less than 0.1. There is thus vague evidence of a pattern of life involving limited movement, and it is possible that territorial boundaries existed. It is known that most Acheulean artifacts were made of local stones (cf. De Mortillet 1883:252; Howell and Clark 1963:510). However, detailed study of patterns of distribution of materials and of distances from sources might prove of interest. Certainly no firm conclusions can be reached until such studies have been made.

Distinctive Styles and Social Entities

Comparisons of the morphology of artifacts, especially bifaces from different sites, indicates to me that, in spite of the evidence of a strong community of craft tradition from the gross content of the tool kits, there were marked differences of a stylistic nature. I later discovered that this aspect of the material had also impressed itself on L. S. B. Leakey:

> I think that whereas the statistical approach can certainly be made to differentiate between this assemblage and that assemblage and to compare this assemblage and that assemblage, I do feel that you have got to be careful to know what in fact in such a comparison you are comparing. I am quite sure that from Acheulian times onward and probably even earlier, the assemblage at any given living site, was very considerably influenced by the tool makers of that particular home and their skill. I am perfectly certain you can find in places like Olorgesailie, on exactly the same horizon, from the same year, with an accumulation of tools made by one family, another by another family; because X was more clever than Y or because X had rather different ideas as to what he wanted than Y, the two things are completely contemporary of the same culture, of the same subculture. Yet statistically they are completely different to look at. (Transcript of verbal statement in a discussion of a paper by de Heinzelin [1962:127])

The statistical verification of these perceptions is discussed in succeeding chapters.

If the worked material at each site were the product of one craftsman, then this variation would be no more than individual idiosyncrasy. However, the bulk of material at some
sites is suggestive of recurrent stoneworking activity by a whole group or band. If this
latter proposition is correct, then culture in the Olorgesailie lake basin exhibits a combination of micro-differences between groups, coupled with a broader conservative uniformity. This is precisely the cultural pattern discussed by Owen (1965) as being usual among
sparse, nonagricultural populations. Owen describes a situation in Baja California, but
provides a convincing case for applicability to Australia and much of aboriginal North
America. He argues that the principal social and economic units within such a population
are commonly a series of fairly small exogamous bands. The identity of bands is generally
maintained by continuity between successive generations of males. Most of the males in
most of the bands are reared within the band, and the male groups are thus a series of partial cultural isolates. The females reared within any band are continually dispersed by
marriage to men outside the band, and are replaced by wives drawn from other bands. The
wives are often taken from appreciable distances, so that the group of wives in a band commonly have varied cultural and linguistic origins. Owen sees this continued cultural hy-
bridization as a social mechanism with high inertia against radical change. Marked diversity in the specifics of local group tradition, especially male traditions, may contrast
with fundamental social and economic uniformity over wide areas.

The data from Olorgesailie are consistent with such a mechanism of social division
and cultural transmission, but it cannot be said that the evidence is conclusive. Only
recently has explicit attention been given to the notion that patterning in artifacts can
reflect aspects of demography and the specific social mechanisms by which craft traditions
were transmitted (see, for example, Binford 1963; Longacre 1964; Owen 1965; Deetz 1965,
1967; David 1973). Much more experimental work will be necessary before the idea is anything more than an interesting line of exploration.

Whatever the sociological explanation, stylistic idiosyncrasy of the kind observed at
Olorgesailie is certainly widespread among Acheulean occurrences where individual occupations can be discerned, for example at Sidi Zin (Gobert 1950) and at Isimila (Howell and
Clark 1963:507). Clearly these considerations have significance also for the taxonomy of
culture in the Pleistocene. The problem is further considered in chapter 9 after treatment
of the details of evidence from the artifact morphology.

Plate 1. Lake Kwennia, a seasonally flooded fault graben that is partially analogous to the former Lake Olorgesailie.

Plate 2. Exposures of the Olorgesailie Formation as seen from the air. Outcrops of Members 1-3 west of the enclosure.

1

2

3

4

Plate 3. Site I 3, sediments of Member 1 banked against a lava ridge, the peninsula.

Plate 4. Site I 3, banded diatomites truncated by a local erosion surface with which the main archeological horizon is associated.

Plate 5. The prehistoric site enclosure and Legemunge Plateau viewed from the air. The mouth of the Koora Graben and Mount Shanamu can be seen in the background.

Plate 6. Air view of the Main
Site complex from the south.

Plate 7. The Catwalk Site viewed from the south, with site H/6 behind. In the background is the Oltepesi Plain and Mount Olorgesailie.

Plate 8. Artifacts littering the eroded surface of the Catwalk Site. These artifacts have been washed out from concentrations at two horizons during the headward erosion of the small gully. A fault cuts into the beds at the start of the Catwalk.

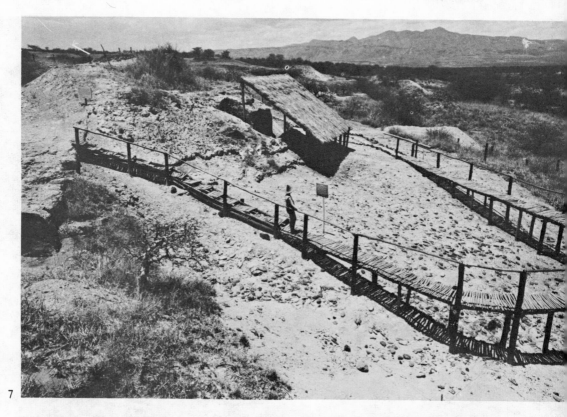

7

8

Plate 9. Site DE/89, a
general view from the south.
The trench cut at right center
is part of Mary and Louis
Leakey's trial trench. The
northeast bank of the small
ephemeral channel within
which the site is situated has
been exposed on the far side
of the Horizon B artifact
concentration.

9

Plate 10. DE/89, general
view along the axis of the
paleochannel. The cutting in
the foreground exposes a
concentration of material
along the central gutter of
the channel incision. This is
Horizon A.

Plate 11. DE/89, a near vertical view of this same part of Horizon A.

Plate 12. DE/89, a close-up of Horizon A showing its burial by a lens of sandy silt (Member 7b) with the thin bed of sand (Member 7c) and archeological Horizon B above.

11

12

Plate 13. DE/89, Horizon B, view from the west. The bank of the paleostream channel can be seen beyond the artifact concentration.

Plate 14. A high angle oblique view of the northwest extremity of the DE/89, Horizon B artifact concentration, seen from the north. The axis of the paleochannel feature passes from left to right. The sediment lens of Member 7b thins so that the scattered artifacts in the center of the photograph rest in a thin layer of sand (Member 7c) directly on Member 5. At the right a minor fault has displaced the horizon downward.

14

15

Plate 15. DE/89, Horizon B, a close-up of bifaces and two *Theropithecus (Simopithecus)* femurs lying among other artifacts and bone fragments.

Plate 16. DE/89, Horizon C, a general view from the east showing the patch of artifacts. In the foreground some large pieces that are part of the occurrence, but which had been removed are replaced balanced on stakes driven in to give them their proper levels. In the rear wall, the paleosol horizon (Member 7f) and the lens that finally silted up the paleochannel can be seen. Above are Member 7g and Member 8.

Plate 17. DE/89, Horizon C, detail of the root cast.

Plate 18. An excavation exposes an archeological horizon adjacent to the Catwalk Site (trench H/6 A).

16

17

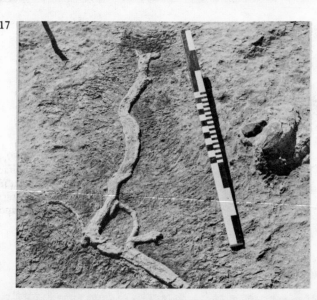

19

20

Plate 19. Site H/9,

Plate 20. Site H/9, a view from the southwest showing the baulks used to control excavation of the complex lenses of horizon A and AM. Linear configuration of material is apparent. The roof in the background covers Mary and Louis Leakey's Mid trench.

Plate 21. Site Trial Trench, Member 10, a view from the south of material left in place as an exhibition by Mary and Louis Leakey. The concentration consists of bifaces, small tools, flakes, cobbles, and some bone. It is situated in the base of a wide channel complex cut into Member 9 and was covered by the coarse sands and granule gravels of Member 10.

Plate 22. The Mountain Foot Site, MFS, a general view from the northwest, showing Members 11 and 13 being stripped by erosion from an interdigitated piedmont rubble, with which are associated numerous artifacts. The excavated soundings were carried out at the far end of the miniscarp.

Plate 23. The Mountain Foot Site, MFS, a large core and other artifacts being exposed as the scarp retreats.

22

23

5. PROBLEMS AND METHODS IN THE STUDY
OF THE ARTIFACT ASSEMBLAGES

Stone artifacts constitute the only class of relics common to all archeological occurrences in the Olorgesailie basin. The sites are recognized in outcrop by the concentration of worked stones, and in many cases the artifacts are the only readily interpretable
traces of prehistoric occupation. Before proceeding to an account of the features and patterns of the Olorgesailie assemblages, it will be useful to discuss briefly what aspects of
culture and behavior I think they may document.

Stone artifacts can be expected to reveal in some incomplete fashion information about
aspects of the behavior that gave rise to them, including (1) technical habits and methods,
(2) design norms, and (3) functional requirements.

The problems that stand in the way of detailed functional interpretation have already
been mentioned in chapter 4. Important though this potential aspect of artifact evidence
is, little can be inferred about it before extensive programs of experimentation and edge-
damage studies have been completed.

Technique and design are largely determined by tradition, and thus their documentation
in stone artifacts constitutes a "fossilized" aspect of culture. Similarities in form and
technique of stone tools have generally been treated in a way closely analogous to the
method of recognizing affinity in biological taxonomy. If a simple equation between degree
of resemblance among artifact samples and degree of cultural affinity held true, then it
might be predicted that all the items in a set of samples from a restricted segment of
space and time would prove to be very similar or be divisible into only a few distinct
groups. This did not prove to be the case at Olorgesailie; factors other than cultural affinity need to be considered as causes of its diversity. (cf. Binford 1972; Isaac 1972b).

Variables which might prevent individual samples of stone artifacts from being directly
representative of widespread cultural norms include:

1. differences in functional requirements of tools at differing places and times,
2. differences in the properties of available raw materials, and
3. idiosyncrasies of individual craftsmen, or the idiosyncrasies of partially
   isolated segments of societies.

In this study, as in most others, the effects of these factors could not be distinguished with complete confidence; consequently it is not yet possible to explain observed
variation. However, a prerequisite for clearer understanding is the accurate definition of
the actual patterns of similarities and differences among the artifact assemblages. Most

of the remainder of this monograph is devoted to reporting on studies made with this objective in mind.

Although the patterns of resemblance among artifacts and artifact aggregates can be
intuitively perceived during sorting and study, it is clear that only by the application
of quantitative methods can these patterns be satisfactorily expressed and defined. A
great deal of numeric data (counts and measurements) was recorded in the laboratory in
Nairobi. Analysis has proceeded through the stage of computation of standard summarizing
statistics, to the application of straightforward tests of significance, such as the
analysis of variance. It is this first round of routine analysis that is outlined in this
volume (for further details, see Isaac 1968b). Much remains to be done in the way of more
sophisticated analyses, including multivariate techniques.

The Meaning of Diversity: Theoretical Considerations

Like a great many archeological studies, this analysis involved groping exploration
as well as specific inquiry into previously accepted propositions; that is to say, the
study has been both inductive and deductive. I began with a clear awareness that certain
assumptions, which had been tacitly accepted for a long time, needed to be tested. First,
I was concerned with the proposition that early culture had been so regularly patterned
that widespread, significant developmental stages could readily be ascertained from small
samples of its material remains. Second, I was interested in inquiring into hypotheses
that interpret recurrent contrasts among contemporaneous assemblages at successive horizons
as being due to the long-term persistence of separate phyla of culture. Third, I wished to
test alternative hypotheses that invoke activity differences to account for these same recurrent contrasts. (See Binford 1972; and Isaac 1972b for general reviews of the theoretical problems.) The structure of the analytical experiment called for comparison of the extent of variation among penecontemporary assemblages (synchronic variation) with differences between groups of assemblages having measurably different ages (diachronic variation).

If the sites are plotted in relation to the rough time scale provided by cumulative
sediment thickness, it can be seen that the known occurrences happen to group naturally
into three sets (see fig. 11, chap. 3). These have been termed the Lower Stratigraphic
Set (of site samples), the Middle Stratigraphic Set, and the Upper Stratigraphic Set, ab-
breviated as LSS, MSS, and USS, respectively. For at least two of the sets, the probable
time difference between the oldest and youngest samples within the set is very much less
than the time difference between the limits of adjacent sets. These sets have been used
in all analyses designed to detect important trends in artifact change.

The first step in analysis has been the assessment of the extent of variation in each
of the stratigraphic sets for any attribute under consideration. A null hypothesis of internal statistical homogeneity has been tested either by chi squares or by the analysis of
variance. It has been found that for very few features do the stratigraphic sets of samples behave as random samples varying about a common norm.

In order to provide a collective preview of evidence on time trends, figures 32 and
33 show examples of the values of selected variables plotted in relation to stratigraphy.
The categories or dimensions are more exactly defined in subsequent chapters. The figures
indicate that there is little tendency for the proportions of major artifact categories to
undergo consistent change in frequency through time (cf. Kleindienst 1961:fig. 5). A
series of plots has shown that in form-defining dimensions and ratios for bifaces, small
tools, and flakes, variation among means for sites within each stratigraphic set covers

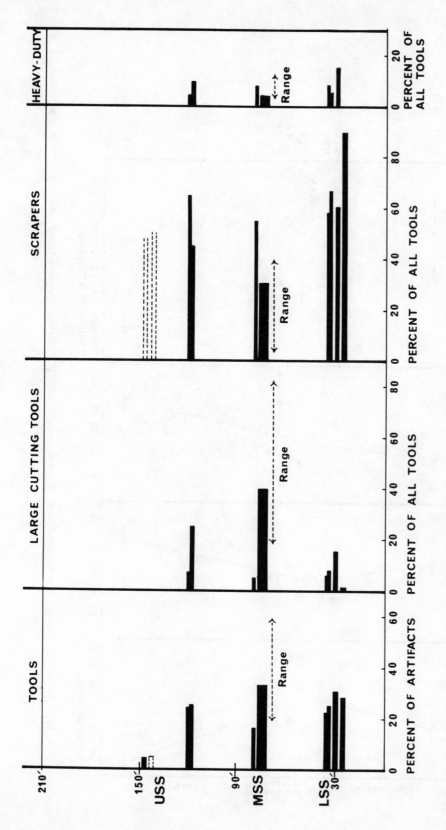

Figure 32. Percentage frequencies of artifact categories plotted against accumulative sediment thickness (α time).

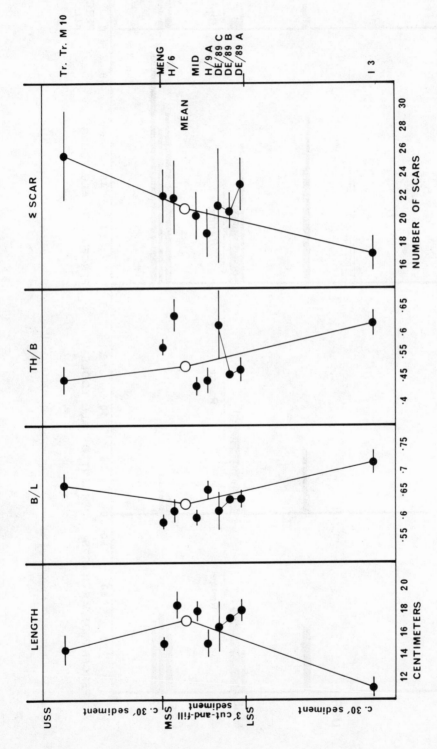

Figure 33. The relationship of cumulative sedimentation and site sample means for biface dimensions, ratios, and scar counts (shown with 95% confidence limits).

almost as wide a range as the total variation. Only the plot of biface attributes is reproduced (see fig. 33). Apparently consistent time trends affect only a small number of
recorded features in the samples; for example, bifaces seem to show a weak tendency toward
reduction in relative thickness and increase in scar numbers; flakes undergo an apparently
uneven but persistent reduction in thickness.

None of these trends can be regarded as being established beyond a doubt. The rarity
and uncertainty of evidence for directional change in a series spanning the time interval
represented by the three stratigraphic sets must lead to doubts about the validity of the
assumption that persistent progressive change was a normal pattern in the Acheulean. Further, it seems unlikely that numerous serial subdivisions are either feasible or meaning-
ful. Other papers contain further discussion of significance of this alleged feature of
the Olorgesailie evidence for cultural taxonomy and for the construction of models of cultural processes in the Middle Pleistocene (Isaac 1972e, 1972b, 1975).

One obvious aspect of diversity is the marked variation in the proportional frequency
of bifaces, the *fossiles directeurs* of the Acheulean. Figure 34 shows the frequency distribution pattern of site sample values for the ratio of bifaces to bifaces plus small
tools. This distribution is compared with the distribution of sample values to be expected
if the samples behaved as random deviates from the aggregate or mean proportion. Clearly
the observed pattern is not a random error pattern. What does it mean? Even before my
analysis began, the opinion of several archeologists who had worked with the Olorgesailie
material was divided (Leakey 1954; S. Cole 1963; Posnansky 1959; Kleindienst 1961). One
group was inclined to regard the two contrasting sets as indicative of two separate and
persistent cultural systems (phyla); another group was exploring activity differences as
an explanation. There are also other possible interpretations. (See Isaac 1972b, for a
review of the issues.)

The precise values of the relative proportions of bifaces and scrapers vary, depending
on whether broken and doubtful pieces are included, but the pattern is clear (table 8).
Two excavated samples, MFS and MPS, include no certain bifaces or biface fragments, though
surface collections indicated that bifaces were in fact present in small numbers on the
relevant horizons. Nine out of sixteen samples have more than three times as many small
tools as bifaces. Four samples show the inverse disproportion with more than three times
as many bifaces as small tools. Three samples at the most show subequal numbers of small
tools and bifaces, and one of these, H/9 AM, is a small sample of dubious significance.

The bimodal tendency is clear at least in the Olorgesailie samples, but it can be seen
that it is not a simple split between some occurrences with bifaces and no small tools
(Acheulean) and other occurrences with small tools but no bifaces (Hope Fountain). The
boundary between artifact assemblages representing the two cultures, if such there were,
lies within a continuum. Both cultures shared all major type design traditions but made
them in different proportions.

Figure 34 shows that the spectrum of biface and scraper proportions is partly dupli-
cated in each stratigraphic set, though biface-dominated assemblages are only well represented in the Middle Stratigraphic Set. This finding could be taken as support for the
hypothesis that the two extremes were maintained by separate ethnic entities persisting
alongside each other with fluctuating boundaries, but other explanations are also possible.

In order to examine the two-culture hypothesis and to explore the character of the
differentiation, the whole series of samples was divided into three sets, each showing a
different degree of biface-to-scraper domination (table 8). In subsequent tests on other

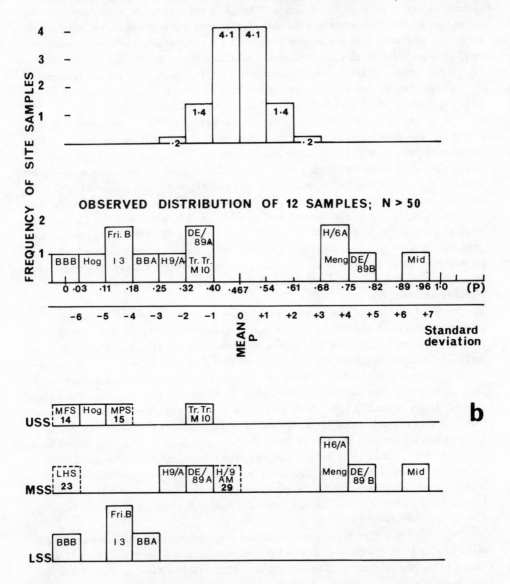

Figure 34. (A) The overall frequency of values of the binomial proportions of large cutting tools and scrapers. Observed frequencies contrasted with expectation for random samples from a single population; (B) Frequencies grouped by stratigraphic sets. Numbers of specimens are shown where sample size is less than 50.

Table 8

*A Rank-Ordered List of the Proportion of Bifaces (Large Cutting Tools) Relative to
Bifaces Plus Small Tools*

The proportions have been calculated in two ways:

Ratio 1: $\dfrac{\text{All large cutting tools (including identifiable broken pieces)}}{\text{All LCT + All small tools (including broken pieces)}}$

Ratio 2: $\dfrac{\text{Large cutting tools (excluding broken pieces)}}{\text{LCT + small scrapers (simple and nosed)}}$

The rank-ordered list for Ratio 1 has been divided into 3 sets:

Scraper-dominated with values from 0 to .15
Intermediate with values from .20 to .50
Biface-dominated with values from .70 to .95

Rank Order	Site	Ratio 1 LCT/LCT+ST	N1	Ratio 2 LCT/LCT+SCR	N2	
1	MFS	(0	14)	0	14	
2	BBB	.013	75	.017	59	
3	LHS	(.086	23)	.071	14	Scraper-
4	Hog	.097	72	.078	51	Dominated
5	Friday Beds	.115	52	.131	38	Set
6	I 3	.121	271	.191	172	
7	MPS	(.133	15)	0	13	
8	BBA*	.216	60	.188	48	
9	H/9 A	.262	217	.307	156	
10	DE/89 C	.328	97	.327	61	Intermediate
11	DE/89 A*	.358	237	.340	197	Set
12	Tr.Tr. M 10	.386	132	.381	118	
13	H/9 AM	.482	29	.518	14	
14	Meng	.742	128	.715	116	
15	H/6 A	.742	70	.774	62	Biface-
16	DE/89 B	.810	624	.896	549	Dominated
17	Mid	.946	94	.976	85	Set

*These assemblages are possibly "compound," but their components cannot be separated
at present (chap. 2).

attributes, these sets were tested for statistical homogeneity and examined for consistent
differences. The tests were largely confined to the small tools and the debitage because
the scraper-dominated samples contain too few bifaces for satisfactory comparison of biface
attributes. Consistent differences between the sets were not readily distinguishable in the
morphology of these classes (see Isaac 1968). Differences that were discerned, such as
relative thinness of flakes and scrapers in the biface-dominated sets, could just as well
have been due to higher incidence of biface trimming flakes in these assemblages.

For a final review of this problem, chapter 9 draws on the details of evidence set out
in the chapters dealing with the type frequencies and artifact morphology. The analysis
clarifies the issues, the choice between an interpretation involving one cultural tradition
with high variability in its manifestations versus an interpretation involving two only
slightly less variable coexistent traditions remains one which will be based largely on personal predilections. However, the evidence undoubtedly shows that patterns of variation are
more complex than has been made fully explicit.

The exploratory aspect of the analysis gains importance from this discovery of complexity. Few extensive studies of Middle Pleistocene assemblage differentiation have been
undertaken under circumstances in which time and space relations are as closely controlled
as in the stratified deposits of a single lake basin. Therefore, it would not have been
appropriate to restrict the investigations at Olorgesailie to the testing of prior hypotheses. The study of this artifact material has suggested various fresh hypotheses about
Middle Pleistocene cultural processes, notably those concerning the mechanisms governing
the apparent existence of numerous stylistically distinct but ephemeral entities within a
single limited network of rather simple craft traditions. Of course, for the purists, the
Olorgesailie data cannot be used to test the fresh ideas, since the hypotheses were suggested by these data.

These theoretical themes run through the chapters dealing with the artifacts, but not
to the exclusion of conventional descriptive reports on the material. The questions being
posed are in fact very subtle, and it would be naive to suppose that they can be settled
conclusively by a few simple tests on a limited body of data.

Composition of the Assemblages

Conventional methods for communicating the character of stone artifact assemblages
have always involved the classification of pieces into more or less standard, named categories present in a given assemblage. However, named categories of artifacts vary greatly
in their nature and properties. Sometimes they coincide with modes in a continuum of attribute variation. The types can then fairly be regarded as natural or intrinsic and the
categories may represent distinguishable design targets, or "mental templates" (J. Deetz
1967) in the culture of the makers. Very commonly, though, named categories are arbitrary
segments of a continuum of variation in form. Such categories have considerable descriptive value and may be of use in quantitative work, but the limitations imposed by their
nature should not be ignored. Any treatment of lists of forms that assumes the existence
of intrinsic types in systems such as those of Bordes (1950b), de Sonneville-Bordes and
Perrot (1954, 1955, 1956), or Tixier (1963), could be dangerously misleading.

Important attempts have been made in recent years to convert the use of inventories
of forms or types from a descriptive procedure into a precise analytical tool and to make
such analytical inventories the principal basis for comparative studies of all kinds
(Bordes 1950b, 1961a). Although I have used this method in the study of Olorgesailie, I
consider it important that other avenues of approach also be explored. The relatively low
degree of standardization apparent in the East African Acheulean industries renders the
value of detailed type inventories especially open to question.

In 1959, M. R. Kleindienst (1962) put forward a comprehensive classificatory scheme
for African Acheulean artifacts. The scheme has the important merit of having been formulated after most of the major collections of Acheulean artifacts from sub-Saharan Africa
had been thoroughly examined.[1] Further, the scheme has already been used in the analysis of
aggregates from Isimila, Kalambo Falls, Kariandusi, Lochard, Montagu Cave, and elsewhere,
so that an extensive corpus of quantitative classificatory data expressed in its terminology
already exists. With suitable modifications, Kleindienst's scheme has been chosen as the
framework for categorizing the Olorgesailie assemblage. Attempts have been made to point
out coincidence with other schemes and to indicate what the main features of the various

---

1. The typological system used by Mary Leakey (1971) for Acheulean assemblages had
not been developed at the time of the laboratory studies on which this monograph is based.

aggregates would be if analyzed in terms of other systems (e.g. Bordes 1961a; Mason 1962).

Table 9 shows the analysis of the Olorgesailie material into a slightly simplified version of Kleindienst's scheme. I experienced great difficulty in applying all the details of the Kleindienst scheme. In the absence of copious illustrations or of extensive consultation over specimens, it may be impossible for several workers to apply such schemes consistently. Even when consistency is achieved, it is not clear that in a situation of low standardization (low attribute cohesion) items classified within a category are homogenous in either their design or their function. Hence it is uncertain whether exegesis of frequency data obtained by the application of an unduly complex system of categorization would have advantages either in relation to cultural taxonomy or in relation to the reconstruction of activities.

These comments notwithstanding, the table provides a useful descriptive device preliminary to quantitative treatment of the morphology of major artifact classes. I do not believe that after the lapse of a few years the exact frequencies of the finer subcategories could be reproduced by another investigator or even by me. However, it seems certain that all analyses would concur in major features, such as the relative proportions of scrapers or bifaces, the percentages of heavy-duty forms, and the ratio of tools to debitage. Interpretation has been restricted to such features. In the future, when intrinsic patterns of morphological variation have been elucidated and when there is information concerning edge morphology and utilization damage, it may be possible to establish typologies with demonstrable validity in relation to more specific problems. Separate schemes dealing explicitly with either design and style or with function may be necessary.

In addition to applying Kleindienst's scheme, I examined the relationship of the categories to intrinsic features in morphological variation, using the frequency distributions of measurable attributes. I have provided information on these studies in chapters 6 and 7, and have published further discussion of the problem elsewhere (Isaac 1972a).

A distinct bimodality in size emerges in the tool series as a whole (fig. 35). Small, predominantly unifacial tools are very numerous and have a size model of about 4 cm. Bifacial tools are predominantly large, with a mode of about 16 cm. Thus the dichotomy that has long been recognized between Acheulean flake tools and core tools corresponds to an intrinsic, not an arbitrary, division. At site complexes such as Isimila and 'Ubeidiya the evidence for this dichotomy is reinforced by strong association of the two modalities with differences in raw material (Kleindienst 1962; Stekelis et al. 1969). Within each of these two sets, intrinsic submodalities have proved difficult to discern and morphological diversity takes on the appearance of an ill-differentiated continuum. The application of a χ^2 test to raw frequencies calculated from Kleindienst's inventories for the Olorgesailie assemblages (1961) shows that it is inconceivable that the samples from any one of the stratigraphic sets could be regarded as random-error deviates from a common norm characteristic of the set (Isaac 1968). Data subsequently compiled by me greatly increases the evidence for statistical heterogeneity of the typological inventories.

Certain of the Olorgesailie assemblages excavated by L. S. B. Leakey and M. D. Leakey in 1943 have been sorted and classified by both Kleindienst (1961) and me (1968, and this monograph). A pattern of minor discrepancies serves to illustrate the difficulties encountered in class analysis. Similar major features emerge in both analyses, but there is extensive divergence between the two over detail. For this reason, my discussion of the significance of class analysis is restricted to the gross proportions of major categories. There is also some discrepancy in the total number of pieces as I included fewer in the

Table 9
Percentage Composition of the Olorgesailie Artifact Samples

Overall Composition of Samples

Site	BBB	BBA	FB FB	FB HL	I3	DE/89A L	DE/89A I	DE/89B L	DE/89B I	DE/89C	H/6	H/9 A	H/9 AM	Mid	Meng	LHS	Tr Tr M10	Hög	MFS
Shaped tools	-	-	-	-	4	-	14	-	13	8	10	4	15	-	-	3	-	-	1
Modified and broken	-	-	-	-	2	-	3	-	3	5	2	1	2	-	-	2	-	-	·
Edge-damaged	-	-	-	-	2	-	2	-	-	4	2	2	1	-	-	2	-	-	1
Hammers etc.	-	-	-	-	·	-	·	-	1	·	2	·	·	-	-	1	-	-	1
Cores	-	-	-	-	2	-	·	-	3	2	2	·	1	-	-	1	-	-	1
Flakes etc.	-	-	-	-	13	-	12	-	15	23	19	15	32	-	-	21	-	-	30
Angular fragments	NR	NR	NR	NR	76	NR	67	NR	63	59	65	78	50	NR	NR	71	-	-	66
All Worked Stone (N)	>272	>234	>326	>63	5001	>584	(360)	>332	(4429)	(1104)	(807)	(5923)	(206)	>212	>426	658	>832	>221	(1426)
Manuports* N	NR	NR	NR	-	≥18	>2	13	NR	433	80	72	103	2	NR	NR	80	>17	>3	252

Composition of Shaped Tools Divided into Major Classes

Site	BBB	BBA	FB FB	FB HL	I3	DE/89A L	DE/89A I	DE/89B L	DE/89B I	DE/89C	H/6	H/9 A	H/9 AM	Mid	Meng	LHS	Tr Tr M10	Hög	MFS
Large cutting tools	2	19	11	-	15	26	68	67	75	31	67	27	48	80	66	9	35	11	-
Heavy-duty tools	2	13	13	-	6	6	2	9	5	6	5	2	3	4	3	14	3	3	-
Large scrapers	-	-	2	-	3	2	6	6	6	4	1	6	8	4	4	18	3	-	10
Other large tools	-	3	11	-	11	3	10	5	3	3	6	12	8	4	5	-	5	10	5
Small tools	97	62	63	-	64	63	14	10	9	53	19	51	43	4	22	59	50	75	84
Spheroids	3	3	-	-	1	1	-	8	1	3	1	2	-	4	-	-	2	2	-
All Shaped Tools	(61)	(68)	(54)	-	(219)	(198)	(50)	(103)	(581)	(77)	(78)	(211)	(30)	(112)	(147)	(22)	(147)	(63)	(19)

Composition of Shaped Tools Divided into Subclasses

Site	BBB	BBA	FB FB	FB HL	I3	DE/89A L	DE/89A I	DE/89B L	DE/89B I	DE/89C	H/6	H/9 A	H/9 AM	Mid	Meng	LHS	Tr Tr M10	Hög	MFS
Hand axes	-	4	6	-	8	18	40	26	42	12	27	7	17	24	31	4	15	3	-
Picklike hand axes	-	-	-	-	3	1	4	1	·	4	9	8	8	3	1	-	-	2	-
Chisel hand axes	4	4	2	-	1	-	-	-	-	3	13	5	8	13	18	-	-	2	-
Cleavers	2	4	2	-	2	2	2	33	26	8	5	5	8	30	1	4	13	2	-
Knives	-	-	-	-	1	2	4	1	6	5	8	2	-	4	1	-	1	-	-
Broken large cutting tools	-	6	2	-	2	4	18	6	1	5	5	4	3	5	8	4	4	5	-
Picks and trièdres	-	-	2	-	2	2	2	2	3	5	5	4	7	1	4	6	5	2	-
Choppers	2	6	11	-	4	4	2	6	3	5	-	1	-	-	2	9	1	-	-
Core scrapers	-	7	-	-	-	6	2	1	1	1	1	1	1	-	1	1	1	-	-
Large flake scrapers	-	-	2	-	3	2	6	2	6	4	1	6	6	4	4	5	3	-	10
Core/bifaces	-	3	9	-	-	2	2	2	·	1	3	6	7	4	4	6	5	2	-
Other large tools	-	-	2	-	11	1	8	3	3	4	4	8	-	1	1	4	3	8	5
Small scrapers (simple)	56	32	24	-	50	39	14	6	5	29	13	40	40	1	16	14	39	54	26
Small scrapers (nosed/pt.)	39	25	37	-	13	23	-	-	4	25	5	11	3	1	6	36	10	21	47
Other small tools	2	4	2	-	1	-	1	3	1	5	1	1	2	2	-	9	2	2	10
Spheroids	3	3	-	-	1	1	-	8	1	3	1	2	-	4	-	-	2	2	-
All Shaped Tools	(61)	(68)	(54)	-	(219)	(198)	(50)	(103)	(581)	(77)	(78)	(211)	(30)	(112)	(147)	(22)	(147)	(63)	(19)

Table 9--Continued

Composition of Miscellaneous Trimmed Pieces (= Modified) and Broken Tools in Det.

M.T.P. lge. bif.	6	–	–	1	–	–	42	31	20	–	8	–	4	25	60	68	–	–	–
lge. unif.	–	–	12	7	6	–	–	31	–	11	–	10	–	–	–	–	–	27	–
sm. bif.	–	12	–	24	18	25	12	–	–	42	14	–	–	–	–	–	–	4	8
sm. unif.	–	12	5	–	–	19	25	13	–	–	71	25	–	–	–	32	–	38	17
Broken large tool	11	12	14	–	42	25	25	25	–	25	25	50	20	20	–	–	4	–	75
Broken small tool	83	62	86	87	53	18	–	25	52	43	–	71	50	20	–	–	73	27	75	100
All "Modified" and Broken	(18)	(8)	(14)	(142)	(34)	(12)	(16)	(127)	(62)	(26)	(77)	(4)	(5)	(19)	(11)	(26)	(24)	(5)

Composition of Edge-damaged and Utilised Pieces

Large planoclinal	4	–	–	42	86	–	50	–	62	4	–	–	–	40	12	67	5	–	4
Small planoclinal	46	–	–	–	–	8	–	4	–	58	100	–	20	58	31	44	54
Large biclinal	–	90	–	26	9	88	17	5	31	23	–	–	40	8	33	–	–
Small biclinal	50	–	74	–	–	–	8	53	–	15	28	–	–	8	–	27	6	12
Écaillée etc.	–	–	26	17	–	–	–	26	–	–	6	–	–	15	–	21	22	4
Hammers, anvils	–	10	–	14	6	12	17	16	7	54	8	–	–	–	–	16	28	27
All Edge-damaged	(26)	(19)	(19)	(113)	(35)	(8)	(12)	(130)	(45)	(26)	(101)	(1)	(5)	(26)	(12)	(85)	(18)	(26)

Composition of Flakes and Flake Fragments

Flakes large	1	2	–	–	10	4	19	16	3	3	2	–	21	9	7	1	1	1
small	63	78	80	90	57	74	51	56	72	51	67	49	70	62	58	77	67	70
very small	7	1	–	2	22	–	–	13	19	17	8	6	11	11	25	12	14
Flake fragments	30	21	18	8	19	17	30	27	12	29	14	42	24	16	20	15	15	20	16
All Flakes	(166)	(85)	(181)	(60)	(643)	(163)	(43)	(32)	(668)	(265)	(156)	(874)	(67)	(56)	(149)	(137)	(326)	(207)	(420)
Cores, regular	–	22	17	33	21	38	20	5	16	10	18	18	40	50	22	50	45
irregular	100	65	56	33	49	27	60	89	48	60	46	100	60	18	86	51	6	50
casual	–	13	26	33	30	24	5	5	4	10	23	–	33	14	20	44	5
fragments	–	54	–	–	11	20	6	32	20	14	–	–	–	–	6	–	–
All Cores	(1)	–	(23)	(3)	(90)	(37)	(5)	(37)	(141)	(25)	(10)	(57)	(2)	(5)	(12)	(7)	(49)	(16)	(20)

*Since the angular fragment category is not fully represented in the material preserved from L. S. B. and M. D. Leakey's excavations, comparable percentages cannot be computed for the overall make-up of these samples.

·Present but less than 0.5.

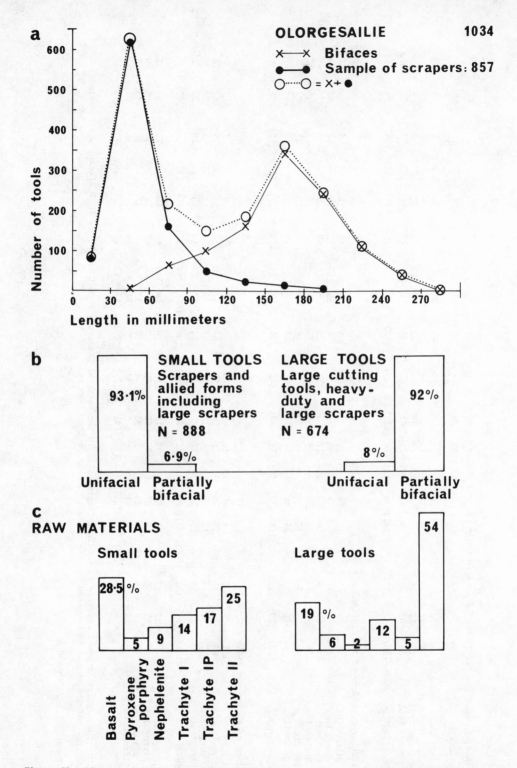

Figure 35. Diagrams illustrating the contrasts between large, predominantly bifacial tools and small, predominantly unifacial tools. (A) Size; (B) Bifacial:unifacial proportions (%); (C) Percentages of various raw materials.

analyses than did Kleindienst. These differences may relate to:

1. Differences in understanding, from some rather cryptic notations which pieces from some sites were recovered from excavations and which from outcrops

2. Rearrangement of the collections between the times the two studies were made.

None of the differences appears likely to affect the results materially.

At several levels of classification, the clearly recognizable categories are conventionally grouped in triads:

Total aggregate--tools, utilized, waste

Shaped tools--large cutting, heavy-duty, small (especially scrapers)

Large cutting tools--hand axes, cleavers, knives

Heavy-duty tools--choppers, picks, and core scrapers.

Small tools show less widely recognized divisions (see chap. 7).

These threefold divisions have the advantage that graphic representation on a triangular coordinate grid facilitates the visual comparison of numerous samples. If for each sample the number of items in each category is expressed as a percentage of the sum of the items in the three categories, then the composition can be represented by a point within the triangle. Points clustering in any corner of the triangle represent samples dominated by the category for which that corner is the 100 % value. Points in the center of the diagram represent subequal quantities of all three components. Points along one or other margin represent varying mixtures of two of the components to the virtual exclusion of the third. This method of representation has advantages over conventional histograms in that a single spatial array of points can present for comparison a large number of samples, whereas a separate histogram would be necessary for each (see Bohmers 1956, 1963).

Figure 36 shows the composition of excavated samples with respect to shaped tools; utilized pieces; and waste, including chips, chunks, and rubble. The array includes only those Olorgesailie samples excavated by Isaac and known not to be depleted by the discarding of angular waste. The diagram makes it clear that almost all excavated Acheulean industries are dominated by waste, as of course are most stone artifact occurrences. The observed values for percentages of waste range from 35.4% (Broken Hill, after Kleindienst 1961) to 99.1% (Montagu Cave layer 3, after Keller 1973). The median for the thirty-two Acheulean occurrences figured is 80% waste. All Olorgesailie sites, despite their distance from raw material sources, have higher proportions of waste than the median value (range 81.5% to 97% waste). Variations in proportions of such gross categories as tools, utilized pieces, and waste could hardly be expected to be closely related to culture-taxonomic divisions. It can be seen that the Lower Acheulean (2 plots), Upper Acheulean (30 plots), Acheulean-Sangoan (3 plots), and the Sangoan (1 plot) all form part of the same scatter pattern without any apparent differentiation. However, the samples of Oldowan and allied industries from Olduvai Beds I and II analyzed and reported by M. D. Leakey (1967) do appear to show a consistently high proportion of utilized pieces.

It has frequently been inferred that sites showing extremes of preponderance of waste over trimmed tools and utilized pieces reflect the special circumstances of an atelier, rather than the more balanced round of activities envisaged as normal for a domestic site. The Olorgesailie samples indicate the need for caution, since they show a strong predominance of waste, but were located so far from outcrops of suitable rock that stoneworking cannot have been a primary determinant of their placement. MFS, because of its location at the point of contact of lake plain and scree slopes, is the only exception. Perhaps

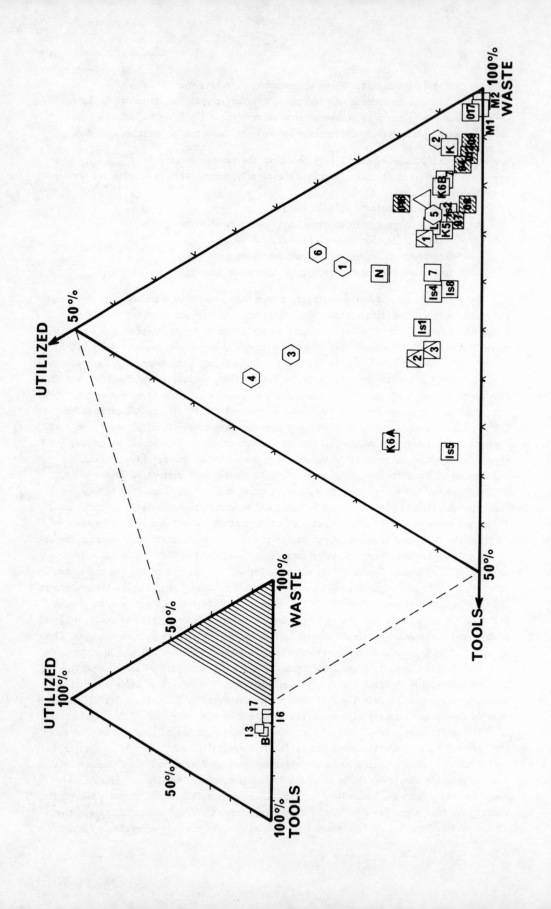

Figure 36. A triangle diagram showing variation in the composition of assemblages with respect to the three supercategories: Tools, Utilized, and Waste (Debitage). Key: hexagon = Oldowan; square = Acheulean; triangle = Sangoan; triangle in a square = Acheulean/Sangoan transition at Kalambo Falls.

ACHEULEAN		OLDOWAN AND DEVELOPED OLDOWAN
Olorgesailie	*Isimila* (Kleindienst 1961)	*Olduvai* (M. D. Leakey 1971)
O1: Basal Bed A	Is1: K19	1: DK 1
O2: Basal Bed B	Is2: K18	2: FLK 1
O3: Friday Beds	Is3: K6	3: FLK N1 (1-2)
O4: I 3	Is4: L-J6-7	4: HWK IIE S conglom.
	Is5: K14	5: BK II
O5: DE/89 A	Is6: H9-J8	6: MNK II
O6: DE/89 B	Is7: J6-7	
O7: DE/89 C	Is8: L-H15	*Early Acheulean*
O8: H/6 A		*Olduvai*
O9: H/9 A	*Kalambo* (J. D. Clark 1964)	7: EFHR (M. D. Leakey 1971)
O10:H/9 AM	K5 5	
O11:Meng	K6a 6a	N: Natron (Isaac 1965)
O12:LHS	K6b 6b	
O13:Mid	K7 7	*Acheulean/Sangoan*
	K8 8	1: Kalambo A/56/4
O14:Tr. Tr. M 10		2: A/56/V
O15:Hog	B: Broken Hill (J. D. Clark 1959)	3: A/56/5B
O16:MPS		
O17:MFS	L: Latamne (J. D. Clark 1969 a and b)	*Sangoan*
		Kalambo B2/54/4
	M1: Montagu Layer (Keller 1973)	

significantly, MFS contains 94% waste--the highest proportion of waste at Olorgesailie. (Olorgesailie plot 17).

Comparative Data Regarding Variation
in the Major Classes of Tool Types

It has become customary to recognize three major classes of "Early Stone Age" (Lower Paleolithic) tools in Africa: large cutting tools (bifaces), heavy-duty tools (massive chunky forms, such as picks and choppers), and small tools (predominantly scrapers).

The relative proportions of these three categories have had fundamental taxonomic significance in the definition and recognition of culture-stratigraphic entities. Figure 60a shows diagrammatically the stereotype or ideal situation as it was understood until excavation of sites such as those at Olorgesailie, Olduvai, Kalambo, and Isimila began to indicate greater complexity than had been anticipated. Figure 37a shows the observed values. It can be seen that only the Oldowan and allied industries form a clearly distinguished cluster. Occurrences that are Acheulean in the classic sense of the term or that are interstratified with such occurrences cover a very wide range of values. The plots for most samples fall along an axis between large cutting tools and small tools, and all but one, Isimila LH/15, contain less than 25% of heavy-duty tools. Overlapping this scatter but toward its heavy-duty margin are the Lower Acheulean plots, Natron and Olduvai EFHR II, and the four Acheulean-Sangoan plots, all from the Kalambo Falls sequence.

The large cutting tools constitute the *fossiles directeurs* of the Acheulean *sensu stricto*, and small tools the *fossiles directeurs* of the Hope Fountain industries. Figure 37b shows that the two extremes of large tool or small tool predominance are linked by a continuous scatter of intermediate values. The Olorgesailie samples, it is true, tend to cluster at the two poles of the scatter, but even here intermediates exist. Since the values of small tool/large tool proportions do not seriate through time (see fig. 32), J. D. Clark (1950, 1959), Posnansky (1959), Kleindienst (1961), and Howell and Clark (1963) all concur in preferring to consider the established variation as being indicative of differences in activity between sites, rather than persistent differences between two or more parallel phyla of culture. However, the latter view was formerly supported by L. S. B. Leakey (1953:86-87).

Kleindienst (1961:44) made the following suggestions:

> At first glance, the extreme variability in percentage of occurrence of any tool type is obvious. . . . Closer inspection shows that two main patterns of grouping of shaped tool components are found, with a suggestion of an intermediate type, and of one other pattern:
> (a) Occupation areas with a high percentage of handaxes/cleavers/knives, consistent low percentages of other large tool components, and low percentages of small implements (Olorgesailie land surfaces 7, 8, 9; Isimila K19, J12, K6, K14, H9-J8, Upper J6-J7).
> (b) Occupation areas with a low percentage of handaxes/cleavers/knives, low percentages of other types of large tools, and high percentages of small implements (Olorgesailie land surfaces 1, 2, 3, 11, 12, 13, and to a lesser degree, 6 and 10; Isimila K18 Tr. 2; Broken Hill Acheulian).
> (c) Occupation areas with approximately equal percentages of handaxes/ cleavers/knives and small implements, and with lower percentages of other large tool types (Isimila Lower J6-J7; Olorgesailie land surfaces 6 and 10 tend toward a position between (a) and (b) as well).
> (d) Occupation areas which have a higher percentage of core scrapers, picks and choppers than is usual in (a), (b), or (c), plus some handaxes/ cleavers/knives and small implements (Isimila Lower H15).

Figure 37 suggests that Kleindienst's patterns or assemblage types are proving to be zones in a fairly even-density continuum, rather than clusters. If one regards the proportions of

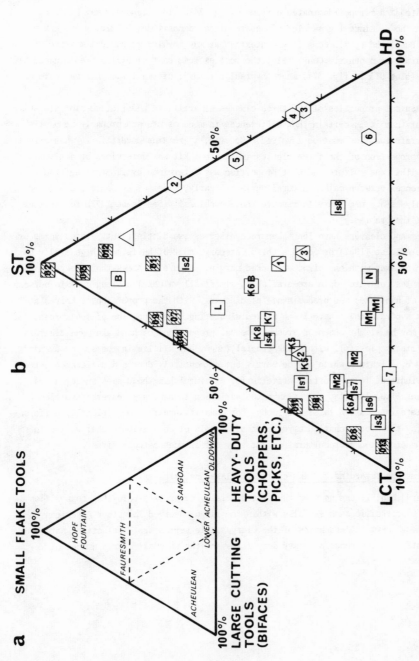

Figure 37. Triangle diagram showing variation in assemblage composition with respect to the three main superclasses of tools: Large Cutting Tools (Bifaces) LCT; Small Tools (Scrapers etc.); Heavy-duty Tools. The taxonomy of early stone age assemblages in Africa has implicitly involved zonation of the mix between these categories, as shown in the inset on the left. Compare the configuration in this figure with the results of a principle components analysis (figure 71). Key as in figure 36.

the categories as indicative of activity bias, then the activities are seen as mixed in all proportions. If one regards such proportions as indicative of cultural differences, then it must be supposed that the traditions were capable of blending completely.

If the Olorgesailie samples are compared with other Middle Pleistocene samples, it can be seen that the Olorgesailie series spans the entire range of values for percentages of large cutting tools, but that it has a lower than usual proportion of heavy-duty tools. Within the Olorgesailie sample range there is some tendency for samples to cluster at the biface-dominated and scraper-dominated extremes (fig. 34). This tendency may be even stronger than shown, since the samples of intermediate composition, Tr. Tr. M 10, H/9 A, DE/89 A, and Basal Bed B, all come from contexts that may involve mechanical mixture of formerly separate components. Conversely, the most extreme case of biface predominance is found at Mid (plot 013 in fig. 37), where hydraulic removal of small elements may have occurred.

The mechanical properties of the three classes of artifacts under discussion are so very different that it is certain that differences in mode of use and probably some differences in craft function must be involved. However, it remains uncertain to what extent the relative proportion of the three classes in the tool kit was determined by activity differences within one culture and what proportion was determined by fluctuating traditional differences between major cultural phyla. Clearly, lines of evidence independent of the class analysis are necessary to resolve these problems. (See Isaac 1972b for further discussion of the problem.)

Hand axes and cleavers have long been recognized as two distinct but related forms of bifaces. Kleindienst (1962) proposed a third category, that of knife, which generally has the form of hand axes with one blunt or backed margin. Figure 38 shows that among the Acheulean samples for which data are available, almost all values lie along an axis between predominance of hand axes and predominance of cleavers, with the proportion of knives at 0-20%, always subordinate. There is no marked clustering in any portion of the spread, though there may be slight bunching around subequal proportions of hand axes and cleavers. The Olorgesailie samples fall within the general range, but all lie in the sector of hand ax predominance, a feature which may be partly but not entirely due to a difference between Isaac and Kleindienst in the sorting criteria for distinguishing hand axes and cleavers.

At Olorgesailie, Isimila, and Kalambo the variation in hand ax/cleaver proportions does not seriate in relation to stratigraphy, nor does it appear to be regionally differentiated. It may therefore constitute yet another example of an attribute that varies in relation to undetermined microcultural or activity differences between sites.

Interim Conclusions regarding the Indication of Class Analysis

In summary then, it can be seen that the diversity of gross typological composition shown by the Olorgesailie samples falls within the range observed for other Acheulean occurrences, though certain tendencies of the Olorgesailie series are distinctive, notably the consistently low incidence of heavy-duty forms and the unusually large number of scraper-dominated samples.

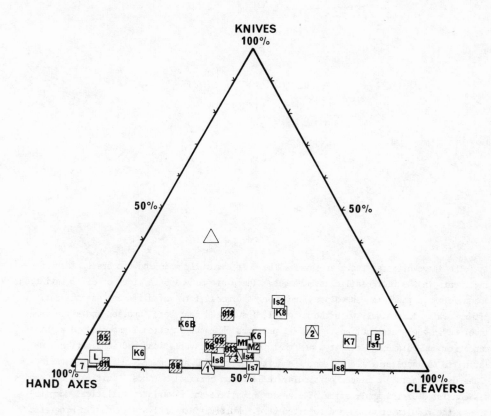

Figure 38. Triangle diagram showing assemblage composition with regard to subdivisions of the Large Cutting Tools (Bifaces): Hand axes; Knives; Cleavers. Key as in figure 36.

6. THE MORPHOLOGY OF BIFACES

The large bifacial tools are by far the most carefully made and elaborate class of
implements in the Olorgesailie assemblages. There are many subtle lines of differentiation
among forms in the same assemblages and among the modal forms of different assemblages.
After working extensively with the material, I surmised that both function and style are
involved in these distinctions. Since I presumed that the functional aspects had significance for understanding activity, and that the stylistic variations had implications relating to sociocultural mechanisms, I undertook a careful attribute study of this varied
class of artifacts. I placed particular reliance on metrical methods. Initially the analysis consisted of the application of classic univariate and bivariate statistical computa-
tions, the results of which are reported here. Multivariate analysis is now in progress.
Aspects of the results of this work have been published elsewhere (Isaac 1972c, d), and
only an outline of the data and results will be presented here as part of a general report
on the morphology of this important tool class.

Archeologists have made several attempts to express aspects of biface forms in numerical terms (e.g., Malvesin-Fabré 1948; Alimen and Vignal 1952; McBurney and West 1954; de
Heinzelin 1960; Bordes 1961a; Roe 1964, 1968; Balout 1967; and Cahen and Martin 1972).
None of these proposed systems has yet become standard. I worked with Roe during the initial development of his system and used the subsequent elaboration (Roe 1964) as the basis
for the Olorgesailie study.

Figure 39 summarizes the measurements used to define plan form and sectional form.
Counts of the scars were undertaken, and in spite of the difficulties of achieving consistency, I believe that the counts are useful numeric indicators. A scheme for scar zonation
is also shown in figure 39c.

Technicalities of the Manufacture of Bifaces

For approximately 60% of the large tools, the blank from which the implement was
formed by trimming cannot be determined with certainty. In 36% (458 specimens), enough of
the platform, bulb, or flake-release surface remains visible to determine that a large
flake served as a blank. It is very probable that most indeterminate specimens in the form
either of conchoidal flakes or of cleavage slabs, were also obtained by percussion. Only
4% show pebble cortex, and most of these are not hand axes or cleavers.

Eighty-six percent of the determinable large flake blanks are side-struck or corner-

116

struck flakes.[1] There are simple patterns of dorsal scars that may approximate Levallois patterns, though they rarely show sufficient intensity of preparation to justify this term. They commonly have rather long, thick, wide-angle platforms. In many of the large tools the first trimming scars, usually reversed, were directed at the removal of the platform vestige. It is not uncommon for tools, especially cleavers, to have this trimming as the only systematic secondary modification (see pls. 26, 44, 45, 60; and fig. 72). The dimensions and morphology of the large tools may well be extensively influenced by the dimensions and form of large flakes.

The characteristics of trimming are highly variable, and scars range from deep, bold stone hammer scars to shallow, invasive cylinder hammer scars. In addition, many specimens, especially those of the slightly fissile lavas, such as trachyte, show pronounced step-fracture trimming. One would guess that a wide range of techniques is represented: anvil, forceful percussion, and controlled percussion with a rounded soft stone or a wood or bone mallet. No attempt has been made to distinguish systematically these varieties of trimming, though the terms are used descriptively in the characterization of assemblages. The scar counts and scar zonation do indirectly define aspects of this variation.

The preparation of large tools from large flakes is a distinctive feature of the Acheulean over most of its distribution. The invention of techniques for obtaining large flakes may have been crucial in the morphological differentiation of the Acheulean from the Oldowan (Isaac 1969). With only a few exceptions, all the large tools from Olorgesailie are made of lava (see appendix B1).

The Structure of the Total Assemblage

How many intrinsic divisions or modalities are there among the bifaces? I became actively interested in this problem during the laboratory phase of the study of the Olorgesailie tools and attempted to use the attribute data to reach an approximate answer. I reported aspects of this inquiry to the 1967 Pan-African Congress (Isaac 1972c), and I will only summarize the conclusions here. These are tentative and subject to modification or revision when full-scale multivariate analyses have been completed.

Analysis has been carried out to determine whether groups of similar forms exist that are isolated from other distinctive forms (a) by relative rarity of intermediates (polymodality), or (b) by showing a standardized combination of measured attribute values that are improbable in relation to the overall frequency distribution of the variables.

Formal statistical tests apart from rank-order tests of consistent differences in variance were not applied, because they are largely meaningless in a situation where the samples compared are obtained by sorting.

I envisage the pattern of variation as being best expressed as a spatial field, with the forms represented as zones that are close together or far apart depending on their similarity. The field can best be explained by taking the classic hand ax form (*coup-de-poing*) as a reference point. The principal attributes for this class are:

1. A variable amygdaloid or oval plan form
2. Lenticular sections

---

1. The overall composition is as follows: flakes with indeterminable orientation of axis, 13.3%; flakes with traces of pebble cortex, 2.4%. Of the 84.3% determinable specimens (n = 386), 48% are normal side-struck flakes, 19% are oblique side-struck flakes, 21% are oblique end-struck flakes, and 12% are normal end-struck flakes.

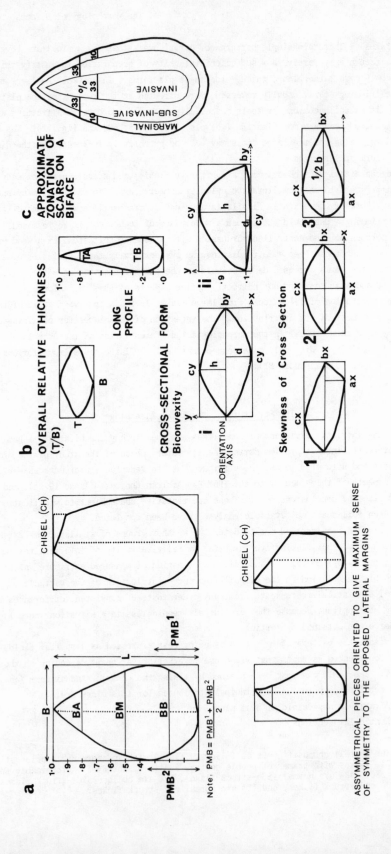

b OVERALL RELATIVE THICKNESS (T/B)

c APPROXIMATE ZONATION OF SCARS ON A BIFACE

LONG PROFILE

CROSS-SECTIONAL FORM

Biconvexity

ORIENTATION AXIS

i

ii

Skewness of Cross Section

1   **2**   **3**

a

Note: PMB = $\frac{PMB^1 + PMB^2}{2}$

CHISEL (CH)

CHISEL (CH)

ASSYMETRICAL PIECES ORIENTED TO GIVE MAXIMUM SENSE OF SYMMETRY TO THE OPPOSED LATERAL MARGINS

Figure 39.

Measured attributes of bifaces.

Cross-sectional form: biconvexity.

i. Index of biconvexity: $\left(1 - \dfrac{h-d}{h+d}\right)$ $\underline{\Omega}$ 1

ii. $\left(1 - \dfrac{h-d}{h+d}\right)$ $\underline{\Omega}$ 0.2

Skewness of cross section.

Index of skewness = $\dfrac{2\left(a-\frac{b}{2}\right)}{b}$ x $\dfrac{2\left(c-\frac{b}{2}\right)}{b}$

1. *Parallelogram forms*

    Signs for $a - \dfrac{b}{2}$ and $c - \dfrac{b}{2}$ differ, giving rise to negative values

    Index of skewness = -0.24 in example shown.

2. *Lens forms*

    Values approximate zero

    Index of skewness 0.0

3. *Wedge forms*

    Same signs for $a - \dfrac{b}{2}$ and $c - \dfrac{b}{2}$, giving rise to positive values

    Index of skewness = +0.24 in example shown.

Scar count records.

   Number of scars in each zone of each face.

   Total of scars on each face.

   Total of scars in each zone on both faces together:

$$i$$
$$si$$
$$m$$

   Total of scars. ΣSc.

Indices

   Index of bifaciality: $\dfrac{Sc.\ \text{on face with least scars}}{Sc.\ \text{on face with most scars}}$

   Index of invasive trimming: $\dfrac{i + si}{\Sigma Sc.}$

3. Trimming scars penetrating most of both faces

4. A sharp edge running all around or almost all around the perimeter.

Hand axes, including chisel-ended forms and picklike forms, make up 57% of the total of all large bifacial tools from Olorgesailie. Among the hand axes, about 28% are classic forms displaying the definitive characters, and 72% represent a more variable fringe of subclassic forms. Among these subclassic hand axes are some that vary from the classic form in the same direction as non-hand ax forms, but to a lesser degree. The subclassic hand axes grade into the following adjoining form categories, distinguished here by the criteria used in recognition:

1. Cleavers, distinguished by the increasing relative magnitude of a sharp transverse untrimmed bit.

2. Knives, distinguished by asymmetry between margins, one side being steep and blunt and the other sharp.

3. Picklike forms, distinguished by the presence of robust thick sections. These forms grade into true picks by increasing robusticity. The latter are extremely rare at Olorgesailie.

4. Trièdres, distinguished by the combination of a delicate apex with a triangular or domed planoconvex section.

5. Corelike discoidal choppers, distinguished by the reduction of length relative to breadth and by the increase in relative thickness. There is also a peculiar and rare group of thin, irregular spindly bifaces, mainly from the earliest stratigraphic levels.

6. Hand axes, cleavers, and knives, all grade into a comparatively rare group, large scrapers, which in turn show a continuous log-normal size gradation with the small scrapers. This group constitutes the principal though tenuous link between the two major supercategories, dominantly large bifacial tools and dominantly small unifacial tools.

Means and standard deviations for type category sets are listed in table 10. Isaac (1972d) gives the individual frequency distributions for each key attribute for each type category. My analysis suggests that the sets of pieces classified into the named forms constitute recurrent improbable combinations of attribute states and that the field of morphological variation is consequently not random. However, the analysis also suggests that, in general, the form categories are not modes, but arbitrary zones within a structured continuum. This concept is partially expressed in figure 40a and 40b. Hand axes appear as a well-defined modal form central to the continuum of variation and display gradational transitions from deviant, subclassic hand axes to a limited number of forms that are sufficiently unlike hand axes to warrant separate designations, such as knives, picklike hand axes, trièdres, corelike bifaces, choppers, and large scrapers. All these form categories are of comparatively rare occurrence, the sum being 20% and the greatest single frequency being 6% for scrapers. However, cleavers do appear to constitute a modality that is weakly separate from hand axes. Cleavers have a frequency of 23%, compared to a 15% frequency for the partially intermediate category of chisel-ended hand axes, and 39% for hand axes other than chisel-ended or picklike forms.

In general, hand axes, including picklike hand axes, show a relatively higher degree of standardization (that is, a smaller standard deviation) than do the other named forms. Important exceptions occur only where there is a clustering about what can be interpreted as a generalized state of an attribute, such as small size or low scar count. A rank-order test of concordance among the variances bears out this assertion (table 11).

Table 10

Mean Values of Measurements and Form-defining Ratios for each Type Category within the Global Series Formed by Pooling All Olorgesailie Samples

	L	(Mean s.d.) B/L	T/B	PMB/L	BA/BB	TA/TB	Σ Sc	Inv Scars Sc	Index of Biconvexity Median and inter-quartile distance
Hand axes N (343-666)	179 27%*	.56 .08	.48 .10	.38 .07	.69 .14	.70 .17	25.4 36%*	.60 .15	.82 .21
Cleavers (162-299)	175 18%	.58 .07	.44 .11	.48 .18	1.02 .18	.71 .19	19.4 51%	.53 .18	.81 .24
Knives (30-65)	174 21%	.58 .08	.47 .11	.38 .10	.73 .16	.71 .20	16.3 44%	.58 .22	.73 .34
Picklike H.A.s (24-35)	169 22%	.53 .07	.65 .13	.36 .06	.67 .12	.66 .16	17.2 41%	.72 .13	.73 .28
Picks and Trièdres (11-23)	140 24%	.60 .11	.56 .15	.31 .08	.58 .16	.64 .15	13.5 51%	.63 .18	.55 .45
Choppers (13-17)	84 18%	.82 .09	.64 .13	.48 .07	1.02 .20	.88 .21	9.4 37%	.89 .19	.73 .60
Large Scrapers (28-73)	122 23%	.54 .13	.44 .12	.44 .13	.84 .20	.95 .31	14.0 47%	.47 .15	.67 .46
Corelike Bifaces (33-40)	84 21%	.62 .10	.56 .13	.44 .10	.87 .16	.89 .18	14.2 32%	.74 .20	.78 .29
Large Flakes (41-54)	125 18%	.60 .08	.47 .12	.43 .14	.84 .21	.77 .27	-- --	-- --	.76 .32
Overall (674-1263)	170 28%	.58 .09	.48 .12	.41 .10	.80 .24	.72 .21	21.0 50%	.55 .19	.80 .25

Note: Values of N are given as ranges, since not all measurements were taken on all specimens. *Coefficient of variation.

Table 11

Means for the Dimensions and Form-defining Ratio of the Bifaces in the Olorgesailie Site Samples
(For definition of the measurements and ratios, see fig. 39 and text)

Site and range of N values	L Mean	C of V	B/L Mean	s.d.	T/B		PMB/L		BA/BB		TA/TB		Σ Sc.		i/Sc.	
Tr. Tr. M 10 (55-64)	145	35%	.62	.11	.45	.12	.44	.14	.83	.23	.78	.24	25.6	56.5%	.51	.17
Meng (83-96)	149	21%	.55	.07	.52	.09	.37	.08	.71	.14	.70	.21	22.1	47.4	.61	.16
Mid (78-86)	177	22%	.55	.08	.44	.09	.46	.08	.92	.26	.76	.24	20.3	45.3	.50	.18
H/9 AM (14-16)	194	25%	.55	.10	.40	.10	.42	.08	.83	.19	.79	.19	19.6	40.9	.41	.16
H/9 A (58-68)	150	33%	.61	.10	.45	.12	.44	.09	.91	.34	.79	.28	18.8	42.4	.43	.19
H/6 A (54-57)	183	24%	.57	.09	.56	.13	.38	.07	.70	.18	.64	.19	21.9	52.1	.61	.16
DE/89 C (15-23)	164	32%	.56	.09	.57	.13	.41	.11	.77	.18	.71	.14	21.6	49.0	.61	.08
DE/89 B (172-520)	172	20%	.59	.07	.46	.10	.41	.10	.82	.24	.70	.19	21.2	47.8	.53	.18
DE/89 A (60-79)	179	24%	.59	.08	.47	.10	.38	.11	.68	.19	.62	.17	23.1	39.0	.53	.16
I 3 (66-74)	104	34%	.67	.11	.57	.12	.44	.10	.83	.22	.80	.19	17.0	35.4	.68	.19
Overall (674-1263)	170	27.5%	.58	.09	.48	.12	.41	.10	.80	.24	.72	.21	21.0	10.2	.55	.19

Note: The first column gives the value of the mean, the second gives the coefficient of variation for dimensions (L and Σ Sc.) and the standard deviation for ratios. The range of values are given for N because not all measurements were taken on all specimens.

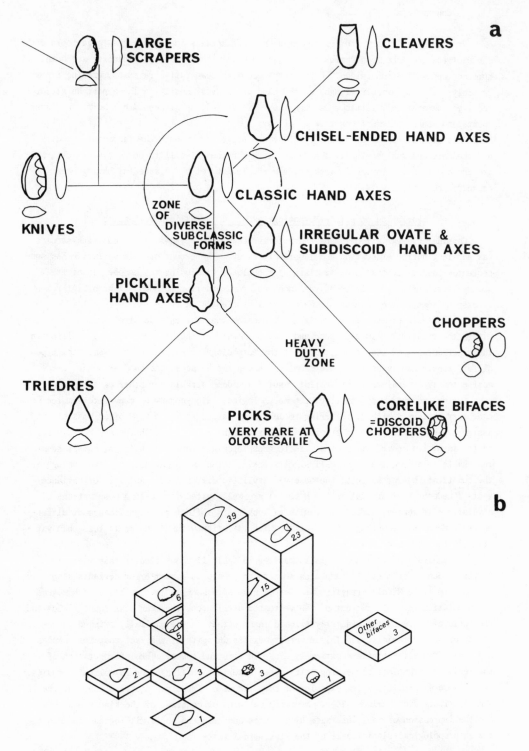

a

LARGE SCRAPERS

CLEAVERS

CHISEL-ENDED HAND AXES

KNIVES

ZONE OF DIVERSE SUBCLASSIC FORMS

CLASSIC HAND AXES

IRREGULAR OVATE & SUBDISCOID HAND AXES

PICKLIKE HAND AXES

CHOPPERS

HEAVY DUTY ZONE

TRIEDRES

PICKS
VERY RARE AT OLORGESAILIE

CORELIKE BIFACES
=DISCOID CHOPPERS

b

39

23

6

15

5

Other bifaces 3

2

3

3

1

1

Figure 40. (A) A diagram illustrating the concept that the various categories of larger tools form zones within a field of morphological gradients; (B) The frequencies of the major categories in the overall Olorgesailie sample. The percentages are represented as a three-dimensional histogram with the forms distributed essentially as in A.

From the preliminary studies reported here, it appears that among the large tools of the Olorgesailie Acheulean series only two categories, hand axes and cleavers, are both numerous and well standardized. Other forms occur as comparative rarities, grading imperceptibly into the variable fringes of the hand ax-cleaver modality. These peripheral forms received comparatively little care when they were shaped, as witnessed by their lower scar counts and weaker internal consistency of form.

This view of Acheulean biface typology was suggested by both the laboratory studies and the metrical analysis. It is advanced as a hypothesis still to be tested by multivariate and quantitative taxonomic methods, and should not yet be regarded as having been demonstrated conclusively.

Variation in Biface Morphology among Olorgesailie Site Samples

Considerable variation in the characteristics of the bifaces in various site samples was apparent during excavation and laboratory study. The extent of this variation has subsequently been demonstrated by statistical techniques, including the comparison of frequency distributions, analysis of variance, and rank-ordering methods. Tables 11 through 13 display some of the results of the metrical studies.

The analysis of measurable variables indicates that not only do site samples from within the relatively limited space and time framework of the Olorgesailie basin differ in their percentages of tool types, but that the morphology of samples of the same tool type differs significantly between site samples. Among the bifaces, the hand axes have been most extensively analyzed, but similar results are demonstrable for other categories.

During excavation and sorting, the morphological idiosyncrasy of many site samples became very obvious. Without referring to labels or catalogs, it is very often possible to assign a piece to its site of origin. Complex combinations of attributes may be involved in the intuitive appreciation of stylistic groupings in a series of bifaces, but it seems reasonable to assume that the small significant differences in parameters of morphology are the quantitative expression of the observed stylistic differences. Analysis of variance tests (Snedecor F or Kruskal-Wallis H tests) are well suited for testing observations of stylistic differences, since the results of such tests reflect the significance of differences in means by measuring the extent to which variation within samples is less than variation in the series as a whole.

The analysis of variance tests summarized in table 11 shows clearly that there is little tendency for the site sample parameters to behave as random-error deviants about a common norm. The Middle Stratigraphic Set of nine site samples is credible as a homogeneous population for only two out of twelve tested attributes, the mean scar count (Σ Sc) and the ratio of scars on the minimally trimmed face to that on the maximally trimmed face (index of scar bifaciality). This diversity exists in spite of the fact that the samples are drawn from sites that are extremely close in time and space. The interpretation of this evident morphological heterogeneity poses a serious challenge for Paleolithic studies.

Figure 41 provides a few examples of comparisons of frequency distributions for the same attribute from various sites. Numerous patterns of contrast of the kind shown, bear out the impression of real intersite differences and heighten one's willingness to accept the anthropological significance of the statistical tests.

Variation in Relation to Stratigraphy

Figure 33 (chap. 5) shows mean values for selected biface attributes plotted in

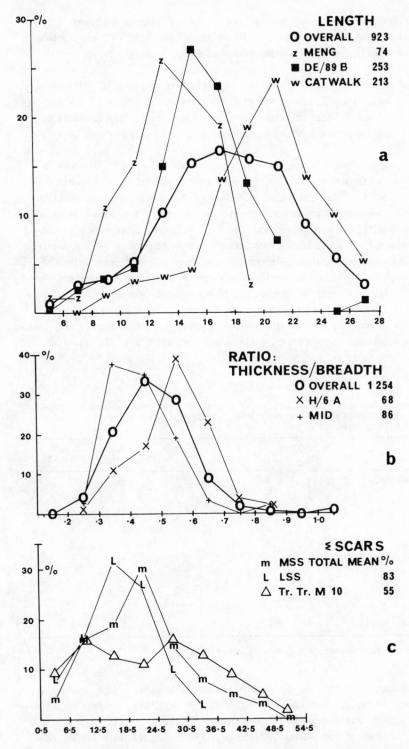

Figure 41. Frequency distribution plots illustrating the extent of between assemblage variation in biface morphology.

relation to stratigraphy. The figure suggests time trends for relative thickness (T/B) and scar counts (Σ S), but not for length or relative elongation (B/L). Clearly, a longer sequence is needed in order to verify whether trends of this kind were persistent or oscillatory.

Table 11 shows the results of tests for the statistical significance of differences between the pooled means of contiguous stratigraphic sets of sites. The means for many attributes are significantly different between sets, but these results are difficult to interpret, considering the proven internal heterogeneity of those sets that are divisible into subsamples.

In addition to the variation among the site sample means, there are differences in dispersal (variance or standard deviation). Table 12 gives a comparison of standard deviations for the site samples. For dimensions L or counts Σ Sc, coefficients of variation are also shown, but coefficients are not appropriate for the standard deviation of ratios. Selected tests of significance between pairs of standard deviations or between a sample standard deviation and the overall standard deviation are reported (table 13). A moderately high incidence of significant differences has been found. A rank-order method has been applied for testing the strong impression that variance in different parameters showed covariation (table 12). The resulting coefficient of concordance (Moroney 1956:337-40) just fails to attain significance at the 5% level. However, it seems likely that while concordance may not be general, certain site samples, notably Meng, consistently show low variance in their morphological parameters, while others, notably H/9 and Tr. Tr. M 10, consistently show high variance.

Table 12

*Rank Orders of the Variability of Site Samples of Bifaces for Various Measurable Attributes, as Indicated by the Values of the Coefficient of Variation of Measurements and the Standard Deviation of Ratios.**

	L	B/L	T/B	PMB/L	BA/BB	TA/BB	Σ Sc	i/Sc	Rank Total	Mean Rank
Tr. Tr. M 10	10	9.5	7	10	7	8	10	6	67.5	10
Meng	2	1.5	1	3	1	7	6	5	26.5	1
Mid	3	3.5	2	4	9	9	5	7	43.5	7
H/9 AM	6	7	4	2	4	6	3	4	36	3
H/9 A	8	8	6	5	10	10	4	10	61	9
H/6 A	5	6	10	1	3	4	9	3	41	5.5
DE/89 C	7	5	9	8	2	1	8	1	41	5.5
DE/89 B	1	1.5	3	7	8	5	7	8	40.5	4
DE/89 A	4	3.5	5	9	5	2	2	2	32.5	2
I 3	9	9.5	8	6	6	3	1	9	51.5	8

*The greater the rank number, the greater the variability.

I consider it suggestive that the two sites with the highest variances are from disturbed stratigraphic contexts, where mixing of material from originally discrete occurrences is a strong possibility. Differences in the variance of measurable aspects of morphology might prove a useful index of homogeneity or heterogeneity for samples for which the mode of aggregation in anthropological terms is uncertain.

Variation in Relation to Biface
and Scraper-Dominated Facies

It is not possible to apply formal tests or comparisons to determine whether biface morphology differs between these facies because only one sufficient sample, site I 3, comes from a scraper-dominated context. The I 3 and the Friday Bed bifaces differ markedly from all other samples, but I provisionally regard these differences as indicative of unreversed changes in morphological conventions that occurred during the time interval separating the Lower from the Middle Stratigraphic Set (Member 1 from Member 7). At present, there is no way to resolve the separate effects of these two confounded factors.

I believe that the numerical data presented in the tables and graphs provides an informative summary of the population characteristics of the biface assemblages. Very elaborate description or extensive illustration would thus be redundant and is precluded by my deliberate policy of minimizing the bulk and cost of this volume. However, a brief verbal commentary on the features of the assemblages follows. I hope that the stereoscopic photographs of bifaces in plates 24 to 60 will provide sufficient material for readers to be able to translate the numerical attributes into an appreciation of the morphology that the numbers represent.

Lower Stratigraphic Set
(pls. 24-28; fig. 72)

The sample derives mainly from site I 3, with a few specimens from the Basal Beds A and B and from the Friday Beds. As a group, the larger bifacial tools from Members 1 and 2 of the Olorgesailie Formation contrast markedly with those from all higher strata. The modal forms of the Lower Stratigraphic Set are smaller and relatively thicker than those for the Middle and Upper Stratigraphic Sets. The trimming scars are characteristically large and deep. The scars are also fewer in number, although a weak regressional relation between size and scar numbers may partly account for this.

The type-category composition of the sample is shown in appendix E3. There is a comparatively low frequency of classic hand axes and cleavers. The large numbers of subclassic hand axes grade into the unusually high frequencies of picklike forms and corelike bifaces.

Numerous corelike bifaces form a conspicuous part of the series. There is a gradation from thick, ovate hand axes to discoid forms that could equally well be classified as cores or bifaces. This series can also be seen to grade into the peculiar group of spindly bifacial forms that were nicknamed "sharp cores" in the laboratory.

Middle Stratigraphic Set
(pls. 29-56)

Individual assemblages from nine occurrences are considered separately.

DE/89 Horizon A (pls. 29-30)

The most conspicuous typological feature of this series is the paucity of cleavers and the presence of a noticeable number of robust picklike forms and trièdres.

Compared to other site samples, the general level of variance of measurements and ratios for this sample is low, the rank-order position being 2 in 9 (table 12). This invariance, along with the idiosyncrasy of the mean values for some variables, suggests origin from a single accumulation.

The distinguishing metrical characters of the series, as compared with other Middle Stratigraphic Set samples, are:

1. A general roughness of execution and usually a thick, partially unretouched butt. This shows clearly in the ratio of Thickness at Apex to Thickness at Butt, which, with a value of 0.62 in a series of means ranging to 0.79, is the lowest value for all sites.

2. A general tendency toward somewhat elongate pointed forms with the margins converging to a narrow ogival or triangular point. This tendency is expressed by the mean value of 0.68 in the ratio BA/BB, in a series of means ranging from 0.68 to 0.92. The common, relatively broad-butted form is also reflected in the low mean value, 0.38, for the ratio PMB/L, where the range for all the site means is 0.37 to 0.46.

3. The bifaces of the series show a marked tendency to be asymmetrical in cross section, and many are planoconvex. The series has the second lowest mean value of all sites for the index of biconvexity, 0.69 in a range 0.55 to 0.78.

The bifaces and related tool forms from this horizon are partly distinguished by the tendency to robusticity and by the crudity of workmanship of butt and body. In this regard they resemble most closely the series from DE/89 C and from H/6; however, they differ in the comparatively delicate conformation of the points.

Although the DE/89 A forms are cruder than those of most of the Middle Stratigraphic Set biface series, they have few specific resemblances to the Lower Stratigraphic Set; for instance, the two series contrast sharply in the virtual absence of short, chunky bifaces from DE/89 A.

DE/89, Horizon B (pls. 33-38)

The collections were recovered from the sandy floor of a silted runnel within Member 7 of the Olorgesailie Formation by the Leakeys in 1943 and by me in 1962 to 1964. More than 500 large tools were excavated from the restricted confines of this remarkable occurrence (see chap. 3). The composition of the measured sample is shown in appendix E3. It is a well-balanced sample that includes examples of all forms. The proportion of hand axes to cleavers is about 2 to 1.

The site evidence does not indicate conclusively whether the material on the horizon was derived from a single accumulation or from several originally distinct aggregates. The question arises whether this collection was a homogeneous assemblage made by one social group during continual or recurrent occupations, or a heterogeneous assemblage of portions of differing artifact sets made by different groups. Significant idiosyncrasy of characteristics among the material would support a hypothesis of manufacture by the members of a single microcultural entity, whereas a generalized scatter of values, approximately defined by the overall parameters of the stratigraphic zone, may indicate a compound origin.

Evidence of idiosyncrasy has been sought in: (1) composition as expressed by form category frequencies (table 13), (2) mean values of morphological measurements, and (3) variances of morphological measurements. In this case, a qualitative aspect of morphological coherence and distinctiveness, together with quantitative demonstrations of significantly low variance for a number of morphological parameters, gives strong evidence of microcultural homogeneity.

It can be seen from table 11 that the mean values for size and for shape-defining ratios among the site sample of large bifacial tools are not markedly different from those for the population comprised of all Olorgesailie bifaces. This similarity is in part a reciprocal relationship, since the site sample is the largest individual component of the overall population, making up approximately half of it. However, for some measured

Table 13

Statistical Tests on Metrical Data for Samples of Bifaces

The Middle Stratigraphic Set of sites (MSS) and various pairs of samples of bifaces were tested to determine whether the individual samples should be regarded as random-sample derivatives of a single population of artifacts. Both parametric and nonparametric analysis of variance or paired comparison tests were used, as shown in the table. Three asterisks denote that the null hypothesis of sample homogeneity has less than one chance in a thousand of being valid. In these cases, it seems almost certain that the samples really do differ from each other with regard to the measured attribute in question.

Measurements and form-defining ratios for all bifaces considered collectively

	L	B/L	T/B	PMB/L	BA/BB	TA/TB	Σ Sc	i/Sc
Kruskal-Wallis H test analysis of variance for 9 site samples of the MSS	***	***	***	***	***	***	-	***
Mann Whitney U test between all MSS and the USS samples	***	***	-	-	-	***	-	-
Mann Whitney U test between the MSS all pooled and the LSS	***	***	***	***	-	***	***	***
Mann Whitney U test between bifaces of Trachyte and of basalt	-	-	***	-	-	-	***	***

Measurements and form defining ratios for hand axes alone

	L	B/L	T/B					
Analysis of variance with Snedecor's F test applied to the MSS samples	***	***	***					
Analysis of variance with Snedecor's F test applied to the MSS vs. USS samples	***	-	-					
Analysis of variance with Snedecor's F test applied to the MSS vs. LSS samples	***	***	***					

attributes, although the means are indistinguishable, the sample dispersal differs from that of the population in a manner analogous to the differences shown by samples that are clearly idiosyncratic in the location of their means. The sample standard deviation is much lower than that of the population in these cases. Figure 41a shows this graphically for the length of hand axes, and table 11 shows that similar relationships hold for the indices of elongation (B/L) and relative thickness (T/B) for all bifaces, although not for hand axes treated separately. These significantly lower deviations are consistent with an hypothesis of unitary, idiosyncratic derivation for the series.

It is possible that hydraulic forces and the kinematic wave effect have resulted in some admixture of materials from formerly distinct occupation sites, but that the admixture has been insufficient to obliterate idiosyncrasy of the principal component.

During field and laboratory work, certain features impressed themselves on me as distinctive; these supplement the quantitative data.

1. A tendency toward the use of coarse trachyte, a partially fissile lava.

2. A marked consistency of length, with most pieces being intermediate in relation to the contrasting standardization of the "small" Meng series and the "large" Catwalk series.

3. A high incidence of chisel-ended forms making an intergrading series between hand axes and cleavers.

4. A tendency for minimal retouch on most of the pieces and for the retouch to form a marginal (<10% of breadth) or subinvasive (<33% of breadth) bevel. Again, this tendency is less marked than it is in pieces from H/9, Mid, or the Catwalk.

5. The common occurrence of battered or chipped portions of edges, which could be the consequence of utilization.

6. The existence on the floor of subsidiary clusters of pieces showing a remarkable resemblance to each other.

DE/89, Horizon C (pl. no. 5, fig. 72)

This series of tools came from a localized occurrence of artifacts in the clayey bed of the DE/89 channel. They were deposited there at a stage when the runnel was almost entirely choked with silt, and although they may have undergone slight concentration by fluvial action, they probably represent a single occupation in the immediate vicinity of their eventual burial. Inasmuch as one can gauge idiosyncrasy from a sample of this size, it would appear that the series is characterized by robusticity and by relatively bold, deep flake scars. There is an unusually high proportion of picklike forms, including a trièdre. In these respects, the series most resembles that of the sites H/6 A and DE/89 A. However, DE/89 C differs from both these in its high proportion of cleavers: 11 hand axes to 6 cleavers, as compared with 31 to 4 and 56 to 2 for H/6 and DE/89 A, respectively.

H/6, Horizon A (pls. 39-41)

A sample of 61 large tools was recovered from a weak unconformity at the base of Member 7 in the area immediately adjacent to the spectacular Catwalk exposure of large tools (chap. 3). The pieces lay on and in a thin, discontinuous sheet of sand that includes derived sediment particles. The excavations are close to the northwest margin of a scatter, the major part of which had been removed by erosion. Thus, it is not known whether the sample is drawn from a structured campsite. However, the series is among the most distinctive recovered at Olorgesailie, a feature favoring origin from the short-term occupation of a single group.

The tools are relatively large, and the mean weight is conspicuously high. The overall mean T/B ratio is higher than the Olorgesailie overall mean by one population standard deviation. With existing sample sizes, the probability of so large a difference in means is about 0.005 (see fig. 41b for comparison of frequency distributions). The mean T/B ratio for 30 hand axes is greater than the overall hand ax mean by an amount that just fails to attain the $p < 0.05$ significance level in a Sheffé multiple comparison test. However, since the relatively large number of picklike hand axes had been excluded from this sample, the series as a whole can probably be regarded as significantly different.

In addition it can be seen that the series shows a tendency to convergent apices (BA/BB = 0.69). There is a somewhat higher than average incidence of invasive scars (i/Σ Sc = 0.61).

In descriptive as well as quantitative terms the distinctive features of H/6 are:

1. A general tendency to robusticity and thick sections, with a relatively high proportion of picklike hand axes.

2. A relatively high incidence of basalt pieces
3. Trimming of deep bold scars covering most of both faces.

The series resembles only DE/89 A and DE/89 C in these regards. It differs from
DE/89 A in the greater mean relative thickness of its pieces, in its T/B ratio, and in its
lesser tendency to planoconvex cross sections. The raw material proportions are also different. The DE/89 C sample is too small and too variable for a firm assessment of its affinities with the H/6 series. Close chronological correlation between H/6 A and DE/89 A
is a possibility.

The H/6 series is of considerable interest because there is little doubt that, had it
been found without clear evidence of contemporaneity with refined and Upper Acheulean assemblages, it would probably have been assigned to a Lower or early Middle Acheulean stage.

H/9, Horizon A (pls. 45-49)

The provenance of the artifacts in the H/9 grid square excavation has proved to be a
complex of thin lenses and silted runnels. The material on the southerly portion of the
complex was patterned in a manner suggestive of fluvial rearrangement.

In 1943, M. D. and L. S. B. Leakey excavated a trench in the adjoining grid square
(G/9). They called the cutting Mid, and the artifact sample recovered from it is strikingly
different than that obtained from H/9; Mid contained very little flake debris and virtually
no small scraper tools. The biface morphology is also different in subtle ways (see table
11).

The most distinctive feature of the H/9 A sample of bifaces is the diversity of sizes
and forms. This characteristic was apparent during laboratory examination, and finds partial numerical expression in a tendency to larger variances; it makes the series difficult
to describe either verbally or by means of a limited series of illustrations. The measured
sample shows that this site sample has subequal numbers of hand axes and cleavers, a feature shared only with Mid, DE/89 C, and Tr. Tr. M 10. It is also one of the few sites with
subequal numbers of bifaces and small scrapers.

The H/9 A pieces tend to be smaller; though the great variation of the H/9 A sample
renders the 2 cm difference in means nonsignificant, the difference between the values for
the standard deviations is highly significant and is consistent with the hypothesis that
H/9 A has a heterogeneous origin.

In view of the strong suggestion of heterogeneity, the average values of morphological
parameters for the sample may have little meaning. The sample is distinguished primarily
by high variance, but other weak idiosyncrasies are relatively small mean size, a high B/L
ratio, and low scar counts (Σ Sc, i/Σ Sc). As already demonstrated, the sample shows little
consistency in size, and there is even a suggestion of bimodality. The low scar density
and the tendency of scars to be confined to the margins appear to be more consistent.

Mid Trench (pls. 42-44)

This series of large tools was recovered by L. S. B. Leakey and M. D. Leakey in 1943.
The field data clearly imply fluvial transport and rearrangement (see chap. 3).

The relative abundance of cleavers, 38 out of 80 large cutting tools, is a notable
feature. The mean values of measurable attributes do not show marked departure from the
overall mean, except for BA/BB and Ch/B, the high values of which give numerical expression
to the high incidence of cleavers. This site sample of large tools along with that from
H/9 AM, also shows the lowest mean relative thickness values, reflecting a tendency to thin
tabular forms that was obvious in sorting.

The variation of measured attributes is generally below the value for the population of all site samples pooled, in accord with an impression of homogeneity and stylistic similarity among the pieces. The hand ax series includes about 12% "double"-ended forms, whereas the usual value is about 5%. This finding is partially reflected in the high values of BA/BB and TA/TB ratios, both of which indicate subequal apex and butt. The cleaver series includes numerous elongate parallel-sided and barrel-shaped examples, though there are also short, stubby specimens.

Four knives form an irregular set without any important group features. Two knives have blunted backs opposed to sharp untrimmed edges and might have been termed "side cleavers" by Kleindienst.

The Mid site sample includes a comparatively high proportion of large pieces (30% are longer than 200 mm), but it is less extreme in this regard than DE/89 A, H/6, or the Catwalk. However, the Mid series is morphologically comparable to the Catwalk series in some ways, and the horizon has been suggested as the stratigraphic source of that aggregate (L. S. B. Leakey, pers. comm.).

H/9 AM (pl. 52)

Occurrence units X and Y in H/9 are thought to represent the southerly extension of the floor of M. D. and L. S. B. Leakey's Mid into my H/9 cutting, and the artifacts from these units have accordingly been isolated as an independent aggregate for comparison (see chap. 3). The sample is too small for any very definite conclusions to be drawn. The sample of 10 hand axes is dominated by 5 chisel-ended hand axes. Other forms include double-ended pieces reminiscent of Mid.

Meng Trench (pls. 53-56)

This subsite, at the southern extremity of the Main Site, was excavated by Dr. and Mrs. Leakey in 1943. A fairly numerous series of large bifacial tools was recovered.

The most notable feature of the series is the paucity of cleavers. The ratio of hand axes to cleavers is about 10 to 1. If the fairly numerous chisel-ended hand axes are classified as cleavers, then the disproportion is reduced (1.3 to 1). However, the mean of the ratio Chisel bit width/Breadth (Ch/B) is very low (0.18). Furthermore, the median of Ch/B for all pieces with chisel (cleaver) bits is relatively low (0.35). Thus it can be seen that most of the chisel bits are extremely small and that the classificatory statement of low incidence of cleavers has real morphological meaning. The ratio of hand axes to cleavers as classified by Kleindienst (1961:49) was 3.5 to 1, indicating the potential ambiguity of classificatory descriptions of a morphological gradation. Presumably the Ch/B ratio is less likely to vary in observations by different workers. In addition to the scarcity of cleavers, the series has relatively few heavy-duty and other large bifacial tools.

The most conspicuous feature of the series is its strong stylistic and morphological consistency. The pieces show marked likeness to each other, a trait that was obvious in the laboratory and that finds clear expression in the low standard deviations of the measurements. Other distinguishing features are as follows.

1. The pieces are relatively small.

2. They are relatively narrow and relatively thick, both these differences being against the trend of the regression of B/L and T/B ratios on size.

3. The apices are relatively narrow and acutely pointed, and the position of maximum breadth is relatively low on the length (low BA/BB).

4. Trimming scars tend to be longer and more invasive (high I/Σ Sc ratio).

Some of these features might be regarded as direct consequences of the predominance of hand axes among the large tools. However, even when the parameters for hand axes alone are compared, similar shifts in the means and variances are observed, though their magnitude is reduced.

It seems likely to me that the morphological coherence of the site sample is best explained by supposing that they are the product of a single craftsman, or of a group of craftsmen who shared well-defined design norms. Unfortunately very little is known of the plan and structure of the site from which the sample was drawn (chap. 3).

In summary, the site series presents a neat and refined general appearance. The pieces are moderately small and compact being both relatively thick and narrow with well-rounded faces. The trimming tends to be invasive and to cover most of both faces with bold and fairly deep scars. Step flaked marginal bevels are comparatively rare.

Upper Stratigraphic Set
(pls. 57-60)

Trial Trench Member 10 (pls. 57-60)

An important but not very large assemblage of artifacts was recovered by M. D. Leakey and L. S. B. Leakey from the sands and fine gravels of member 10 in the Main Site. I made further excavations in 1962 to 1963 but did not recover any additional bifaces.

The artifacts rested on a weak erosion surface, which may have been a floor, at the base of the sands. However, because of the relatively coarse grade of the sediment above, the pronounced channel features in the containing deposit, and signs of abrasion on some of the flakes, it seems unlikely that this assemblage represents a single, undisturbed campsite.

Because the Tr. Tr. M 10 sample comes from a stratigraphic level appreciably higher than the Middle Stratigraphic Set, the question arises whether it lies outside the range of variation of the Middle Stratigraphic series in a way that might represent an unreversed time trend. Clearly, in view of the strong evidence of variability between sites at the same horizon, this point cannot be settled until further sites within the Upper Stratigraphic zone are located and excavated.

The site sample does present some features that distinguish it from the Middle Stratigraphic Set of site samples. For example, a subjective evaluation of the refinement of the bifaces would place the sample outside the range of the Middle Stratigraphic Set; the quantitative data show that this impression has some factual basis, though they do not prove the matter conclusively.

Cleavers and hand axes together make up two-thirds of the large bifacial tools, and they are subequal in numbers (19 to 25). This may in part account for the high variances, though other assemblages with large numbers of cleavers, such as Mid and DE/89 B, do not show a comparable increase in variance.

One extreme form, which in other contexts would merit separate typological classification, is a very long, delicate biface reminiscent of Congo basin Lupemban daggers (pl. 57). The piece is marked as a surface find from the outcrop of the Member 10 horizon. Other less refined but comparable pieces have been recorded only in surface material from the Catwalk and LHS. The significance of the similarity of these pieces to Lupemban forms is considered below.

Detailed reports on the arrangement and grouping of pieces from Tr. Tr. M 10 are not available. However, the geological context of sands and fine gravels make a degree of transport and mixing of pieces from different occupation sites a strong possibility. The fact that the sample from this context shares with H/9 A the feature of extremely high variances possibly has significance in this regard.

This site sample has the highest mean rank for the variance of its morphological parameters. The estimates of standard deviation generally exceed even those of the population formed by pooling all the differing individual sites, and they are radically different from the values for stylistically homogeneous sites like Meng. Yet despite their variance, there is a certain stylistic commonality among the pieces, which takes the form of a refinement and neatness of execution, exceeding even that of the Meng series.

Catwalk Surface Aggregate

A spectacular aggregate comprised of more than 550 large bifacial tools covers the surface of a restricted area of the Main Site (see pls. 7, 18). Being a surface aggregate, it is not strictly comparable to the excavated series. However, because it has very obvious distinctive features that lie outside the range of variation of other samples, the aggregate has been included in parts of the analysis of variation. Whatever the extent of heterogeneity in the origin of this surface accumulation, it provides strong additional evidence that the parameters of even very large Acheulean site samples do not behave as random deviants from a population norm for a given region at a given time.

Excavations indicate that more than one artifact-bearing horizon existed above the surface aggregate, though the only concentration of which sufficient remained for effective excavation was H/6, Horizon A. Unfortunately for simplicity of interpretation, the artifacts from H/6 A proved to have distinct idiosyncratic features that appear to differentiate the assemblage from the totality of the surface aggregate.

It seems likely that an occurrence of approximately the same size and density as DE/89 B must have existed more or less exactly on the site of the present concentration. The disconformity identified in cutting H/6 may represent one edge of the former occurrence, since a few large tools were recovered at this level.

The most striking feature of the aggregate is the very large size of the hand axes and cleavers. The largest specimens exceed 300 mm, and the mean for hand axes is 216 ± 6 mm (95% confidence). This is almost 2 cm larger than the next highest hand ax mean of 199 ± 15 mm (95% confidence) for H/6 A. Another obvious feature of the Catwalk sample is the high degree of elongation in the specimens. The B/L ratio is 0.52 ± 0.01 (95% confidence), compared with a range of 0.54 to 0.58 for the hand axes of other MSS sites. This is a correlate of the extreme length, but it is nonetheless worth comment.

The form range resembles that of Mid: amygdaloidal shapes are commonest, but delicate ficron types are also present. Cleavers are especially elongate and tend to be barrel-shaped or parallel-sided. Chisel-ended forms are fairly numerous.

Morphological Comparisons of Olorgesailie Hand ax and Biface Samples with Other Acheulean Samples

Comparison of the morphological character of bifaces has long been the principal basis for the classification of Acheulean industries. Characterizations of hand ax plan form and evaluations of refinement have been particularly important. Most of the literature contains only generalized descriptive information and partially subjective comparative statements. Illustrations tend to portray special rather than representative examples, so that it is very difficult to make reliable comparisons without direct study of the relevant collections. Furthermore, the extent of penecontemporaneous variation demonstrated for sites

such as Olorgesailie and Isimila makes it clear that qualitative judgments may be trust-
worthy only for extreme differences.

Fortunately, in recent years there has been a growing tendency to report sample parameters or frequency distributions for at least some of the dimensions of hand axes and
other bifaces. Tables 14 through 17 show some of the data currently available. These
compilations are not exhaustive; however, they cover much of the relevant African data and
a sufficient quantity of other data to indicate a wider context. It can be seen that the
data are most complete for size (length) and that decreasing amounts of information are
available for elongation (B/L) and relative thickness (T/B).

Full discussion of the implications of the comparative data for assessing the relationships of the Olorgesailie samples is deferred until the concluding chapter, but the
present treatment serves to document the features that will then be discussed. Only hand
axes (*sensu lato*) and cleavers are sufficiently numerous and well-reported to justify detailed consideration.

Table 14 shows a rank-ordered compilation of data from African assemblages for hand
ax size. The columns of the table represent provisional culture-stratigraphic assignments,
such as early Acheulean, Acheulean, or terminal Acheulean.

Some available data for European and Asiatic assemblages are included in the table for
comparison. The samples for which the mean lengths have been recorded cannot provide a
balanced representation of the African Acheulean, but they offer some guide to general features. The available sets of sample means range from 93 mm (85-100, 95% confidence) for
Lochard (G. Cole 1961:292) to 216 mm (210-220, 95% confidence) for the surface sample from
the Olorgesailie Catwalk. The median for the set is about 154 cm. Only one Olorgesailie
sample has a mean length less than this median value; the LSS mean of 117 cm.

Tentative grouping of the samples into culture-stratigraphic divisions does not indicate any clear cut long-term trends in size. It is apparent that even if extremes of small
and large size prove to be restricted in their time distribution, the ranges overlap extensively. The data may indicate that hand axes in very late and post-Acheulean industries--
Fauresmith, Sangoan, or Lupemban--are generally relatively small. However, given the variations demonstrated within the Middle and Upper Acheulean, this criterion can only be used
as a supplement to others, such as the presence of additional tool forms or the rising importance of Levallois techniques. Compared with most European and West Asian Acheulean
samples, the African hand axes in general and the Olorgesailie ones in particular are
large.

If the mean lengths of cleavers are plotted against the mean lengths of hand axes in
the same sample, the correlation is so close that no separate discussion of cleaver size
is called for. This proves to be the case for all gross aspects of cleaver form, so that
no further comment on cleavers is made.

Elongation

The taxonomic relevance of varying degrees of elongation has long been recognized and
treated by description in terms such as broad or narrow. McBurney and West (1954) demonstrated the potential of quantitative expressions of this attribute as a discriminant
between Acheulean and Mousterian hand axes. Subsequently, G. Cole (1961:325) used the B/L
ratio as one of the quantitative ingredients in the formula he devised for seriating Late
Acheulean and First Intermediate industries of south central Africa. Cole, like McBurney
and West, suggested that late hand ax forms, especially post-Acheulean ones, were relatively

Table 14

Hand Ax Length, Rank-Ordering Lists of Sample Means for Olorgesailie and Other Sites

mm	EAST AFRICA			SOUTH AFRICA	NORTH AFRICA AND PALESTINE	SELECTED EUROPEAN
	Lower Pleist.	Middle Pleist.	?Late Middle or Early Upper Pleist.			
70						Oldbury
80						Caddington
90		Olduvai SHK		Inhoek		
100		Olduvai TK Upper		Meirton Rooidam		Swanscombe MG
110				Waterval	Deb Deb	Swanscombe UL Hoxne
120		Olorg. LSS		Three Rivers Cave of Hearths Wonderboompoort	Ma'Ayan Baruch	Atelier Commont
130				Blaaubank Riverview Cornelia	Ubeidiya Adrar Bous AE	Cuxton Furze Platt
140	Olduvai EFHR Olduvai FC	Isimila H20 Isimila K18	Baringo (LHR)	Amanzi Montagu L 3	Termifine	Fordwich
150	Olduvai TK lower	Kariandusi Olorg. Meng	Kalambo A5 B Kalambo B6			Farnham Terr. A
160		Olorg. Tr.Tr. M 10 Olorg. H/9 A	Nsongezi MN Kalambo A5	Wagenmaker Vallei	Latamne	
170	Peninj Olduvai MNK	Olorg. DE/89 C Isimila J 12		Hangklip Montagu L 5		
180		Olorg. Mid Olorg. DE/89 B Isimila K 6	Kalambo A6 Kalambo B5			

Table 14--Continued

190	Isimila K 14 Olorg. DE/89 A	190
200		200
210		210
220		220
230	Olorg. Catwalk	230

Sources: Olduvai, M. D. Leakey (1971, 1975); Peninj, Isaac (1967); Isimila, Kariandusi and Kalambo, Kleindienst (1959); Baringo, Margaret C. Leakey et al. (1969); Nsongezi, Cole (1967); South Africa, Deacon (1975); Ubeidiya, Stekelis et al. (1969); Adrar Bous, Clark et al. (1973); Ternifine, Balout et al. (1967); Latame, Clark (1966); Atelier Commont, Bordes and Fitte (1953); Abbeville and St. Acheul, Malvesin-Fabré (1948); other European from Roe (1967).

small and broad. Roe (1964, 1968) incorporated the B/L ratio into his system of form definition.

Regression analysis has shown that within the Olorgesailie series of bifaces, size
(length) and elongation are not independent characters: long implements tend also to be
relatively narrow. That is to say, there is a negative regression of B/L ratio on length.
Figure 42 shows the relation of means for B/L ratios to means for length of the same sample.
It is clear that among those Acheulean industries for which data are available, a regression
relationship holds that is similar to that of the Olorgesailie series. The time trend reported by G. Cole (1961) probably involves selective reduction in the proportion of the
larger implements without any change in the basic pattern of form determinants. Table 15
shows the data according to tentative stratigraphic divisions within the hand ax tradition.
It is clear that the Olorgesailie plots form part of a scatter of values within which Lower,
Upper, and terminal Acheulean are only weakly segregated. All the post-Acheulean hand axes
and hand ax-like forms appear to be smaller and broader than any Olorgesailie sample, other
than those of the I 3 sample. Consistent time trends are not obvious among occurrences
where the sequences are known through stratigraphy.

Relative Thickness

This aspect of biface form has long been included in descriptive accounts of assemblages by means of more or less vague adjectives, such as thick or robust. Considerable
classificatory importance has been attached to qualitative evaluations of the attribute,
along with the general supposition that thick crude forms are early and thin and that refined forms are late (Malvesin-Fabré 1948). The attribute is most readily expressed quan-
titatively by the Thickness/Breadth ratio.

There is less published data for relative thickness than for length or elongation.
However, sufficient data is available for some comparative consideration. Table 16 provides
a rank-ordered array of the available T/B ratio sample means. As is evident from the table,
the mean values for the two Lower Acheulean samples for which data are available, Ternifine
and Natron, lie at the uppermost extreme or outside the limits for Middle-Upper Acheulean
industries such as those of Olorgesailie and Isimila. Based on rock-stratigraphic evidence,
the Kalambo Falls, Nsongezi, and Montagu Cave Acheulean samples are known to be drawn from
terminal Acheulean industries. Their range of mean values spans the entire range of Middle
or Upper Acheulean samples and may extend somewhat beyond it. Mean T/B ratios are available
for very few post-Acheulean biface assemblages. Fauresmith industries probably fall within
the Acheulean range or are thinner. Sangoan industries are likely to have relatively high
mean values for this ratio; the samples reported by G. Cole (1961) do show this feature. The
Olorgesailie site samples belong with the other Middle or Upper Acheulean samples--Isimila,
Kalambo, Kariandusi, and so on--and in fact help to define the range of the group.

Plan-form

A full and satisfactory comparison of biface plan-form will not be possible until
metrical work has been done on a wider range of assemblages. Howell and Clark (1963:508)
published tables comparing the incidence at Olorgesailie and Isimila of 20 plan-form categories of hand axes and 24 categories of cleavers. These tables show that both the

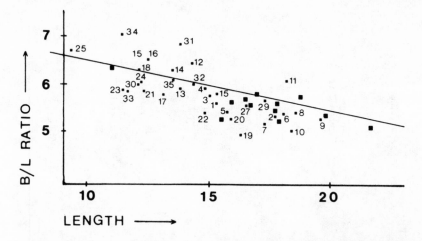

Figure 42. A bivariate plot showing that the Length and B/L ratio of bifaces are not independent variables. Each plotted point represents the mean values for one assemblage. The regression line is that obtained from bivariate analysis of individual bifaces in the overall Olorgesailie sample. Rectangles represent Olorgesailie sample means.

1. Kariandusi	13. Isimila H 20	25. Lochard
2. Kalambo A6	14. Isimila L 19	26. Montagu L 3
3. Kalambo B	15. Cave of Hearths	27. Montagu L 5
4. Kalambo A5b	16. Wonderboompoort	28. Hangklip
5. Kalambo A5	17. Blaaubank 2	29. Natron (Peninj)
6. Kalambo B5	18. Blaaubank 3	30. Three Rivers
7. Isimila J 12	19. Homestead	31. 'Ubeidiya
8. Isimila K 14	20. Pniel	32. Ternifine
9. Isimila H 9	21. Canteen Kopje	33. Atelier Commont
10. Isimila K 6	22. Larsen	34. Ma'Ayan Barukh
11. Isimila H 15	23. Riverview	35. Angola Sangoan
12. Isimila K 18	24. Newmans Port	Lupemban
		36. Nsongezi

Olorgesailie and Isimila hand ax aggregates are dominated by almond-shaped (long ovate) forms.[2] The almond-shaped forms grade in one direction into ovates and in another direction into relatively elongate or lanceolate forms. Both show much smaller and variable incidence of other forms, such as those with delicate concave-defined points and cordiforms. The cleavers from Olorgesailie differ markedly from the Isimila cleavers in being dominated by convergent parallel-sided or divergent cleavers. These tables also serve to emphasize the limitations of class analysis for comparing assemblages. The number of subdivisions renders comparisons difficult. Assignment to discrete forms is highly subjective, as indicated by the fact that 10% of triangular forms are shown for the Olorgesailie series, as opposed to less than 1% for Isimila. Yet the form-defining indices BA/BB and PMB/L show conclusively

2. Kleindienst (1962) used "ovate" for approximately almond-shaped forms and "broad ovate" or *limande* for what in my view would normally be termed ovates in Britain. In this respect she may have been following Bordes (1961a).

Table 15

B/L Ratio for Hand Axes; Rank-Ordered Lists of Sample Means for Olorgesailie and Other Sites

	EAST AFRICA			SOUTH AFRICA	NORTH AFRICA AND PALESTINE	SELECTED EUROPEAN
	Relatively early	Undiff.	Relatively late			
.40						Abbeville
.45						
.50		Isimila K6 Isimila J12 Isimila H9 Olorg. Meng H/6 A Isimila K14	Kalambo B5 A5	Homestead (C) Phiel (C) Riverview Estate (C) Larsen (C) Inhoek		Fordwich Farnham Terr. A
.55	Peninj Olduvai EFHR	Olorg. DE/89 C Mid Kariandusi Olorg. DE/89 B Tr. Tr. M 10 H/9 A DE/89 A Isimila H20	Kalambo A6 B6 Nzongezi Kalambo A5 B	Montagu L5 Riverview Est. VI Blaaubank 2 Hangklip Canteen Kopje Waterval		Furze Platt Cuxton St. Acheul
.60	Olduvai TK lower	Isimila H15 Olorg. LSS Isimila K18				Tilehurst Swanscombe MG Hoxne
.65	Olduvai TK upper			Three Rivers Amanzi Glen Elliot Elands Kloof Montagu L3 Rooidam Blaaubank 3		Caddington Swanscombe UL
.70	Olduvai SHK MNK BK			Cave of Hearths Wonderboompoort Lochard (C)	'Ubeidiya	
.75				Luangwa (C) Meirton		
.80						Oldbury

Sources: As for table 14. C = Cole, G. H. (1961).

Table 16
T/B Ratio for Hand Axes: a Rank-Ordered List of Sample Means for Olorgesailie and Other Sites

	Lower Pleistocene	Middle Pleistocene	Late Middle or Early Upper Pleistocene	Other Areas
.40			Baringo (LHR)	
.41				Oldbury
.42			Kalambo A6	
.43		Kariandusi		
.44		Olorg. Mid.		High Lodge
.45		Olorg. DE/89 A Olorg. Tr. Tr. M 10		
.46		Olorg. DE/89 B	Kalambo A5 Kalambo B5	Swanscombe U.L.
.47		Olorg. C.W.		St. Acheul
.48		Isimila H 9	Kalambo B6	Hoxne
.49		Isimila K 14		
.50		Olorg. Meng	Kalambo A5 B	Ma'Ayan Barukh
.51		Olorg. I 3		
.52		Isimila K6		
.53		Olorg. H/6 Isimila H 20		
.54		Isimila K 18 Olorg. DE/89 C		Ternifine Swanscombe M.G.
.55	Olduvai TK.1		Nsongezi	
.56				Wolvercote
.57		Isimila L 19		Farnham Terr. A
.58	Olduvai EFHR Olduvai TK.u			
.59				Furze Platt
.60	Olduvai SHK			
.61	Olduvai BK			Cuxton
.63	Peninj			
.65	Olduvai MNK			
.66	Olduvai FC			
.69				Latamne Fordwich
.80				Abbeville

Sources: See table 14.

that less than 0.1% of Olorgesailie bifaces approach a triangular form by having a maximum breadth within 0.4 of the length from the base, or BA/BB less than 0.3. Quantitative methods of the kind proposed by Roe (1964) have far more promise as a means of achieving satisfactory comparisons of plan-form, but unfortunately these methods have not yet been widely applied. Appendix F shows plots of some of the Olorgesailie assemblages and other assemblages presented according to a simplification of Roe's diagrams.

Qualitative Comparison of Certain Distinctive Plan-Forms

Among the large tools at Olorgesailie there are some comparatively rare forms that have taxonomic interest in spite of their rarity. Several sites, Catwalk, Tr. Tr. M 10 surface, LHS surface, and Mid, have yielded extremely elongate bifacial forms reminiscent of the long bifacial foliate daggers of the Lupemban (pl. 51). All the Olorgesailie speci- mens are thicker than the most delicate Congo or Angola examples. Similar specimens are also figured from the Acheulean of Bed IV Olduvai (Leakey 1951 nos. 68, 73, 77, and 91), so that the presence of the form may not have any significance as an Upper Pleistocene zone fossil. Nenquin (1967) shows similar specimens from Nyarunazi in a context that may be transitional from Acheulean to Lupemban (for example, fig. 33, items 4, 5; fig. 38, chap 5). Pointed trihedral forms, trièdres, are present in small but persistent numbers in the Olorgesailie samples. These forms are prominent in the earlier Acheulean industries of the Maghreb, Casablanca Acheulean I-III and Ternifine. Until more is known of their distribu- tion in space and time in the remainder of Africa, no conclusions can be based on their presence at Olorgesailie.

Trimming Characteristics

Intuitive evaluation of the density and character of trimming scars on bifaces has long been an established criterion in the taxonomy of biface assemblages. The distinction between Abbevillian (Chellean) and Acheulean forms has depended on discrimination between stone hammer and cylinder hammer technique. The extreme expressions of these two trimming techniques are unmistakable, but a very large number of specimens shows a debatable inter- mediate condition. A complex of attributes is involved in the discrimination between tech- niques. However, scar number is a relatively simple index of trimming character that proves to be closely related to intuitive evaluations. Stone hammer technique is charac- terized by large, deep, subcircular scars that are relatively few in number. Cylinder hammer trimming consists of shallow, elongate scars that cut one another and interpenetrate, thereby producing a much higher number of scars (facets). Table 17 shows available scar count means for biface assemblages. Unfortunately, complete data are available only for samples studied by me from Natron, Olorgesailie, and Ternifine, and for a few more recently studied assemblages. Some spot checks have been made on three other small samples in the collections at Berkeley.

From these preliminary observations it appears that there is a marked difference between earlier and later Acheulean samples, in the mean scar numbers per piece and in the maximum scar numbers per piece. Further work may well establish a widespread tendency toward increase in scar numbers per piece through time, which could be a useful index of relative chronology. However, as with other attributes, the extent of variation among the Olorgesailie hand axes and among Late Acheulean industries shows that chronological fixes should involve the intersection of several independent lines of evidence.

Table 17

Flake Scar Counts on Hand Axes: A Rank-Ordered List of Sample Means for the Olorgesailie Stratigraphic Sets and Some Other Sites

	Lower Pleistocene	Middle Pleistocene	Late Middle or Early Upper Pleistocene	Other Areas
8-9	Peninj			
10-11	Olduvai EFHR WK			
12-13				
14-15				
16-17				Ternifine*
18-19		Olorg. LSS		
20-21				
22-23				
24-25		Olorg. MSS		Montagu* L.5
26-27				
28-29				
30-31				
32-33		Olorg. USS		
34-35				
36-37				
38-39				
40-41				Tabun Ea*
42-43				
44-45			Kalambo var.*	
46-47				
...				
56			Baringo (LHR)	

*Small samples determined by Isaac (1968a) for comparative purposes. LSS, MSS and USS = Lower, Middle and Upper Stratigraphic sets.

Sources: Other sources as for table 14.

It is clear from the available data that the bifaces from the Middle and Upper Stratigraphic Sets at Olorgesailie fall into the later or cylinder hammer segment of the hand ax continuum. Greater precision is not possible at present. The Lower Stratigraphic Set bifaces have low scar counts, close to the range of early hand ax assemblages. This evidence corroborates the intuitive impression of relatively simple and forceful trimming. Other lines of evidence also suggest affinities with Early Acheulean occurrences.

Other aspects of the morphology of trimming scars on bifaces have less well-established value for chronological and cultural taxonomic interpretations, perhaps because systematic observations have not yet been made.

Similarly, comparative data for quantitative characterizations of cross sections (index of biconvexity, index of skewness) are not available for samples other than Olorgesailie and Ternifine.

The Culture-Stratigraphic Implications of Biface Morphology

The values for no single attribute seriate with perfect consistency in relation to the available independent stratigraphic evidence, but if the attributes are considered together, then the data support the tentative definitions of the following culture-stratigraphic zones.

Post-Acheulean (for example Sangoan-Lupemban). A zone principally characterized by the appearance of new forms, such as the core ax (J. D. Clark 1963), but also by a partial recrudescence of earlier biface morphology; namely relatively short, broad, and thick bifaces. This appears to have a regional distribution, and it may be in part laterally equivalent to the terminal phases of the Upper Acheulean and to a Fauresmith that cannot currently be defined.

Upper Acheulean. A zone characterized by great variability. On available data, samples believed to be of Upper Pleistocene date (Kalambo Falls, Cave of Hearths, Nsongezi MN) cannot be consistently distinguished from samples of supposed Middle Pleistocene age (Olorgesailie, Isimila). Bifaces are generally of moderate to large size, showing moderately high to very high scar counts.

Lower Acheulean. A zone characterized by a tendency for bifaces to be robust and to show a relatively low number of trimming scars. All the African Acheulean samples that are demonstrably of Lower Pleistocene or early Middle Pleistocene age show these features.[3] In gross morphology the bifaces are least distinct from those of the post-Acheulean Sangoan facies of the Sangoan-Lupemban.

Neither in sub-Saharan Africa as a whole nor in the East African province is it possible at present to differentiate on strictly morphological criteria a distinct Middle Acheulean category of assemblages. A twofold division is all that can be justified for the subcontinent, though provincial substages of the Upper Acheulean may be recognizable in some areas.

In Atlantic Morocco a three fold culture-stratigraphic categorization has been possible by using the presence and degree of development of the *méthode levalloise* as the principal criterion. In sub-Saharan Africa, this discriminant is known to be applicable only in the Vaal River Basin (Söhnge, Visser, and Lowe 1939).

Possible time scales for the two divisions of the Acheulean in East Africa and models for the interpretation of variation within the zones are discussed in the final chapter.

Conclusion

I anticipate that morphometric data such as that reviewed here can be used to throw light on other matters that I find more interesting than culture-stratigraphic divisions. As already indicated, the stylistic idiosyncrasy of individual occupation sites appears to have intriguing sociocultural implications. Do the consistently distinctive forms of Meng and H/6 for example, represent the work of individual craftsmen or of small bands that developed particular fashions in partial isolation? Or can we find mechanical or functional explanations for these features?

The whole question of the function of the large bifacial tools remains obscure. In chapter 4 I briefly discussed the idea that these tools tend not to be associated with

3. Olduvai EFHR (M. D. Leakey 1967), Peninj (Isaac 1965, 1967a), Sidi Abderahman layer M, Casablanca STIC (Biberson 1961a), Ternifine (Balout et al. 1967), ? Three Rivers and Sterkfontein extension (Mason 1962). Of these, suitable quantitative data are available only for Peninj and Ternifine (Balout et al. 1967, and records made in Paris by Isaac in 1966).

traces of butchery or of extensive meat eating. The site of DE/89 B is one of the most important exceptions to this tendency. Many of the hand axes and cleavers at this site appear too delicate to be used for digging or woodwork, but this may be an illusion. Experiments may help us ascertain the potential utility of these forms. Many of the specimens show extensive chipping and battering around the edges, which may have resulted from use. The damage needs to be more closely investigated.

7. SCRAPERS AND OTHER SMALL TOOLS

Morphology and Classification

Scrapers and small tools are numerically the most important categories of artifacts in many site aggregates from Olorgesailie. They constitute approximately 40% of all secondarily trimmed tools. However, as a class, the scrapers are variable in form and are standardized relatively little. Because most are made of lava, they are often difficult to recognize, and details of retouch may be obscure because of surface irregularity and weathering. The lack of clearly defined reiterating forms with an obvious conventional design is the leading feature of the Olorgesailie scraper series. Movius (1948:396) makes a similar comment on the Choukoutien small tools: "The general impression one receives on examining a large series of them is that for the most part they are the result of the artisan having taken advantage of the accidental shape of the splinters and chips produced by primary flaking, rather than following a definite technique of shaping the stone."

Recent writings on the Lower Paleolithic have emphasized the wealth of small tool forms (J. D. Clark 1964; Howell et al. 1962; Kretzoi and Vértes 1965; Vértes 1965; M. D. Leakey 1967, 1971). This stress is a healthy corrective to the tendency to consider the industries of the period as characterized solely by choppers, hand axes, and so on. However, it should be realized that the number of forms is partly a function of the low degree of standardization, in contrast to many assemblages of later periods, in which several varieties of scrapers are readily recognized as standardized tool forms. Among the Olorgesailie artifacts, there do occur rare well-executed pieces that can fairly be compared with the more familiar scrapers of Upper Pleistocene industries (see fig. 51:6, pls. 54:6). Still more rarely within site aggregates, small distinctive groups occur, with pieces closely similar to each other and conspicuous by their contrast to the casual appearance of most of the small tools (see fig. 54:1,2,4). Line drawings of scrapers (figs. 50-54) follow this chapter.

Although I know of no satisfactory formal definition of scrapers, there is little difficulty in recognizing members of the genus, which is numerically the most important class in most stone industries. The generic term, when first used in the formative years of paleolithic studies, was prompted by the conjecture that the forms were used for dressing skins. The scrapers from the classic Mousterian and Upper Paleolithic assemblages, made under subarctic conditions of Europe during last glacial times may have been used in this way. However, such scanty ethnographic data as we have for recent stone-using peoples suggests that under temperate and tropical conditions, pieces with comparable retouch and edge morphology are much more often used as whittling and adzing tools (J. D. Clark 1958; D. F. Thompson 1964; Gould 1968, Gould et al. 1971). This possible functional diversity within the class probably does not seriously affect its overall morphological coherence. The essential feature of all scrapers is the presence of a beveled margin, asymmetric to the horizontal (maximum projection) plane of the piece. For this relationship the term "planoclinal" is suggested. The condition is contrasted to the "biclinal" edges of cutting tools (fig. 43). The asymmetry of the edge bevel is functionally related to movements sub-parallel to a surface that is modified by the removal of shavings. Such a pattern of tool movements can aptly be termed scraping, regardless of the substratum involved.

CROSS SECTIONS

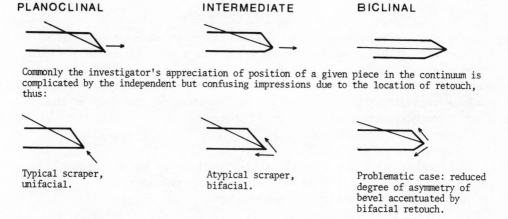

PLANOCLINAL   INTERMEDIATE   BICLINAL

Commonly the investigator's appreciation of position of a given piece in the continuum is complicated by the independent but confusing impressions due to the location of retouch, thus:

Typical scraper,   Atypical scraper,   Problematic case: reduced
unifacial.   bifacial.   degree of asymmetry of
                                                     bevel accentuated by
                                                     bifacial retouch.

Figure 43. Relationships of edge bevels to the plane of maximum projection of tools.

It is of interest to note that Gould (1968:44) reports that the aborigines of the western Australian desert "classify their flaked stone tools into two categories, basing this distinction on the cross-sectional shape of the working edge (*yiri*) of the stone flake from which the tool is fashioned. A fairly thick flake with a steep working edge suitable for adzing or scraping in making wooden objects is called *purpunpa*. A knifelike flake with a thin, sharp edge suited for slicing or cutting is termed *tjimari*.

Intensity of Trimming

Scrapers grade into the utilized categories by decreasing intensity of retouch, and during the present study, the scrapers were assigned to one of four grades as follows:

1. *Intensive*. Bevel due largely to the retouch scars; scars relatively large in the sense of not being confined to a few millimeters from the edges; general subjective impression of purposive modification.

2. *Subintensive*. Scraper bevel only partly due to retouch, scars partly confined to the edge; less clearly purposive impression.

3. *Casual*. Bevel irregular, with intermittent scars only, mainly close to the edge, and possibly partly due to utilization.

4. *Utilized I*. Intermittent serial edge scars only, attributed to damage, rather than to deliberate trimming.

Figures 50-54 illustrate these graded categories. Only grades 1 through 3 have been analyzed as tools. Rated grades are given for all figured specimens. The boundaries of these
grade divisions could not be readily defined so as to be exactly reproducible, but the system may have some value for describing the assemblages in semiquantitative terms. It also
keeps to the fore the important fact that the gradation exists, and that most of the
Olorgesailie scrapers, while trimmed, have been shaped casually and are thus not entirely
comparable with the familiar, more intensive and more highly standardized *racloirs* and
grattoirs of Middle and Upper Paleolithic industries. Devising means of measuring casual-
ness and standardization in scrapers is an important project for future research.

Small Tools and Pseudo-outils

Many of the unstandardized Olorgesailie pieces can be matched in the series illustrated by Bordes (1961a) as *pseudo-outils* and interpreted by him as the outcome of cryotur-
bation or *piètinement*. From many field contexts, the artifactual nature of the secondary
scars could be in doubt, and the possibility remains that a proportion of the Olorgesailie
specimens are *pseudo-outils*. The principal forces that could have been agents of edge
damage or modification at Olorgesailie can be listed as follows:
    1. Deliberate trimming by man.
    2. Deliberate use of an edge by man.
    3. Trampling by the feet of man and animals, the flakes and angular fragments being
pressed against hard particles in the substratum or against each other.
    4. Concussions occurring during stream transport.

Although factors 3 and 4 cannot be eliminated as causes of edge damage among the materials
at Olorgesailie, it is likely that they were of minimal importance, given the peculiar context of the artifact assemblages.

From the foregoing, it can be seen that a gradation exists between undoubted tools
and debatable tools and that different authorities are likely to place the boundary at different points. Only further experiment and observation of natural processes under known
conditions can lead to greater precision.

Morphological Variation and Subdivisions

The variation among the small predominantly unifacial tools involves many variables.
Like the bifaces, they can be considered to comprise a multidimensional field in hypergeo-
metric space, but two principal variables have been used to structure a two-dimensional
simplification of the field of variation (fig. 44). They are ratios partially expressing
(1) elongation in relation to the line(s) of retouch and (2) degree of flexure of the line
of retouch.

I found it convenient to base the classification of pieces on qualitative and quantitative appreciation of the two variables and to recognize eight zones, or categories,
within the field. Figure 45 shows the forms central to each of the zones and indicates
the criteria used for separating them. An additional category, given the number 7, is comprised of composite pieces, potentially classifiable into two categories by virtue of their
two unconnected lines of retouch. In figure 45, a three-dimensional (isometric) histogram

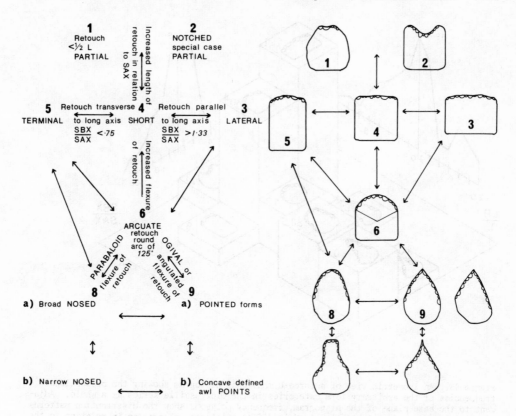

1
Retouch
<½ L
PARTIAL

Increased length of retouch in relation to SAX

Increased flexure of retouch

2
NOTCHED
special case
PARTIAL

5
TERMINAL

Retouch transverse to long axis
SBX/SAX <·75

4
SHORT

Retouch parallel to long axis
SBX/SAX >1·33

3
LATERAL

6
ARCUATE
retouch
round
arc of
125°

PARABALOID flexure of retouch

OGIVAL or angulated flexure of retouch

8
a) Broad NOSED

9
a) POINTED forms

b) Narrow NOSED

b) Concave defined
awl POINTS

Figure 44.   Categories of small tools shown as zones within a morphological field.

shows the relative frequencies of specimens as classified into the form categories. The figure suggests that only two intrinsic, modal form classes are present in the material and that these intergrade. The two natural classes are (1) simple forms, with a single line of retouch (categories 1-6) and (2) apical forms, in which a nose or point is defined by the flexure or angulation of the retouch (categories 8 and 9).

The system of classification constitutes a departure from the system of Bordes (1950b, 1961a) and that of Kleindienst (1962). The step was taken because the Olorgesailie small tools and other Acheulean small tool assemblages are not closely comparable with the classic European assemblages, the features of which are conveyed by standard typological usages and by the more closely defined meanings given them by Bordes. Kleindienst's system made use of the standard terms, such as side-scraper and end-scraper, and although I have in effect retained these categories, I have renamed them lateral scraper, terminal scraper, and so on, in order to make it clear that the forms are classified simply by reference to the relationship of the long axis to the line of retouch and that the resultant sets of specimens bear little resemblance to the side-scrapers and end-scrapers of Europe. I introduced the category short scraper because I found it impossible to assign the equidimensional pieces to either the lateral scrapers or the terminal scrapers.

Table 18 relates my proposed new terms to Bordes's categories, as I understand them. On the basis of available definitions, a maximum of 64% of the small tools were found to be

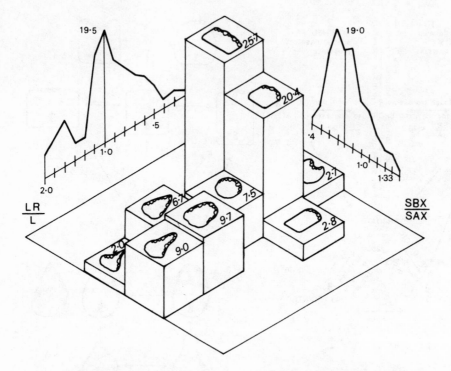

Figure 45. An isometric view of a three-dimensional histogram showing the proportional frequencies of the arbitrary form categories in the Olorgesailie series as a whole. Adjacent to the base plane of the histogram, frequency polygons show the distribution patterns of the two principal variables involved in differentiation: elongation in relation to the line of retouch (SBX/SAX) and the length of retouch in relation to the length (LR/L). A weak bimodality is apparent in the degree of edge flexure as indicated by the ratio, LR/L and the histogram. For explanation of the measurements, see figure 46. For sorting criteria, see appendix C.

classifiable according to the *système Bordes*. The approximate incidence of these classifiable tools for the various site samples is also shown in tables 18 and 19.

The notion that the small tools comprise a variable series lacking standardized types and with only two weak modalities is one that will require further testing.

The coefficients of variation of dimensions and the standard deviations of ratios are in general larger for the scrapers than for the bifaces (table 20). This fact strengthens my conviction that these small forms show a lower degree of standardization. Among the bifaces, the hand axes and cleavers emerge as fairly constant, reiterating designs. There is no equivalent among the small tools. In consequence of this greater variability, site sample idiosyncrasy, though detectable, is less obvious than for bifaces.

Variation in the Frequency of Forms

Table 19 shows the inventory of pieces for each site, classified into the nine form categories. Despite wide variation, a certain overall pattern and consistency emerge. The two major categories, scrapers with a single line of retouch (forms 1-6) and scrapers and other tools with the retouch flexed around a nose or point (forms 8,9), are present in the series in the approximate proportions of 70:30. Very few samples lie outside the range

Table 18

Approximate Equivalence of Categories Used at Olorgesailie with European Usage (from Bordes 1950b). The numbers shown for each site are the numbers classifiable into the the specified category of Bordes.

Comparable Categories of Bordes (1950b)	Designation in System Used by Isaac	BBB	BBA	FB	I 3	DE/89 A	DE/89 B	DE/89 C	H/6 A	H/9 A and H/9 AM	Meng	LHS	Tr. Tr. M 10	Hog	MPS	Total
Racloir, various subtypes 7,12,13,14	Lateral 3,4,6 Short Arcuate	4	2	3	5	8	3	1	1	12	4	1	5	5	2	56
Racloir transversal type 11	3,4 or 6 "	8	3	4	20	7	4	3	3	16	3	2	3	7	4	87
Grattoirs types 18,19	4,5 or 6 Short Terminal Arcuate	2	2	2	9	10	6	5	-	1	-	-	3	-	1	41
Grattoirs à museau	8 Nosed	10	9	7	18	25	16	14	2	17	5	1	6	8	3	141
Racloir convergent type 9	9	8	2	7	4	13	4	-	1	2	1	-	3	1	1	47
Racloir déjeté type 10	9	-	-	2	4	-	1	1	-	3	1	-	3	1	-	16
Percoirs types 22,23	9 Pointed sub-categories distinguished in table 6	4	-	-	3	5	3	-	-	1	-	1	-	-	1	18
Point de Tayac	9	1	5	-	4	3	1	2	1	4	-	1	7	3		32
Outil Comp. and *Racloir* double type 8	7 Double or compound	2	2	4	10	28	16	1	-	16	5	1	18	7	1	111
Pièces à encoché	2 Notched	-	-	-	2	3	5	2	-	4	-	-	1	-	-	17
																566
% of Sample Classifiable in Bordes's system	%	66	60	85	57	78	98	71	53	63	58	54	66	68	100	67%
Denticulé Type 32	No.	3	9	3	22	21	25	10	3	30	8	7	25	6	2	174
	%	5	21	9	16	16	42	24	20	25	25	24	34	13	15	21%

Table 19

The Percentage Frequency of Form Categories

	Partial	Notched	Lateral	Short	Terminal	Arcuate	Multiple	Nosed	Pointed	Total Classified	Number Unclassified
MPS	-	-	23.1	23.1	-	7.7	7.7	23.1	15.4	13	-
Hog	-	-	28.3	26.1	-	2.2	15.2	21.7	6.5	46	-
Tr. Tr. M 10	-	1.2	31.2	18.8	1.2	1.2	22.5	13.8	10.0	80	-
U.S.S. Total	-	0.7	29.5	21.6	0.7	2.2	18.7	17.3	9.4	139	-
LHS	-	-	23.0	15.4	-	15.4	7.7	30.8	7.7	13	-
Meng	-	-	45.7	17.1	-	2.9	14.3	14.3	5.7	35	-
H/9 AM	6.7	6.7	13.3	-	20.0	13.3	33.3	6.7	-	15	-
H/9 A	-	2.5	35.0	21.7	1.7	11.7	9.2	13.3	5.0	120	-
H/6 A	-	-	21.4	42.9	-	7.1	-	21.4	7.1	14	-
DE/89 C	-	4.9	17.1	24.4	-	4.9	2.4	39.0	7.3	41	-
DE/89 B	1.0	5.0	25.2	10.1	4.0	14.1	16.2	16.2	8.1	99	-
DE/89 A	1.6	2.3	11.8	15.8	3.1	7.1	22.0	21.3	15.0	127	2
MSS Total	0.9	3.0	24.4	17.2	2.8	9.7	14.4	19.0	8.6	464	2
I 3	1.4	1.4	31.6	26.8	5.5	6.2	6.9	13.8	6.2	145	2
FB	-	-	26.4	11.8	-	8.8	11.8	20.6	20.6	34	-
BBA	-	-	15.8	23.7	2.7	10.5	5.3	36.8	5.3	38	-
BBB	1.7	-	19.0	29.3	3.4	3.4	3.4	19.0	20.7	58	1
LSS Total	1.0	0.7	26.0	24.9	4.0	6.5	6.5	18.8	10.8	275	3
Total (all sets)	0.7	2.7	25.7	20.4	2.8	7.5	12.6	18.7	9.5	878	5

Table 20

Mean Dimensions and Shape-Defining Ratios for Small Scrapers and Other Small Tools (Olorgesailie Site Samples)*

	N	L	SGX	T	T/B	SBX/SAX	TM/SSX	RL/SGX
MPS	19	42.1	41.3	16.1	.53	.86	.44	1.21
		7.6	7.3	5.0	.15	.46	.15	.40
Hog	46	50.1	48.2	15.5	.44	.75	.40	1.19
		12.0	12.0	5.8	.14	.20	.15	.41
Tr. Tr. M 10	80	64.0	62.4	19.6	.44	.72	.38	1.11
		21.3	21.7	8.9	.13	.14	.14	.38
USS	144	56.9	55.2	17.9	.45	.75	.39	1.14
		13.3	19.5	7.8	.14	.23	.14	.39
LHS	13	47.9	47.0	15.8	.52	.69	.44	1.26
		10.3	10.1	4.4	.18	.19	.16	.43
Meng	35	76.0	74.3	22.8	.42	.76	.35	1.06
		34.9	35.2	11.4	.10	.18	.10	.42
H/9 AM	15	104.9	101.7	23.8	.36	.85	--	.97
		49.9	50.8	8.6	.06	.29		.44
H/9 A	120	62.8	61.4	16.9	.40	.79	--	.97
		31.7	31.6	7.8	.11	.23		.33
H/6 A	13	61.5	59.8	18.1	.43	.80	.36	1.03
		48.9	47.6	10.8	.07	.20	.09	.43
DE/89 C	41	48.8	47.4	15.0	.44	.82	.36	1.06
		18.9	17.7	5.4	.14	.23	.13	.38
DE/89 B	103	78.4	67.8	22.9	.45	.77	.37	1.10
		51.6	50.9	14.7	.11	.22	.10	.41
DE/89 A	71	49.9	49.8	16.6	.45	.85	.42	3.19
		22.6	21.3	9.0	.13	.24	.12	.36
MSS	411	65.2	60.0	18.9	.43	.80	.38	1.45
		39.4	36.2	10.8	.12	.23	.12	.75
I 3	146	48.8	46.8	15.2	.45	.80	.37	1.04
		20.2	20.2	8.0	.12	.26	.14	.38
FB	38	--	49.8	--	--	.76	.49	--
			19.0			.16	.13	
.BBA	38	--	41.4	--	--	.82	.54	--
			14.1			.20	.14	
BBB	50	--	38.9	--	--	.81	.45	--
			11.1			.20	.14	
LSS	267	49.6	45.0	15.6	.46	.80	.43	1.04
			18.3	8.4	.12	.24	.14	.38

*The two figures given for each entry are arranged thus: mean s.d.

between 60:40 and 80:20. This overall pattern of composition for the small tools is quite
distinct from the patterns defined for Middle and Upper Paleolithic industries.

No important time trends in the incidence of form categories have been discerned.
There is no obvious difference between the biface- and scraper-dominated sets with regard
to the proportions of the form categories.

Large Scrapers

Scrapers over 100 mm in length are classified as large scrapers by Kleindienst (1962)
and J. D. Clark (1964). For the purpose of this analysis, they have been included with the
others, although they may be present as minor second modalities to some small scraper
series, rather than as tails to the positively skew distributions. In many respects, they
are more like large cutting tools than like small scrapers, so they have been included in
the analysis of both categories. Core scrapers are numerically unimportant at Olorgesailie
and have not been distinguished in this analysis.

Measured Attributes

Measurements were taken of eight linear dimensions, the weight, and the edge angles
(fig. 46). The problems of measuring edge angles are such that the results have been
treated, in effect, as ordinal data. Eight ratios, based on the linear measurements, define form and proportion. Table 20 summarizes site means and standard deviations. Table
21 summarizes analysis of variance tests. Sets are based on stratigraphy or on the hypothetical facies divisions of Acheulean and Hope Fountain. Most of these prove heterogeneous in their dimensions but less so in their form-defining ratios.

Edge Angles

Steep edge angles have long been commented on as a prominent characteristic of Hope
Fountain industries (J. D. Clark 1950:82), so I made an attempt to obtain measurements defining this aspect of morphology. Because the angles are difficult to measure, the data in
figure 47 must be regarded with caution. All the angles show comparatively high modal
values for their edge angles, which range from 75 to 85 degrees. There is a faint indication of reduction in angles through time, but it could well be illusory. There appears to
be no consistent association of steep edge angles with scraper-dominated Hope Fountain
assemblages.

Denticulation

Denticulation is here treated as an attribute of scrapers, whereas Bordes (1950b,
1961a) uses it as the criterion for inclusion in a distinctive type category.

The retouched edges on Olorgesailie scrapers tend to be somewhat irregular, and most
of them show a degree of serration comparable to the least extreme examples labeled as
denticulé by Bordes (1961a:pl. 40, nos. 10, 11). Clearly denticulation is a gradational
phenomenon, not a clear-cut, present-or-absent attribute. Table 22 shows the incidence of
pieces with denticulation sufficiently marked to have prompted recording. The proportion
ranges from 5 to 47% with both extremes having a small number of samples; but observed
values cluster mainly around the aggregate proportion of 18.8%. If denticulation is correlated with form categories, 20.9% of single line of retouch scrapers are denticulate, but
only 13.2% of nosed and pointed ones are.

There are no obvious time trends or facies division for this attribute.

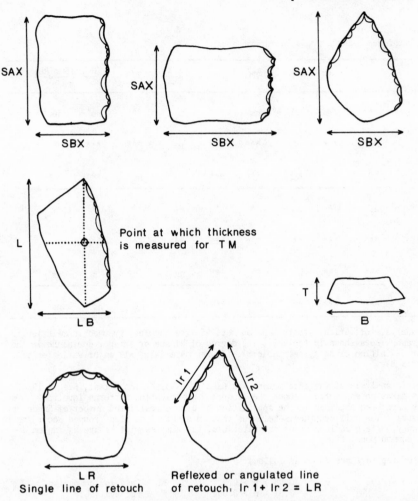

Figure 46. Measurements taken on scrapers and allied small tools. SAX = Scraper A axis; SBX = Scraper B axis; L = maximum length; B = containing rectangle breadth; T = thickness; TM = thickness at the mid point; LR = length of retouch; SGX = greater, SAX, SBX; SSX = smaller, SAX, SBX.

Primary Forms

More than half the pieces (55.9%) cannot be positively identified as flakes with a definable orientation. The remainder is divided subequally between side-struck and end-struck flakes (22.2% and 21.0%, respectively). These proportions are very close to the overall proportions for side- and end-struck flakes in the Olorgesailie industries. The difference is not significant in a χ^2 test. Lack of a careful choice of standardized blanks to serve as the basis for the small tools is apparent: any suitable stone fragment was seemingly regarded as a satisfactory basis for modification. This lack of standardized use of flake blanks is a point of contrast with the classic paleolithic industries of Europe and the Mediterranean, and is among the factors that render the European typological systems inapplicable to the Olorgesailie material.

A small number of scrapers, 0.9%, were made directly on pebble fragments.

Table 21

Analysis of Variance: Small Tools (Scrapers)

	L	SGX	T	TM	Wt.	$\dfrac{SBX}{SAX}$	T/B	$\dfrac{TM}{SSX}$	$\dfrac{Sum(RL)}{SGX}$
USS 3 samples	***	***	*	ns	***	ns	**	ns	ns
MSS 8 samples	***	***	***	***	***	ns	***	***	*
LSS 4 samples	NC	**	NC	***	***	ns	ns	***	NC
BDS 4 samples	ns	*	ns	**	*	ns	**	*	ns
Int. S. 5 samples	***	***	**	***	***	***	*	***	*
SDS 5 samples	***	***	ns	**	***	ns	*	*	ns
Raw Material	***	***	**	***	***	ns	ns	ns	ns

Results of analysis of variance tests made on sets of site samples, grouped in relation to (1) stratigraphy (sets shown in table 5), (2) degree of biface or scraper dominance in the samples (for definition of sets, see table 8), (3) raw materials, all major varieties of lava (appendix B).

A nonparametric analysis of variance method was used (Kruskal-Wallis H test, Siegel 1956) because this makes no assumptions about the frequency distribution patterns involved. Similar results have been obtained in the application of a more restricted number of Snedecor F test analyses. The null hypothesis tells us that in a set of samples grouped according to stratigraphy, biface dominance, or raw materials, the samples will behave as random deviants of a common population.

The results of the test are coded as follows:

ns	$p > 0.05$	*	$0.05 > p > 0.01$	NC	Data for comparison
		**	$0.01 > p > 0.001$		not available
		***	$p < 0.001$		

The number of asterisks indicates the strength of evidence indicative of significant differences among the samples in the given set.

Conclusions Concerning Internal Variation

The scrapers and allied small tools are an important part of the evidence relevant to an exact definition of the extent of differences between the biface-dominated set of samples and the scraper-dominated set. These are the only trimmed tools that are sufficiently numerous in both sets to be compared.

The results of the comparisons are not entirely conclusive; there appears to exist a poorly standardized pattern common to all the small tool samples. This pattern covers the presence and approximate proportions of form categories, the general tendency being toward steep edge angles and technical features, such as the proportions of various primary blanks. There are slight differences in measurable variables: the scraper-dominated sets tend to lack the distribution tail of large scrapers; they tend also to have relatively thicker

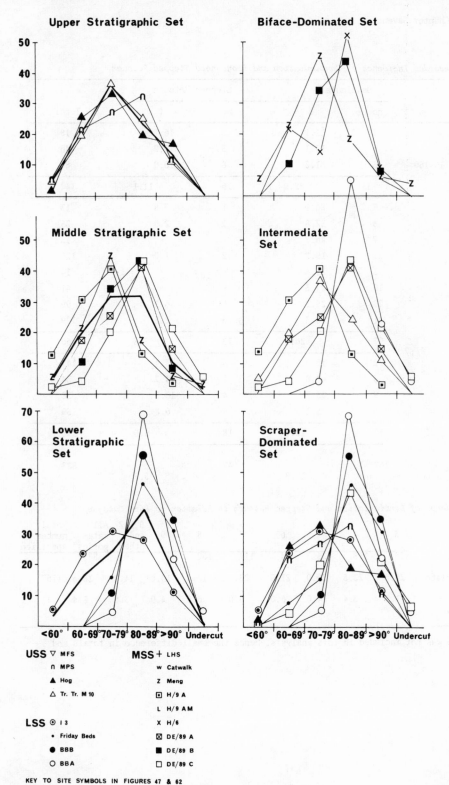

Figure 47.   Frequency distributions of scraper edge angles, shown in relation to classification of the samples into stratigraphic sets (left) and degree of biface-dominated sets (right).

Table 22

a) The Recorded Incidence of Denticulation and Pronounced Stepped Retouch

Site	Denticulate		Stepped Retouch		Total
	no.	%	no.	%	
MPS	2	İ1.1	3	16.7	18
Hog	6	13.1	5	10.9	46
Tr. Tr. 110-160	25	31.2	8	10.0	80
	33	22.9	16	11.1	144
LHS	7	53.9	1	7.8	13
Meng	8	22.8	1	2.9	35
H/9 AM	7	46.7	-	-	15
H/9 A	23	19.2	2	1.7	120
H/6	3	21.4	-	-	14
DE/89 C	10	24.3	-	-	41
DE/89 B	25	25.2	6	6.1	99
DE/89 A	21	16.3	3	2.3	129
	97	20.8	13	2.8	466
I 3	22	15.0	5	3.4	147
FB	3	8.8	5	14.7	34
BBA	9	23.7	4	10.5	38
BBB	3	5.1	4	6.8	59
	37	13.3	18	6.5	278
	167	18.8	47	5.3	888

b) Incidence of Denticulation and Stepped Retouch in Relation to Form Category

	3	4	5	6	7	8	9	0,1,2 and other	All categories	Total number specified
Total No.	224	178	25	64	111	162	82	29	875*	
% Denticulate	20.6	22.5	20.0	21.9	23.5	12.4	14.6	14.2	18.3	(167)
% with step retouch	1.0	3.4	4.0	6.0	9.0	6.8	4.9	3.6	5.4	(47)

*LHS was not included in this analysis, hence the small difference in totals and % values.

cross sections. Both these differences can be attributed either to cultural differences or
to differences in activity and the characteristics of the available primary blanks.

The poorly standardized scraper samples provide even less evidence of consistent
trends of change in artifact traditions through time than do the bifaces. Faint indications of increase in size, reduction of edge angle, and increase in the partly subjective
intensity rating may well be illusory.

Comparison with Other Selected
Small Tool Assemblages

The qualitative and quantitative description of the Olorgesailie small tool series can
now be used as a basis for considering the relationships of the series to comparable artifacts in other assemblages. Two issues, (1) the relationship of the Olorgesailie small
tools to other Acheulean small tools and (2) the features of Acheulean small tools in relation to those of other major paleolithic traditions, will be discussed.

The scope of this discussion is severely limited by the scarcity of comparable data.
In recent years, the excavation of various complexes of African Acheulean sites, such as
Kalambo and Isimila, has led to an awareness of the numerical importance of small tools in
many Acheulean industries. Little detailed information and few illustrations have been
published for any of these sites.

Outside Africa, information is similarly fragmentary. J. D. Clark (1966a, b, 1969)
has given a well-illustrated account of Acheulean small scrapers from Latamne, Syria.
Qualitative illustrated descriptions also exist for the scrapers of a fair number of European and Levantine sites. Notable among these are the Atelier Commont (Bordes and Fitte
1953), Swanscombe (Wymer 1964), and Levantine cave sites, such as Tabun and Jabrud (Garrod
and Bate 1937; Rust 1950). Howell (1966) has published a series of classificatory percentage figures for European Lower Paleolithic sites, including Torralba and Vertésszöllös, but
illustrations are not available.

Comparison with non-Acheulean industries is selectively made to place the features of
the Olorgesailie scrapers in a wider context. The relatively standardized classic forms
of the Mousterian and Upper Paleolithic of Europe provide one useful reference point, while
the scrapers from such poorly standardized industries as the Clactonian, Tayacian, Chou-
koutenian, and the earliest phase of the Australian Stone Age provide convenient yard-
sticks by which to gauge widespread, generalized features, which have little significance
for defining specific traditions.

Size

Some quantitative information on scraper length is available, and selected data are
presented in figure 48. The Olorgesailie series is generalized, in that it covers a range
from microlithic to extremely large. The mode and mean are at a larger size level than
that of the relatively standardized small forms of the later Pleistocene and Holocene of
both Africa and Europe (for example, Montagu Cave, layers 1 and 2, after Keller 1973;
Oakhurst Smithfield B, after Fagan 1960; and a European Mesolithic site, Oirschott V, after
Bohmers 1963). However, the mode, median, and mean length are appreciably less than those
of available examples of classic Mousterian and Upper Paleolithic of Europe. It appears
that the Acheulean situation itself is subject to considerable variation.

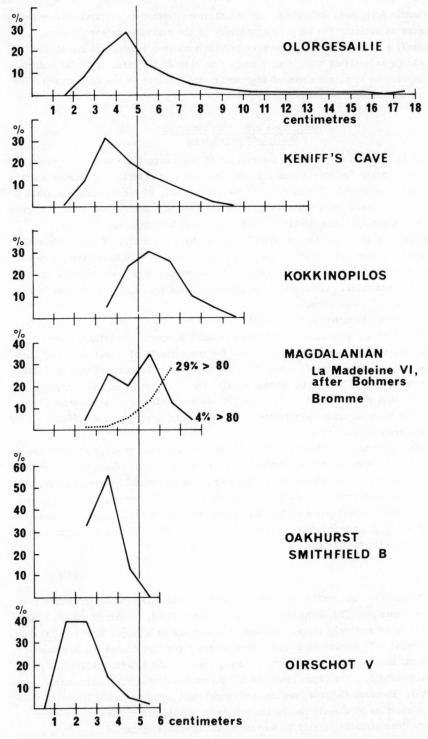

Figure 48. The size distribution of scrapers from Olorgesailie in relation to distributions for selected examples of sites for which data is available: Keniff's Cave, Queensland, Australia, after Mulvaney and Joyce (1965); Kokkinopilos Mousterian *racloirs*, after Mellars (in Dakaris et al. 1964); two Late Magdalenian assemblages, after Bohmers (1963).

Elongation

It is my impression that the Olorgesailie scrapers and those of many other generalized industries, such as Choukoutien and Keniff's Cave, Queensland, contrast with classic European Middle and Upper Paleolithic scrapers in exhibiting a much lower degree of elongation. Middle and Upper Paleolithic forms contrast in that elongation is parallel to the trimming in the former and at right angles to the trimming in the latter.

Published data relevant to these comparisons have proved hard to obtain, but figure 49 shows a comparison of frequency polygons for the B/L ratio, B axis/A axis of scrapers in the Olorgesailie series, two samples from the Mount Carmel sequence (Berkeley collections), and a miscellaneous sample of European Upper Paleolithic scrapers (also in the Berkeley collections). The validity of the samples as representative of Middle and Upper Paleolithic industries is open to question. However, the figure is presented because it makes explicit the otherwise vague statement that the Olorgesailie Acheulean samples contrast with both Middle and Upper Paleolithic form patterns.

Ranges and Frequencies of Forms

Part of the difference between Olorgesailie samples and those of European industries is that the Olorgesailie Acheulean scrapers seem to lack the pronounced elongation that characterizes the *racloir* and *grattoir*. However, because pieces from other nonclassic assemblages have been forced into either the one or the other of these two categories, the classificatory data of conventional reports do not reflect this difference. Inspection of figures and collections suggests that equidimensional short scrapers are prominent, if not predominant, in other generalized assemblages, namely, the Broken Hill Acheulean and Hope Fountain (J. D. Clark 1959), Sidi Zin (Gobert 1950), Fontéchevade (Henri-Martin 1957), Choukoutien (Movius 1948), Ternifine, Isimila, Vértésszöllös (personal inspection). However, certain Acheulean assemblages contrast by showing a clear predominance of elongate *racloirs*, as in Tabun layer E (Garrod and Bate 1937, and measurements in fig. 49) and Latamne (J. D. Clark 1966a, b, 1969a). For the Atelier Commont, Bordes and Fittes (1953) show numerous *racloirs* and *grattoirs* comparable with the classic forms of these categories.

The narrow-nosed and awl-pointed forms comprise a numerically subordinate but conspicuous morphological set in the Olorgesailie samples. Data published by F. C. Howell (1966: figs. 5, 13, 14, 17, 22, 26) suggest that several European Lower Paleolithic sites, Torralba 1962-63 excavations (11.8%), the lower unit at Ambrona (15.5%), Swanscombe (21.4%), and Torre in Pietra (14.7%), also show a noticeable proportion of *becs* and borers. (All these percentage values have been converted to proportions of the small tools, not of the total tool kit.) This feature was also obvious to me when I was privileged to examine the Vértésszöllös collection in Budapest in 1965, and a frequency of 32% of small tools is calculated from Howell (1966: fig. 5). The Olorgesailie overall value is about 15%. The prominence of spurs and beaks is also apparent in other generalized assemblages for which quantitative data are not available: Choukoutien (Movius 1948), and the lower layers of Keniff's cave (Mulvaney and Joyce 1965: figs. 17, 18).

In addition to the Olorgesailie series, many other Acheulean small tool assemblages give the appearance of being irregular ad hoc tools. This is not invariably the case; notable exceptions are the illustrated series from the Mount Carmel Acheulean (Garrod and Bate 1937, and personal observation).

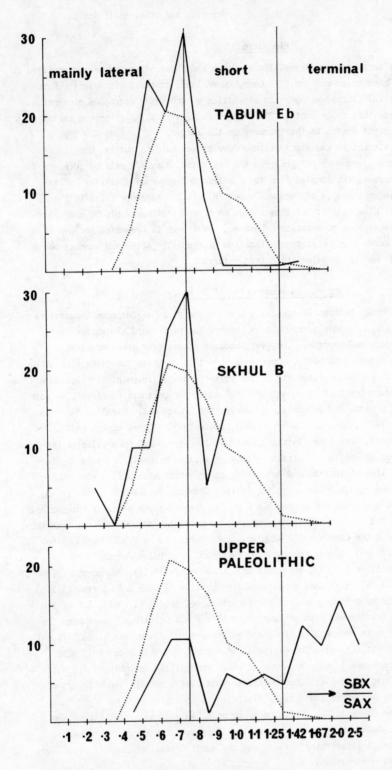

Figure 49. Frequency distributions of scraper elongation in relation to retouch. The Olorgesailie series (stippled trace) compared with small samples of Late Acheulean (Tabun Eb, 75 specimens), Levalloisian-Mousterian (Skhul B, 20 specimens) and a miscellaneous, unselected series of French Upper Paleolithic scrapers (Lowie Museum collections, 46 specimens).

Conclusion

The available qualitative and quantitative data concerning Acheulean small tools is inadequate as a basis for even tentative proposals regarding distinctions between strati-graphic or geographic zones. It seems clear that many, but not all such small-tool kits show a lower degree of standardization than do the industries that succeeded them in the Upper Pleistocene. However, until measurement becomes a routine part of describing assem-blages and until attention is devoted to the development of quantitative methods for analy-zing and expressing standardization, we shall not be able to trace the history of the transformation from one condition to the other.

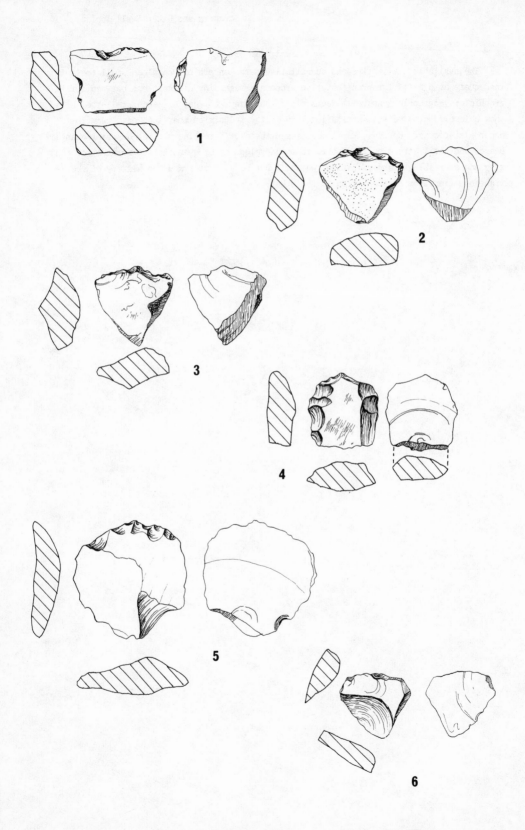

1

2

3

4

5

6

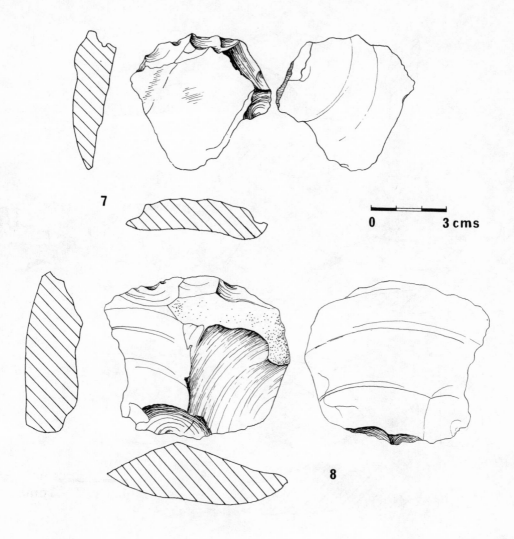

0   3 cms

7

8

Figure 50. (1) *Scraper, short, casual*. Concave retouch or intensive utilization. On a fragment. Trachyandesite B. I 3; (2) *Scraper, short, intensive*. Denticulate retouch. On a fragment. Trachyandesite B. Friday Beds; (3) *Scraper, short, casual*. On a fragment. Basalt. I 3; (4) *Scraper, short, intensive*. On a corner-struck flake (oriented with long axis vertical instead of with the scraper axis horizontal.) Trachyandesite A. Friday Beds; (5) *Scraper, short, intensive*. On a side-struck flake. (= ? *Grattoir*) Trachyandesite. H/9 A; (6) *Scraper, short, intensive*. The reverse, not shown, is a plain cleavage surface. On a fragment. Basalt. I 3; (7) *Scraper, short/arcuate, subintensive*. Retouch lateral to an end-struck flake. Trachyte. H/9 A; (8) *Scraper, short, subintensive*. On a side-struck flake. (= ? *Grattoir*) Trachyandesite. H/9 A.

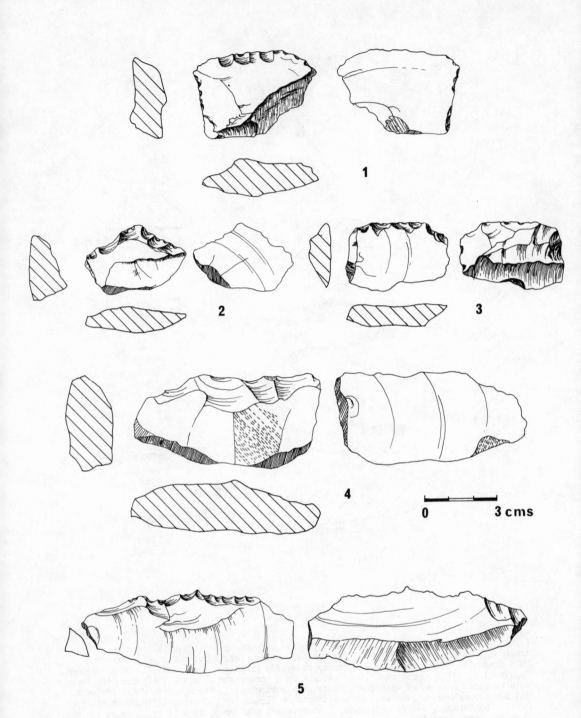

1

2   3

4   0 |——————| 3 cms

5

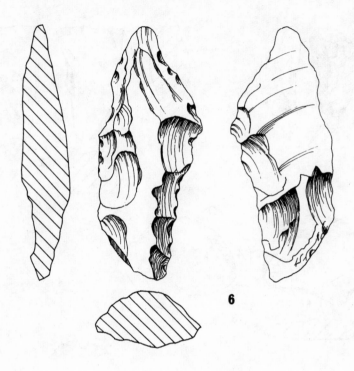

6

Figure 51. (1) *Scraper, lateral, intensive.* Subdenticulate. On a side-struck flake (= *Racloir transversal*). Basalt. I 3; (2) *Scraper, lateral, intensive.* Retouch angulated to form a spur. On a corner-struck flake. Andesite. DE/89 A; (3) *Scraper, lateral, casual.* With reversed retouch, on an end-struck flake, plain, irregular platform (= *Racloir* surface plan.) Basal Bed B; (4) *Scraper, lateral, subintensive.* With subdenticulate retouch and utilization damage. On an end-struck flake (= *Racloir normal*) Phonolite. H/9 A; (5) *Scraper, lateral, subintensive.* With reversed, denticulate retouch. On an end-struck flake (= *Racloir à retouche inverse*). Trachyandesite. H/9 A; (6) *Scraper, double, intensive.* Double, lateral scraping edges partly bifacial consequent on invasive bulb thinning retouch at the butt. On an (?) end flake. Trachyte. H/9 A.

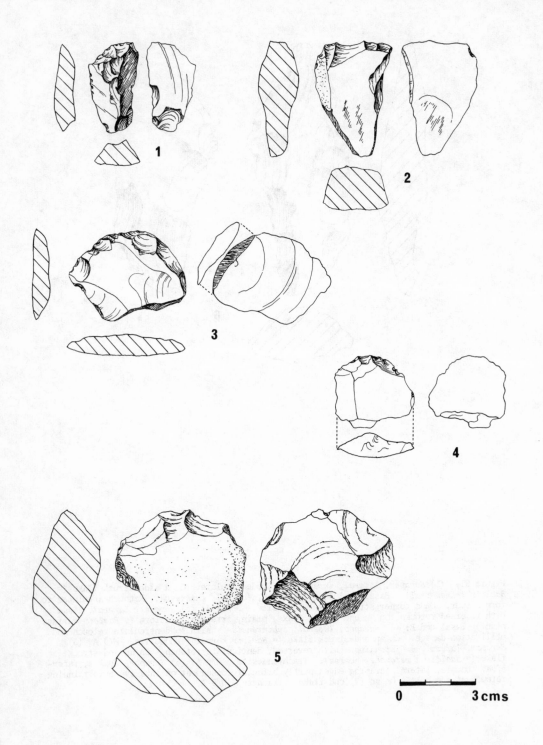

1

2

3

4

5

0   3cms

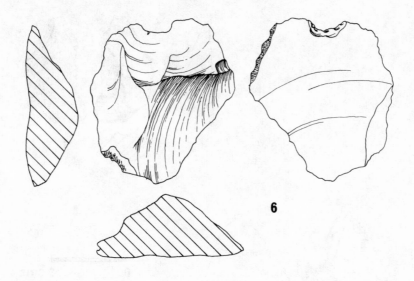

6

Figure 52. (1) *Scraper, terminal, subintensive*. Normal and reversed retouch reversed
bulbar thinning. (?) Corner-struck side flake. Andesite. Basal Bed B; (2) *Scraper,
terminal, subintensive*. With a technical burin blow. On a fragment. Nephelenite. Basal
Bed B; (3) *Scraper, arcuate, intensive*. Subdenticulate retouch. On an end-struck flake
(? = *Grattoir atypique*). Trachyandesite B. Friday Beds; (4) *Scraper, arcuate, subintensive*. Transverse to a side-struck flake. (= *Grattoir*) Fine-grained lava. H/9 A; (5)
Scraper, arcuate, intensive. With a plano-clinal, bifacial retouch. On a side-struck
flake with cortical dorsal surface and a (?) dihedral platform. Quartzite. Friday Beds;
(6) *Scraper, notched (partial), casual*. On a fragment. Basalt. H/9 A.

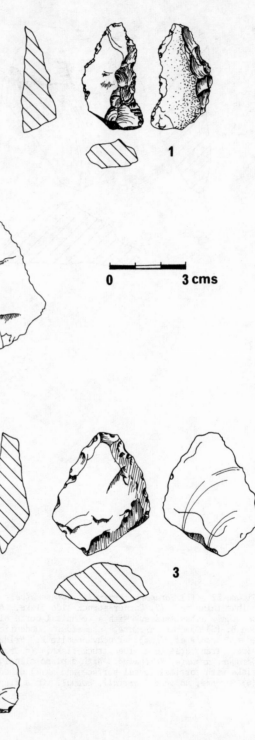

0 ___ 3 cms

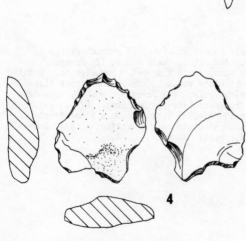

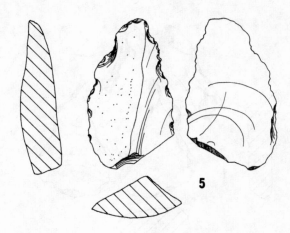

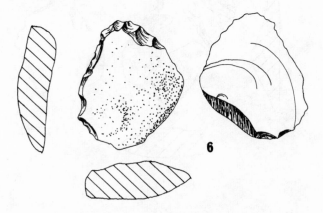

Figure 53. (1) *Scraper, nosed (and double lateral), intensive*. Normal and reversed retouch. Primary form indeterminable (cf. *Bec*). Chert. Tr. Tr. 140-150 floor; (2) *Scraper, nosed, intensive*. Convergent, subdenticulate lines of retouch defining a narrow nose/point. On a fragment. ? Phonolite. Tr. Tr. 140-150 floor; (3) *Scraper, nosed, intensive*. Subdenticulate retouch. On a fragment. ? Basalt, abraded. Tr. Tr. 120-130 floor; (4) *Scraper, nosed (paraboloid), intensive*. Denticulate. The character of the double notch-defined opposite the nose is obscure due to rounding by weathering or rolling. Basalt. DE/89 B; (5) *Scraper, nosed, subintensive*. Denticulate retouch. On an end-struck flake. Basalt. DE/89 B; (6) *Scraper, nosed (paraboloid), intensive*. On a corner-struck flake. Basalt. DE/89 B.

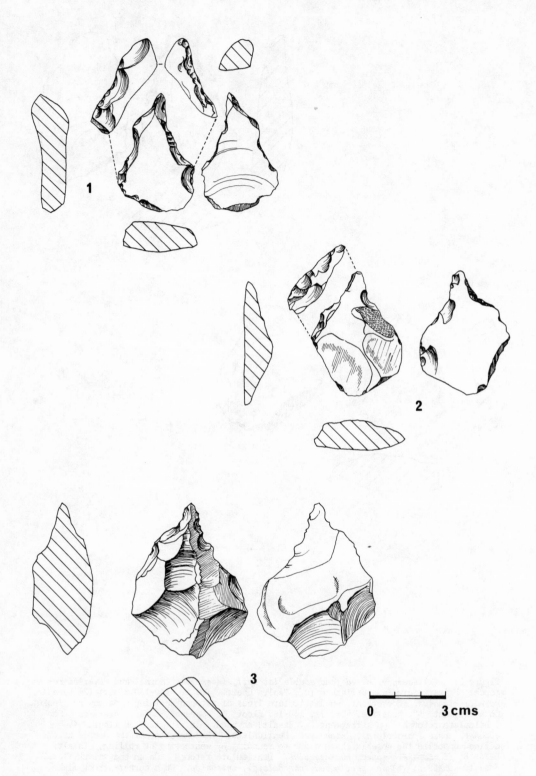

1

2

3

0   3 cms

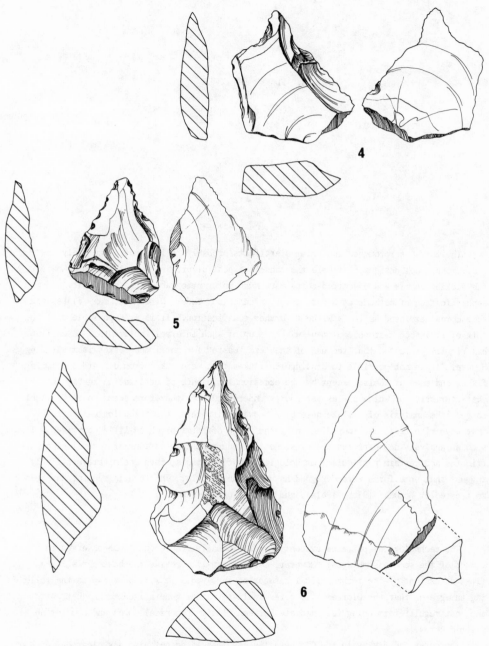

Figure 54. (1) *Awl/scraper, convergent, pointed, intensive*. A singular piece with a beak-like apex. On an end-flake. Trachyandesite A. DE/89 A; (2) *Awl/scraper, convergent, pointed, intensive*. On a fragment. Trachyte. DE/89 A; (3) *Awl/scraper, convergent, pointed, intensive*. Partially bifacial retouch on an indeterminable primary form. ? Basalt. Tr. Tr. Ext. S1A; (4) *Awl/scraper, convergent, pointed, intensive*. On a corner-struck flake. Basalt. DE/89 A; (5) *Awl/convergent scraper, pointed, intensive*. Subdenticulate. On a side-struck flake. Fine-grained lava. I 3; (6) *Scraper/awl, pointed, intensive*. Convergent lines of retouch angulated in relation to corner-struck side flake axis. (= *Racloir déjeté*). ? Andesite. Tr. Tr. 140-150.

8. FLAKES AND CORES

The forms of retouched and trimmed artifacts probably reflect most accurately the traditional tool designs that were the conscious goal of prehistoric craftsmen. However, the flaking debris and discarded cores give much information about the regularity and sophistication of methods used for achieving conscious ends. Of course, many flakes and some cores were used as tools without further modification. It is even possible that the bulk of Pleistocene stone equipment was made up of such informal implements. Mason (1967) has rightly protested that the use of the term "waste" for untrimmed flakes is misleading. However, it is not possible to distinguish flakes that were taken from discarded trimming flakes and used as tools, except by the occasional presence of utilization scars, the characteristics of which are as yet poorly understood. It therefore seems most profitable to gear the analysis of a flake assemblage toward discerning the technological patterns that gave rise to it and toward defining the range of forms of which it is comprised. If such an analysis demonstrates the existence of recurrent combinations of technological attributes and certain particular morphological configurations, then one might justifiably suggest that some forms were designed as unretouched tools. The Levallois point has been so treated by Bordes (1950b, 1961a), and is a plausible example.

Cores

The technological patterns evident in cores usually complement those observed in the flakes of the same assemblages. However, cores generally provide the best basis for a first assessment of the technological categories involved. It will be shown in the following paragraphs that the Olorgesailie cores indicate rather generalized techniques, with the most regular form being intermediate between Clacton biconical cores and Mousterian discoid cores.

The cores and flakes in the Olorgesailie assemblages do not give any clear evidence of sophisticated preformation of flake forms struck from cores with elaborate standardized designs. The three classic paleolithic patterns of core preparation, Mousterian disc preparation, Levallois preparation, and blade preparation are represented only by doubtful and presumably fortuitous examples. Figure 55 represents the field of morphological variation observed among the cores. Figures 63 through 68, line drawings of cores and flakes, follow this chapter.

The form and flake patterning on poorly standardized cores used for more or less ad

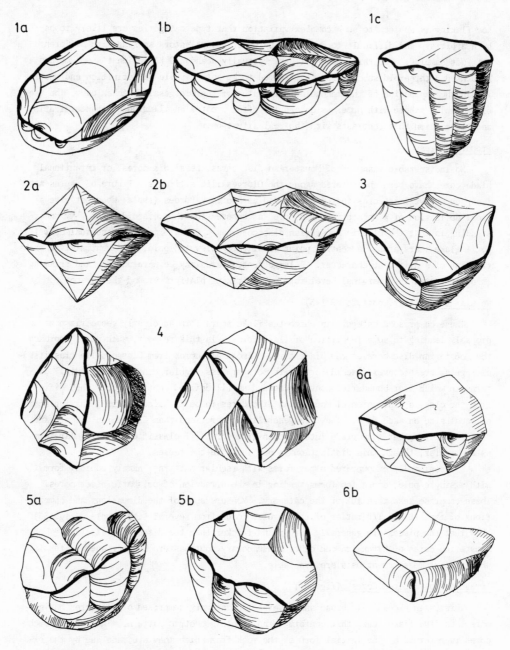

Figure 55.
1. *Regular ("prepared") cores*
   A. Levallois (tortoise core); not definitely represented in the
   Olorgesailie industrial series.
   B. Disc core, with prepared platform. Not represented at Olorgesailie.
   C. Blade core. Rare and ambiguous examples only.
2. *Regular (radial) cores*
   A. Biconical cores.
   B. Biconvex discoid core.
3. *Subregular cores*
   e.g. high-backed discoid cores.
4. *Polyfaceted (multidirectional) cores*
   e.g. polyhedral and subspherical examples.

5. *Polyfaceted bidirectional cores*
   e.g. A. Single flaking edge core/
   chopper
   B. Two flaking edge core.
6. *Casual cores* (less than 5 scars)
   e.g. A. Single flaking edge.
   B. Two flaking edges.

hoc flaking is subject to such complex variation that type categories are likely to be both arbitrary and difficult to duplicate by other investigators working with different artifact samples. For this reason, I have virtually abandoned Kleindienst's scheme and have used a threefold subdivision that seemed to be both capable of definition and meaning-ful in the expression of the technological status of the Olorgesailie Acheulean. The use of a complex scheme with numerous categories often creates an illusion of standardization and elaboration that contrasts with the real situation.

Prepared Cores

No indisputable examples of Mousterian disc cores, Levallois cores, or intentional blade cores have been encountered among the Olorgesailie artifacts. Figure 63 represents two pseudo Levallois cores that are regarded as sports. Bordes (1961a) does not give a clear definition of a Mousterian disc core, as opposed to other discoid cores. My under-standing is that the classic Mousterian disc core has a dorsal face with subequal centri-petal flake scars around a central point or slightly elevated pole. The ventral face shows trimming of a different character. A large central area may be unretouched, and trimming is concentrated in a marginal bevel forming a striking platform around the perimeter.

Regular Cores (figs. 63:1,2; 69:1-3)

These comprise a category in which the flake scars form an orderly geometric pattern, probably leading to some repetition of flake forms. In this respect, such cores approach the Mousterian disc core or the blade core. Almost all cores from Olorgesailie classified as regular are biconvex discoid forms with more or less regular centripetal (radial) pat-terns in which scar boundaries converge toward an ill-defined central pole. They differ from the classic expression of Mousterian disc cores in being bifacial and in having scars of equal size on each face. They are generally more refined than Clactonian discoid and biconical cores, but they grade into Clacton-like forms. I classified less regular forms as subregular, though this distinction is not shown in the tables.

I occasionally encountered other forms with regular patterns, namely conical forms with a single pole, and a few forms tending in the direction of prismatic blade cores. These comprise less than 10% of the category. Measurements of the dimensions and computa-tions of the B/L and T/B ratios of the regular cores from several site samples (fig. 56) show that the pieces are generally larger and thicker than the discoid Levalloiso-Mousterian cores of Cyrenaica and other contemporary southeastern Mediterranean sites for which useful measurement data are available.

Irregular Polyfaceted Cores (fig. 65)

This is an exceedingly broad and diversified category comprised of all cores having more than five flake scars that conform to no simple geometric pattern. The form of such cores is governed by the initial form of the rock from which they are made and by the ex-tent to which they were worked. In general, one gets an impression of ad hoc flaking on every suitable angle that developed or could be contrived. If this impression is correct, elaborate typological categorization would be meaningless. In part, cores in this broad category can be seen to constitute a series from irregular angular forms to battered equi-dimensional forms, tending to be subspherical or cuboidal. These latter may be either worked-out cores or deliberately shaped tool forms.

Casual cores (fig. 67)

These are blocks of stone with less than five discernible major flake scars. Many

OVERALL SHAPE OF CORES

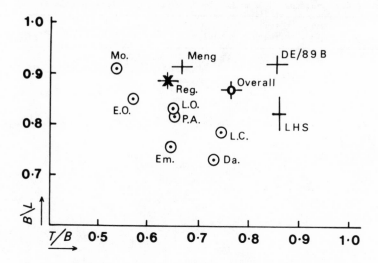

Figure 56. Bivariate plot of mean B/L ratio versus mean T/B ratio for a series of core samples. The overall mean for Olorgesailie is shown, plus extreme individual site sample variants and the overall mean for regular biconvex discoids as a separate class. The comparative data are for the cores from different levels at the Haua Fteah (McBurney 1967). Mo = Mousterian; E O = Early Oranian; L O = Late Oranian; P A = Pre-Aurignacian; L C = Late Capsian; Da = Dabban.

casual cores in the Olorgesailie series may have been angular unmodified stones scarred while in use as hammers or anvils; Kleindienst would probably have designated some as bashed or battered chunks.

Intergradation of Cores with Other Classes

The large bifacial tools in the Olorgesailie series undoubtedly grade into the cores. The distinction between thick chunky ovates, discoid bifaces, and biconvex cores is necessarily arbitrary. Similarly, the distinction between choppers and cores depends in part on subjective evaluation of the maker's intentions. In general, where a piece could, in my opinion, be classified as either a core or a tool, I have assigned it to the latter category. Examples of an intergrading series are shown in plate 47. This series has been selected from the Lower Stratigraphic Set, for which the intergradation is an important feature.

Table 23 provides a summary of core measurements and of form-defining ratios. Figure 56 shows how mean values for two such ratios compare with values for other sites.

Flakes

In this study little importance has been attached to typological category systems for the flakes, and the features of the assemblages have been defined largely by the systematic observation of quantitative and qualitative attributes.

Table 24 shows the approximate frequency of occurrence of the form categories used by Mason (1957) and other authors (J. D. Clark 1964, 1966a,b, and c, 1969; Keller 1973). Given the variability observed in the Acheulean flakes at Olorgesailie, the rare items falling

Table 23

Mean Dimensions and Form-Defining Ratios of Site Samples of Cores [*] *from Olorgesailie*

	N	Wt(g)	Mean L(mm)	Coeff. of var.	B/L	T/B
MFS	21	253	67.6	26.0%	.850	.753
					.085	.125
Hog	10	173	49.8	21.7	.867	.745
					.092	.115
Tr. Tr. M 10	36	263	72.0	22.8	.854	.767
					.119	.156
LHS	9	249	63.8	41.2	.821	.862
					.063	.102
Meng	8	258	71.6	26.2	.908	.665
					.069	.133
Mid	7	244	73.4	17.2	.852	.786
					.089	.145
H/9 A	40	282	69.2	33.5	.872	.743
					.072	.151
H/6 A	3	437	86.3	37.8	.899	.712
					.045	.180
DE/89 C	15	395	78.1	30.9	.905	.778
					.076	.168
B	35	761	96.7	20.3	.918	.855
					.062	.127
A	29	274	70.1	31.5	.903	.766
					.231	.305
MSS	137	415	78.1	30.9	.895	.777
					.123	.194
I 3 T	5	680	60.6	40.5	.891	.741
					.084	.075
O	26	172	64.6	28.5	.851	.745
					.077	.144
M	28	144	55.8	34.9	.864	.756
					.095	.139
FB	17	169	63.6	31.0	.867	.788
					.102	.180
BB A2	21	317	71.9	30.7	.871	.810
					.071	.181
A	16	122	55.4	32.7	.873	.728
					.083	.172
LSS	113	180	62.2	32.6	.865	.764
					.085	.157
Overall	296	244	67.2	26.4	.856	.762
					.113	.147
Regular (biconvex)						
Tr. Tr. M 10	11		64.5		.86	.62
DE/89 A	14		61.7		.88	.62
I 3	18		59.8		.88	.67

[*] "Casual cores" excluded   [†] There are two samples from BBA.

Note: Mean values for breadth and thickness have not been presented but are closely estimated from $\bar{B} = \bar{L} \times \bar{B}/L$ and $\bar{T} = \bar{L} \times \bar{B}/L \times \bar{T}/B$.

Table 24

Classification of Flake Forms in the Measured Samples

	Total	Side-struck	End-struck	Long Quadrilateral	Short Quadrilateral	Triangular	HA Trimming Flakes	Flakes with radial dorsal patterns
MFS	93	52%	48%	-	-	-	4.3%	5.4%
MPS	33	42	58	-	-	-	NC	9.1
Hog	137	59	42	-	0.7%	0.7%	14.6	2.2
Tr. Tr. M 10	175	49	51	-	3.3	1.7	10.4	1.1
USS	438	51	49		1.6	0.9	9.6	3.0
LHS	61	36	65	-	-	-	1.6	6.6
Meng	53	47	53	-	3.8	-	3.8	1.9
H/9	107	65	35	0.9%	4.7	-	29.0	1.9
H/6	37	50	50	-	-	-	5.5	-
DE/89 C	45	71	28	...Not recorded...				
B	129	77	23	-	-	0.8	5.5	0.8
A	45	57	42	-	4.4	2.2	4.5	2.2
MSS	435	61	38	0.2	2.3	0.5	10.8	2.1
FB HL	50	38	62	-	-	-	12.0	4.0
FB	48	43	57	2.1	-	2.1	12.5	8.3
I 3	190	60	40	-	1.6	1.6	18.0	0.5
BBA	48	45	55	-	-	-	2.1	-
BBB	40	45	55	-	2.5	-	20.1	-
LSS	376	53	47	0.3	1.1	1.1	14.6	1.9
ALL	1249	57	43	0.16	1.7	0.8	12.3	2.3
Ternifine	129	41	59	1.5	5.5	8.5	4.6	5.4
Isimila	58	50	50	-	3.4	3.4	5.1	3.4
Abri Ohla	57	37	63	-	5.2	8.8	-	24.5

Note: All flakes were classified either as side-struck or end-struck and the complementary percentages of each are shown. The incidence of flakes which also show special form characteristics are shown in the other columns. The remainder of the samples are simply undifferentiated irregular flakes.

into regular classes such as quadrilateral or triangular flakes can probably be regarded as fortuitous. A few examples of flakes from the Olorgesailie assemblages are illustrated in figure 68.

Figure 57 shows diagrammatically the features of flakes which were systematically recorded on more than 1,500 flakes from seventeen site samples. Table 25 summarizes the

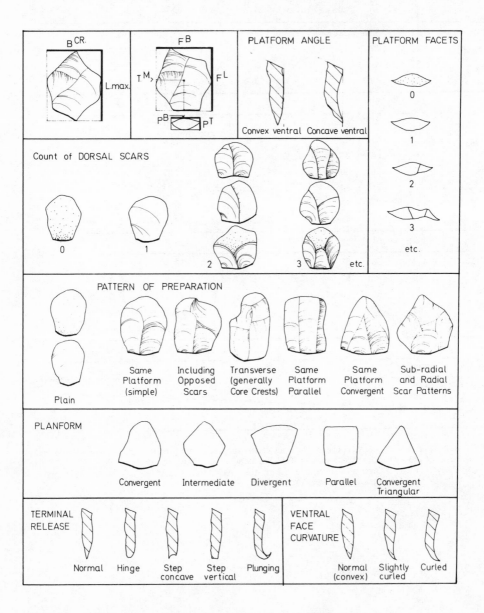

Figure 57.   The attribute system and categorization of flakes.

Table 25

Mean Measurements and Form-Defining Ratios for Flakes

	N	L(Max)		B/L		T/B		FB/FL		Angle
MFS	93	46.1	13.0	.770	.138			1.010	.288	
MPS	33	47.7	13.6	.804	.118			.977	.229	
Hog	137	44.7	12.3	.768	.132	.358	.125	1.052	.305	109.8
Tr. Tr. M 10	175	52.5	16.0	.748	.124	.374	.113	1.030	.353	109.8
LHS	61	51.7	14.7	.747	.124			.968	.283	
Meng	53	47.5	14.3	.782	.127	.369	.137	.993	.262	105.9
H/9 AM	47	45.6	14.2					1.160	.359	
H/9 A	330	48.5	13.1					1.139	.322	
H/6 A	37	47.4	13.4	.706	.124	.388	.124	1.072	.369	112.4
DE/89 C	45	50.4	17.7	.763	.110	.349	.094	1.123	.319	
DE/89 B Leakey	23	55.8	18.9	.798	.105	.346	.092	1.076	.268	111.7
Isaac	106	45.5	12.8	.777	.123	.363	.101	1.243	.588	107.5
DE/89 A	45	49.0	13.7	.770	.092	.399	.083	1.033	.277	111.9
MSS	747	47.7	15.0	.763	.124	.355	.109	1.133	.394	109.0
I 3 O	116	43.8	12.3	.736	.131	.397	.110	1.068	.295	109.7
I 3 M	74	43.0	12.1	.716	.149	.399	.129	1.068	.396	108.2
FB HL	50	51.9	13.3	.768	.124	.396	.095	.934	.249	108.1
FB	48	48.5	13.2	.779	.121	.362	.106	.961	.240	106.8
BBA	48	45.6	12.5	.760	.104	.442	.111	1.023	.306	111.9
BBB	40	42.1	12.1	.772	.126	.387	.127	1.000	.230	105.4
LSS	376	44.9	12.7	.744	.133	.397	.116	1.034	.315	108.7

Note: The samples for which the parameters were measured and computed excluded chips, i.e., flakes for which L+B/2 < 25 mm. This was done to secure comparability between samples collected by Isaac and those collected by the Leakeys.

A supplementary table (E4) in the appendix gives mean values for other attributes (L, TM, TM/B, PB/FB, PT/TM) and of logarithmic transformations of the data, i.e., Log FL, Log TM, Log TM/B.

Results of Analysis of Variance Tests on Flake Sample Sets

Tests[1] for the significance of variation in means among samples in the following sets:

	Log FL	Log TM	FB/FL	Log TM/B	No.
Within the Upper Stratigraphic Set	***	*	ns	**	4
Within the Middle Stratigraphic Set	***	***	***	***	8
Within the Lower Stratigraphic Set	****	***	*	***	5
Between Stratigraphic Sets	***	ns	***	***	3
Biface-dominated Set	*	ns	**	ns	4
Intermediate Set	***	***	***	***	5
Scraper-dominated Set	***	***	ns	*	8
Between-dominance Sets	***	ns	***	***	3

1. Snedecors F. Symbols as in Table 21.

statistics that were compiled. The attributes used were chosen both for their general descriptive value (eg., L, B, Th) and for their relevance to comparison of the Olorgesailie assemblage with others that incorporate disc core, Levallois and blade techniques.

Comparisons with other assemblages are limited by a paucity of data. Because very little comparable information on measurement or attribute frequency from other assemblages has been published, I have used the data from a series of samples that I have had the opportunity to study. The small size of most of these samples renders the results less secure than is desirable. The comparison made in this chapter should be regarded as exploratory, and the conclusions as hypotheses for testing.

Length

For reasons explained in appendix C, flakes with an average length of less than 25 mm were excluded from the Olorgesailie samples that were subjected to intensive measurement and attribute analysis. Figure 58 shows a size analysis for a complete and probably representative population.

Size distribution data for flakes is plotted in figures 58 and 59. One graph shows the overall frequency pattern for maximum length in all Olorgesailie samples combined. A cumulative frequency plot of the same data on probability paper shows a reasonable but imperfect approximation to log-normal distribution (Daniels 1967). However, although the available samples of unretouched flakes show unimodal log-normal distributions with modes situated between 3 and 5 cm, this pattern is probably a distorted version of a bimodal distribution (see Isaac 1968:X-10-11). Figure 35 (chap. 5) shows frequency distribution of length for tools that are predominantly based on flakes, and it can clearly be seen that distinct, separate modalities exist at 4 to 5 cm, and at 15 to 17 cm. It is postulated

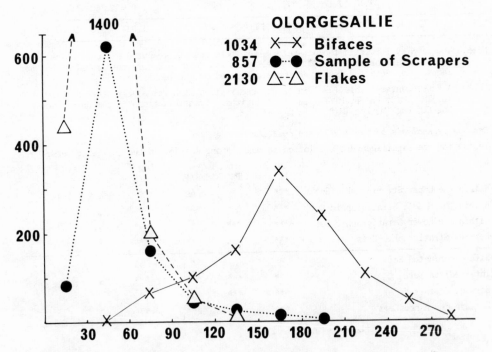

Figure 58. Frequency distributions of size (length) for various categories showing the the bimodal character of the assemblage.

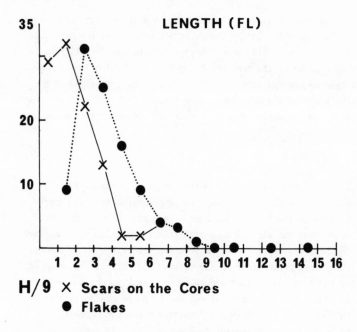

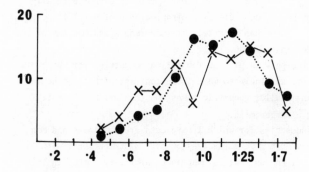

Figure 59. Size and shape of scars on the cores and the flakes from a single site: H/9, Horizon A.

that the large flakes were deliberately struck as blanks for large bifacial tools and that, in spite of the numerical preponderance of smaller flakes, a second mode exists in this size range. The Ternifine assemblage shows comparable bimodality. In some instances, for example the Peninj Acheulean industry, the appearance of a skew, unimodal distribution may well result from the overlap of the tails of more closely spaced major and minor modalities.

The bimodal tendency in flake size is regarded as a fundamental feature of Acheulean industries in Africa and is one that may prove to distinguish them from preceding Oldowan industries and from succeeding Middle and Later Stone Age industries.

Figure 59 shows the frequency distribution of flake scar lengths, as measured on a sample of 51 cores and on the accompanying flakes. This distribution is markedly skew, and has its mode at the lower limit of measurement; scars smaller than 1 cm in length were

ignored. The marked shift toward smaller sizes is interpreted as a consequence of many of
the cores being worked out. Theoretically, during the reduction of a core, the mean scar
size should progressively diminish from a value above the population mean for all the
flakes removed to a value very much below it, the core being finally abandoned when flakes
of a useful size could no longer be removed from it. The frequency distributions of B/L
ratio for loose flakes and the scars on the H/9 cores agree closely. Possibly there is a
slight tendency toward an increased proportion of side-struck and stepped scars on the
worked-out cores.

Variation in Flake Length in Relation
to Stratigraphy and Facies Set

The statistical parameters of samples (means, geometric means, and standard deviations) are summarized in table 25. The differences between sample means are not numerically large; there is 11.4 mm between the highest and lowest geometric means. However,
analysis of variance tests shows that the variation is statistically significant. Neither
the stratigraphic sets nor the biface/scraper dominance sets are credible as homogeneous.
This kind of pattern has already been encountered in the bifaces and scrapers and need not
be discussed separately. For the purposes of most archeological comparisons, a common
pattern with modes between 32 and 40 mm, and means between 36 and 45 mm can be said to
prevail. It can also be seen that there is remarkable consistency between Olorgesailie
and other Acheulean sites, since the means or medians of many samples fall within the
range of variation of the Olorgesailie site samples.

The data given by Mason (1962) for Transvaal sites clearly reflect either a totally
different technological situation or pronounced selective disappearance of small flakes
between manufacture and measurement. Mason has reported only the ranges and medians of
his assemblage and these are included in table 26.

Abri Ohla and Haua Fteah are the only samples of Mousterian industries for which
comparable flake length statistics are available to me. These contrast with the Acheulean
values, the Haua Fteah samples having smaller geometric means and the Abri Ohla sample,
which may be a selected one, having a larger mean.

Two African Middle Stone Age industries for which I have data are Chaminade and Montagu Cave Howiesonspoort. These show much more markedly skew size distributions, with the
modes at or below the 25 mm average dimension that is used as an arbitrary cutoff in this
study.

Elongation

Many African Acheulean industries contrast markedly with Upper Pleistocene industries
in the degree of elongation of flakes. As figure 60 shows, Acheulean industries are commonly dominated by flakes with subequal length and breadth axes. This can probably be regarded as a generalized feature, since flakes ordinarily do not show elongation unless
special care is taken in core preparation.

The available Acheulean samples from Africa south of the Sahara consistently show
this lack of elongation. However, J. D. Clark (1966:215-17) and others have pointed out
that certain Mediterranean Acheulean industries may have included appreciably larger proportions of long, regular quadrilateral flakes, which might be regarded as the forerunners
of blades. Clark states that the Middle Pleistocene assemblage from Latamne in Syria appears to show an early stage of this technological trend. Stronger subsequent expressions
of the tendency have been reported at such important Upper Pleistocene sites as Tabun

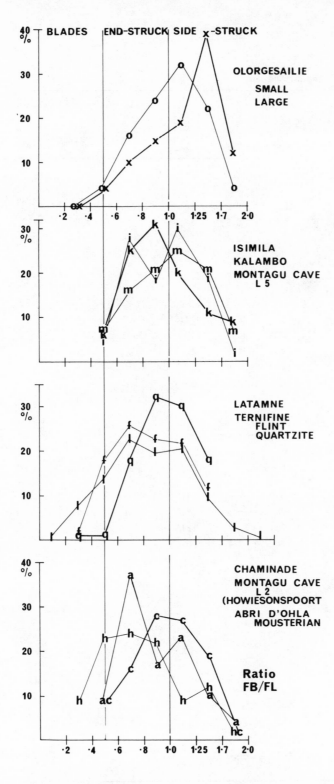

Figure 60. The degree of elongation of Acheulean flakes and selected comparative data. In the top frame x=large, o=small. In the other frames i=Isimla, K= Kalambo, etc.

Table 26
Flake Size and Shape: Selected Comparative Data

	N	Arithmetic Mean	Standard Deviation	Geometric Mean	Median
1. Flake Length					
<u>Olorgesailie</u>					
All small flakes (1)	1815	39.5	13.4	37.5	38.0
H/9 A (most complete sample) (2)	416	36.8	17.3		34.0
I 3 (lowest sample mean) (1)	190	36.4	12.4	34.8	35.2
LHS (highest sample mean) (1)	61	45.1	13.8	43.2	43.5
<u>Other Acheulean</u>					
EFHR (8)	147	56.6			
Isimila (1)	58	40.9	14.5	38.7	38.8
Ternifine (1)	130	40.7	12.6	39.2	38.9
Kalambo Falls A4/62 (1)	35	44.5	15.3		39.5
Montagu Acheulean (1)	63	51.8	16.7		41.8
Amanzi (7)	628	62.1	29.6		54
Cave of Hearths L5 (5)					80.0
Wonderboompoort (5)					45.0
Canteen Kopje (5)					100.0
Kliplaatdrif (5)					55.0
<u>Post-Acheulean</u>					
Abri Ohla (1)	57	51.4	14.7	49.3	52.5
Rooiberg M.S.A. (3)	209	75.3	28.7	69.1	65.0
Chaminade M.S.A. (1)	82	27.2	12.3		25.1
Montagu Cave L 2 (1)	36	28.4	16.0		25.3
Cave of Hearths L 4 (5)	435				80.6
Cave of Hearths L 5 (5)	1570				55.1
Cave of Hearths L 6-9 (5)	399				48.6
Magabeng (5)					15.0
<u>Developed Oldowan</u> (8)					
M N K	226	43.6			
TK Lower	84	43.9			
Upper	183	42.0			
BK	652	37.8			
<u>Oldowan</u>					
DK (8)	198	33.2			
DK (9)	40	34.9			

Table 26 (Continued)

	N	% Sidestruck flakes	Arithmetic Mean B/L	S.D.
2. *Relative Elongation* (f^B/fL)				
Olorgesailie (overall)	1561	57	1.076	0.366
Olorgesailie (lowest site sample value)	50	38	0.934	0.249
Olorgesailie (highest site sample value)	129	75	1.21	0.542
Other Acheulean samples				
Isimila (1)	58	50	0.993	0.304
Kalambo (1)	36	39	1.04	0.38
Various samples (4)	71-481	42-69		
Montagu Cave L 5 (1)	81	63	1.088	0.317
Report by Keller (1966)	16,814	52		
Ternifine (1)	130	41	0.948	0.275
Latamne (10)	180	34	0.875	0.360
EF-HR (8)	147		0.95	
Cave of Hearths L 3 (5)	1180	30		
Wonderboompoort (5)	704	28.6		
Blaaubank (5) (Later Acheulean)	214	11		
Kliplaatdrif (5)	?	28		
Peninj (Lower Acheulean)(1)	76	67		
Middle Stone Age and Mousterian				
Abri Ohla (1)	57	37	0.932	0.304
Rooiberg (3)	209	10	0.678	0.271
Cave of Hearths L 5 (5)	1570	2		
Montagu Cave L 2 (1)	34	24	0.83	0.32
Report by Keller (1966) (4)	9047	37		
Mossel Bay (4)	539	12		
Haua Fteah Lev. Moust. (6)	398		0.75	
Developed Oldowan (8)				
MNK	226	23	0.87	
TK Lower	84	32	0.89	
Upper	183	38	0.89	
BK		28	0.90	
Oldowan				
DK lava (8)	198	33	0.84	
DK lava (1)	40	39	0.95	0.28

Table 26 (Continued)

1. Samples, measured by Isaac, comprised of flakes larger than chips, that is with mean dimension greater than 25 mm. Most of these samples did not include large flakes (greater than 100 mm). For comparability, the large flakes were omitted from Olorgesailie samples unless otherwise stated.

2. Sample including chips and large flakes.

3. From data in Daniel 1967.

4. Isaac and Keller 1968.

5. From Mason 1962.

6. From McBurney 1967.

7. Deacon 1970.

8. M. D. Leakey 1971.

9. A sample measured by G. Isaac, not excluding chips.

10. From a scattergram in Clark 1967a.

(Garrod and Bate, 1937); Jabrud (Rust, 1950), where the Acheulean shows a blade element; and Amudian (pre-Aurignacian), where blade industries occur in a partly Acheulean context. Similar evidence has been encountered at the Haua Fteah; a general review of all these sites is given by McBurney (1967:90-100).

With this situation in mind, it is of interest to compare the data from Latamne and Ternifine with the sub-Saharan pattern. Using length/breadth scattergrams (from J. D. Clark, 1969a) I have prepared the statistical parameters and a frequency distribution polygon of the ratio of Flake length to Breadth for the Latamne flake assemblage. Table 26 shows that the mean and median lie outside the range of recorded values for most sub-Saharan industries and that they reveal an appreciably lower FB/FL ratio (i.e., greater elongation). However, the frequency distribution in figure 59 shows that this does not represent any drastic contrast in the form of the flakes, but indicates instead a slight shift of the mode and a marked extension of the distribution tail into ratios below 0.5. The Ternifine flakes, both the sandstone-quartzite subseries and the flint-chert subseries, are more closely similar to the sub-Saharan pattern, showing only a slightly higher frequency of end-struck flakes.

Margaret Leakey et al. (1969) have reported one Acheulean industry from Kapthurin in East Africa that does include markedly elongate flakes and that may even have blades as a separate modality. The form of the frequency distribution for the B/L ratio in this case has not been determined, so that detailed comparisons with North Africa and the Levant are not yet possible.

The Olorgesailie site samples vary among themselves to a statistically significant degree (table 25), and the differences in elongation, though slight, are perceptible in sorting.

Mason (1962) has not given measurement statistics on the form of his flake assemblages, but he has given data for the relative frequency of side- and end-struck flakes (see table 24). All the assemblages reported by him are dominated by end-struck flakes. The frequencies are so different from those observed in other Acheulean sites that it will be necessary to check the possibility of nonequivalence of classificatory criteria. If Mason's criteria are comparable, then the Transvaal Acheulean assemblages show a more marked degree of elongation than the Middle Eastern series, for which this feature has already been stressed (J. D. Clark 1966a; see also Isaac and Keller 1968).

Figure 59 presents comparisons between the Olorgesailie frequency distribution patterns and those of other industries for which I have data. Great variability is indicated for many regions and time periods; however it seems that some later industries, such as the MSA, Mousterian, and Upper Paleolithic, are comprised of flake series with a much stronger tendency to elongation than is shown by the Olorgesailie samples.

Relative Thickness

Relative thickness can be assessed from the ratio of the thickness at the midpoint to the breadth of a containing rectangle (see fig. 56). Values for the mean of this ratio in the Olorgesailie samples and for various other assemblages are shown in table 25. There is little variation among the Olorgesailie samples, though there is some tendency for flake populations from biface-dominated assemblages to be thinner than those from scraper-dominated sites. This may perhaps be due to the preponderance of biface trimming flakes at the former sites. There also does not appear to be much meaningful difference between the Olorgesailie sample and the other Acheulean industries for which I have obtained data.

There is some tendency for relative thickness to diminish through the stratigraphic sequence, as is shown by the series of set means. This effect is partly confounded with the biface dominance effect, since most of the scraper-dominated sites are in the Lower Stratigraphic Set.

Reconstruction of Flaking Practices

It has long been customary to draw conclusions about the technological basis of a flake assemblage from the number and patterning of the primary scars. However, a typological approach has often been used, with the characterization of flakes as Levallois blades, and so on, on the basis of an intuitive appreciation of constellations of attributes. Only rarely (McBurney, 1948) have attempts been made to analyze a complex by recording separately the individual technological components of the complex. For the purpose of this study, I have recognized four separate multistate attributes as being of primary importance:

1. Scar counts, with (a) primary facets on the talon or, with (b) major (>5 mm length) primary scars and facets on the dorsal face
2. Conformation of the dorsal scars in relation to one another and to the axis of the flake
3. Plan-form of the flake in relation to its talon
4. Flaking angles.

Only a brief summary is presented here. For details see Isaac (1968).

Scar Counts, Platform Facets, and Flake Form

Figure 61 summarizes the results of recording the attributes, defining the number and disposition of the primary scars on flakes. It can be seen that little meaningful variation was found among the Olorgesailie assemblages and that in these aspects, too, the Olorgesailie flake populations are generalized ones, sharing attributes of many early stone industries.

Plan-Form

Partly inspired by a system used by M. D. Leakey, I devised a basis for the analysis of shape among the flakes. Figure 56 shows the scheme of categories, which depends on the position of maximum width in relationship to the flake axis, as outlined below.

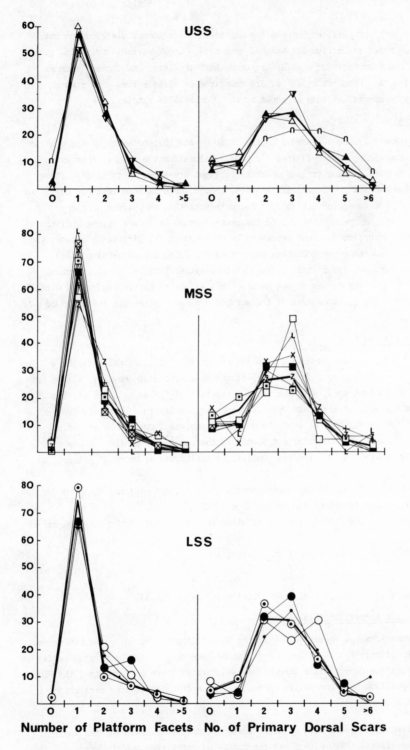

Figure 61. The frequency distributions of platform (left) and dorsal scar counts (right) in Olorgesailie site samples, arranged by stratigraphic sets. The Olorgesailie overall sample is shown in the bold line. See key to site symbols after figure 47.

1. Convergent: a flake with its greatest width at the platform. Two major subforms can be distinguished by (a) curvilinear, ogival, paraboloid, or arcuate edges or (b) straight edges meeting at a point (triangular form).

2. Medially expanded: a flake with its greatest width in the middle third of the length.

3. Parallel: a flake with subequal widths in all three segments.

4. Divergent: a flake with its greatest width in the distal segment, the last third of the length.

In the analysis of the Olorgesailie, Isimila, Ternifine, and Abri Ohla samples, the distinction between la (curvilinear) and lb (triangular) was not recorded. Reexamination of the H/9 series, for which outlines were drawn, shows that category lb represents less than 5% of the forms at Olorgesailie. However, Montagu Cave Layer 5 and Layer 2 and a Middle Stone age sample did show higher incidences (17 to 22%) of irregular triangular forms (see table 27).

Platform Angles

The angle between the platform and the bulbar surface of flakes was measured with a contact goniometer; figure 62 shows a plot of the measurements. This angle corresponds closely with the "re-entrant flaking angle" of S. H. Warren (1914:416). In the Olorgesailie series individual values ranged from 60 to 140°, but the means for all samples cluster fairly closely around the overall mean of 109.1° (standard deviation 14.2°, standard error 0.04°). Table 28 provides some comparative data. It is clear that the pattern observed at Olorgesailie is common to many other Acheulean industries. Many but not all later industries have mean angles closer to 90°.

Stratigraphic Sets and Biface/
Scraper-Dominated Sets

If all the foregoing attributes are considered collectively, it can be seen that at Olorgesailie there is only ambiguous evidence for trends of diachronic change. With the exception of the I 3 sample, the Lower Stratigraphic Set of samples has high means for relative thickness. But the same degree of contrast does not separate the middle and upper sets. Other slight shifts in the means for the stratigraphic sets may indicate increasing size and an increasing number of primary facets, but the range of means within the sets overlaps to such an extent that the set means cannot be regarded as representative.

The scraper-dominated set of samples tends to be relatively thicker than the biface-dominated set. This is true also of DE/89 A and Basal Bed A, both of which may be compound in origin (see chap. 3). This set of samples may also tend to have relatively short, broad talons. Both of these differences might be attributed to the paucity of biface trimmers. There are certainly no differences in flake attribute frequencies or core types suggestive of any radically divergent technological differences.

Because of the unequal distribution of biface- or scraper-dominated sets among the stratigraphic sets, the apparent differences partly confound one another so that, for instance, it becomes uncertain whether the Lower Stratigraphic Set flakes are relatively thick because of a time trend or because most of them came from scraper-dominated sets, and vice versa.

Conclusions on the Technology Represented

This attribute analysis was conducted partly in order to define the technological

Table 27

Classificatory Categories of Flake Plan-Form (After M. D. Leakey 1971)

Site	N	Convergent (mainly rounded)	Medially Expanded	Divergent	Parallel
Olorgesailie					
MFS	96	35%	23%	20%	22%
MPS	33	33	30	18	18
Hog	137	27	28	29	17
Tr. Tr. M 10	270	26	31	27	16
USS	537	29	29	25	17
LHS	79	39	18	22	22
Meng	60	25	35	23	17
H/9 AM	37	44	12	24	20
H/9 A	385	26	26	29	19
H/6 A	37	27	40	22	11
DE/89 C	Not recorded				
B	100	26	32	27	15
A	58	41	22	26	10
MSS	744	29	27	27	17
I 3	303	28	26	26	20
FB HL	51	28	16	33	24
FB	51	29	16	35	20
BBA	48	23	21	38	19
BBB	41	44	12	24	20
LSS	224	29	23	28	20
Olorgesailie total	1847	29	26	27	17
Isimila	54	33	26	11	30
Kalambo A4/62	36	30	14	33	22
Montagu L 5	76	44	13	23	18
Ternifine	105	32	31	18	18
Chaminade	45	40	25	20	18
Montagu L 2	46	29	9	17	46
Abri Ohla	55	44	16	18	22

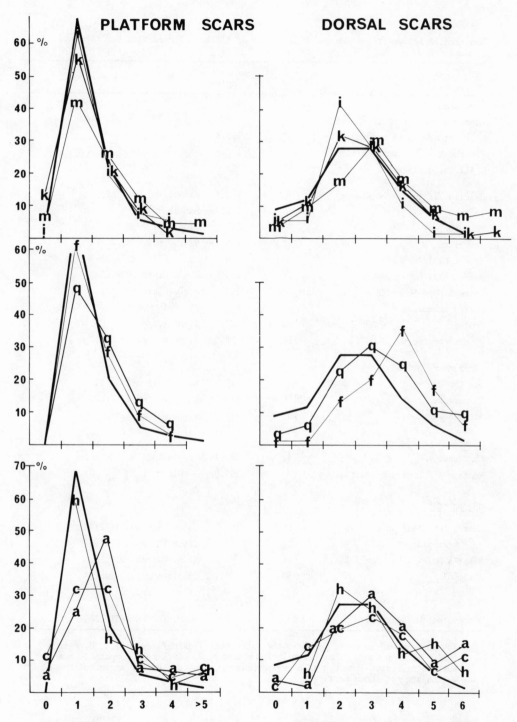

Figure 62. Frequency distributions for numbers of platform scars and dorsal scars in the Olorgesailie sample overall (bold line) compared with samples from other sites. i=Isimila; k=Kalambo Falls; m=Montagu Cave Acheulian; q=Ternifine quartzite; f=Ternifine flint; h=Montagu Cave Howiesonspoort; c=Chaminade; a=Abri Ohla Mousterian.

Table 28

Mean Angles between the Talon and Bulbar Face of Flakes: Olorgesailie and Selected Comparative Data

	N	Mean Angles	
Acheulean			
Olorgesailie all small flakes	1561	109.1	
Lowest sample mean (BBB)	40	105.4	
Highest sample mean (H/6A)	37	112.4	
All large flakes	56	112.0	
Isimila K18 to 2, and K14	56	109.1	Sample msd GI, Chicago
Kalambo	30	106.3	Sample of A4/63
Montagu L 5	75	110.7	Sample of sfc. X
Ternifine	128	110.4	Sample msd. GI, Paris
Broken Hill Acheulean	36	108	J. D. Clark 1959:21
Broken Hill Hope Fountain	25	110	J. D. Clark 1959:21
Zambezi Hope Fountain	unspec.	113	J. D. Clark 1950:81
Kharga Acheulean	81	114	Caton-Thompson 1952:70
Peninj	58	103.0	Isaac 1967a
Upper Dovercourt	150	110.5	S. H. Warren 1951:122
Clactonian (Britain)			
Clacton	213	119	S. H. Warren 1951:122
Swanscombe Lower Gravel	150	110.5	S. H. Warren 1951:122
Stoke Newington	208	111	S. H. Warren 1951:122
Middle Stone Age etc. (Africa)			
Chaminade	41	100.4	Sample msd. GI, Berkeley
Montagu L 2 Howiesonspoort	27	105.0	Sample of L 2
Levalloisian and Mousterian (North Africa and Europe)			
Kharga Levalloisian	86	104	Caton-Thompson 1952:78
Aterian	52	104	Caton-Thompson 1952:87
Baker's Hole	45	92	S. H. Warren 1951:122
Abri Ohla	58	109.1	Sample msd. GI, Paris
Other			
Broxbourne (Mesolithic)	149	103	S. H. Warren 1951:122

The angle measured corresponds to the "reentrant flaking" angle of S. H. Warren 1914. It is presumed that Caton-Thompson and J. D. Clark took comparable measurements. Caton-Thompson also measured the more obtuse bulbar angle but these values are not shown here.

features of some Acheulean flake assemblages and partly in order to set up, as a standard for comparison, an example of attribute frequencies in a technologically generalized industry. These data may be useful in assessing the extent and intensity of regular patterned flake preparation in other assemblages where the matter is in doubt.

It is thought that the generalized patterns detected in this study arose from a variety of elementary flaking procedures. These included (1) the trimming of the 60 to 90° edge angles of large tools with either a stone or a bar hammer, (2) the more or less ad hoc working at the edges of suitable angular blocks or split cobbles, with the eventual reduction of these to multifaceted subspherical polyhedral cores with irregular flaking patterns, and (3) perhaps some conscious regularization of method in the exploitation of the flaking potential of both faces of discoid cores. Rare examples of both the tool trimming flakes and flakes from the biconvex discoid cores resemble Levallois flakes. Intensification of the regular patterns of work could easily have given rise to either a Levallois or a Mousterian disc core type of debitage.

Very few running elongate flakes appear to result from this kind of technical situation, and the predominance of equidimensional flakes may well be a distinguishing feature of Lower Paleolithic industries in Africa and elsewhere (Isaac and Keller 1968). The possible existence of this distinction has not been made explicit before.

It has already been shown that the bimodal frequency distribution of the length of flakes and flake tools implies that the production of the two groups of flakes could be regarded as separate processes. Furthermore, by comparison with the small flakes, the large flakes have a slight tendency toward a subradial dorsal preparation pattern and toward more primary scars. It is quite possible that some of these large flakes derive from simple "proto-Levallois" cores of the kind that characterize the Middle Acheulean in Morocco (Biberson 1961b:447-62) or the Vaal (Söhnge, Visser, and Lowe 1937). Only two cores of a size suitable for yielding large flakes have been recovered from Olorgesailie. These are more in the nature of gigantic discoid cores than Levallois cores. The question cannot be settled until sites are located at the outcrops where the large flakes were struck.

The features of the flake industry have limited relevance for taxonomic purposes, partly because suitable comparative data is scarce and partly because the patterns appear to be widespread and generalized. However, further study is certainly called for, and it may be that attribute analysis, such as that reported here, will help to define technological trends leading from generalized patterns to the more elaborate procedures of many Upper Pleistocene industries.

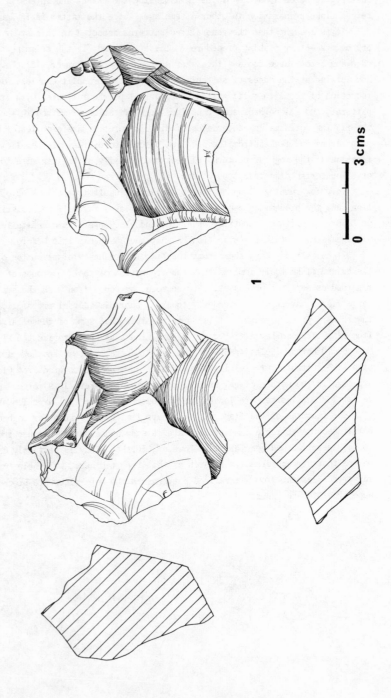

3 cms

0

1

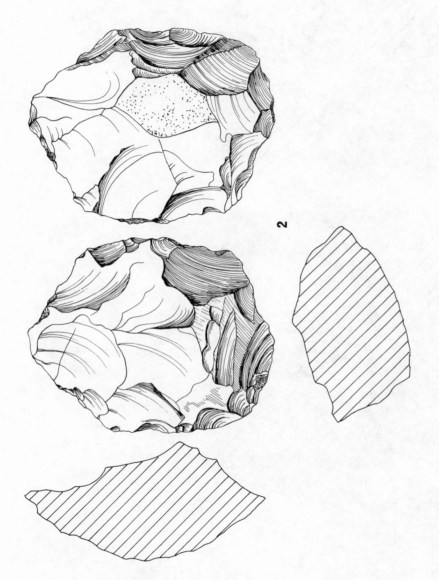

2

Figure 63. (1) *Core, "pseudo-levallois."* Subregular biconvex disc (cf. "Clacton biconical") with a subradial scar pattern partially dished by a large bold scar on face (ii).
6/5 (scars on opposing faces). MFS; (2) *Core, regular biconvex discoid.* Slightly sinuous
sharp edge; centripetal (radial) scar patterns on both faces with slightly asymmetric poles.
11/12 scars. MFS.

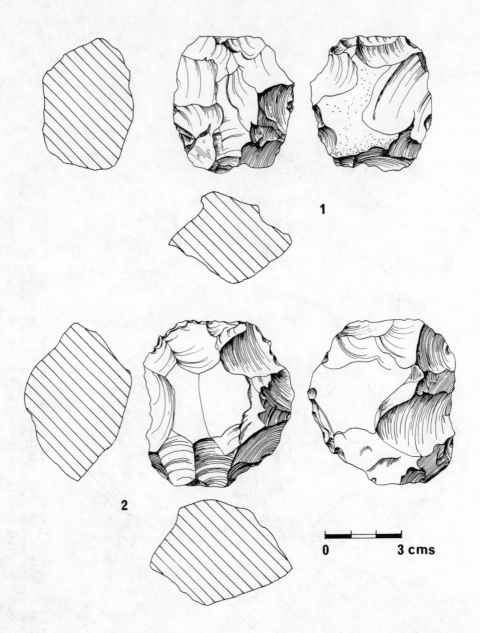

1

2

0   3 cms

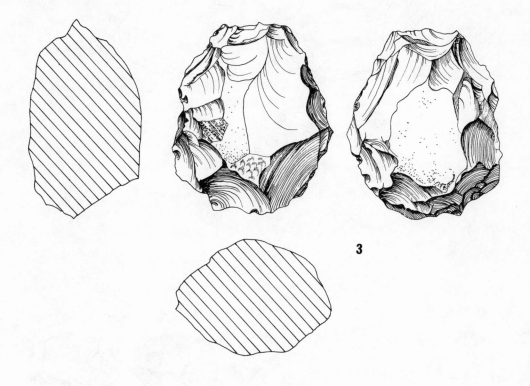

3

Figure 64. (1) *Core, subregular biconvex discoid.* ? On a cobble fragment slightly sinuous sharp margin; subregular centripetal flaking on each face with the pole distorted to a minor keel. 7/6 scars. MFS; (2) *Core, subregular biconvex disc*, approaching biconical form. 11/7 scars. DE/89 A; (3) *Core, biconvex, discoid.* A worked-out core with domed faces and a battered perimeter. 10 major scars/9 major scars. MFS.

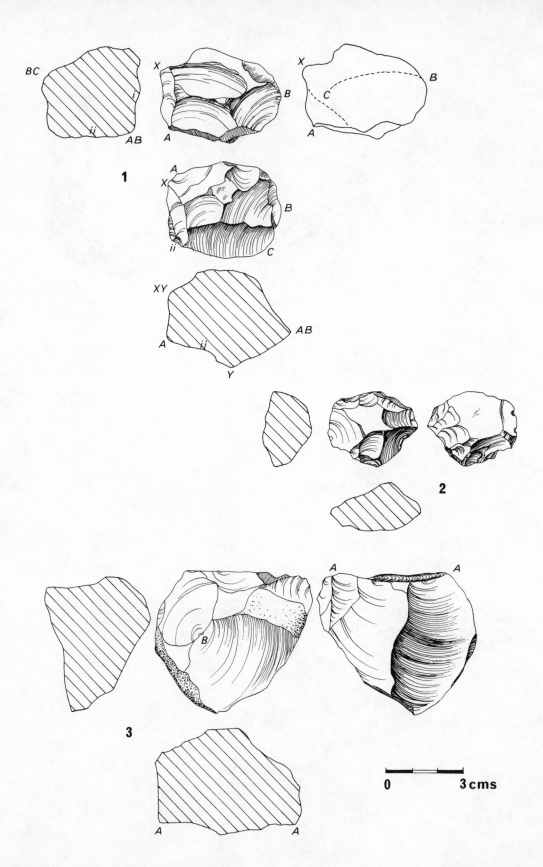

1

2

3

0   3 cms

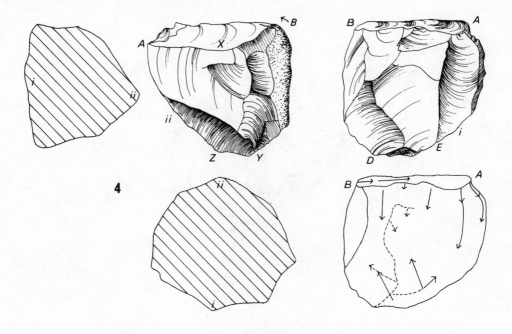

Figure 65. (1) *Core, multifaceted (irregular polyhedral)*. Two arcuate edges set obliquely
to one another: a-b-c spiraled "bifacial" edge; 4/5 scars. x-y arcuate edge, 3/2 scars.
LHS; (2) *Core, polyfaceted irregular bipolar discoid*. With a single sinuous equatorial
edge. 5/4. BBA; (3) *Core, irregular, multifaceted multidirectional*. On a cobble segment;
two edges: a-a', 4/1 scars. b, 1/1 scars. Tr. Tr. B4; (4) *Core, irregular polyfaceted
multidirectional*. Two edges at more or less right angles on a subtetrahedral form; a-b
arcuate, 1 platform preparatory scar (B) and 5 unidirectional scars; x-y-z sinuous bifaci-
ally flaked edge 3/3. Tr. Tr. B4.

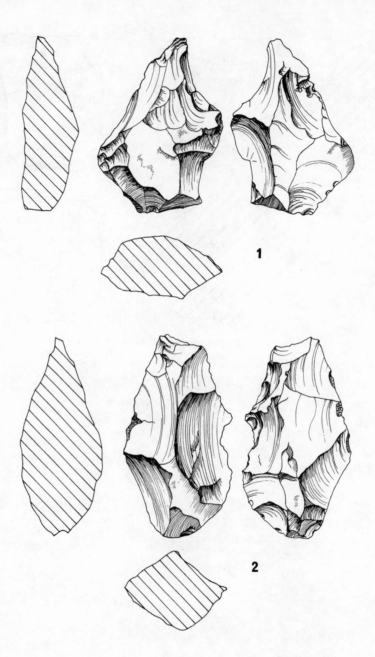

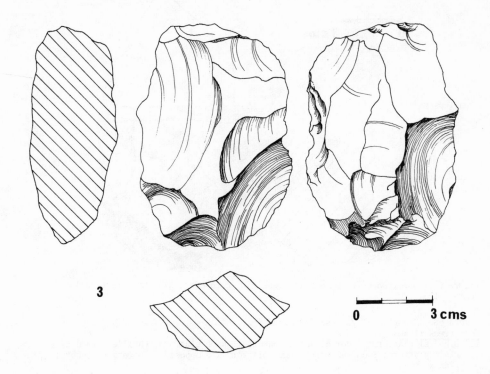

3

0   3 cms

Figure 66. (1) *Core, sharp/"spindly biface."* With an awl point. I 3 M; (2) *Core,
spindle/"chunky biface."* I 3; (3) *Core, sharp bipolar/"chunky biface."* I 3.

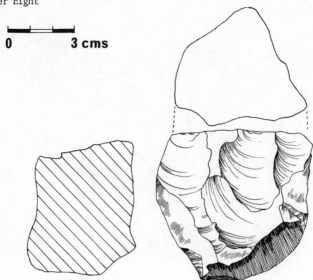

0   3 cms

Figure 67. *Core, casual.* On a split cobble; single edge, a-b, unidirectional 4 or 5 scars. LHS.

Figure 68. *Examples of flakes: H/9 A, various.*
End-struck flakes
1. Dihedral platform; 3 dorsal scars, parallel, same platform. Parallel-sided plan form
2. Plain platform; 3 dorsal scars, same platform and opposed. Convergent (subtriangular) plan form
3. Plain platform; 4 dorsal scars, same platform and parallel scar pattern. Parallel-sided plan form (? = short quadrilateral flake of Mason 1958)
4. Plain platform; more than 4 dorsal scars, same platform and parallel scar pattern. Medially expanded plan form
5. Plain platform; 3 dorsal scars, same platform and parallel scar pattern. Divergent side plan form
6. Plain platform; 4 dorsal scars, convergent pattern, convergent (curvilinear) plan form
7. Dihedral platform; 3 dorsal scars, same platform and indeterminate, divergent plan form
8. Plain platform; 5 dorsal scars, same platform and opposed/near subradial pattern. Intermediate plan form
Side-struck flakes
9. Plain platform; 2 dorsal scars (i.e., 1 + plain) same platform. Convergent (a) plan form
10. Plain platform; 3 dorsal scars (i.e., 2 + plain) same platform. Convergent (a) plan form
11. Plain platform (edge strip); two dorsal scars, same platform. Parallel plan form
12. Cf. hand ax trimming flake. Plain platform (edge strip); 4 dorsal scars, opposed and same platform. Medially expanded plan form
13. Dihedral platform; 3 dorsal scars, same platform. Parallel plan form. Step vertical terminal release
14. Plain platform; 4 dorsal scars, subradial pattern. Divergent plan form
15. 3 facets to platform (2 + cortex); 4 dorsal scars, same platform convergent. Convergent (b/a) plan form
Examples of "hand ax trimming flakes"
16. Side-struck, plain platform (edge strip); 4 dorsal scars, same platform scar pattern. Intermediate plan form
17. Side-struck, plain platform; 2 dorsal scars, same platform scar pattern. Divergent side plan form. Step-fractured terminal release
18. Side-struck, plain platform; 3 dorsal scars, same platform scar patterns. Divergent side plan form. Curled axial section
19. Side-struck, plain platform (edge strip); 2 dorsal scars (1 + plain surface). Convergent (a) edge plan form. Curled axial section
20. Side-struck, plain platform (edge strip); 5 dorsal scars, same platform and opposed scar pattern. Curled axial section
21. End-struck, platform with 3 facets; 3 dorsal scars, same platform/convergent scar pattern. Irregular convergent sided platform. Curled axial section

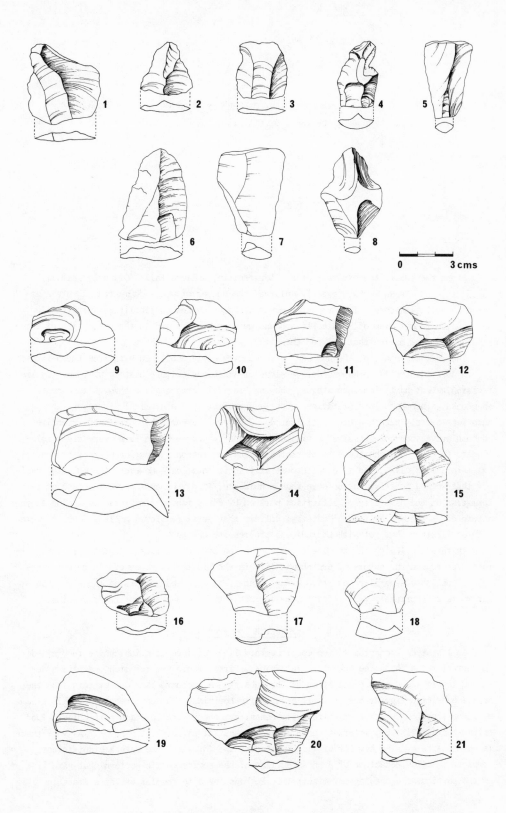

0   3 cms

9. A COMMENTARY ON THE CONTRIBUTION
OF THE OLORGESAILIE EVIDENCE

Since the 1950s, the excavations at Olorgesailie, Kalambo Falls, Olduvai, Isimila, Kapthurin, and elsewhere have greatly enlarged the number of well-documented Acheulean artifact association sets. This research movement opens up new possibilities for precision and realism in our view of Middle Pleistocene culture history and in the perception of the kind of cultural milieu that existed then.

The initial impact of the new and as yet incompletely published data from these sites is, in part, disruptive. Many older versions of Acheulean culture history will now require revision. Neat partition into stages, showing "logical" progressions through time must be abandoned, since such interpretations grossly oversimplify a historical situation that was much less orderly than had been anticipated. The newer research has disclosed extensive noncumulative, non-"progressive" variation. Further, because there is no very clear relation to geography, a challenge is presented to the conventional practice whereby archeological material is classified into culture-stratigraphic entities. However, the puzzling variety that we now perceive may be more than a nuisance, it may be an important source of information on the diversity of activities pursued by early man. It may also be a clue to the nature of protohuman systems of material culture that persisted for a million years or more with oscillations but yet without radical, progressive changes.

In this concluding chapter I want to comment on how the Olorgesailie data fit into current research on the nature of protohuman life in the Middle Pleistocene. In recent years I have published several comparative essays that treat selected aspects of the same issues, and where appropriate I will refer to these, rather than repeat the entire discussion.

Research Concerns

As I stated in chapter 1, two complementary lines of investigation can be recognized in current research on the Acheulean in Africa. First, there are research operations designed to provide direct elucidation of the subsistence economy, land use pattern, and the socioeconomic configurations of early prehistoric hominids. The data needed for this kind of reconstruction consists of paleoenvironmental evidence, site location particulars, food refuse characteristics, information on intrasite spatial patterns, and so on. As yet, there is no one site or site complex of Mid-Pleistocene age for which the data are sufficiently complete to allow deduction of even an outline of the socioeconomic pattern that gave rise to the particular archeological materials. Perhaps the site complex of Terra Amata in southern France comes closest to this ideal, but as yet we have only preliminary reports by which to judge (de Lumley 1969, 1975). Under these circumstances, it seems to me that we are obliged to adopt an explicit strategy of compiling fragmentary information in the belief that from an accumulation of related evidences we will be able to discern patterns. The chief importance of the Olorgesailie evidence summarized in this volume is that it, along with that from Olduvai, Isimila, Kalambo, and so on, comprises a major contribution to the stockpile of information. These are much more complete records than anything we have had until recently, but even so, interpretation must remain tentative until we have even more data.

The second line of research is focused on the collections of artifacts themselves. Most paleolithic archeologists, myself included, tend to believe that the assemblages of humanly flaked stones that we recover in quantities from sites such as Olorgesailie preserve a great deal of valuable information about the craft traditions, the cultural affinities, and the economic life of the hominids who made them. This belief is in part a matter of faith, and there is a danger that in our enthusiasm we may overextend the exegesis of stone artifacts. It sometimes appears that all of us treat stone artifacts as infinitely complex repositories of paleocultural information and assume that it is only the imperfections of our present analytical systems that prevent us from decoding them. But is this really so? In this monograph I have sought to make a contribution toward an answer to this question by formally examining the nature and degree of orderly morphological differentiation among the specimens in each major artifact class. It seems to me that we need a better assessment of regularity and pattern among artifacts before we can estimate how much information artifact assemblages may have locked-up inside themselves.

Among paleolithic archeologists in general, attention has come to be firmly focused on a particular issue with broad implications, namely the question of the meaning of variety among assemblages. Conventional culture-historic classificatory systems allowed for contrasts between assemblages of the same age but in different regions. However, paleolithic archeology has run into the recurrent problem of perceiving extensive variety among assemblages of indistinguishable age and from the same region. How can this be explained? There is a mounting body of literature dealing with this problem in both Europe and Africa. Important early contributions concerned with Africa were those of Louis Leakey (1934, 1953), J. D. Clark (1959), Kleindienst (1961), and Howell and Clark (1963). Isaac (1972b) and L. R. Binford (1972) have provided general theoretical reviews, each written from a rather different standpoint. I currently recognize three main competing lines of interpretation:

1. The view that distinct contemporaneous but contrasting sets of artifact assemblages represent distinct cultural systems maintained over time through the coexistence of more than one hominid species.

2. The view that in many cases the differentiation between contemporaneous and contiguous assemblages reflects the fact that various activities within the same cultural system may have resulted in the discard of different tool kits at different sites.

3. The view that perhaps the critical functions of stone tools during the Middle Pleistocene could be fulfilled by a wide range of forms and that therefore the characteristics of assemblages were free to vary within broad limits in response to influences such as raw material characteristics, stylistic idiosyncrasy, and random walk oscillation of norms.

There is healthy debate going on as to the relative importance of each of these factors. As Cole and Kleindienst (1974) point out, it is to be anticipated that variation was determined by a complex multiplicity of influences. One effect of the debate has been that the

study of the artifacts has been brought into closer conjunction with research into economy
and ecology. The debate has also served to emphasize our great need for more objective
evidence concerning the function of the stone tools that are so painstakingly studied.
Later in the chapter I will review the specific contribution of the Olorgesailie evidence
to this discussion.

These then, are general questions that currently engage the attention of archeologists
who study Acheulean material in Africa. I will confine all further commentary to specific
remarks on how the Olorgesailie data affects the issues. I will first continue with consideration of the artifact studies and then return to questions regarding early human ecology and behavior.

The Implications of the Artifact Studies

Research on the stone artifacts from Olorgesailie can be thought of as involving three
hierarchic levels:

1. Intra-assemblage variation, the study of intrinsic patterns of differentiation
among artifact forms.

2. Interassemblage variation among Olorgesailie samples, as measured both by their
typological composition and by the statistics of appropriate attributes and measurements.

3. Comparisons of the data on the Olorgesailie spectrum of forms and assemblages with
such data as are available for other relevant assemblages.

Each of these topics has been treated in each of the four chapters devoted to the specifics of the artifacts, and only a very brief integrating commentary is necessary here.

Intra-assemblage Differentiation

If we consider the assemblage of humanly modified stones as a whole, we can conceive
of it as a constellation in multidimensional morphological space. Each important aspect of
differentiation can be thought of as a Cartesian axis:

Axis 1--core/flake dichotomy.

Axis 2--tools/nontools (an axis dependent on the intensity of deliberate modification;
        shaped tools grade through casually trimmed and modified pieces into items
        lacking secondary trimming, the so-called debitage).

Axis 3--utilized (edge-damaged)/nonutilized (undamaged).

These axes of differentiation are common to many assemblages, but the particular configuration of forms is specific to Olorgesailie and perhaps a number of other Acheulean assemblages.

I currently recognize four intrinsic artifact modalities within the Olorgesailie assemblages. These are: large, predominantly bifacial tools (bifaces); small, predominantly unifacial tools (especially scrapers); cores; and flakes and flake fragments.

Each of these modalities has been considered in a separate chapter, except for cores
and flakes, which, following convention, have been arbitrarily lumped together as debitage.
Each of the modalities has a pattern of internal morphological differentiation of its own,
which has been graphed and discussed in the appropriate chapter. As already explained in
chapters 6 and 7, each of the two major tool classes comprises a series of intergrading subforms with what appears to me to be only weak and incomplete division into distinct subsidiary modalities. I offer the hypothesis that internal differentiation is less advanced than
in many, but not all, later paleolithic industries. This hypothesis needs to be tested by
the development of appropriate techniques of measurement (Isaac 1972a, b, c).

Interassemblage Variation at Olorgesailie

By 1961, Maxine Kleindienst had already perceived that there were probably two aspects to the differences among site samples. First, there were gross differences in composition of the assemblages with regard to entirely distinct tool classes, such as large cutting tools, scrapers, choppers, picks, and so on. Second, there were subtle differences on the level of subtypes. My own studies convince me of the correctness of this view of the variation. Perhaps one of the most valuable contributions of the artifact data reported in this volume is the inclusion of statistics that provide formal measures of the subtle second level of variation. Until recently such data has not been available.

Chapter 5 contains the data on typological composition and triangle graphs that help to put this in comparative perspective. Suffice it to say here that, although there is a multivariate situation, the principle axis of variation is easily recognized as one determined by the relative proportion of bifaces and small scrapers. This view was arrived at by myself and others intuitively, but subsequently it has received support from a principal components analysis (see below). The two artifact classes tend to show inverse correlation, so that if one is present in large or even moderate proportions, the other tends to be scarce. This effect is of course exaggerated by the fact that the two classes are the two major constituents in percentage tables, and therefore their values must show a partially inverse relationship. But this does not account for the fact that these two classes occur only rarely in subequal numbers within assemblages, even though the ratio in the overall aggregate is 0.53 scrapers to 0.47 bifaces. Figure 69 displays the Olorgesailie data on this aspect of variation in the context of data from other East African sites. A tendency to a bimodal pattern is apparent.

Thus the existence of variety among the assemblages is clear enough, but it is a fair question to ask whether the Olorgesailie research helps to resolve the problem of how the differences in assemblage composition are to be explained. It seems to me that although the research makes a very useful contribution, it does not lead to a definite solution. There are several explanatory models that can be tested for their applicability to the Olorgesailie assemblage composition. These models can best be expressed as a series of questions and answers.

1. Does the scraper to biface ratio show any consistent trend of change through time (stratigraphy)? Present indications are that they do not; they seem to oscillate (see fig. 32 and Kleindienst, 1961).

2. Does the scraper to biface ratio show consistent patterning in relation to the context of the sites from which the artifact samples derived? Table 29 examines this proposition with regard to (a) topography and (b) substratum. The results are interesting, if inconclusive. There is a strong tendency for the sites yielding biface-dominated artifact assemblages to be associated with watercourses and sand. This in turn suggests other hypotheses. For instance, could the proportion of bifaces to small tools at these sites have been severely distorted by hydraulic forces? Perhaps so, but because proportion of flakes is not distorted to the same extent (table 29), one cannot embrace this explanation without reservations. Another hypothesis might involve a functional (activity) connection between biface-dominated assemblages and the gallery woods that perhaps grew along the watercourses. The Olorgesailie data suggest such hypotheses but cannot also be used to test them.

3. Does the scraper to biface ratio show any clear relationship to economic patterns such as might be indicated by the abundance of bone food refuse? Within the Olorgesailie series no such correlation emerges, though faint indications of a relationship have been

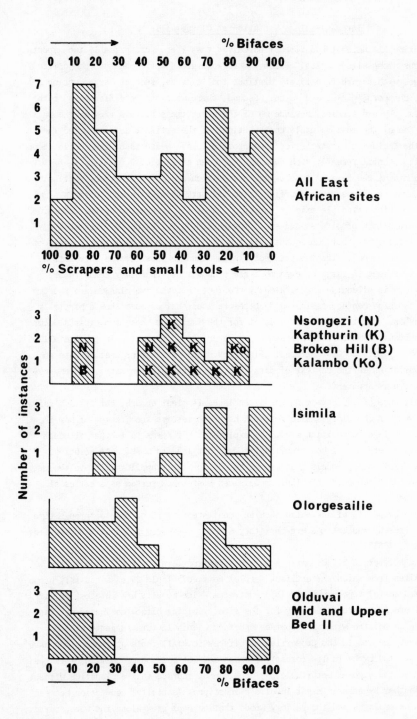

Figure 69. The frequency distribution of an index of biface to small tool dominance in various East African assemblages (after Isaac 1975:518). In the construction of the diagram, percentage bifaces = number of bifaces x 100 ÷ no. of bifaces + no. of small tools; percentage small tools = 100 - percentage bifaces.

Table 29

Relationships between Artifact Sample Composition and Site Characteristics

	Biface-Dominated Samples	Intermediate	Scraper-Dominated Samples
A. *Topographic Location*			
Water courses traversing lake-side flood plains	Meng H/6 A DE/89 B Mid	H/9 A DE/89 C DE/89 A Tr. Tr. M 10	
Floodplain (without clear channel associations)			LHS FB (?)
Rocky ridge flanked by floodplains			I 3
Basin Margin			MFS
Lakeshore zone (?)			Hog ? MPS ?
B. *Substratum/Matrix*			
Sand	Meng H/6 A DE/89 B Mid	Tr. Tr. M 10	Hog MPS
Sand and silt		H/9 A DE/89 C DE/89 A	
Clay (soil) or silt			MFS LHS
Rocky soil			I 3

suggested from the totality of Middle Pleistocene data (Clark and Haynes 1969; Binford 1972; Isaac, 1975).

In short, the contributions of the Olorgesailie data to the question of the meaning of variety in composition are valuable, but they do not provide definitive answers. Clearly, to make progress with this inquiry we need patience and a larger stock of data. It should be pointed out that we cannot classify the Olorgesailie sites with regard to important contextual variables, such as season of occupation, character of plant food consumed, character of nonstone artifacts prepared, and so on. As Kleindienst (1961:45-46) foresaw, these variables remain untested potential explanatory factors.

The matter of subtle differences in the tool morphology of individual samples has been treated in detail in earlier chapters, especially in chapter 6. I find the clear pattern of idiosyncrasy for so many of the sites extremely provocative. It seems very possible that this will prove to be an important clue to the nature of the sociocultural milieu that prevailed in East Africa during the part of the Middle Pleistocene represented by Olorgesailie. I have argued elsewhere that this phenomenon of site idiosyncrasy may reflect a pattern of microcultural differentiation of individual bands or social groups, which in turn may indicate a cultural transmission system that combined high inertia to large-scale change, with kaleidoscopic variability of material culture habits at a local level (see chap 4 and Isaac 1972b, e). I regard this insight as potentially the most important outcome of my part in the Olorgesailie research.

Kleindienst (1961:44) has suggested that "when dealing with short-time-span sites variability on the level of sub-types is more likely to be related to stylistic cultural differences, and that variation on the level of major types is more likely to be related to functional differences." I find this hypothesis to be extremely plausible, but it must be stressed that it has not yet been confirmed. As we have seen, such tests as can be applied at Olorgesailie have proved inconclusive. Following the work of Binford and Binford (1966, 1969) and of L. R. Binford (1972), many observers seem to have assumed that activity differences have been proved to be the crucial determinants of diversity among broadly contemporaneous, sympatric sets of Paleolithic industries. However, despite the attractiveness of the model as an explanatory principle, there are as yet very few cases where independent contextual evidence has provided substantiation. Perhaps the best described and documented case comes from Australia (Gould, in press) (see Bordes and Bordes 1970; Mellars 1970; Isaac 1972b). I remain convinced of the likelihood that activity differences will prove to be an important factor, but I am also inclined to think that paleolithic prehistorians may have an exaggerated sense of regularity in the determinants of stone artifact morphology. Let us imagine that a very wide variety of assemblages of sharp stones could fulfill equally well the basic requirements of nonagricultural humans, namely cutting up carcasses, making spears and digging sticks, and so on. Might we not then expect a fair amount of erratic variation both in assemblage composition and in the details of morphology? In recognition of this possibility, I have floated the alternative hypothesis of random walk variation (Isaac 1969, 1972a, b, c). This is in the nature of a null hypothesis, a nonexplanation. I will be perfectly content to see it rejected by the demonstration that positive explanations can apply.

What bearing does the Olorgesailie data reported here have on the proposition that more than one distinct cultural system (tradition), may be represented among the sites? As mentioned in chapter 1, it has long been considered a possibility that the scraper-dominated assemblages derive from a culture separate from that which gave rise to the hand ax-dominated assemblages. The second culture has been called African Tayacian (Leakey 1953) or Hope Fountain (S. Cole 1963; Posnansky 1959), while the hand ax-dominated assemblages are treated as part of the far-flung Acheulean entity.

More recently, a somewhat analogous dichotomy between groups of assemblages has been demonstrated among the material from Middle and Upper Bed II, Beds III and IV, and the Masek Beds at Olduvai. Mary Leakey regards the distinct assemblage types as indicative of two separate cultural systems, the Developed Oldowan and the Acheulean (M. D. Leakey 1971, 1975). Personally I am skeptical of the coexistence of contrasting, stable cultural traditions that maintained their separate identity over hundreds of thousands of years. My skepticism is reinforced by the complexity of variation now known to exist. As shown earlier, the report dividing the sites into biface- and scraper-dominated sets does not help very much to produce homogeneous entities. These are matters of opinion, not of fact, and inasmuch as we are dealing with a bio-social condition that was not yet fully human and a situation that possibly involved species diversity among hominids, I think that the two-culture hypothesis needs to be retained as one alternative, to be tested whenever possible.

The argument might be advanced that since many of the Olorgesailie assemblages have been partially disturbed by geological agencies, the variation among them is likely to be due to the differential action of hydraulic forces. If the only distinctions between assemblages were connected with the relative proportions of objects of different sizes, then the argument might be taken as a substantial objection to either activity difference or random walk interpretations. However, it is difficult to imagine that natural processes could separate out, from homogeneous sources, sets of specimens with such subtle distinguishing features as have been observed among the site samples of bifaces at Olorgesailie. Presumably, compound aggregates would tend to average the features of diversified source assemblages. As has already been pointed out, those assemblages at Olorgesailie that show signs of both disturbance and transport (e.g., H/9 A and Tr. Tr. M 10), also show close to average values for most attributes, but they tend to show much larger variances for these attributes than do other sites. This is consistent with the notion that they are in fact mixtures of material derived from a series of idiosyncratic source assemblages. All that was claimed for the Olorgesailie artifact aggregates is that they represent sufficiently small space-time segments to be worthwhile units of comparative study. The results seem to bear this out, though it is clear that processes of distortion and blurring have intervened between the manufacture of the pieces and their archeological discovery.

Olorgesailie Assemblages in Relation
to Others from East Africa

Comparative data and discussion has been included in chapters 5 to 8, and the specifics need not be repeated here. Taken as a whole, the comparison of typological composition, biface morphology, small tool morphology, and debitage characteristics show that there is extensive overlap in the range of values observed at Olorgesailie for almost all variables and those recorded for site clusters such as Kalambo Falls and Isimila. Clearly the Olorgesailie series belongs within the Acheulean Industrial Complex of eastern Africa. However, there are distinctive tendencies that differentiate the series from all other described sets; for example heavy-duty tools such as choppers, core-scrapers, and picks are less prominent in the Olorgesailie assemblages than in the Kalambo or Isimila series. Perhaps the overall differences are sufficient to justify the designation of an Olorgesailie Industry, but since it is entirely possible that this entity will never be found anywhere but at Olorgesailie, I prefer to keep it as an informal category, rather than offer an elaborate definition as required in the resolution of the 1965 Burg Wartenstein symposium (Bishop and Clark 1967:879-90).

The Olorgesailie assemblages are generally more refined than those from Lower Pleistocene sites, such as Olduvai EF-HR (M. D. Leakey 1971) or Peninj (Isaac 1967a). That is to say, the bifaces show higher mean scar counts, are thinner relative to their breadth, and so on. They are therefore to be classified as Upper Acheulean. However, since they are somewhat less refined than some other assemblages, such as those from Kapthurin, one might be tempted to designate them as Middle Acheulean, but in fact reliable chronological distinctions among these later sites are not possible (Isaac 1969, 1975; M. D. Leakey 1975). Figure 70 shows the best estimation of time relationships between Olorgesailie and the other Acheulean sites in East Africa.

Multivariate Analyses

L. R. Binford (1972) has published a factor analysis of data on the East African Acheulean. His study includes the Olorgesailie assemblage samples reported by Kleindienst (1961). R. N. Corruccini and I have repeated the experiment, using a principal components analysis (PCA). Both of these multivariate studies are of interest here because they were done after the conventional univariate analysis already reported in this volume, and they thus provide a kind of cross-check on some of the conclusions reached. Details and a full

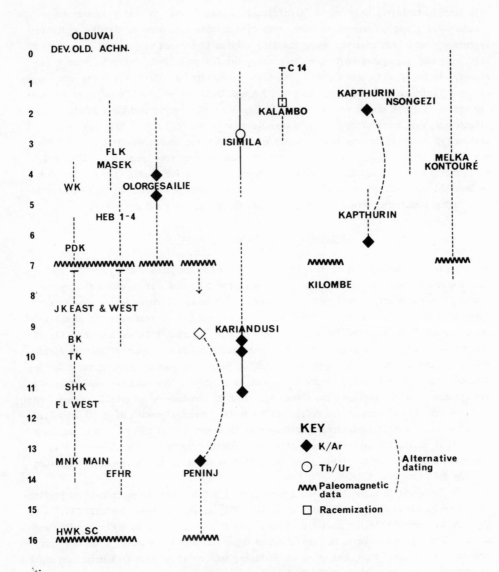

Figure 70. Estimation of time relationships between Olorgesailie and other Acheulean sites in East Africa.

discussion of the limitations of the methods are being prepared for publication elsewhere.

The principal components and the factor analyses in question both involve a search for structure in a matrix of correlation coefficients between variables (see table 5 in appendix E). In this case the primary variables were the percentage frequencies of tool categories in each of the individual assemblages. This procedure provided (1) information on sets of artifact frequencies that show a tendency to mutual correlation or inverse correlation (R-mode analysis) and (2) information on interrelationships among the assemblages, as expressed by their positions along the component or factor axes (Q-mode analysis) (fig. 71). For a more complete explanation of the application of PCA or factor analysis to archeology, see Binford and Binford 1966; Hodson 1969; Doran and Hodson 1975:chap. 8.

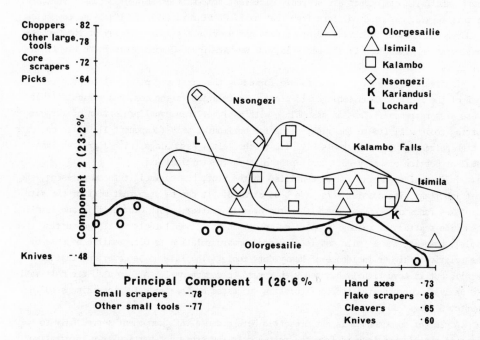

Figure 71. A graphic display of the results of a principal components analysis done by Corrucini and Isaac (unpublished). The input data were the percentage values of tool categories in 32 assemblage samples from various sites in East Africa. Data from Binford (1972:tables 1-4). The plot presents the values of original data x eigenvector (P component) for each sample. Alongside the axes values are presented for the coefficient of correlation of individual input variables with the particular principal component (eigenvector). This serves as a guide to the archeological meaning of the axes. More detailed information, a key, and numerical data are presented in appendix E5. B = Broken Hill.

The tables in appendix E show that among the East African assemblages the frequencies of tools that are commonly based on large flakes--namely hand axes, cleavers, knives, and (large) flake scrapers--form a weakly but positively correlated set. This set as a whole is inversely correlated with another set comprised of small scrapers and other small tools. This pattern in the data is identified by the analysis as the major component of variation among the assemblages, and some 27% of all variation is associated with it. This feature of the computer study thus offers confirmation of the long-recognized distinction between large cutting tool-dominated assemblages and small tool-dominated assemblages.

The second principal component is determined largely by intercorrelations between picks, choppers, core scrapers, and other large tools, that is to say, the heavy-duty tools. There is no set of tools that is inversely correlated with the heavy-duty tools, though knives and spheroids show a weak tendency to opposing trends. This component also coincides with an aspect of variation that was picked out by Kleindienst.

The third principal component has discoids as the main associated category. However, scrutiny of the primary percentage data shows that one extreme value for the percentage of discoids, that for the site of Lochard, has largely determined the component, thus rendering it of doubtful value for this comparative study.

On the advice of R. Corruccini, I am not attempting to interpret components beyond the third one, because in this particular analysis the eigenvalues associated with the fourth and fifth components are scarcely different from that of an average input variable. In this regard, our study differs from that of L. R. Binford (1972). (See also comments by Doran and Hodson 1975:204.) Binford does not provide a graphic display of the Q-mode configuration discovered by the analysis, but we have found Q-mode plots to be highly informative.

In figure 71 the Cartesian axes are formed by the first two principal components. Each of the individual assemblages is plotted in relation to the compound variables that these axes represent. Thus an assemblage with a higher than usual proportion of large cutting tools will lie to the right along the horizontal axis (component 1), while one with a high percentage of small tools will lie to the left. Assemblages with a greater than usual proportion of heavy-duty tools plot high on the vertical axis.

Individual assemblages are identified on the plot, but to facilitate comparisons, the most important site complex sets have been circled. It can be seen that most of the site complexes tend to occupy a zone within the overall scatter. Both Olorgesailie and Isimila show wide scatters of values in relation to component 1 (small tools vs. large cutting tools); however, the Isimila set is displaced upward relative to Olorgesailie because of the relatively higher incidence of heavy-duty tools. The Kalambo set overlaps that of Isimila but is more tightly bunched with regard to component 1. All in all, the multivariate analysis corroborates the configuration suggested by the triangle plots discussed in chapter 5 (figs. 36-38).

A plot of component 3 is not presented here because this component serves only to separate the site of Lochard from the rest and is therefore not particularly informative in interpreting data from Olorgesailie.

Our principal components analysis follows closely the outcome of L. R. Binford's factor analysis. Binford (1972) argues that these results overthrow the "traditionalist's paradigm," that is, he claims that the data contradict the expectation that "associations between things, the coincidence of recognized classes of tools at sites, will exhibit directional patterns of gradual replacement and drift in their relative proportions when plotted accurately either temporally or spatially." I certainly agree that the entirety of observed variation cannot be accommodated within an orthodox culture-historic taxonomy in which all important variants are segregated in space and/or time, but I also think that the configuration may in some degree reflect such patterning.

We do not have unequivocal measures of the time relations among the assemblages in this analysis, but of course we do know their geographic distribution. The site complex sets shown in figure 71 are in fact drawn from widely spaced localities. The partial clustering of contiguous samples in the diagram could be taken to indicate that differentiation in relation to space and very possibly time are important aspects of the total observed variation. The results obtained seem to me to favor the kind of multistranded interpretation supported by Cole and Kleindienst (1974).

A multivariate analysis such as this provides a useful clarification of both pattern among the variables and of comparative relationships between assemblages and between assemblage sets. However, the results in and of themselves do not throw light on the causes of variation. For that we are thrown back, as in a conventional study, on the context of the archeological material.

The Context of the Sites

The opportunity to pursue detailed paleoanthropological research at Olorgesailie derives from the preservation of archeological materials in the context of the comparatively
fine-grained sediments of a small lake basin. However, in view of the extensive evidence
for partial rearrangement and disturbance of the assemblages, questions should be asked
about the degree to which inferences concerning the association patterns of the artifacts
are anthropologically valid. There are no simple answers to these questions, but the
Olorgesailie study does perhaps help to make explicit issues that also affect other important sites, such as Amanzi, Isimila, Kalambo Falls, Olduvai, and Latamne. Most archeological studies of early Pleistocene sites tend rather naively to distinguish between undisturbed occupation floor sites on the one hand and redeposited materials in geological context on the other. In fact, the studies at Olorgesailie show that in this site complex
some kind of intermediate condition is most frequent. I suspect that this will also prove
to be the case in many other Pleistocene open-air sites, and readers should be alert for
the possibility even when it is not discussed in the reports.

In chapter 4 strong arguments have been presented in favor of the view that the Olorgesailie assemblages have been subject to rearrangement and local redistribution, rather
than to extensive transport. I do not think that, for the most part, the assemblages have
been formed by secondary combination of materials from widely scattered sources. However,
since this is an hypothesis, not a direct empirical observation, alternatives need to be
kept in mind.

If this position regarding a lack of long-distance transport is accepted as a working
hypothesis, then it follows that inferences can be made from the distribution of materials
within the sample sector of the lake basin. On this basis, I advance the secondary hypothesis that the association of concentrations of archeological materials with watercourses
is a functional, anthropological association that reflects the propensity of the prehistoric peoples to establish camps along the banks and beds of the ephemeral streams. This
proposition requires further testing at Olorgesailie and elsewhere.

Similarly, the nature of associations between artifacts and bone remains must be ques-
tioned. In the most important instance, DE/89 B, a highly unusual bone assemblage consist-
ing of the fragmented bones of all body parts of a large number of *Theropithecus* baboons
was concentrated in exactly the same area as the dense occurrence of artifacts. It is
hard to imagine that this represents a composite aggregate drawn from formerly widely dispersed materials, but of course there is a small, finite possibility that this occurred.
Meanwhile, I offer as a working hypothesis the interpretation that the artifact concentration and the baboon bone concentration were functionally associated. The broken bones
presumably became mixed with the artifacts because they were the food refuse of at least
some of the tool-makers. This seems to be a reasonable interpretation, but it is not an
established fact. I currently and tentatively make similar judgments regarding other artifact concentrations where the density of broken bones is noticeably higher than background for the beds as a whole. The importance of scavenging relative to hunting is unknown.

From the foregoing, it can perhaps be appreciated that one of the contributions of
the Olorgesailie study has been to raise the level of awareness of these kinds of inter-
pretational problems,which although they are all too seldom discussed, are in fact widespread. I have explicitly developed the method of presenting the interpretations that I
favor as one set of alternative hypotheses, rather than as privileged visions of the past.

Contribution to Economic and
Ecological Interpretations

The Olorgesailie research has yielded a variety of data with implications for our understanding of protohuman life during the Middle Pleistocene. The most important lines of
evidence are the distribution pattern of sites within the sedimentary basin, the paleotopographic setting of sites, and the presence of introduced raw materials from varying sources.
Of particular interest are the quantities and characteristics of bone and food refuse,
which has direct implications for reconstructing subsistence economy and perhaps also for
inferences about social configurations.

In chapter 4 the specifics of the evidence is discussed and interpretation is carried
to limits that verge on speculation. Here one might legitimately ask what the Olorgesailie
research has taught us about life in the Middle Pleistocene that is interesting to know?
The answer that one can offer is not a resounding one, and yet the findings do represent a
valuable first-stage exploration of a period of prehistory for which until recently only
information on selected aspects of stone artifact morphology existed. The findings can be
briefly listed.

1. Archeological materials can be mapped within a segment of an ancient landscape.
They occur both as a general broadcast scatter and as concentrated patches. These latter
attest the organization of hominid movements around spatial foci, some of which were presumably home bases. This organization is a distinctive and fundamental characteristic of
human behavior that arose during evolutionary differentiation (Washburn 1965; Isaac 1969,
1972a,b). It was already becoming established as a pattern in the early Pleistocene (M. D.
Leakey 1971).

2. The universal low density scatter of artifacts in all terrestrial facies of the
Olorgesailie Formation attests the persistent presence of hominids in the basin. They were
presumably not rare creatures; one might imagine them as being present among prehistoric
fauna in the same proportions as lions have been among recent fauna.

3. Some sites suggest recurrent usage over a period of time; others, with smaller
quantities of materials, may represent only one or a very few brief occupations. The configurations are consistent with a model of life patterns that involved frequent movement of
the base of operations but intermittent return to favored localities.

4. The study suggests hominid preferences for certain kinds of topographic settings
as locales for camps, notably the sandy channels of ephemeral watercourses. Perhaps these
were preferred in part because they were tree-lined. Other favored spots were rocky prom-
ontories jutting into the alluvial flats.

5. The Middle Pleistocene hominids were habitual tool users. Over the period of time
represented by some of the sites, they transported literally a ton or more of stones for a
distance of several miles. Presumably this aspect of their behavior is indicative of the
mounting importance of equipment. The quantities of transported stone exceed anything so
far observed in the Lower Pleistocene (cf. M. D. Leakey 1971; Isaac, 1975), and one would
guess that such transport implies the invention of bags or baskets--devices of fundamental
importance for the human way of life (Lee 1968).

6. The artifacts show that the early humans who frequented the basin were moderately
skilled craftsmen. Most of the material reflects a deft but opportunistic exploitation of
the principles of conchoidal fracture, but the biface series shows that these early humans
were also cognizant of a limited but very specific repertoire of arbitrary designs.

7. The variety among the vestiges of stone tool kits is hard to interpret as yet, but

at least it seems to imply either a flexible strategy of forms created in relation to varied needs or a varied set of norms and rules belonging to particular groups, or most likely, some combination of both. In any event, the patterning is distinctly nonrandom.

8. Meat was clearly an important food item at some sites (e.g., DE/89 B, I 3). At sites where bone refuse is sparse we are left uncertain about whether this sparseness reflects a dietary pattern that did not include much meat. This is a difficult conclusion to reach, since preservation is so uncertain. However, it can be said that the archeological observations at Olorgesailie are consistent with a model of a subsistence system that involved opportunistic acquisition of substantial quantities of meat, but which may well have had gathered foodstuffs as its staple (cf. Isaac 1971, 1975).

9. The mass of *Theropithecus* bones from DE/89 B presumably attests skillful hunting, which probably involved group coordination and cooperation. This document joins an older one from Olduvai site BK, and roughly contemporary ones from Torralba, Terra Amata, Vértesszöllös, and Choukoutien. Together they have considerable importance for our understanding of the dynamics of the later phases of human evolution.

One million years ago, there already existed upright, bipedal, tool-making hominids. They seem to have lived in cooperating groups and to have hunted and shared food, but the archeological record suggests that by our standards their capacity for culture was slight. Very probably they lacked effective language and did not have the mind-brain configuration that we regard as human. By the end of the Middle Pleistocene, some fifty to one hundred thousand years ago, both the archeological and osteological evidence attest the emergence of hominids with fully human capabilities.

From this view of the record, it can be seen that during the intervening time span, the so-called Middle Pleistocene, the last crucial evolutionary changes that culminated in mankind as we know it, took place. In spite of that, the Middle Pleistocene is not a particularly glamorous period to study. It lacks the drama that surrounds the pursuit of origins in the Lower Pleistocene and Pliocene. By comparison with the later Pleistocene it also lacks artifacts with a strong aesthetic appeal, such as that of some upper Paleolithic material, the art and fastidious craftsmanship of which allows us to identify ourselves with its makers. Many aspects of the Middle Pleistocene record strike even enthusiasts as monotonous--it lacks well-defined culture-historic patterns. For almost a million years, tool kits tended to involve the same essential ingredients seemingly being shuffled in restless, minor, directionless changes. Nonetheless, the social and economic milieu of life in the Middle Pleistocene unquestionably molded many important aspects of our species, and it seems to me that in order to understand the evolutionary dynamics that were involved, we need to build up a file of case studies. None will be complete, but from a sufficient set we can surely gain useful insights. The investigation reported in this volume should be viewed simply as a part of the groping exploration of a vast formative period of prehistory. All interpretations are offered as hypotheses to be rejected or refined through further research.

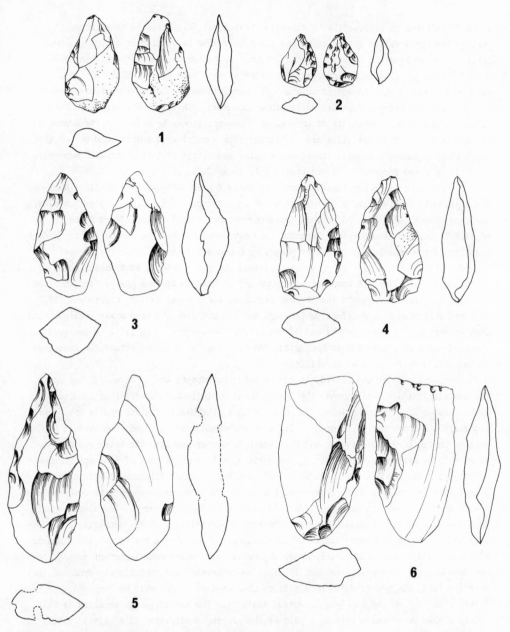

Figure 72. (1) Typological designation: Hand ax, subclassic; Primary form (blank): cobble; Material: basalt; Length: 100 mm; B/L: 0.62; BA/BB: 0.65; BA/B: 0.56; T/B: 0.5; Sc.: 16; Scar Bifac.: 0.5; Site: I 3; Field Cat. no.: 289. (2) Typological designation: Hand ax, subclassic; Primary form: indet.; Material: trachyte; Length: 55 mm; B/L: 0.73; BA/BB: 0.56; BA/B: 0.50; T/B: 0.57; Sc.: 19; Scar bifac.: 0.9; Site: I 3; Field Cat. no: 41. (3) Typological designation: Picklike biface; Primary form: indet.; Material: trachyte; Length: 130 mm; B/L: 0.57; BA/BB: 0.92; BA/B: 0.51; T/B: 0.74; Sc.: 31; Scar bifac.: 0.8; Site: I 3; Field Cat. no: MS 982. (4) Typological designation: Hand ax, classic; Primary form: indet.; Material: trachyandesite deeply altered; Length: 131 mm; B/L: 0.52; BA/BB: 1.07; BA/B: 0.94; T/B: 0.56; Sc.: 22; Scar bifac.: 0.7; Site: I 3; Field Cat. no: 74. (5) Typological designation: Hand ax, subclassic/trièdre; Primary form: side-struck flake; Material: basalt deeply altered; Length: 196 mm; B/L: 0.41; BA/BB: 0.49; BA/B: 0.43; T/B: 0.58; Sc.: -; Scar bifac.: -; Site: DE/89 C; Field Cat. no: MS 991. (6) Typological designation: Cleaver; Primary form: side flake; Material: Magadi trachyte; Length: 172 mm; B/L: 0.55; BA/BB: 1.25; BA/B: 0.91; T/B: 0.46; Sc.: 16; Scar bifac.: 0.8; Site: I 3; Field Cat. no: 184.

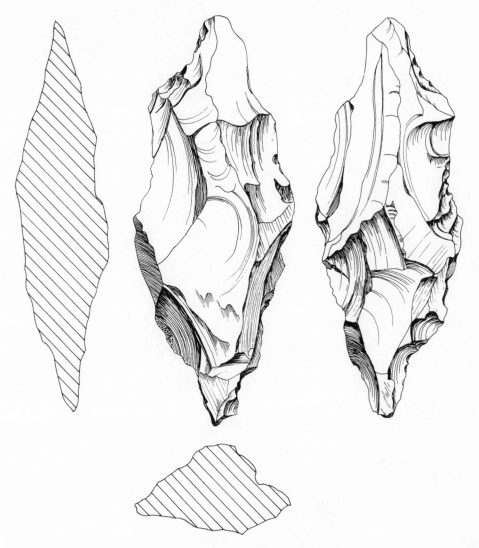

Figure 73. Typological designation: Biface, other/hand ax subclassic; Primary form: indet.;
Material: trachyte; Length: 149 mm; B/L: 0.42; BA/BB: 1.00; BA/B: 0.75; T/B: 0.56; Sc: 23;
Scar bifac.: 0.9; Site: I 3, surface; Field Cat. no: -.

APPENDIX A

A Brief Summary of the History
of Quarternary Research at Olorgesailie

<u>1919</u>

The first record of the Olorgesailie Formation and of the presence of artifacts in
the area was made by J. W. Gregory (1921:221)

> During our journey from Naivasha to Magadi Mr. Hobley and I found independently
> near our camp at the Ol Keju Nyiro, at the northern foot of Mount Ol Gasalik,
> some large roughly chipped axes similar in size and character to those found by
> Harrison. The specimens collected (Pl. IV, Fig. C, reduced 1.3 dia.) were lying
> on a bank of white diatomaceous earth which seemed to have been dug by such im-
> plements. The earth was probably used as a paint, and these thin stone axes
> would make effective hand hoes in digging it. One specimen was in two pieces
> lying 4 ft. apart, showing that it had been broken at the place. These flakes
> are certainly suggestive of Paleolithic workmanship. They are not to be ex-
> plained as unfinished implements which were to be ground and used elsewhere,
> since no ground stones of this type have been found in the country. They indi-
> cate the occupation of the Rift Valley N. of Magadi by Paleolithic man.

<u>1941-42</u>

Dr. and Mrs. Leakey were restricted to the Nairobi area by wartime duties and patrol
rationing. Aware of Gregory's discovery and of the archeological potential of the Olorgesailie area, they devoted as many weekends as they could to a systematic search for artifacts and fossils. They were assisted by Italian prisoners of war and by various volun-
teers (L. S. B. Leakey in MS and pers. comm.). Dr. Leakey (in MS) records the discovery
of the Main Site and its subsequent investigation and preservation as follows:

> On April 20, 1942 Mrs. Leakey who was exploring in one direction with Miss M.
> Davidson (now Mrs. Fagg) suddenly came upon an incredible concentration of hand-
> axes (see Plate) lying on the surface, while almost simultaneously the writer and
> Mr. F. Mengetti who were exploring in a slightly different direction came upon
> two other, but small concentrations a little distance away. Thus was discovered
> the now famous Olorgesailie Prehistoric Site which is now a 'Museum on the Spot'
> in the care of the Kenya National Park Trustees.
>   In 1943 a period of 18 days local leave was utilised to start excavation
> work. The party consisted of Dr. and Mrs. Leakey, Mr. A. S. Arkell of the Sudan,
> Miss M. Davidson, Miss M. Paine, Mr. F. de V. Kirk and Mr. G. Alkins together
> with a number of trained native excavators.
>   Excavation was continued in 1944 and 45 with the help of some Italian Pris-
> oners of War who were in charge of a Senior Prisoner of War, Mr. Giuseppe Della
> Giustina, who is now the curator of the site under the National Parks organisation.
>   In 1946 Dr. (now Professor) Robert Shackleton was specially flown out from
> England to complete a detailed geological survey and map of the site upon which he
> had done some preliminary work in 1944 while employed by the Kenya Geological Depart.[1]

---

1. See Isaac, in press.

(In 1944) as a result of negotiations with the Masai elders in whose Reserve the site is situated, the Masai gave the site to the Nation - to be fenced in and protected for all time - and the Kenya Government provided annual grants to enable the fencing of the site, and the erection of shelters over some of the trenches . . . in order to make a Museum on the spot.

Early in 1948 Mr. F. Andrews was appointed warden of the site which by that time was attracting many visitors, but in the latter part of the year he resigned owing to ill health.

Towards the end of 1948 the care of the site was vested in the Kenya National Parks Trustees and gazetted as a National Park and Mr. Della Giustina was brought out from Italy to be the new warden.

In January 1947 the Delegates to the Pan African Congress on Prehistory paid a formal visit to the site and on that occasion Sir Gilbert Rennie formally declared the site as open to the Public as a Museum on the Spot.

1948

Mr. Andrews, first warden of Prehistoric Sites, excavated two trenches in Member 1 at the northern end of the enclosure. These trenches were adjacent to the Basal Bed A site of Leakey (chap. 3) and exposed the fragmentary hippopotamus carcass and the gigantic *Elephas recki* humerus, which are preserved in situ as an exhibition. No excavation records are available.

1948-57

Mr. G. della Giustina, as warden of Prehistoric Sites, was engaged mainly in construction and maintenance work. He excavated a small trench adjacent to the Meng site. The small patch of flakes and tools discovered there, is preserved in situ under a roof. No excavation records are available, and the material has not been included in this study.

1952

Mr. Brian Baker, then of the Geological Survey of Kenya, undertook the mapping of the Magadi area, which was defined to include most of the Olorgesailie lake basin. Mr. Baker reported the principal results of Dr. R. M. Shackleton's previous work and did the necessary work to relate them to his own findings concerning the regional sequence (Baker 1958).

Dr. Merrick Posnansky served as warden of Prehistoric Sites during these years. He excavated a site in Member 11 (termed MPS) (Posnansky 1959).

1959-61

Mr. Richard Wright served as National Parks Warden of Prehistoric Sites, with Olorgesailie as his principal charge. Mr. Wright excavated a long narrow sounding trench to the west of the Main Site (Grid Squares HKL/11). No notes on results have been obtained, but draft sections were found among the papers in the warden's office. Workmen reported the trench entirely sterile. Mr. Wright and the geologist Mr. Briscoe also studied exposures of sediments on Mt. Shanamu that resemble the Olorgesailie Formation and contain Acheulean artifacts. He located a site in the brown silts of a piedmont fan deposit in the Koora (post-Olorgesailie Formation) where numerous Levalloisian flakes and neat discoid and tortoise cores occur (Koora Levallois Site). Mr. Wright has expressed his intention to publish accounts of these finds.

1961-65

In October 1961, I was appointed National Parks Warden of Prehistoric Sites and was based at Olorgesailie. In making the appointment on behalf of the National Parks, Dr. L. S. B. Leakey gave me every encouragement to seriously undertake the completion of researches and the publication of a full report. Subsequently both he, Mrs. Leakey, and the Trustees of the Museum and of the Parks gave their full cooperation to the research.

After the renovation of facilities, a start on fieldwork was made in 1962. However, for financial reasons, the National Parks abolished the post of warden and gave the site over to the administration of the Museums Trustees of Kenya in July of 1962. With the support of small grants from the Wenner-Gren Foundation, the Boise Fund, the British Institute of History and Archaeology in East Africa, and the British Academy, I was able to remain as honorary warden and continue excavation and research.

In January 1963, I accepted an appointment as deputy director in the newly established (National Museum) Centre for Prehistory and Palaeontology in Nairobi, under the direction of Dr. L. S. B. Leakey. A principal duty remained the Olorgesailie research. Field seasons were possible in 1963, 1964, and 1965.

Excavations were undertaken first in Member 1 (Site I 3) and then on the Main Site (DE/89, H/9, H/6, and other smaller trenches). Finally, some further work was undertaken outside the enclosure (MFS and LHS). During the 1965 season, detailed stratigraphic research was the principal undertaking.

In September 1965, I left Kenya to spend a year at Cambridge University preparing a report on the Olorgesailie research. I completed the work while serving on the staff of the Department of Anthropology, University of California at Berkeley. The report (Isaac 1968) was accepted as a Ph.D. thesis at Cambridge University.

The archeological sites continue to be administered by the National Museums of Kenya, but as far as I am aware, no extensive scientific studies have been undertaken at Olorgesailie since 1965. Much remains to be done. The publication of this monograph should permit new and more specific questions to be formulated and appropriate investigations organized.

APPENDIX B
Technical Reports

1. Petrological Identification of Six Samples of the
Principal Varieties of Lava of Which Artifacts
and Manuports are Composed

A brief report by J. Walsh of the Kenya Geological Survey, September 1965, with supplementary description of weathering[1] added by Glynn Isaac.

Sample A--a variety denoted as Trachyte II (Tr. II) in notes. This lava is slightly fissile
and exfoliates in sheets.

"*Trachyte*. Hand specimen: Fine-grained black lava with rare small phenocrysts.

Microscope slide: Phenocrysts of anorthoclase and green aegirine-augite in trachyte-
textured groundmass of anorthoclase laths with interstitial aegirine-augite and
magnetite."

Alteration: to slightly greenish gray or yellowish gray. Phenocrysts and granular
matrix become more obvious.

Sample B--denoted Trachyte I (or fine Trachyte) in notes, etc.

"*Trachyandesite*. Hand specimen: Fine-grained black lava with rare small phenocrysts.

Microscope slide: Phenocrysts of andesine and greenish gray augite in trachytic-
textured groundmass of anorthoclase laths with interstitial augite and magnetite."

Alteration: to pale yellow gray color.

(A subsidiary variety with more phenocrysts was termed Trachyte IP. Not examined
petrographically.)

Sample C--denoted Basalt or B1 in notes.

"*Basalt*. Hand specimen: Fine-grained black lava with small phenocrysts.

Microscope slide: Numerous phenocrysts and microphenocrysts of pale greenish gray
augite, magnetite, and red brown iron mineral which has apparently replaced
olivine, in fine-grained granular groundmass of labradorite, augite, and magnetite."

Alteration: to a rather dirty ochrous yellow color with the surface tending to spall
off and the center tending to crumble.

---

1. Refers to alteration under conditions of burial in the volcanic silts of Member 1
or Member 7 at Olorgesailie.

Sample D--termed Nephelenite (N) or green trachyte in notes.

"*Phonolite*. Hand specimen: Fine-grained black lava with elongated black glassy phenocrysts.

Microscope slides: Phenocrysts of gray green augite and nepheline in very fine-grained granular groundmass of nepheline, felspar, green aegirine-augite and magnetite."

Alteration: Undergoes deep alteration (with loss of morphological detail) to a strong green color. The large nepheline phenocrysts become conspicuous white cavities.

Sample E--termed Pyroxene Porphyry (PP) in notes.

"*Andesite*. Hand specimen: Fine-grained brownish black lava with numerous black phenocrysts.

Microscope slide: Phenocrysts of augite, brown hornblende, andesine, and magnetite in semi-trachytic groundmass of andesine, augite, and magnetite."

Alteration: to pale grayish yellow with conspicuous black phenocrysts.

Note: None of these samples can be identified with particular outcrops, but rocks with these characteristics occur in abundance in the varied suite of volcanics that compose Mount Olorgesailie (see Baker 1958).

2. Molluscan Fossils

Mollusk fossils are exceedingly rare in the Olorgesailie Formation. The following list summarizes identifications made by Dr. B. Verdcourt, then of the East African Herbarium.

Member 1 at I 3	*Bithynia neumanni*
GS 406 Members 5-8 at Loc. F.	*Bithynia neumanni*
GS 573 Members 5-8 at LHS	*Bithynia neumanni*
GS 541 Member 9, "Basal Ash"	*Biomphalaria* sp.
loc. 1	*Bithynia neumanni*

Main diatomite or lateral equivalents

GS 579 Lateral equivalent of diatomites, Main Site, trench D/10ii	*Bithynia neumanni*
GS 484 Member 9 lower diatomite	
GS 415 Loc. T.1.	*Bithynia neumanni*

Upper diatomite

GS 496 Member 9 at Loc. J 1	*Bithynia neumanni*
	Biomphalaria sp.

Post-Olorgesailie Formation calcareous deposits

GS 422	*Melanoides tuberculata*
GS 577	*Biomphalaria cf sudanica*
	? *Lymnaea*

Dr. Verdcourt states in a letter dated 26 October 1966 that the common species is *Bithynia* (Gabbia) sp. cf. *neumanni* Van Martens, a member of the family Hydrobiidae which is not distinguished with any certainty from the specimens of *Gabbia cf. subbadiella* found in quantities in the early Middle Pleistocene Humbu Formation (Verdcourt, in Isaac 1967a). He adds

"The material is extremely poorly preserved. In the case of *Gabbia* it is not possible to sort out the recent material, let alone the fossil."

These forms are all either widely distributed and occupy diverse environments (*Melanoides tuberculata, Biomphalaria* sp., *Lymnaea* sp.) or have unknown ranges of environmental tolerance.

3. Pollen Analysis

In 1962 samples were submitted to Dr. E. Van Zinderen Bakker for pollen analysis. Dr. Bakker was unable to carry out tests at the time, and further samples were submitted to Dr. D. A. Livingstone of Duke University, North Carolina. Following tentative identification of small numbers of grains in a series of pilot samples, the sampling of the entire formation was undertaken by D. A. Livingstone and me. Samples were taken at approximately one foot intervals.

Dr. Livingstone and his assistants have recovered very small quantities of pollen from some samples:

Sample	K2B	Member 2	Locus F	Diatomite
	K5-8F	Members 5-8	Locus F	Volcanic silt
	K9F	Member 9	Locus F	Diatomaceous silt
	K11A	Member 11	Locus D	Diatomaceous silts
	K13B	Member 13	Locus E	Brown clays
	K14C	Member 13	Locus E	Diatomaceous silts

Livingstone, in a letter dated 20 September, 1965, reports that the quantities range

> between one and ten grains per gram. . . . The pollen is not well preserved but recognizeable. Podocarpus[2] is the commonest grain I've seen yet.
> . . . It seems unlikely that there will be enough pollen to tell us anything. In all likelihood we shall be left speculating about whether there was Podocarpus nearby in Olorgesailie time, or whether Podocarpus pollen just happens to be resistant to the bugs that break down pollen under the prevailing conditions.

Elsewhere Livingstone points out that

> it is likely that the diatomite at least of the Olorgesailie Lake contained thousands or tens of thousands of grains per cc. If there are only tens or hundreds of grains left, much of the pollen must have been destroyed by weathering and it is at least possible that the few grains remaining are not original ones but are later contaminants, added, perhaps at the time of collection.

It is conceivable that in samples obtained by drilling, better conditions of preservation might be encountered. Meanwhile, pollen analysis provides no assistance for paleoecological reconstruction.

4. Microscopic Charcoal (information in a letter from D. A. Livingstone, 2 July 1964)

During preliminary searches for pollen grains, laboratory assistants found "quite a bit of charcoal (reportedly too much to be contamination) in the following samples: DE/89 Member 8 'Red Bed,' DE/89 Member 7 'Mid green clay' (M7f), Locus d Member 2 pure diatomite." The DE/89 Member 7c, the grit associated with the Horizon B occupation apparently lacked charcoal.

It is uncertain whether this charcoal is the result of human activity or wild fire, but the question deserves further attention.

---

2. In East Africa, *Podocarpus* is a montane forest genus. At present, no such forests are growing within 20 mi of Olorgesailie (Trump 1967).

5. The Mineralization of Bone

Dr. K. P. Oakley requested samples of fossil bones from Olorgesailie and has kindly furnished the results of uranium assays on four samples.

$\underline{e}$ U_3O_8 ppm

B.S.1	Stratum	M 1 Land Surface 2	
	Locality	Hippo carcass exhibition trench, north end of enclosure.	
	Matrix	Weakly diatomaceous tuff.	
	Sample	Portion of Hippo rib.	72
B.S.2	Stratum	M 1 Land Surface 3	
	Locality	Peninsula Site, north of enclosure, excavation I 3, trench 1	
	Matrix	Basal calcretion against basalt below diatomaceous tuff silts.	
	Sample	Indeterminate bone.	169
B.S.3	Stratum	M 7 Land Surface 7	
	Locality	Main Site excavation DE/89	
	Matrix	A grit at the base of tuffaceous silts and immediately overlying the sandy layer K 6.	
	Sample	A chip from MS 2223. Long-bone fragment indeterminate.	50
B.S.4	Stratum	M 10 Land Surface 10	
	Locality	Main Site. L. S. 10 exhibition trench	
	Matrix	A pumice gravel overlying tuff and covered by pumice sands and gravels.	
	Sample	Indeterminate bone.	123

Other examples of $\underline{e}$ U_3O_8 assays for East African fossil bones are:

Holocene	Elmenteita (Bromheads site) Human skull A	16
Upper Pleistocene	Eyasi Hominid 2, occipital	208
Middle Pleistocene	Kanjera fauna and hominid	11-113
Lower Pleistocene	Fauna from Kanam	60-214

(Comparative data from Oakley and Campbell 1967)

6. Diatoms

For information on identifications by Dr. J. L. Richardson, see Isaac (in press).

7. Skeletal Remains of *Theropithecus (Simopithecus) oswaldi* from the Site DE/89, Horizon A by Meave G. Leakey

Following is a list of the remains, classified into anatomical categories, with indications of the degree of completeness. Following the list is a brief discussion of the minimum number of individuals represented.

Isolated Permanent Teeth

	Side	Complete Specimens	Frags.	Teeth in small mand or Maxillae frags.	Total
Incisors, upper I^1	L	25	--	--	25
	R	27	--	--	27
I^2	L	16	--	--	16
	R	20	--	--	20
lower I^1	L	21	--	--	21
	R	18	--	--	18
I^2	L	20	--	--	20
	R	20	--	--	20
Incisor frags., indet.		--	7	--	7
Upper canines ♂	L	14	8	--	22
	R	9	4	--	13
♀	L	5	1	--	6
	R	13	2	--	15
Lower canines ♂	L	13	4	1	18
	R	11	4	1	16
♀	L	23	3	--	26
	R	14	10	--	24
Indet. canine frags.			12	--	12
Upper premolars P^3	L	13	3	2	18
	R	6	3	1	10
P^4	L	12	5	3	20
	R	15	--	1	16
Lower premolars P^3 ♂	L	6	4	2	12
	R	11	3	2	16
P^3 ♀	L	10	2	--	12
	R	6	--	1	7
P^4	L	23	1	1	25
	R	23	5	6	34
Upper P^3 or P^4 frags.		--	7	--	7
Lower P^3 or P^4 frags.		--	3	--	3
Molars, upper M^1	L	9	--	--	9
	R	27	--	1	28
M^2, M^3	L	24	--	--	24
	R	28	--	1	29
Molars, lower M_1	L	29	--	3	32
	R	21	--	3	24
M_2	L	21	--	1	22
	R	25	--	2	27
M_3	L	10	--	--	10
	R	15	--	1	16
upper frags.		--	17	--	17
lower frags.		--	34	--	34
indet. frags.		--	77	--	77
			Total nondeciduous teeth		855

Isolated Deciduous Teeth

	Side	Complete Specimens	Frags.		Total
Incisors, upper dI^1	L	4	--	--	4
	R	5	--	--	5
dI^2	L	5	--	--	5
	R	6	--	--	6
lower $dI_{1,2}$		5	--	--	5
Canines, upper dc̲	L	14	--	--	14
	R	11	--	--	11
lower dc̄	L	6	--	--	6
	R	11	--	--	11
Premolars, upper dM^1	L	4	--	--	4
	R	3	--	--	3
lower dM_1	L	8	--	--	8
	R	12	--	--	12
upper dM^2	L	8	--	--	8
	R	16	1	--	17
lower dM_2	L	9	1	--	10
	R	8	--	--	8
Deciduous premolar frags.		--	16	--	16
			Total deciduous teeth		153

Cranial Parts

		Teeth present	Total
Mandible frags.	L	$(C, P_3, -, M_1, M_2, -\ )$	1
	L	$(-, P_3, P_4, M_1, -, -\ )$	1
	L	$(-, -, dM_2, M_1, -, -\ )$	1
	R	$(C, P_3, P_4, -, -, -\ )$	1
	R	$(-, P_3, P_4, M_1, -, -\ )$	1
	R	$(-, P_3, P_4, M_1, M_2, M_3\ )$	1
	R	$(-, -, P_4, M_1, M_2\ )$	1
	R	$(-, -, P_4, -, -, -\ )$	1
Maxillae frags.	L	$(-, P^3, P^4, -, -, -\ )$	1
		$(-, P^3, P^4, -, -, -\ )$	1
		$(-, -, P^4, -, -, -\ )$	1
	R	$(-, P^3, P^4, M^1, M^2, -\ )$	1
		$(-, -, dM^2, M^1, -, -\ )$	1

	Total
Skull frags., frontal	9
temporal	6
maxilla	1
inion region	3
indet.	12
Total cranial parts	44

Axial and Pelvic Bones

	Total
Vertebrae (centrum), caudal	10
Rib, proximal end	1
Innominate frags.	12
Total axial and pelvic bones	23

Limb Bones

	Rel. complete	Frag. Shaft	> 1/4 shaft and prox. end	> 1/4 shaft and distal end	< 1/4 shaft and prox. end	< 1/4 shaft and distal end	Total
Clavicle	1	--	--	--	--	--	1
Scapula	--	--	--	--	--	5	5
Humerus	1	8	--	1	--	9	19
Ulna	--	8	4	--	6	1	19
Radius	--	5	--	1	3	--	9
Femur	4	24	4	--	4	--	36
Patella	9	--	--	--	--	--	9
Tibia	--	12	--	--	--	2	14
Fibula	--	2	--	--	--	2	4
Metacarpals I	1	--	1	--	--	--	2
II	1	--	2	--	--	--	3
III	--	--	5	--	--	--	5
IV	--	--	2	--	--	--	2
V	--	--	--	--	4	--	4

Limb Bones (continued)

	Rel. complete	Frag. Shaft	> 1/4 shaft and prox. end	> 1/4 shaft and distal end	< 1/4 shaft and prox. end	< 1/4 shaft and distal end	Total
Metatarsals I	5	--	--	--	--	--	5
II	2	--	6	--	10	--	12
III	2	--	8	--	10	--	18
IV	1	--	4	--	10	--	15
V	2	--	4	--	3	--	9
Metacarpal/tarsal frags.	--	--	--	--	--	--	51
Phalanges, proximal	38	--	2	12	1	1	54
middle	30	4	1	10	--	3	48
distal	8	--	--	--	--	--	8
Phalangeal frags. indet.	--	--	--	--	--	--	11

	Rel. complete (> 3/4)	Fairly complete (< 3/4>1/4)	Sm. Frag. (< 1/4)	Total
Tarsals, calcaneum	10	10	12	32
talus	23	12	3	38
middle cuneiform	5	--	--	5
medial cuneiform	6	--	--	6
lateral cuneiform	1	3	--	3
cuboid	5	3	--	4
navicular	9	14	1	16
Carpals, trapezoid	1	--	--	1
trapezium	1	--	--	1
lunate	9	1	--	10
scaphoid	3	2	--	5
capitate	8	3	--	11
hamate	10	2	--	9
sesamoids	2	--	--	2

Total of specimens from the limbs and extremities   505

Indeterminable bone fragments, probably *T. oswaldi*, large   32
small   62
Total   1674

Minimum number of individuals

The absolute minimum is given by the highest observed overall number of any one element. This is the left lower canine:

adult   44
juvenile   6
          50

A larger estimate is obtained by using different teeth for adults and juveniles:

adults (left $\overline{c}$)   44   (6 possibly unerupted)
juveniles (right dM^2)   17   (5 moderately worn)
                          61

However, since it is possible for a worn dM^2 to occur with an adult canine in a single individual, corrections should be made by discounting the 5 moderately worn dM^2. The best estimate is thus 56 individuals. (This appendix presents an amplification and revision of the material previously published in M. G. and R. E. F. Leakey 1973.)

APPENDIX C

Additional Information on the Classification of Artifacts
and the Analysis of Morphology

As explained in chapter 5, a modified version of the system of Kleindienst (1962) has been used. It is believed that the major categories (primary and secondary divisions) correspond closely with Kleindienst's usages. The scheme has diverged extensively in the classification of scrapers and allied small tools because of a conviction that for poorly standardized fields of variation, systems that expressed measurable aspects of form were necessary. The classification of cores has also been radically simplified to one expressing flaking patterns rather than the often irrelevant variation in the overall shape of the cores. The hierarchical scheme is summarized below. Some notes on distinguishing criteria follow:

Primary Classes	Secondary Classes	Form Categories
Shaped Tools		
	Large Cutting Tools	Hand axes
		Chisel hand axes
		Cleavers
		Knives
		Picklike hand axes
		Other
	Heavy-Duty Tools	Trièdres
		Picks
		Choppers
		Core-Scrapers
		Other
	Scrapers and Small Tools	Large Scrapers
		Small simple scrapers
		Small nosed and pointed forms
	Other Tools	ad hoc
Miscellaneous Trimmed and Broken		ad hoc
Utilized	Edge-Damaged	Biclinal
		Planoclinal
	Battered	eg. Spheroids (bolas), hammerstones, anvils

233

Primary Classes	Secondary Classes	Form Categories
Debitage	Cores	Regular Irregular polyfaceted Casual
	Flakes	Large Small Chips Fragments
Artifactual Rubble		ad hoc
Manuports		ad hoc

Primary Classes

Shaped Tools. Stone artifacts, with trimming or retouch, the form of which is judged to be the result of purposive human activity, and which conforms to one of a limited number of morphologically defined tool categories,[1] known to be recurrent in relevant assemblages of artifacts.

Miscellaneous Trimmed Pieces (= Modified of M. R. K.) and Broken Indeterminable Tools. All artifacts showing some trimming or retouch, which do not conform to any existing relevant tool category, and of which the degree of purposive modification and the low frequency of occurrence do not justify the creation of new specific categories, and artifacts judged to be fragments of larger tools, but presenting inadequate portions for the identification of these. Ad hoc subdivisions only are employed.

Utilized Pieces. Natural and artifactual stone pieces showing distinct signs of wear or damage assumed to be due to human usage but not classifiable as shaped tools or MTPs; includes hammerstones, etc. (see Secondary Classes).

Debitage. Artifacts such as cores, core fragments, flakes, and recognizable flake fragments not conforming to any tool class, nor showing retouch or utilization. Artifactual rubble and angular waste not having (a) bulb and platform, or (b) any intact flake scar, are excluded.

Artifactual Rubble (Angular Waste).[2] All stone pieces that are neither (a) demonstrably shaped by man, nor (b) demonstrably natural forms. That is, tools, utilized pieces, flakes, and cores are excluded under a. (Bulb and platform or negative scars make a convenient objective sorting criterion.) Rounded pebbles, etc. are excluded under b.

Manuports. All stones, the form of which is demonstrably due to natural processes, without subsequent damage by utilization or flaking, but the presence of which at a site is attributable to human activities (eg., rounded pebbles and cobbles).

Secondary Classes

Large Cutting Tools.[3] A convenient compound category comprising all those artifacts falling within the definition of (1) Hand axes and hand ax-like, (2) cleavers, (3) knives, (4) other large sharp bifacial forms (see below).

---

1. Cores are trimmed, but where use other than the production of flakes is not indicated by utilization, they are conventionally excluded from being tools.

2. This group can only be recognized for industries from sealed sites in fine-grained stratigraphic context. It appears that Kleindienst used a less rigorous definition in separating waste from chips and chunks. That is, she did not demand a portion of platform and bulb.

3. Large denotes that the modal value for maximum length is generally in excess of 10 cm. Comparatively small numbers of items within the morphological series may be less than 10 cm. in length, but are nevertheless included.

Heavy-Duty Tools. Compact shaped tools, with robust functional zones and generally with minimal trimming. May be large or medium small (i.e. greater than 5 cm.). Overall morphology may be used as a criterion in marginal cases (i.e., where the edge character is marginal and indecisive). The Th/Br ratio can be used as a decisive factor.

Scrapers and Allied Small Tools. Shaped tools having a planoclinal scraping edge judged to be dominant and not made on compact rock masses with very robust edges (see Core-Scrapers). Large or small. Includes composite forms with angulated points, awl points, or noses, where these are combined with scraping edges.

Note: Intensity of retouch grades have been used to qualify the form categorizations (see chap. 7).

Other Tools (Large and small). Shaped tools other than the 3 previous categories, judged to be of sufficient significance to be excluded from MTP. Ad hoc descriptive subdivision.

Edge-Damaged. Flakes and other relatively thin pieces showing chipping snaps and small scars along the edges but with a form and intensity not suggestive of retouch.

Battered Forms. Pebbles, cobbles, or chunks with battering, shatter scars, or peck marks (eg. hammerstones, etc.).

Cores (and core fragments). Pieces other than tools having flake scars that are large relative to the piece and that are judged to result from the purposive removal of flakes.

Flakes (and flake fragments). Pieces having a recognizable striking platform (talon) or part thereof, but not significantly retouched or utilized. (Kleindienst does not define flakes, but her counts suggest that any piece with a portion judged to be ventral surface was counted as a flake.)

Tool Form Categories ("Types")

Hand Axes (Classic). Approx. synonyms: biface classique (Bordes 1961a), sharp-rimmed implements (Evans 1897); in part coup-de-poing (de Mortillet 1883; Burkitt 1921).

This category was probably not closely defined when it first came into technical usage, but it was taken as an equivalent of the French coup-de-poing. It is a typological category, the modal forms of which are universally recognized, but the boundaries of which have hitherto not been sufficiently well defined for use in a quantitative analysis of such varied bifacial forms as occur in many African Acheulean assemblages. Clearly the attributes of hand axes constitute a complex polythetic set, as defined by D. L. Clarke (1968). Experience with Olorgesailie material suggests that the typological category can usefully be split into two subclasses: classic forms comprising specimens that correspond closely to the modal type; and hand ax-like forms comprising specimens that depart significantly from the central type but are related in their morphology and would be classified as hand axes by most workers. This division is arbitrary, but should serve to give a more accurate and readily understood description than would be provided either by lumping all the diversity into one class or by creating new classes for the variety of subtypical forms. A similar division is in fact employed by Bordes (1961a) in the arrangement of his chapters on bifaces.

Classic, Acheulean Hand ax. A bifacial tool showing some degree of elongation (Br/L < .76); having a flattish biconvex or lenticular cross-section over most of its length, with a maximum thickness/breadth ratio < .67; having a plan profile that is even and generally rounded, with or without a pointed apex; having edges that are continuous around the

perimeter, dominantly sharp (< 75°), and biclinal in
relation to the tool axis.

The chisel-ended/nonchisel-ended division cuts across the classic/subclassic division.
A specific category has also been used for thick-sectioned picklike hand axes. Abbevillian
and Chellean hand axes will generally fall into the categories hand ax-like or picks under
the proposed scheme.

Subclassic Hand Ax. A tool resembling a hand ax in its general morphology but which
may depart from the classic form in some or all of the above attributes.

Cleavers. Large cutting tools, commonly but not always bifacial, having a clean cutting edge, commonly unretouched, transverse or subtransverse to the major axis. The cutting
edge should be greater than 1/2 of the maximum breadth. Unretouched "cleaver flakes" with
predetermined form cannot be included, but should be cited in conjunction with this category.
In the system that I have employed, the category passes into chisel hand axes with a bit
less than 1/2 Br, and into knives with an obliquity greater than 45°. For Kleindienst, all
chisel-ended hand axes are convergent cleavers.

Picklike Hand Axes. An arbitrarily demarcated segment of the subclassic hand ax form
range. Pieces so designated are generally robust (T/B usually > 0.6) with thick butts,
stout pointed apices, and often with coarse trimming.

Other Large Cutting Tools. Related large, partially bifacial cutting tools falling outside the categories. Generally nonstandard types requiring ad hoc description.

Trièdres. Forms intermediate between picklike hand axes and picks with moderately
acute pointed apices and relatively thick biconvex or subtriangular sections. May be partially bifacial or unifacial (cf. Biberson 1961, especially 437-41; Balout 1967:723-27).

Picks. Generally large tools having a prominent robust apex. Breadth and thickness
subequal. Commonly with minimal retouch and sinuous chopping edges. Grades into trièdres
with flattening of section, and into picklike hand axes when Th is less than 2/3 Br.

Choppers (and chopping tools of Movius 1948:351). Compact robust implements with a
dominant chopping edge that is judged to be purposive or shows signs of use, i.e., not primarily a core. In Africa generally restricted to bifacial tools.

Core Scrapers. Compact stone masses having a robust scraping edge. Will be generally
distinguished from large scrapers by having Th/Br ratio greater than 2/3 and by edge trimming being along a subvertical or undercut edge. It is often problematic to decide whether
these forms are tools or cores.

Other Heavy-Duty Tools. Any artifacts on compact rock masses with subsharp or obtuse
nonscraping, nonchopping edges. A numerically small class requiring ad hoc descriptive subdivision.

Scrapers, large and small. Definitions depend on oriented measurements using the line
of retouch as the A-axis (see chap. 7 and figs. 44 and 46).

Regular Cores. Cores with repetitive patterns of scars approximating some simple geometric pattern, for example, (1) a radial pattern with scars centripetal about a pole on
one or two faces (i.e., disc core, discoid core, or regular biconic core), (2) a convergent
pattern (segment of a radial system) (not found at Olorgesailie), (3) a parallel fluted pattern from one or more platforms.

Irregular Polyfaceted Cores. Cores with more than 5 scars forming irregular apparently
ad hoc patterns often involving several flaking edges at odd angles to one another. Such
cores may be subspherical, polyhedral, cuboidal, or irregular.

Casual Cores. Cores, pebbles, or blocks with so few (> 5) scars that both pattern and
purpose can be in doubt (includes some battered chunks of Kleindienst 1962).

APPENDIX D

Notes on Pilot Samples of Flakes
from Sites Other than Olorgesailie*

Ternifine.   From the sands with an Acheulean industry and the *Atlanthropus* fossils
               (Arambourg 1957; Balout et al. 1967). A random sample approximating one-
               third of the collections in the Institut de Paléontologie Humaine, Paris.
               Measured by courtesy of Prof. L. Balout.
                       Simple quartzite and allied rocks   73 specimens
                       Flint/chert   57 specimens.

Isimila.   (Howell et al. 1962) Specimens seen in the collections at the Department
               of Anthropology, University of Chicago, by courtesy of Dr. F. C. Howell.
               K 18, trench 2, clay contact floor, a random sample of 29 specimens (2/5
                   of the series).
               K 14, various units, all specimens (29).
               These two subsamples have been treated together for most purposes.

Kalambo Falls. (J. D. Clark 1964) Unit A4/63/184 "River face extension *in situ* coarse
               sand--base between start of the big Acheulian stringer dipping east."
               Collections in the Lowie Museum, Berkeley, by courtesy of Dr. J. D. Clark.
               Sample of 35 (1/3 of the series).

Montagu Cave. Cape Province S. A. (Keller 1966).
               Acheulean industry, layer 5, surface X.
               Sample of 63, approximately 1/3 sample of an unselected series. All attri-
               butes recorded for only 55 flakes. All available large flakes included for
               some purposes.

               Howiesonspoort industry, layer 2.
               Sample of 36 (1/6 sample from whole series,
               1/3 of the size-ranked sample).

Chaminade.   Malawi (unpublished), a Middle Stone Age collection being studied in
               Berkeley. Sampled by courtesy of J. D. Clark. Sample of 82, from which
               38 chips were excluded for most attribute counts.
               (1/3 from Main Floor, grid squares H3, H6, and I 3.)

Abri Ohla.   Basses Pyrénées, France. A small series of a Mousterian industry housed in
               the Musée de l'Homme, Paris. Chosen because it includes quartzite artifacts.
               Marked *foyer superieur* 38 quartzite flakes, 19 flint flakes.

*For comparability, all samples were restricted to flakes for which L + B > 50 mm.

237

APPENDIX E

Supplementary Quantitative Data

Table E1.   Presents the raw numbers from which the percentage values in table 9 were computed. These are the actual counts of objects in the assemblages.

Table E2.   A supplement to table 10. It provides (1) rank-order data for the degree of standardization as indicated by a low standard deviation or a low coefficient of variance, and (2) tabulates the numbers of items in the sample for each category and each attribute.

Table E3.   A table showing the composition by category of the biface series with all sites lumped, on which computation of metric statistics were performed.

Table E4.   A supplement to table 25. Mean values and standard deviation for site-samples of flakes. The attributes are ones not included in table 25. These include means and standard deviations for logarithmetically transformed variables.

Table E5.   Supplementary data regarding the principal components analysis (see fig. 71). Particulars of procedure, the matrix of correlation coefficients, the eigen values associated with the first five eigen vectors and the correlation coefficients linking each of the variables with the first 3 eigen vectors.

Table E1

Actual Counts of Artifacts (supplement to table 9, chap. 5)

Site	BBB	BBA	FB	FB HL	I3	DE/89 A L	DE/89 A I	DE/89 B L	DE/89 B I	DE/89 C	H/6	H/9 A	H/9 AM	Mid	Meng	LHS	Tr Tr M 10	Hog	MFS
Overall Composition of Samples																			
Shaped tools	61	68	54	-	219	198	50	103	581	77	78	211	30	112	147	22	147	63	19
Modified and broken	18	8	14	-	124	34	12	16	127	62	12	77	4	5	19	11	26	24	5
Edge-damaged	26	17	14	-	97	33	7	10	109	42	12	93	1	5	26	12	71	13	19
Hammers etc.	-	2	5	-	16	2	1	2	21	3	14	8	-	5	-	-	14	14	7
Cores	1	54	23	3	90	37	5	37	141	25	10	57	2	5	12	7	49	16	20
Flakes*	166	85	181	60	643	163	43	32	668	265	156	874	67	56	149	137	326	207	420
Angular fragments*	NR	NR	(35)	NR	3812	>117	242	>132	2782	680	525	4603	102	>(29)	>(73)	469	(200)	(73)	936
ALL Worked Stone	>272	>234	>326	>63	5001	>584	360	>332	4429	1154	807	5923	206	>212	>426	658	>833	401	1426
Manuports*	NR	NR	NR	NR	18	(2)	13	NR	433	80	72	103	2	NR	NR	80	(17)	(3)	252
Composition of Shaped Tools Divided into Major Classes																			
Large cutting tools	1	13	6	-	33	51	34	69	435	24	52	57	14	89	97	2	51	7	-
Heavy-duty tools	1	9	7	-	14	11	3	7	30	5	4	5	1	5	4	3	4	2	-
Large scrapers	-	-	1	-	6	5	3	4	38	2	1	12	2	5	6	7	7	1	1
Other large tools	-	2	6	-	24	6	5	5	20	2	5	25	-	4	7	4	8	6	-
Small tools	59	42	34	-	139	124	7	10	50	41	15	108	13	4	33	13	74	47	16
Spheroids	-	2	-	-	3	1	1	8	8	2	1	4	-	5	-	-	3	1	-
ALL Shaped Tools	61	68	54	-	219	198	50	103	581	77	78	211	30	112	147	22	147	63	19
Composition of Shaped Tools Divided into Subclasses																			
Hand axes	-	-	-	-	6	1	2	1	2	3	7	-	2	3	2	-	-	1	-
Picklike hand axes	-	3	3	-	17	36	20	27	245	9	21	15	5	27	46	1	22	2	-
Chisel hand axes	-	3	1	-	3	-	-	-	-	2	10	11	5	15	29	-	3	-	-
Cleavers	1	3	1	-	5	1	1	34	148	6	4	18	2	34	7	-	19	1	1
Knives	-	-	-	-	2	1	2	1	33	-	6	4	-	4	1	1	1	1	1
Broken large cutting tools	-	4	1	-	-	9	9	6	7	4	6	9	-	6	12	1	6	3	-
Picks and trièdres	-	-	-	-	4	2	1	1	9	1	4	3	1	9	-	1	1	-	-
Choppers	-	4	6	-	9	7	1	6	18	4	1	3	1	4	3	2	2	2	2
Core scrapers	-	5	1	-	1	1	-	1	-	4	3	3	-	-	1	1	1	-	2
Large flake scrapers	-	-	1	-	6	5	3	4	38	2	1	12	2	5	6	7	7	1	1
Core/bifaces	-	2	5	-	20	4	4	2	20	1	2	9	2	-	6	-	7	-	1
Other large tools	-	-	1	-	4	2	1	3	-	1	3	16	-	4	1	3	4	1	-
Small scrapers (simple)	34	22	13	-	110	78	7	6	20	22	10	85	12	1	24	8	58	34	5
Small scrapers (nosed/pt.)	24	17	20	-	29	45	9	21	29	19	4	23	1	1	9	5	15	13	9
Other small tools	1	3	1	-	-	1	1	3	-	2	1	4	2	2	-	-	3	1	2
Spheroids	-	2	-	1	3	1	1	8	8	2	1	-	5	5	-	-	3	1	-
ALL Shaped Tools	61	68	54	-	219	198	50	103	581	77	78	211	30	112	147	22	147	63	19

Table E1--Continued

Composition of Miscellaneous Trimmed Pieces (= Modified) and broken tools indet.

Lge. bifac.	-	1	-	-	-	1	2	5	5	25	-	1	3	1	3	13	-	-
Lge. unif.	1	-	-	-	-	-	8	-	-	-	7	5	8	-	-	-	7	-
Sm. bifac.	-	1	-	-	-	10	6	-	-	-	15	5	-	-	-	-	1	2
Sm. unif.	-	1	2	-	-	7	-	4	5	15	8	3	11	1	1	6	10	4
Broken large tool	2	1	12	-	-	-	18	3	32	32	3	11	55	1	1	6	3	8
Broken small tool	15	5	-	-	-	124	18	2	4	55	3	55	-	2	1	18	7	7
All "Modified" and Broken18	18	8	14	-	-	142	34	12	16	127	62	12	77	4	5	19	11	26

Composition of Edge-damaged and utilized pieces

Large planoclinal	1	-	-	-	-	48	30	-	6	-	28	1	-	-	-	3	8	4
Small planoclinal	12	17	-	-	-	-	3	1	1	-	14	59	59	1	1	15	4	26
Large biclinal	13	-	17	-	-	30	3	7	2	6	14	6	-	-	2	2	4	23
Small biclinal	-	-	14	-	-	-	-	-	1	69	-	4	28	-	-	2	-	18
Ecaillée etc.	-	2	-	-	-	19	2	1	-	34	-	-	6	-	-	4	-	14
Hammers, anvils	-	-	5	-	-	16	1	2	2	21	3	14	8	-	-	-	-	-
All Edge-damaged	26	19	19	-	-	113	35	12	12	130	45	26	101	1	5	26	12	85

Composition of Flakes and Flake Fragments

Flakes large	1	-	3	54	-	-	15	8	5	30	8	4	14	-	12	14	-	24
small	105	66	145	1	-	377	120	22	23	377	136	104	426	47	35	89	82	250
very small	11	18	1	1	-	143	-	13	-	88	50	27	71	4	-	16	34	4
Flake fragments	49	18	33	5	-	123	28	13	4	173	71	21	363	16	9	30	21	48
All Flakes	166	85	181	60	-	643	163	32	43	668	265	156	874	67	56	149	137	326
Cores, regular	-	12	4	1	-	19	14	1	2	22	4	1	10	2	2	6	-	11
irregular	1	35	13	1	-	44	10	3	33	77	12	6	26	-	3	2	6	25
casual	-	7	6	1	-	27	9	-	2	33	1	1	13	-	-	4	1	10
fragments	-	-	-	-	-	-	4	1	-	9	8	2	-	-	-	-	-	3
All Cores	1	54	23	3	-	90	37	5	37	141	25	10	57	2	5	12	7	49
Angular fragments	NR	NR	35	3	NR	3812	(117)	242	(132)	2782	680	525	4603	102	29	73	469	200

Table E2

Supplement to Table 10.

	Rank Order of Standardisation*										Values of N								
	L	B/L	T/B	PMB/L	BA/BB	TA/TB	Sc	inv/Sc	i.Bic	Mean	L	B/L	T/B	PMB/L	BA/BB	TA/TB	Sc	inv/Sc	i.Bic
Hand axes	8	3	1	3	2	3	2	2	1	2	669	666	664	561	583	404	343	343	409
Cleavers	2	2	2	8	6	5	8	4	2	3	299	299	294	281	269	181	162	162	179
Knives	4	4	3	6	4	6	5	8	5	5	65	63	63	55	56	33	30	30	32
Picklike H.A.s	5	1	6	1	1	2	4	1	3	1	34	32	35	30	29	30	24	24	30
Picks, etc.	7	7	8	4	3	1	7	5	6	7	22	23	23	18	18	13	11	11	14
Choppers	1	5	7	2	7	7	3	6	8	6	17	17	16	17	17	13	17	17	13
Large scrapers	6	8	4	7	8	8	6	3	7	8	72	73	71	57	54	41	28	28	49
Corelike bifaces	3	6	5	5	5	4	1	7	4	4	40	40	40	40	39	39	33	33	35
Large flakes	1-2	4-5	4-5	7-8	>8	7-8	--	--	4-5	7-8	54	54	54	53	53	43	--	--	41
Overall	>8	4-5	3-4	7-8	>8	6-7	6-7	6-7	2-3	7-8	1263	1263	1254	1126	1126	804	674	674	795

* As indicated by low values of CV or SD.

Table E3

Composition of the Computed Sample of Bifaces

	I 3	Oth LSS	DE/89 A	DE/89 B	DE/89 C	H6/A	H9/A	H9/AM	Mid	Meng	C.W.	Tr. Tr. M 10	Hog	Total
Hand Axes														
Classic	2	2	16	52	6	5	10	2	11	22	49	16	2	195
Chisel, Classic		1	6	19		5	5		12	19	20	2	1	90
Subclassic	15	4	30	128	3	16	5	3	16	24	36	6		286
Chisel, Subclassic	3	3	4	42	2	5	6	5	3	10	15	1		99
Cleavers	5	5	3	178	6	6	17	2	34	7	17	19		299
Knives	2		6	33		4	4		4	1	9	1		64
Picklike Hand Axes	6		3	3	3	7		1		2	6		1	32
Triêdres	2	1	3	10	1					1	4	1		23
Picks	2					1								3
Choppers	6			5		2			1			2	1	17
Large Scrapers	6	1	4	37		1	11	2	4	5		6		77
Corelike Bifaces	20	1	1	2	1	2	7			2	2	4	1	40
Other Bifaces	4	3	3	14	1	2	3			1	1	4		32

The composition by "types" and sites of the total sample of Olorgesailie bifaces used in computations. Some of the data cited for hand axes alone are based on a larger series, some of which were subsequently excluded due to incompleteness of records or other reasons.

Table E4

Supplement to Table 25 (chap. 8). Means and standard deviations of flake measurements

Site	FL		TM		TM/B		PB/FB		PT/TM	
MFS	40.2	12.5	10.0	4.2	.290	.107	.708	.259		
MPS	43.0	13.5	12.4	4.7	.333	.111	.665	.244		
Hog	38.1	12.1	9.6	8.3	.288	.114	.579	.256	.84	
Tr. Tr. M 10	44.6	14.8	10.8	7.0	.274	.134	.716	.196	1.001	.576
LHS	45.1	13.8	11.9	5.1	.310	.089	.741	.211		
Meng	41.7	13.8	10.7	5.0	.293	.105	.632	.239	1.06	.133
H/9 AM			9.6	3.9						
H/9 A			9.6	4.5						
H/6 A	39.6	14.4	9.2	4.6	.281	.123	.619	.198	.948	.541
DE/89 C	41.0	14.7	11.6	5.1	.308	.085	.586	.277	.778	.430
DE/89 B										
Leakey	47.2	16.6	12.3	4.5	.289	.086	.594	.270	.736	.377
Isaac	35.0	11.2	9.9	6.6	.297	.172	.733	.280	1.003	.483
DE/89 A	41.9	11.9	12.6	3.9	.342	.075	.681	.226	.801	.352
MSS	38.9	13.1	10.1	5.1	.287	.123	.658	.278	.912	.619
I 3 O	36.8	11.5	9.6	3.4	.308	.084	.679	.260	.938	.493
I 3 M	35.9	13.7	8.6	3.5	.287	.095	.739	.317	1.013	.436
FB/HL	46.6	14.5	12.3	3.9	.316	.071	.614	.238	.785	.385
FB	42.7	12.1	11.1	3.8	.303	.092	.633	.308	.781	.396
BBA	39.2	12.3	12.5	4.8	.374	.121	.710	.241	.810	.324
BBB	36.3	11.2	10.6	5.3	.328	.112	.567	.280	.688	.416
LSS	38.3	13.0	10.1	4.1	.311	.096	.677	.282	.893	.448

Log Data*	Log FL		Log TM		Log 100 x TM/B	
MFS	3.645	.314	2.215	.426	3.308	.345
MPS	3.717	.298	2.455	.375	3.460	.297
Hog	3.593	.306	2.165	.439	3.285	.395
Tr. Tr. M 10	3.743	.336	2.227	.536	3.222	.414
USS	3.681	.326	2.223	.483	3.278	.385
LHS	3.765	.300	2.392	.416	3.395	.288
Meng	3.682	.308	2.277	.421	3.322	.329
H/9 AM	3.553	.305	2.170	.528	3.305	.373
H/9 A	3.611	.318	2.175	.376	3.231	.344
H/6 A	3.620	.346	2.102	.480	3.249	.423
DE/89 C	3.654	.346	2.368	.397	3.391	.274
DE/89 B (All)	3.500	.348	2.201	.446	3.301	.397
DE/89 A	3.696	.283	2.491	.300	3.510	.219
MSS	3.612	.328	2.232	.426	3.295	.354
I 3 (All)	3.547	.323	2.145	.374	3.355	.292
FB/HL	3.797	.278	2.466	.304	3.428	.232
FB	3.716	.296	2.344	.367	3.368	.304
BBA	3.623	.292	2.466	.355	3.566	.343
BBB	3.549	.298	2.260	.451	3.435	.341
LSS	3.593	.320	2.239	.396	3.402	.307
Overall	3.626	.330	2.231	.435	3.316	.356
Biface-dominated set	3.568	.338	2.184	.449	3.299	.386
Intermediate set	3.657	.326	2.246	.449	3.285	.366
Scraper-dominated set	3.630	.321	2.246	.419	3.353	.327

Anti-Logs	FL		TM		100 x TM/B	
	Mean	SD	Mean	SD	Mean	SD
USS	39.5	1.38	9.3	1.62	26.6	1.47
MSS	37.0	1.42	9.3	1.53	26.9	1.42
LSS	36.2	1.38	9.4	1.49	30.0	1.36
Biface-dominated Set	35.5	1.40	8.9	1.57	27.1	1.47
Intermediate Set	38.9	1.39	9.5	1.57	26.7	1.44
Scraper-dominated Set	37.8	1.38	9.5	1.52	28.6	1.39
All	37.54	1.390	9.31	1.544	27.6	1.427

*Napierian (natural) logarithms of diversions in millimeters.

Particulars of the principal components analysis summarized in fig. 71.

1. The input data were taken without change from Binford 1972: table 1. The site samples are: 1 = Lochard; 2 = Kariandusi; 3 = Broken Hill; 4-6 = Nsongezi; 7-14 = Kalambo Falls; 15-23 = Isimila; 24-32 = Olorgesailie. Binford derived his data from Kleindienst 1961, J. D. Clark 1964, G. Cole 1967, Howell and Clark 1963 with adjustments.

2. The variables were standardized at the outset of the analysis.

3. The *matrix of correlation coefficients* among variables was determined as follows.

	1	2	3	4	5	6	7	8	9	10	11	12
1. Hand axes	1.00											
2. Cleavers	.18	1.00										
3. Knives	.50	.26	1.00									
4. Flake scrapers	.23	.40	.18	1.00								
5. Discoids	.01	-.11	-.09	-.25	1.00							
6. Core scrapers	-.31	-.11	-.35	-.40	-.13	1.00						
7. Picks	.09	-.08	-.15	.27	-.18	.41	1.00					
8. Choppers	-.28	.00	-.43	-.10	.46	.40	.34	1.00				
9. Spheroids	-.15	-.12	-.09	-.37	-.03	-.34	-.18	-.15	1.00			
10. Other large tools	-.05	-.17	-.22	.06	.20	.30	.45	.71	-.19	1.00		
11. Small scrapers	-.65	-.46	-.40	-.41	.06	.03	-.22	-.07	.19	-.32	1.00	
12. Other small tools	-.52	-.61	-.36	-.49	-.06	-.11	-.27	-.12	.08	.01	.38	1.00

4. The first five eigen vectors (principal component axes) were as follows.

Component	1	2	3	4	5
Eigen values	3.193	2.789	1.572	1.127	.958
% of variance	26.6	23.2	13.1	9.4	8.0
1. Hand axes	.41	-.14	-.24	.35	.04
2. Cleavers	.36	-.06	-.01	-.57	-.15
3. Knives	.34	-.29	-.11	.17	.17
4. Flake scrapers	.38	.15	.36	-.14	.11
5. Discoids	-.10	.11	-.61	-.27	.31
6. Core scrapers	.00	.43	.39	-.12	.10
7. Picks	.14	.38	.15	.34	-.35
8. Choppers	-.08	.49	-.33	-.21	-.08
9. Spheroids	-.18	-.23	-.14	-.04	-.79
10. Other large tools	.01	.47	-.27	.29	-.06
11. Small scrapers	-.44	-.08	.20	-.24	.06
12. Other small tools	-.43	-.07	.09	.34	.25

For most practical purposes, this is accepted as a 2 component solution (Doran and Hodson 1975:191).

5. Correlation coefficients between the variables and the first three eigen vectors (components) were as follows.

	First Principal Comp.	Second Principal Comp.	Third Principal Comp.
1. Hand axes	.73	-.24	-.30
2. Cleavers	.65	-.09	-.01
3. Knives	.60	-.48	-.14
4. Flake scrapers	.68	.26	.45
5. Discoids	-.17	.18	-.77
6. Core scrapers	.00	.72	.49
7. Picks	.25	.64	.18
8. Choppers	-.14	.82	-.42
9. Spheroids	-.33	-.38	-.17
10. Other large tools	.02	.78	-.38
11. Small scrapers	-.78	-.14	.25
12. Other small tools	-.77	-.12	.12

APPENDIX F

Bivariate Plots of Ratios
Defining Biface Form

This appendix presents summarizing representations of numerical data regarding the
frequency of variant biface forms. The representations are based on the method devised by
D. A. Roe (1964), with modifications as shown in the diagram.

Figure F1

(a) shows three ratios as the orthogonal axes of a three-dimensional cartesian graph.
The small biface forms drawn adjacent to the axes provide reminders of the measurements
used to define the ratios. (b) the block diagram on the left represents a solid rectangle
bounded by the three axes, and cut open so as to display the biface plan forms defined by
a series of different intercept values for the ratios in question. (c) the block diagram
on the right shows an array of plotted values for one Olorgesailie assemblage (H/9 A + Mid)
projected onto the cut faces of the solid rectangle. Note the regression relation between
BA/BB and BA/B. Note also that since BA cannot be greater than B there is a zone within
the 3-D graph for which no biface forms exist. This is indicated in the small inset.

Figure F2

(a) provides a representation, exactly in the manner of Roe (1964, 1968). For each
assemblage bivariate plots are drawn of values of the ratio BA/BB against the ratio B/L.
Three frames are given for each assemblage so that the plotted points for biface forms
with markedly different values of the PMB/L ratio can be represented on a separate frame.
(b) shows the same plot simplified by omitting the distinction between differing PMB/L
values. This relation is, in any case, highly correlated with BA/BB and therefore in a
sense is redundant. R = 0.61. (c) shows a contour representation of the density of plotted points in (b). The contours are drawn so as to delimit the sectors with plot densities
of 5 and 10 plots per 0.1 interval on each axis. Where less than 5 plots occur in a square,
the number present is represented by an equivalent number of dots. (d) provides contoured
diagrams for each of the Olorgesailie assemblages of bifaces drawn in the manner of (c),
plus a plot for the Ternifine bifaces provided for comparison. (e) the frames on the lower
right show the approximate location of verbal designations of the forms represented by different sectors of the frames. The labels given are based on (b) Bordes 1961: figs. 8-9;
(k) Kleindienst 1962: fig. 1; and (i) the usage employed in this volume.

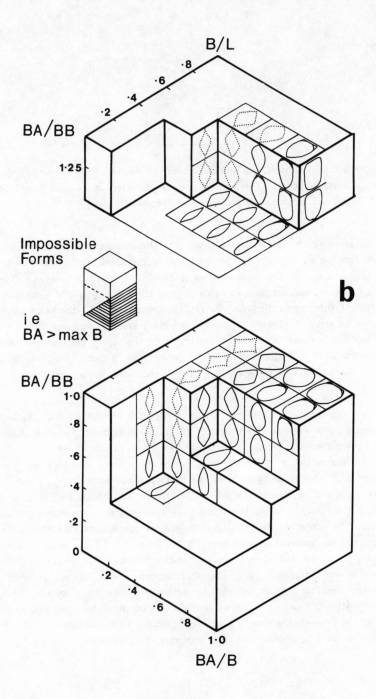

B/L

BA/BB

·2   ·4   ·6   ·8

1·25

Impossible
Forms

i e
BA > max B

BA/BB

1·0
·8
·6
·4
·2
0

·2   ·4   ·6   ·8   1·0

BA/B

b

Figure F1.

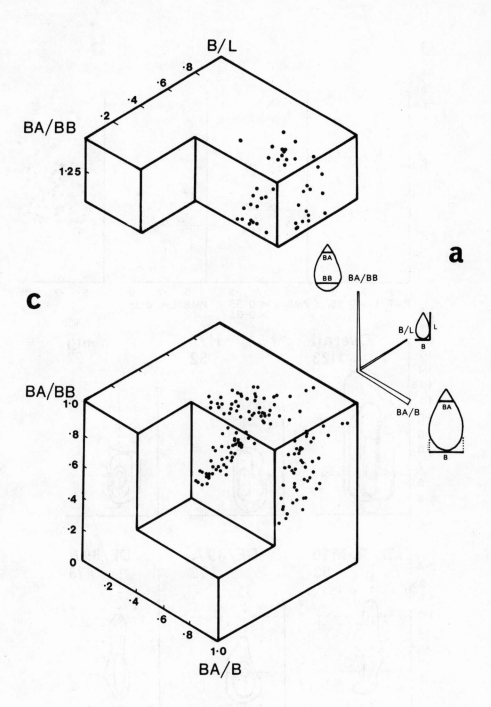

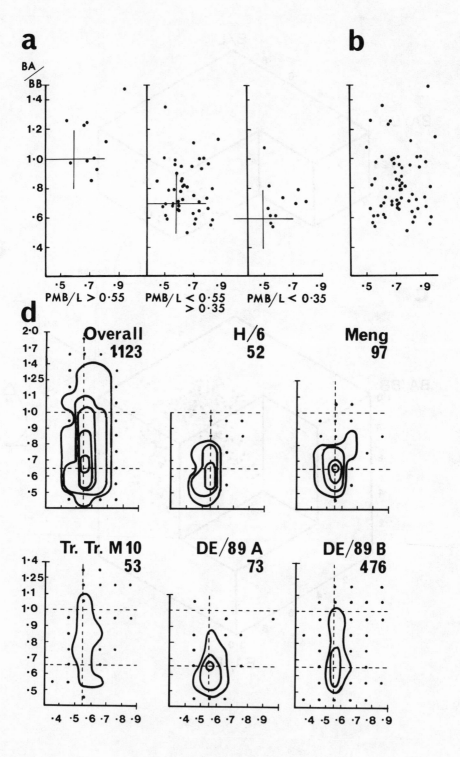

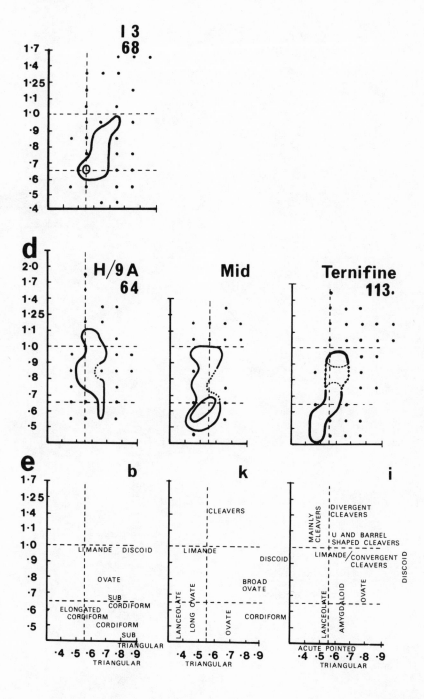

BIBLIOGRAPHY

Alimen, H. 1957. *The prehistory of Africa*. Trans. A. H. Brodrick. London: Hutchinson.

Alimen, H., and Vignal, A. 1952. Etude statistique de bifaces acheuléens: essai d'archéo-métrie. *Bulletin de la Société Préhistorique Française* 49:56-72.

Arambourg, C. 1957. Les fouilles du gisement de Ternifine et l'Atlanthropus (1954-56). *Compte Rendu du Congrès Préhistorique de France*, 15th session, pp. 171-77.

Baker, B. H. 1958. Geology of the Magadi area. *Geological Survey of Kenya*, rept. 42. Nairobi: Government Printer.

Baker, B. H., and Mitchell, J. G. 1976. Volcanic stratigraphy and geochronology of the Kedong-Olorgesailie area, and the evolution of the Southern Kenya Rift Valley, *Journal of Geological Society* 132:467-84.

Baker, B. H.; Mohr, P. A.; and Williams, L. A. J. 1972. Geology of the eastern rift system of Africa. *Geological Society of America*, special paper 136.

Balout, L. 1967. Procédés d'analyse et questions de terminologie dans l'étude des ensembles industriels du Paléolithique inférieur en Afrique du Nord. In *Background to evolution in Africa*, ed. W. W. Bishop and J. D. Clark, pp. 701-35.

Balout, L.; Biberson, P.; and Tixier, J. 1967. L'Acheuléen de Ternifine (Algérie), gisement de l'Atlanthrope. *L'Anthropologie* 71:217-37.

Beaumont, P., and Vogel, J. 1972. Revised radiocarbon chronology for the Stone Age in South Africa. *Nature* 237:50-51.

Biberson, P. 1961a. *Le cadre paléogéographique de la préhistoire du Maroc Atlantique*, no. 16. Rabat: Publications du Service des Antiquités du Maroc.

_____. 1961b. *Le paléolithique inférieur du Maroc Atlantique*, no. 17. Rabat: Publications du Service des Antiquités du Maroc.

_____. 1967. Some aspects of the Lower Palaeolithic of Northwest Africa. In *Background to evolution in Africa*, ed. W. W. Bishop and J. D. Clark, pp. 447-75.

Binford, L. R. 1963. "Red ochre" caches from the Michigan area: a possible case of cultural drift. *American Anthropologist* 19:89-107.

_____. 1972. Contemporary model building: paradigms and the current state of Palaeolithic research. In *Models in archaeology*, ed. D. L. Clarke, pp. 109-66. London: Methuen.

Binford, L. R., and Binford, S. R. 1966. A preliminary analysis of functional variability in the Mousterian of Levallois facies. In *Recent studies in paleoanthropology*, ed. J. D. Clark and F. C. Howell, pp. 238-95.

For the reports of symposia or congresses where numerous contributions are cited, full publication particulars are entered only under the name(s) of the editor(s).

Binford, S. R., and Binford, L. R. 1969. Stone tools and human behavior. *Scientific American* 220, no. 4:70-82.

Bishop, W. W., and Clark, J. D., eds. 1967. *Background to evolution in Africa*. Chicago: University of Chicago Press.

Bishop, W. W., and Miller, J. A., eds. 1972. *Calibration of hominoid evolution*. Edinburgh: Scottish Academic Press.

Bishop, W. W., and Posnansky, M. 1960. Pleistocene environments and early man in Uganda. *Uganda Journal* 24:44-61.

Black, D., ed. 1933. Fossil man in China: the Choukoutien cave deposits with a synopsis of our present knowledge of the late Cenozoic in China. Contributions by D. Black, T. de Chardin, C. C. Young, and W. C. Pei. *Memoirs of the geological survey of China*, ser. A, no. 11. Peking.

Bohmers, A. 1956. Statistics and graphs in the study of flint assemblages, I-III. *Palaeohistoria* 5:1-38.

_____. 1963. A statistical analysis of flint artefacts. In *Science in archaeology*, ed. D. Brothwell and E. S. Higgs, pp. 469-81.

Bonadonna, F. P. 1965. Further information on the research in the Middle Pleistocene diatomite quarry of Valle dell'Inferno (Riano, Rome). *Quaternaria* 7:279-99.

Bordes, F. 1950a. L'évolution buissonnante des industries en Europe occidentale: considérations théoriques sur le Paléolithique ancien et moyen. *L'Anthropologie* 54:393-420.

_____. 1950b. Principes d'une méthode d'étude des techniques de débitage et de la typologie du Paléolithique ancien et moyen. *L'Anthropologie* 54:19-34.

_____. 1953. Essai de classification des industries "Moustériennes." *Bulletin de la Société Préhistorique Francaise* 50:226-35.

_____. 1961a. *Typologie du Paléolithique ancien et moyen*. Bordeaux: Imprimeries Delmas.

_____. 1961b. Mousterian cultures in France. *Science* 134:803-10.

Bordes, F., and Fitte, P. 1953. L'Atelier Commont. *L'Anthropologie* 57:1-45.

Bordes, F., and Sonneville-Bordes, D. de. 1970. The significance of variability in palaeolithic assemblages. *World Archaeology* 2:61-73.

Bourgon, M. 1957. Les industries moustériennes et prémoustériennes du Périgord. *Archives de l'Institut de Paléontologie Humaine*, rept. 27. Paris: Masson.

Brain, C. K. 1967. Bone weathering and the problem of pseudo tools. *South African Journal of Science* 63:97-99.

Breuil, H. 1932. Les industries à éclats du Paléolithique ancien. *Préhistoire* 1:125-90.

_____. 1939. Bone and antler industry of the Choukoutien *Sinanthropus* site. *Palaeontologia Sinica*, n.s. D, no. 6. Peking.

Brothwell, D., and Higgs, E. S., eds. 1963. *Science in archaeology*. London: Thames and Hudson.

Burkitt, M. C. 1921. *Prehistory: A study of early cultures in Europe and the Mediterranean Basin*. Cambridge: Cambridge University Press.

_____. 1928. *South Africa's past in stone and paint*. Cambridge: Cambridge University Press.

_____. 1933. *The Old Stone Age: A study of palaeolithic times*. Cambridge: Cambridge University Press.

Butzer, K. W. 1964. *Environment and archaeology*. London: Methuen.

Butzer, K. W., and Isaac, G. Ll., eds. 1975. *After the Australopithecines: stratigraphy, ecology and culture change in the Middle Pleistocene*. The Hague: Mouton.

Butzer, K. W.; Isaac, G. Ll.; Richardson, J. L.; and Washbourn-Kamau, C. 1972. Radiocarbon dating of East African lake levels. *Science* 175:1069-76.

Cahen, D., and Martin, P. 1972. Classification formelle automatique et industries lithiques: interprétation des hachereaux de la Kamoa. *Annales (Série in-8°)Sciences Humaines*, no. 76. Musée Royal de l'Afrique Centrale, Tervuren.

Calvert, S. E. 1966. Accumulation of diatomaceous silica in the sediments of the gulf of California. *Geological Society of America*, bull. 77, no. 6, pp. 569-96.

Caton-Thompson, G. 1952. *Kharga Oasis in prehistory*. London: University of London, Athlone Press.

Cerralbo, Marquis de. 1913. Torralba, la plus ancienne station humaine de l'Europe? *Congrès International d'Anthropologie et d'Archéologie Préhistorique*. Comptes Rendus XIVe Session (Geneva, 1912), 1:277-90.

Chavaillon, J. 1974. Etat actuel des recherches au site paléolithique de Melka-Konturé (Choa) in IV Congresso Internazionale di Studi Etiopici. *Academia Nazionale dei Lincei Quaderno*, no. 191. Rome.

Clark, J. D. 1950. *The Stone Age of northern Rhodesia; with particular reference to the cultural and climatic succession in the upper Zambezi Valley and its tributaries*. Cape Town: South African Archaeological Society.

_____. 1954. An early Upper Pleistocene site on the northern Rhodesia-Tanganyika border. *South African Archaeological Bulletin* 9:51-56.

_____. 1958. Certain industries of notched and strangulated scrapers in Rhodesia: their time range and possible use. *South African Archaeological Bulletin* 13:56-66.

_____. 1959. Further excavations at Broken Hill, northern Rhodesia. *Journal of the Royal Anthropological Institute* 89:201-32.

_____. 1963. *Prehistoric cultures of northeast Angola and their significance in tropical Africa*. 2 vols. Museu do Dundo, Publicacões Culturais, no. 62. Lisbon: Diamang.

_____. 1964. The influence of environment in inducing culture change at the Kalambo Falls prehistoric site. *South African Archaeological Bulletin* 19:93-101.

_____. 1966a. Acheulian occupation sites in the Middle East and Africa: a study in cultural variability. In *Recent studies in paleoanthropology*, ed. J. D. Clark and F. C. Howell, pp. 202-29.

_____. 1966b. The Middle Acheulian occupation site at Latamne Northern Syria. *Annales Archéologiques Arabes Syriennes* 16:31-74.

_____. 1966c. Further excavations (1965) at the Middle Acheulian occupation site at Latamne, northern Syria: general results, definitions, and interpretations. *Annales Archéologiques Arabes Syriennes* 16:75-113.

_____. 1969a. The Middle Acheulian occupation site at Latamne, northern Syria (second paper). Further excavations (1965): general results, definition, and interpretations. *Quaternaria* 10:1-71.

_____. 1969b. *Kalambo Falls prehistoric site*. Vol. 1, *The geology, palaeoecology, and detailed stratigraphy of the excavations*. With contributions by G. H. Cole; E. G. Haldemann; M. R. Kleindienst; and E. M. van Zinderen Bakker. Cambridge: Cambridge University Press.

_____. ed., assisted by S. Cole. 1957. *Third Pan-African Congress on Prehistory, Livingstone 1955*. London: Chatto and Windus.

_____. comp. 1967. *The atlas of African prehistory*. Chicago: University of Chicago Press.

Clark, J. D., and Haynes, C. V. 1969. An elephant butchery site at Mwanganda's village karonga, Malawi, and its relevance for palaeolithic archaeology. *World Archaeology* 1:390-411.

Clark, J. D., and Howell, F. C., eds. 1966. Recent studies in paleoanthropology. Special
    Publication. *American Anthropologist* 68, no. 2, pt. 2.

Clark, J. D., and van Zinderen Bakker, E. M. 1964. Prehistoric culture and Pleistocene
    vegetation at Kalambo Falls, northern Rhodesia. *Nature* 196:639-42.

Clark, J. D.; Williams, M. A. J.; and Smith, A. B. 1973. The geomorphology and archaeology
    of Adrar Bous, Central Sahara: a preliminary report. *Quaternaria* 17:245-97.

Clark, J. G. D. 1954. *Excavations at Star Carr: an early Mesolithic site at Seamer near
    Scarborough, Yorkshire.* Cambridge: Cambridge University Press.

Clark, J. G. D.; Higgs, E. S.; and Longworth, I. H. 1960. Excavations at the Neolithic
    site at Hurst Fen, Mildenhall, Suffolk, 1954, 1957, and 1958. *Proceedings of the
    Prehistoric Society,* n.s. 26:202-45.

Clarke, D. L. 1962. Matrix analysis and archaeology with particular reference to British
    beaker pottery. *Proceedings of the Prehistoric Society,* n.s. 28:371-82.

Cole, G. H. 1961. Culture change in the Middle-Upper Pleistocene transition in Africa south
    of the Sahara. Ph.D. dissertation, University of Chicago. Microfilm Thesis no. 8411.

_____. 1967. The later Acheulian and Sangoan of southern Uganda. In *Background to evo-
    lution in Africa,* ed. W. W. Bishop and J. D. Clark, pp. 481-528.

Cole, G. H., and Kleindienst, M. R. 1974. Further reflections on the Isimila Acheulian.
    Quaternary Research 4, no. 3:346-355.

Cole, S. 1963. *The prehistory of East Africa.* New York: Macmillan.

Commont, V. 1908. Les industries de l'ancien Saint-Acheul. *L'Anthropologie* 19:527-72.

Cook, S. F., and Heizer, R. F. 1965. The quantitative approach to the relationship between
    population and settlement size. *Reports of the University of California Archaeological
    Survey* 64:1-97.

Cooke, C. K. 1963. Report on excavations at Pomongwe and Tshangula Caves, Matopo Hills,
    Southern Rhodesia. *South African Archaeological Bulletin* 18:73-151.

Cooke, H. B. S. 1967. The Pleistocene sequence in South Africa and problems of correlation.
    In *Background to evolution in Africa,* ed. W. W. Bishop and J. D. Clark, pp. 175-84.

Curtis, G. H. 1967. Notes on some Miocene to Pleistocene potassium/argon results. In
    Background to evolution in Africa, ed. W. W. Bishop and J. D. Clark, pp. 365-69.

Cuscoy, L. D., ed. 1966. *Actas del V congreso Panafricano de Prehistoria y de Estudio del
    Cuaternario,* vols. 1 and 2. Publicaciones del Museo Arqueologico Santa Cruz de
    Tenerife, nos. 5 and 6.

Dakaris, S. I.; Higgs, E. S.; and Hey, R. W. 1964. The climate, environment, and industries
    of Stone Age Greece, part 1. *Proceedings of the Prehistoric Society,* n.s. 30:199-244.

Daniel, G. E. 1950. *A hundred years of archaeology.* London: Duckworth.

Daniels, S. H. 1967. Statistics, typology, and cultural dynamics in the Transvaal Middle
    Stone Age. *South African Archaeological Bulletin* 22:114-25.

Darwin, C. 1859. *The origin of species by means of natural selection or the preservation
    of favoured races in the struggle for life.* London: J. Murray.

David. N. 1973. On Upper Palaeolithic society, ecology and technological change: the
    Noaillan case. In *The explanation of cultural change: models in prehistory,* ed. C.
    Renfrew, pp. 277-303. London: Duckworth.

Davison, D. 1934. *Men of the dawn.* London: Watts.

Day, M. H. 1965. *Guide to fossil man.* Cleveland: World Publishing.

Deacon, H. J. 1970. The Acheulian occupation at Amanzi Springs Uitenhage district, Cape
    Province. *Annals of the Cape Provincial Museums* (Natural History) 8, pt. 11:89-189.

Deacon, H. J. 1975. Demography, subsistence and culture during the Acheulian in Southern Africa. In *After the Australopithecines: stratigraphy, ecology and culture change in the Middle Pleistocene,* ed. K. W. Butzer and G. Ll. Isaac, pp. 543-69. The Hague: Mouton.

Deacon, J. 1966. An annotated list of radiocarbon dates for sub-Saharan Africa. *Annals of the Cape Provincial museums* 5:5-83.

Deetz, J. 1965. *The dynamics of stylistic change in Arikara ceramics.* Urbana, Ill.: University of Illinois Press.

_____. 1967. *Invitation to archaeology.* Garden City, N.Y.: Natural History Press.

DeVore, I., ed. 1965. *Primate behavior.* New York: Holt, Rinehart and Winston.

DeVore, I.; and Hall, K. R. L. 1965. Baboon ecology. In *Primate behavior,* ed. I. DeVore, pp. 20-52.

DeVore, I., and Washburn, S. L. 1963. Baboon ecology and human evolution. In *African ecology and human evolution,* ed. F. C. Howell and F. Bourlière, pp. 335-67.

Evans, J. 1860. Letter. In J. Prestwich, On the occurrence of flint implements, associated with the remains of extinct species in beds of a late geological period, in France at Amiens and Abbeville and in England at Hoxne. *Philosophical Transactions of the Royal Society of London* 150:310-12.

_____. 1897. *The ancient stone implements, weapons and ornaments of Great Britain.* 2d ed. London: Longmans, Green.

Evernden, J. F., and Curtis, G. H. 1965. Potassium-argon dating of Late Cenozoic rocks in East Africa and Italy. *Current Anthropology* 6:343-85.

Evernden, J. F.; Curtis, G.; and Savage, D. 1964. Potassium-argon dates and the Cenozoic mammalian chronology of North America. *American Journal of Science* 262:145-98.

Fagan, B. M. 1960. The Glentyre shelter and Oakhurst re-examined. *South African Archaeological Bulletin* 15:80-94.

Flint, R. F. 1957. *Glacial and Pleistocene geology.* New York: John Wiley.

_____. 1959a. Pleistocene climates in East and southern Africa. *Bulletin of the Geological Society of America* 70:343-74.

_____. 1959b. On the basis of Pleistocene correlation in East Africa. *Geological Magazine* 96:265-84.

Flint, R. F., and Gale, W. A. 1958. Stratigraphy and radiocarbon dates at Searles Lake, California. *American Journal of Science* 256:689-714.

Fox, R. 1967. In the beginning: aspects of hominid behavioural evolution. *Man* 2, no. 3: 415-33.

Freeman, L. G. 1975. Acheulian sites and stratigraphy in Iberia and the Maghreb. In *After the Australopithecines: stratigraphy, ecology and culture change in the Middle Pleistocene,* ed. K. W. Butzer and G. Ll. Isaac, pp. 661-743. The Hague: Mouton.

Freeman, L. G., Jr., and Butzer, K. W. 1966. The Acheulian station of Torralba (Spain): a progress report. *Quaternaria* 8:9-21.

Funnel, B. M. 1964. The Tertiary period. *Quarterly Journal of the Geological Society, London* 120:179-91.

Garrod, D. A. E., and Bate, D. M. A., 1937. *The Stone Age of Mount Carmel.* London: Oxford University Press.

Glass, B.; Ericson, D. B.; Heezen, B. C.; Opdyke, N. D.; and Glass, J. A. 1967. Geomagnetic reversals and Pleistocene chronology. *Nature* 216:437-42.

Gobert, E. G. 1950. Le gisement paléolithique de Sidi Zin. *Karthago,* vol. 1.

Goodwin, A. J. H., and Lowe, C. van Riet. 1929. The Stone Age cultures of South Africa. *Annals of the South African Museum*, vol. 27.

Gould, R. A. 1968. Chipping stones in the outback. *Natural History* 77, no. 2:42-49.

_____. In press. Where do the models come from? In *Stone tools as cultural markers*, ed. R. V. Wright. Canberra: Institute of Aboriginal Studies.

Gould, R. A.; Koster, D. A.; and Sontz, A. H. L. 1971. Lithic assemblage of the Western Desert Aborigines of Australia. *American Antiquity* 36:149-69.

Gregory, J. W. 1921. *The rift valleys and geology of East Africa*. London: Seeley, Service.

Hansen, C. L., and Keller, C. M. 1971. Environment and activity patterning at Isimila karongo, Iringa District, Tanzania: a preliminary report. *American Anthropologist* 73:1201-11.

Hay, R. L. 1965. Comment on Dr. Leakey's comment. *Current Anthropology* 6, no. 4:381.

_____. 1966. Zeolites and zeolitic reactions in sedimentary rock. *Special papers of the Geological Society of America*, no. 85. New York.

_____. 1967a. Hominid-bearing deposits of Olduvai Gorge. In *Time and stratigraphy in the evolution of man*, a symposium sponsored by the Division of Earth Sciences, National Academy of Sciences, National Research Council, Washington, D.C., pp. 30-42.

_____. 1967b. Revised stratigraphy of Olduvai Gorge. In *Background to evolution in Africa*, ed. W. W. Bishop and J. D. Clark, pp. 221-28.

_____. 1968. Chert and its sodium silicate precursors in sodium-carbonate lakes of East Africa. *Contributions to mineralogy and petrology* 17:225-74.

_____. 1971. Geologic background of Beds I and II: stratigraphic summary. In M. D. Leakey, ed., *Olduvai Gorge*, 3:9-18. Cambridge: Cambridge University Press.

_____. 1976. *The geology of Olduvai Gorge*. Berkeley: University of California Press.

Heinzelin de Braucourt, J. de. 1960. Principes de diagnose numérique en typologie. *Académie Royale de Belgique, classe des sciences, Mémoires*, 2e serie, no. 14.

_____. 1962. Comptages typologiques par catégories: entension aux indystries eurafricaines. In *Actes du IVe Congrès Panafricain de Préhistoire et de l'Etude du Quaternaire*, ed. G. Mortelmans and J. Nenquin, pp. 113-27.

Henri-Martin, G. 1957. La grotte de Fontéchevade. *Archives de l'Institut de Paléontologie Humaine*, Memoire 28. Paris: Masson.

Hodson, F. R.; Sneath, P. H. A.; and Doran, J. E. 1966. Some experiments in the numerical analysis of archaeological data. *Biometrika* 53:311-24.

Howell, F. C. 1965. *Early man*. New York: Time-Life.

_____. 1966. Observations on the earlier phases of the European Lower Paleolithic. In *Recent studies in paleoanthropology*, ed. J. D. Clark and F. C. Howell, pp. 88-201.

Howell, F. C., and Bourlière, F., eds. 1963. *African ecology and human evolution*. Viking Fund Publications in Anthropology, no. 36. Chicago: Aldine.

Howell, F. C., and Clark, J. D. 1963. Acheulian hunter-gatherers of sub-Saharan Africa. In *African ecology and human evolution*, ed. F. C. Howell and F. Bourlière, pp. 458-533.

Howell, F. C.; Cole, G. H.; and Kleindienst, M. R. 1962. Isimila: an Acheulian occupation site in the Iringa Highlands, Southern Highlands Province, Tanganyika. In *Actes du IVe Congrès Panafricain de Préhistoire et de l'Etude du Quaternaire*, ed. G. Mortelmans and J. Nenquin, pp. 43-80.

Isaac, G. Ll. 1964. Olorgesailie: a study of the natural history of a Middle Pleistocene lake basin. *Proceedings of the East African Academy: First Symposium, Makerere, June 1963*. Nairobi: Longmans.

Isaac, G. Ll. 1965. The stratigraphy of the Peninj Beds and the provenance of the Natron Australopithecine mandible. *Quaternaria* 7:101-30.

_____. 1966a. The geological history of the Olorgesailie area. In *Actas del V Congreso Panafricano de Prehistoria y de Estudio del Cuaternario*, ed. L. D. Cuscoy, pp. 125-33.

_____. 1966b. New evidence from Olorgesailie relating to the character of Acheulian occupation sites. In *Actas del V Congreso Panafricano de Prehistoria y de Estudio del Cuaternario*, ed. L. D. Cuscoy, pp. 135-45.

_____. 1967a. The stratigraphy of the Peninj Group: early Middle Pleistocene formations west of Lake Natron, Tanzania. In *Background to evolution in Africa*, ed. W. W. Bishop and J. D. Clark, pp. 229-57.

_____. 1967b. Towards the interpretation of occupation debris: some experiments and observations. *Kroeber Anthropological Society Papers* 37:31-57.

_____. 1968a. Traces of Pleistocene hunters: an East African example. In *Man the hunter*, ed. R. B. Lee and I. DeVore, pp. 253-61.

_____. 1968b. The Acheulean site complex at Olorgesailie, Kenya: a contribution to the interpretation of Middle Pleistocene culture in East Africa. Ph.D. dissertation, Cambridge University.

_____. 1969. Studies of early cultures in East Africa. *World Archaeology* 1:1-28.

_____. 1971. The diet of early man: aspects of archaeological evidence from lower and middle Pleistocene sites in Africa. *World Archaeology* 2:278-98.

_____. 1972a. Chronology and tempo of cultural change during the Pleistocene. In *Calibration of hominid evolution*, ed. W. W. Bishop and J. A. Miller. Edinburgh: Scottish Academic Press, pp. 381-430.

_____. 1972b. Early phases of human behaviour: models in Lower Palaeolithic archaeology. In *Models in archaeology*, ed. D. L. Clarke, pp. 167-99. London: Methuen.

_____. 1972c. Comparative studies of Pleistocene site locations in East Africa. In *Man, settlement and urbanism*, ed. P. J. Ucko, R. Tringham and G. W. Dimbleby, pp. 165-76. London: Duckworth.

_____. 1972d. Some experiments in quantitative methods for characterising Acheulian assemblages. In *Congrès Panafricain de Préhistoire, Dakar 1967: Actes de 6ᵉ Session*, ed. H. J. Hugot, pp. 547-55. Paris: Chambéry.

_____. 1972e. Identification of cultural entities in the Middle Pleistocene. In *Congrès Panafricain de Préhistoire, Dakar 1967: Actes de 6ᵉ Session*, ed. H. J. Hugot, pp. 556-62. Paris: Chambéry.

_____. 1975. Middle Pleistocene stratigraphy and cultural patterns in East Africa. In *After the Australopithecines: stratigraphy, ecology and culture change in the Middle Pleistocene*, ed. K. W. Butzer and G. Ll. Isaac, pp. 495-542. The Hague: Mouton.

_____. In press. The Olorgesailie Formation: stratigraphy, tectonics and the paleogeographic context of the Middle Pleistocene archaeological sites. In *Geological background to fossil man in East Africa*, ed. W. W. Bishop. Edinburgh: Scottish Academic Press.

Isaac, G. Ll., and Curtis, G. H. 1974. Age of early Acheulian industries from the Peninj Group, Tanzania. *Nature* 249:624-27.

Isaac, G. Ll., and Keller, C. M. 1968. Note on the proportional frequency of side- and end-struck flakes. *South African Archaeological Bulletin* 23:17-19.

Jones, N. 1929. A hitherto undescribed Early Stone Age industry near Hope Fountain, Rhodesia. *South African Journal of Science* 26:631-47.

Keller, C. M. 1973. Montagu Cave in prehistory. *University of California Anthropological Records* 28:1-98.

Kelling, G., and Williams, P. F. 1967. Flume studies of the reorientation of pebbles and shells. *Journal of Geology* 75:243-67.

Klein, R. G. 1966. Chellean and Acheulean on the territory of the Soviet Union: a critical review of the evidence as presented in the literature. In *Recent studies in paleoanthropology*, ed. J. D. Clark and F. C. Howell, pp. 1-45.

Kleindienst, M. R. 1959. Composition and significance of a Late Acheulian assemblage based on an analysis of East African occupation sites. Ph.D. dissertation, University of Chicago. Microfilm Thesis no. 4706.

————. 1961. Variability within the Late Acheulian assemblage in East Africa. *South African Archaeological Bulletin* 16:35-52.

————. 1962. Components of the East African Acheulian assemblage: an analytic approach. In *Actes du IVe Congrès Panafricain de Préhistoire et de l'Étude du Quaternaire*, ed. C. Mortelmans and J. Nenquin, pp. 81-105.

Kretzoi, M., and Vertes, L. 1965. Upper Biharian (Inter Mindel) pebble industry occupation site in western Hungary. *Current Anthropology* 6:74-87.

Lal, B. B. 1956. Palaeoliths from the Beas and Banganga valleys, Punjab. *Ancient India* 12:59-92.

Langbein, W. B., and Leopold, L. B. No date. River channel bars and dunes: theory of kinematic waves. Manuscript.

Leakey, L. S. B. 1931. *The Stone Age cultures of the Kenya Colony*. Cambridge: Cambridge University Press.

————. 1934. *Adam's ancestors*. London: Methuen.

————. 1951. *Olduvai Gorge: a report on the evolution of the handaxe culture in Beds I-IV*. Cambridge: Cambridge University Press.

————. 1952. The Olorgesailie prehistoric site. In *Proceedings, First Pan-African Congress on Prehistory, 1947*, ed. L. S. B. Leakey and S. Cole, p. 209.

————. 1953. *Adam's Ancestors*. 4th edition. London: Methuen.

————. 1957. Preliminary report on a Chellean I living site at BK II, Olduvai Gorge, Tanganyika Territory. In *Proceedings, Third Pan-African Congress on Prehistory, Livingstone, 1955*, ed. J. D. Clark, pp. 217-18.

————. 1958. Some East African Pleistocene Suidae. *Fossil Mammals of Africa*, no. 14. London: British Museum of Natural History.

————. 1965a. A comment on S. L. Washburn's contribution to the symposium, *The origin of man*, ed. P. L. DeVore, p. 98. New York: Wenner-Gren Foundation (private circulation).

————. 1965b. *Olduvai Gorge, 1951-61*, vol. 1. A preliminary report on the geology and fauna. Cambridge: Cambridge University Press.

————. 1974. *By the evidence: memoirs 1932-1951*. New York and London: Harcourt Brace Jovanovich.

————. Various notes and draft reports in the files of the Centre for Prehistory and Palaeontology, Nairobi.

Leakey, L. S. B., and Cole, S., eds. 1952. *Proceedings, First Pan-African Congress on Prehistory, 1947*. Oxford: Blackwell.

Leakey, L. S. B., and Whitworth, T. 1958. Notes on the genus *Simopithecus*, with a description of a new species from Olduvai. *Coryndon Memorial Museum Occasional Papers*, no. 6.

Leakey, M. C.; Tobias, P. V.; Martyn, J. E.; and Leakey, R. E. 1969. An Acheulian industry with prepared core technique and the discovery of a contemporary hominid mandible at Lake Baringo, Kenya. *The Prehistoric Society* 35:48-76.

Leakey, Mary D. 1967. Preliminary survey of the cultural material from Beds I and II, Olduvai Gorge, Tanzania. In *Background to evolution in Africa*, ed. W. W. Bishop and J. D. Clark, pp. 417-46.

Leakey, Mary D. 1971. *Olduvai Gorge*. Vol. 3, *Excavations in Beds I and II, 1960-1963*. Cambridge: Cambridge University Press.

_____. 1975. Cultural patterns in the Olduvai sequence. In *After the Australopithecines: stratigraphy, ecology and culture change in the Middle Pleistocene*, ed. K. W. Butzer and G. Ll. Isaac, pp. 477-93. The Hague: Mouton.

Leakey, M. G., and Leakey, R. E. F. 1973. Further evidence of *Simopithecus* (Mammalia, Primates) from Olduvai and Olorgesailie. In *Fossil vertebrates of Africa*, ed. L. S. B. Leakey, R. J. G. Savage, and S. C. Coryndon, pp. 101-20. London and New York: Seminar Press.

Lee, R. B. 1968. What hunters do for a living, or, how to make out on scarce resources. In *Man the hunter*, ed. R. B. Lee and I. DeVore, pp. 30-48.

Lee, R. B., and DeVore, I., eds. 1968. *Man the hunter*. Proceedings of a symposium held in Chicago, April 1966, sponsored by Wenner-Gren Foundation for Anthropological Research. Chicago: Aldine.

Leopold, L. B.; Emett, W. W.; and Myrick, R. M. 1966. Channel and hillslope processes in a semiarid area, New Mexico. *Geological Survey Professional Paper*, no. 352-G, pp. 193-253. Washington, D.C.

Leroi-Gourhan, A. 1966. *La Préhistoire*. Paris: Presses Universitaires de France.

Lindley, D. V. 1965. *Introduction to probability and statistics from a Bayesian viewpoint*. Cambridge: Cambridge University Press.

Livingstone, D. A. 1965. Sedimentation and the history of water level change in Lake Tanganyika. *Limnology and Oceanography* 10 (no. 4): 607-10.

Longacre, W. A. 1964. Archaeology as anthropology: a case study. *Science* 144:1454-55.

Lowe, C. Van Riet. 1937. See Sönghe et al. 1937.

_____. 1952. *The Pleistocene geology and prehistory of Uganda, Part II. Prehistory*. Geological Survey of Uganda, Mémoire 6.

Lubbock, J. 1865. *Prehistoric times*. London: Williams and Norgate.

Lumley, H. de. 1969. A Paleolithic camp at Nice. *Scientific American* 220, no. 5:42-50.

_____. 1975. Cultural evolution in France in its paleoecological setting during the Middle Pleistocene. In *After the Australopithecines: stratigraphy, ecology and culture change in the Middle Pleistocene*, ed. K. W. Butzer and G. Ll. Isaac, pp. 745-808. The Hague: Mouton.

McBurney, C. B. M. 1948. The tools of Neanderthal man: a comparative study of Middle Palaeolithic material from European cave deposits. Ph.D. dissertation. Cambridge University.

_____. 1950. The geographical study of the older Palaeolithic stages in Europe. *Proceedings of the Prehistoric Society*, n.s. 16:163-83.

_____. 1967. *The Haua Fteah (Cyrenaica) and the Stone Age of the south-east Mediterranean*. Cambridge: Cambridge University Press.

McCall, G. J. H.; Baker, B. H.; and Walsh, J. 1967. Late Tertiary and Quaternary sediments of the Kenya Rift Valley. In *Background to evolution in Africa*, ed. W. W. Bishop and J. D. Clark, pp. 191-220.

MacCalman, H. R., and Grobbelaar, B. J. 1965. Preliminary report of two stone-working Ovatjimba groups in the northern kaokveld of South West Africa. In *Cimbebasia*, South West Africa Research Publication, no. 13, pp. 1-39. Windhoek: Administration of S.W.A.

MacCurdy, G. C. 1924. *Human origins: a manual of prehistory*. 2 vols. New York: D.Appleton.

Malvesin-Fabré, G. 1948. Essai de discrimination des bifaces abbévilliens et acheuléens par un indice numérique. *Bulletin de la Société Préhistorique Française* 45:58-63.

Marsden, M. In preparation. A report on the geomorphology of the Olorgesailie-Magadi sector of the Rift Valley.

Martyn, J. 1967. Pleistocene deposits and new fossil localities in Kenya. *Nature* 215: 476-79.

Mason, R. J. 1957. The Transvaal Middle Stone Age and statistical analysis. *South African Archaeological Bulletin* 12:119-43.

_____. 1961. The Acheulian culture in South Africa. *South African Archaeological Bulletin* 16:107-10.

_____. 1962. *Prehistory of the Transvaal*. Johannesburg: Witwatersrand University Press.

_____. 1967. Analytical procedures in the Earlier and Middle Stone Age cultures in southern Africa. In *Background to evolution in Africa*, ed. W. W. Bishop and J. D. Clark, pp. 737-69.

Mellars, P. A. 1965. Sequence and development of Mousterian traditions in southwestern France. *Nature* 205:626-27.

_____. 1970. Some comments on the notion of "functional variability" in stone-tool assemblages. *World Archaeology* 2:74-89.

Miller, J. A. 1967. Problems of dating East African Tertiary and Quaternary volcanics by the potassium-argon method. In *Background to evolution in Africa*, ed. W. W. Bishop and J. D. Clark, pp. 259-72.

Mitchell, S. R. 1949. *Stone age craftsmen: stone tools and camping places of Australian Aborigines*. Melbourne: Tait Book Co.

Morgan, W. T. W. 1967. *Nairobi: city and region*. Nairobi: Oxford University Press.

Moroney, M. J. 1956. *Facts from figures*. Harmondsworth Middlesex: Penguin Books.

Mortelmans, G., and Nenquin, J., eds. 1962. *Actes du IVe Congrès Panafricain de Préhistoire et de l'Étude du Quaternaire*. 2 vols. Musée Royal de l'Afrique Centrale, Annales Série, Sciences Humaines, no. 40. Tervuren, Belgium.

Mortillet, G. de. 1883. *Le Préhistorique: antiquité de l'homme*. Bibliothèque des Sciences Contemporaines. Paris: C. Reinwald.

_____. 1890. *Origines de la chasse, de la pêche, et de l'agriculture*. Bibliothèque Anthropologique, no. 12. Paris: Lecrosnier et Babe.

Mortillet, G. de, and Mortillet, A. de. 1910. *Préhistorique: origine et antiquité de l'Homme*. Paris: Librairie Schleucher.

Movius, H. L. 1948. The Lower Palaeolithic cultures of southern and eastern Asia. *Transactions of the American Philosophical Society* 38:329-419.

Mulvaney, D. J., and Joyce, E. B. 1965. Archaeological and geomorphological investigations on Mt. Moffat Station, Queensland, Australia. *Proceedings of the Prehistoric Society*, n.s. 31:147-212.

Nenquin, J. 1967. *Contributions to the study of the prehistoric cultures of Ruanda and Burundi*. Musée Royal de l'Afrique Centrale (Serie in-8°) Sciences Humaines, no. 59. Tervuren, Belgium.

Oakley, K. P. 1956. The earliest fire makers. *Antiquity* 30:102-7.

Oakley, K. P., and Campbell, B. G. 1967. *Catalogue of fossil hominids: part 1, Africa*. London: British Museum (Natural History).

Obermaier, H. 1925. *Fossil man in Spain*. New Haven: Yale University Press.

Osborn, H. F. 1916. *Men of the Old Stone Age: their environment, life, and art*. New York: Charles Scribners.

Owen, R. C. 1965. The patrilocal band: a linguistically and culturally hybrid social unit. *American Anthropologist* 67:675-90.

Paterson, T. T. 1937. Studies in the Palaeolithic succession in England: no. 1, the Barnham sequence. *Proceedings of the Prehistoric Society*, n.s. 3:87-135.

————. 1945. Core, culture, and complex in the Old Stone Age. *Proceedings of the Prehistoric Society*, n.s. 11:1-19.

Paterson, T. T., and Fagg, B. E. B. 1940. Studies of the Palaeolithic succession in England (Elveden). *Proceedings of the Prehistoric Society*, n.s. 6:1-29.

Peake, H., and Fleure, J. H. 1927. *Apes and men: corridors of time*, no. 1. Oxford: Clarendon Press.

Posnansky, M. 1959. The Hope Fountain Site at Olorgesailie, Kenya Colony. *South African Archaeological Bulletin* 16:83-89.

Reed, C. A. 1963. Osteo-archaeology. In *Science in archaeology*, ed. D. Brothwell and E. S. Higgs, pp. 204-16.

Reed, O. M. 1967. Cephalometric studies of the growth, development, and eruption patterns of the baboon. In *The baboon in medical research*, vol. 2, ed. H. Vagtborg, pp. 181-86.

Richardson, J. L. 1966. Changes in lake level in Lake Naivasha, Kenya, during postglacial times. *Nature* 209:290-91.

Richardson, J. L., and Richardson, A. E. 1972. History of an African lake and its climatic implications. *Ecological Monographs* 42:499-534.

Roe, D. A. 1964. The British Lower and Middle Palaeolithic: some problems, methods of study, and preliminary results. *Proceedings of the Prehistoric Society*, n.s. 30: 245-67.

————. 1967. A study of handaxe groups of British Lower and Middle Palaeolithic periods. Ph.D. dissertation, Cambridge University.

————. 1968. British Lower and Middle Palaeolithic handaxe groups. *Proceedings of the Prehistoric Society*, n.s. 34:1-82.

Rust, A. 1950. *Die höhlenfunde von Jabrud (Syrien)*. Neumünster: K. Wachholtz.

Sackett, J. R. 1966. Quantitative analysis of Upper Paleolithic stone tools. In *Recent studies in paleoanthropology*, ed. J. D. Clark and F. C. Howell, pp. 356-94.

Sampson, C. G. 1974. *The Stone Age archaeology of Southern Africa*. New York and London: Academic Press.

Savage, D. E., and Curtis, G. H. 1970. The Villafranchian Stage-age and its radiometric dating. *Geological Society of America*, special paper 124, pp. 207-31.

Shackleton, R. M. 1945. Geology of the Nyeri area. *Geological Survey of Kenya*, rept. 12.

————. 1955. Pleistocene movements in the Gregory Rift Valley. *Geologische Rundschau* 43:257-63.

————. In press. A geological map of the Olorgesailie area. In *Geological background to fossil man in East Africa*, ed. W. W. Bishop. Edinburgh: Scottish Academic Press.

————. Maps and stratigraphic profiles made available to the author. Copies of these will be lodged in the library of the Louis Leakey Memorial Institute, Nairobi.

Shawcross, W. 1964. Stone flake industries in New Zealand. *Journal of the Polynesian Society* 73:7-25.

————. 1967. An investigation of prehistoric diet and economy on a coastal site at Galatea Bay, New Zealand. *Proceedings of the Prehistoric Society*, n.s. 33:107-31.

Siegel, S. 1956. *Non-parametric statistics: for the behavioral sciences*. New York: McGraw-Hill.

Simpson, G. G. 1941. Large Pleistocene felines of North America. *American Museum Novitates* 1136:1-27.

Simpson, G. G.; Roe, A.; and Lewontin, R. G. 1960. *Quantitative Zoology*. New York: Harcourt, Brace and World.

Söhnge, P. G.; Visser, D. J. L., and Lowe, C. Van Riet. 1937. *The geology and archaeology of the Vaal River basin*. Union of South Africa Geological Survey, Memoire 35.

Sokal, R. R., and Sneath, P. H. A. 1963. *Principles of numerical taxonomy*. San Francisco: W. H. Freeman.

Sollas, W. J. 1911. *Ancient hunters and their modern representatives*. London: Macmillan.

Sonneville-Bordes, D. de. 1960. *Le Paléolithique Supérieur en Périgord*. 2 vols. Bordeaux: Delmas.

Sonneville-Bordes, D. de, and Perrot, J. 1954, 1955, 1956. Lexique typologique du Paléolithique supérieur, outillage lithique. *Bulletin de la Société Préhistorique Française* 51:327-35; 52:76-79; 53:408-12, 547-59.

Spaulding, A. C. 1953. Statistical technique for the discovery of artifact types. *American Antiquity* 18:305-13.

_____. 1960. Statistical description and comparison of artifact assemblages. In *The application of quantitative methods in Archaeology*, ed. R. F. Heizer and S. F. Cook, pp. 60-83. Viking Fund Publications in Anthropology, no. 28. New York: Wenner-Gren Foundation.

Stekelis, M. 1966. *Archaeological excavations at 'Ubeidiya, 1960-63*. Jerusalem: Israel Academy of Sciences and Humanities.

Stekelis, M.; Bar-Yosef, O.; and Schick. T. 1969. *Archaeological excavations at 'Ubeidiya, 1964-1966*. Jerusalem: Israel Academy of Sciences and Humanities.

Stekelis, M., and Gilead, D. 1966. *Ma'ayan Barukh: a Lower Palaeolithic site in Upper Galilee*. Jerusalem: Metqufat Ha-even, 8.

Stewart, D. R. M. 1967. Fauna. In *Nairobi: city and region*, ed. W. T. W. Morgan, pp. 48-56.

Survey of Kenya. 1959. *Atlas of Kenya: a comprehensive series of new and authentic maps*. Nairobi: Survey of Kenya.

Thompson, B. W., and Sansom, H. W. 1967. Climate. In *Nairobi: city and region*, ed. W. T. W. Morgan, pp. 20-38.

Thompson, D. F. 1964. Some wood and stone implements of the Bindibu tribe of central Western Australia. *Proceedings of the Prehistoric Society*, n.s. 30:400-422.

Thompson, J. 1885. *Through Masai Land: the narrative of the Royal Geographical Society's expedition to Mount Kenya and Lake Victoria Nyanza, 1883-1884*. London: Sampson Low, Marston.

Tixier, J. 1957. Le hachereau dans l'Acheuléen nord-africain. In *Congrès Préhistorique de France: Compte rendu de la XVᵉ Session (1956)*, pp. 914-23. Paris: Bureau de la Soc. Prehist. Francaise.

_____. 1963. *Typologie de l'Epipaléolithique du Maghreb*. Paris: Arts et Métiers Graphiques.

Trump, E. C. 1967. Vegetation. In *Nairobi: city and region*, ed. W. T. W. Morgan, pp. 39-47.

Turnbull, C. M. 1962. *The forest people*. Garden City, N.Y.: Doubleday Anchor Books.

_____. 1968. The importance of flux in two hunting societies. In *Man the hunter*, ed. R. B. Lee and I. DeVore, pp. 132-37. Chicago: Aldine.

Tyrrell, G. W. 1926. *The principles of petrology*. London: Methuen.

Vagtborg, H., ed. 1967. *The baboon in medical research*. Austin: University of Texas Press.

Vayson de Pradenne, A. 1937. Les denominations de l'outillage du Paléolithique inférieur. *Revue Anthropologique* 47:91-112.

Vertes, L. 1965. Typology of the Buda industry, a pebble-tool industry from the Hungarian Lower Palaeolithic. *Quaternaria* 7:185-95.

Vogel, J. C., and Waterbolk, H. T. 1967. Groningen radiocarbon dates VII. *Radiocarbon* 9: 145.

Walker, D., and Sieveking, A. de G. 1962. The Palaeolithic industry of Kota Tampan, Malaya. *Proceedings of the Prehistoric Society*, n.s. 28:103-39.

Warren, S. H. 1914. The experimental investigation of flint fracture and its application to problems of human implements. *Journal of the Royal Anthropological Institute* 44: 412-50.

_____. 1951. The Clacton flint industry: a new interpretation. *Proceedings of the Geologists Association* 62:107-35.

Washburn, S. L. 1957. Australopithecines: the hunters or the hunted. *American Anthropologist* 59:612-14.

_____. 1965. An ape's eye view of human evolution. In *The origin of man*, a symposium sponsored by the Wenner-Gren Foundation for Anthropological Research, ed. P. L. DeVore. New York: Wenner-Gren Foundation (private circulation).

West, R. G., and McBurney, C. B. 1954. The Quaternary deposits at Hoxne, Suffolk, and their archaeology. *Proceedings of the Prehistoric Society*, n.s. 20:131-54.

Williams, L. A. J. 1967. Geology. In *Nairobi: city and region*, ed. W. T. W. Morgan, pp. 1-19. Nairobi and London: Oxford University Press.

Woodburn, J. 1968. An introduction to Hadza ecology. In *Man the hunter*, ed. R. B. Lee and I. DeVore, pp. 49-55.

Wymer, J. 1964. Excavations at Barnfield Pit, 1955-1960. In *The Swanscombe Skull*, ed. C. D. Ovey, pp. 19-62. Occasional paper no. 20 of the Royal Anthropological Institute, London.

Yellen, J., and Harpending, H. 1972. Hunter-gatherer populations and archaeological inference. *World Archaeology* 4:244-53.

Bibliography

PHOTOGRAPHS AND STEREOPHOTOGRAPHS OF LARGE TOOLS

The three-dimensional effect can be achieved by using a small stereoscopic viewer or by holding a card between the two images so that each eye sees only the image on its side of the card. Plates 24-45 are stereo pairs; plates 46-51 are non-stereo photographs usually showing faces of each specimen; plates 52-60 are stereo pairs.

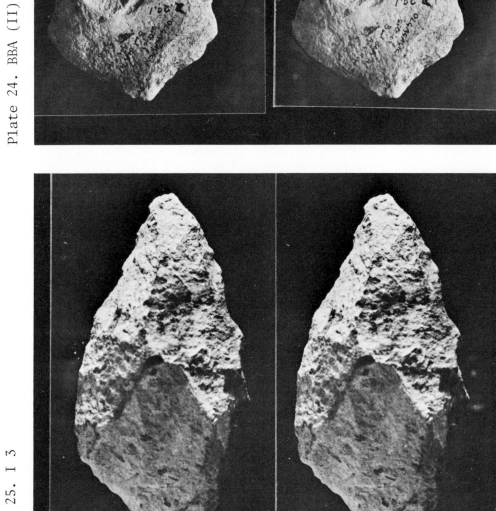

Plate 24. BBA (II)

Plate 25. I 3

Plate 26. I 3

Plate 27. I 3

Plate 28. I 3

Plate 29. DE/89 A

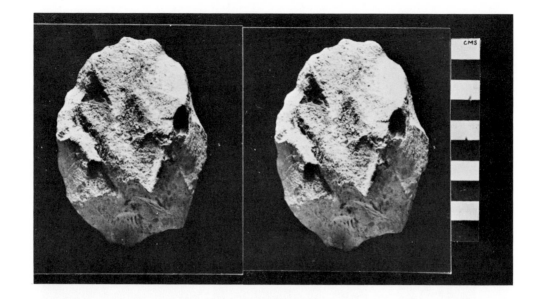

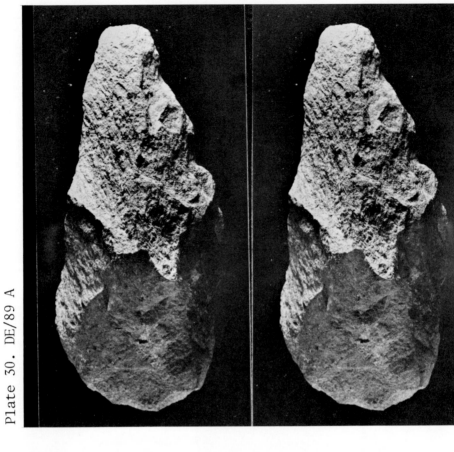

Plate 30. DE/89 A

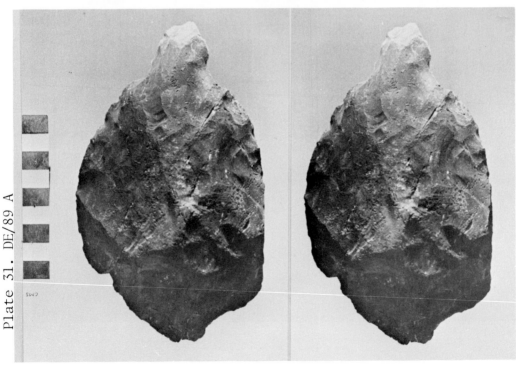

Plate 31. DE/89 A

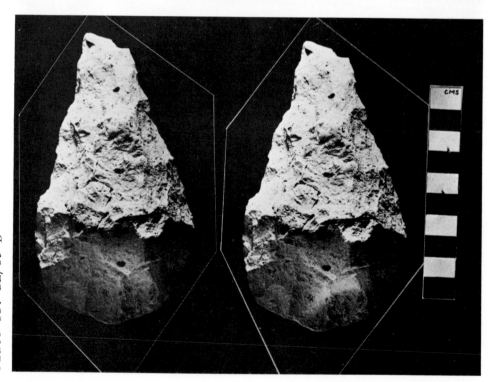

Plate 32. DE/89 A

Plate 33. DE/89 B

Plate 34. DE/89 B

Plate 35. DE/89 B

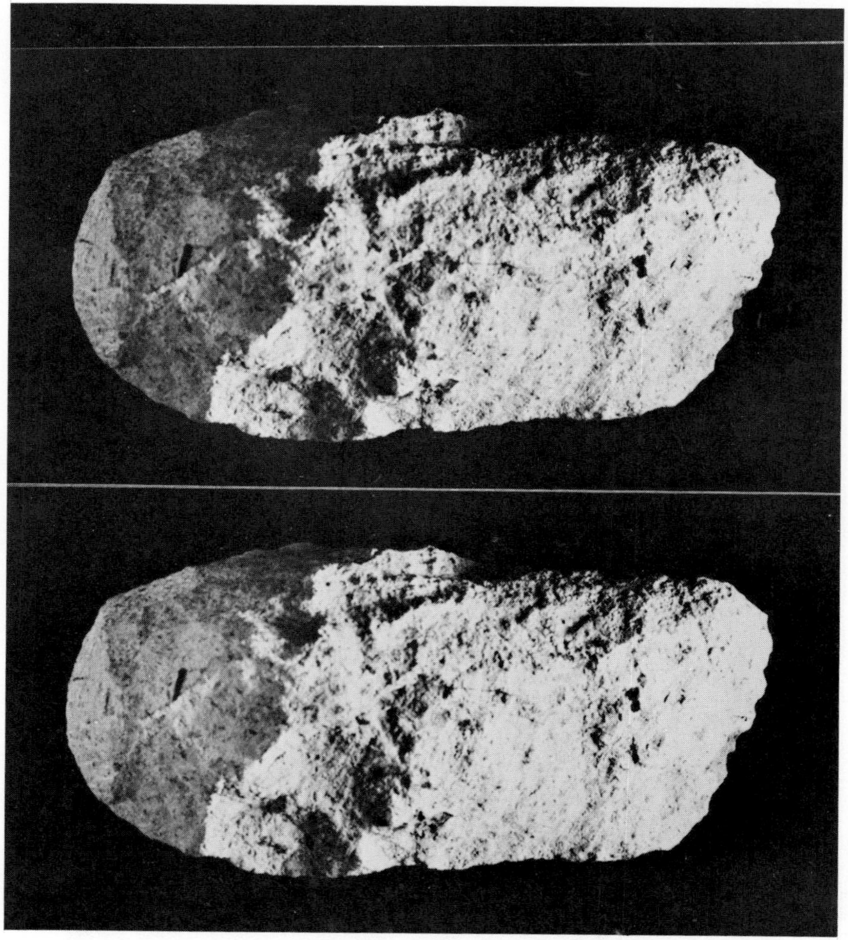

Plate 36. DE/89 B

Plate 37. DE/89 B

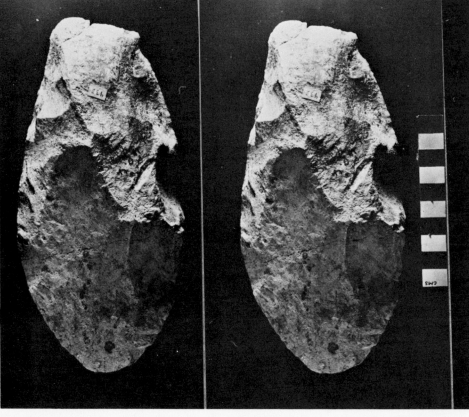

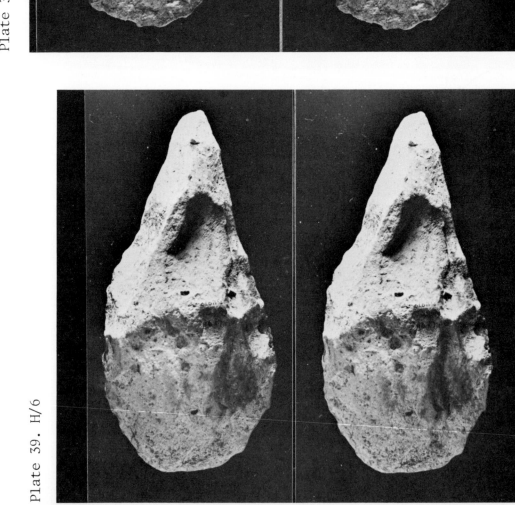

Plate 38. DE/89 B

Plate 39. H/6

Plate 40. H/6

Plate 41. H/6

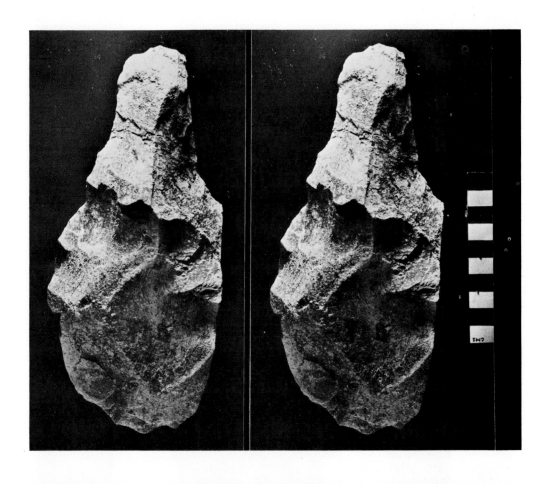

Plate 42. Mid

Plate 43. Mid

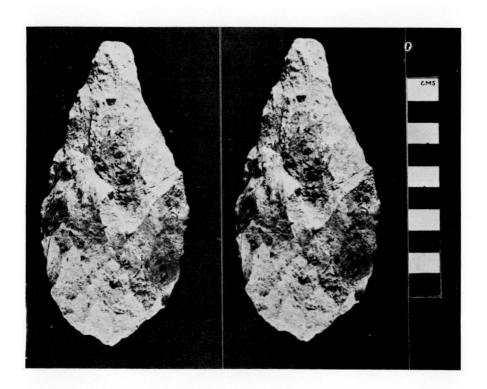

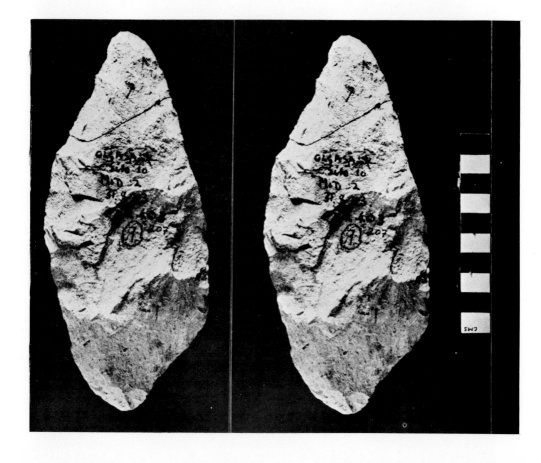

Plate 44. Mid

Plate 45. H/9 A

Plate 46. H/9 A

Plate 48. H/9 A

Plate 49. n/5 A

Plate 50. H/9 A

Plate 51.

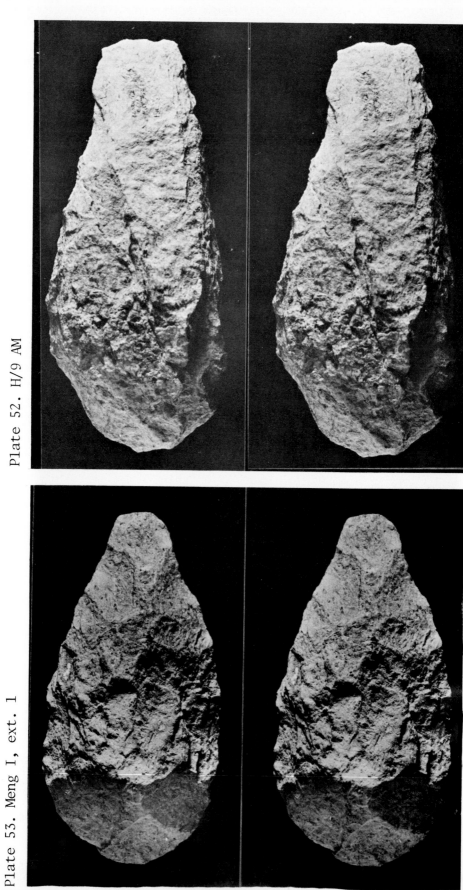

Plate 52. H/9 AM

Plate 53. Meng I, ext. 1

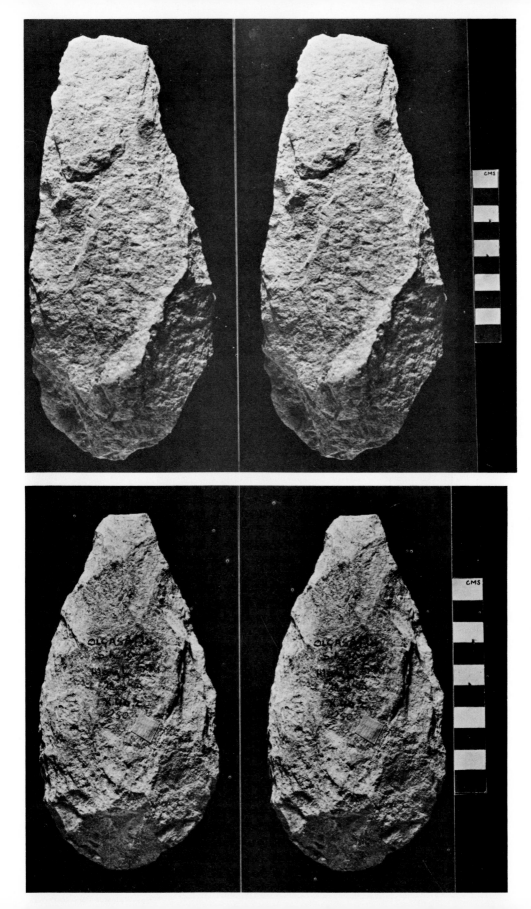

Plate 54. Meng II

Plate 55. Meng I

Plate 56. Meng II

Plate 57. Tr. Tr., E surface

Plate 58. Tr. Tr., 140-150 floor

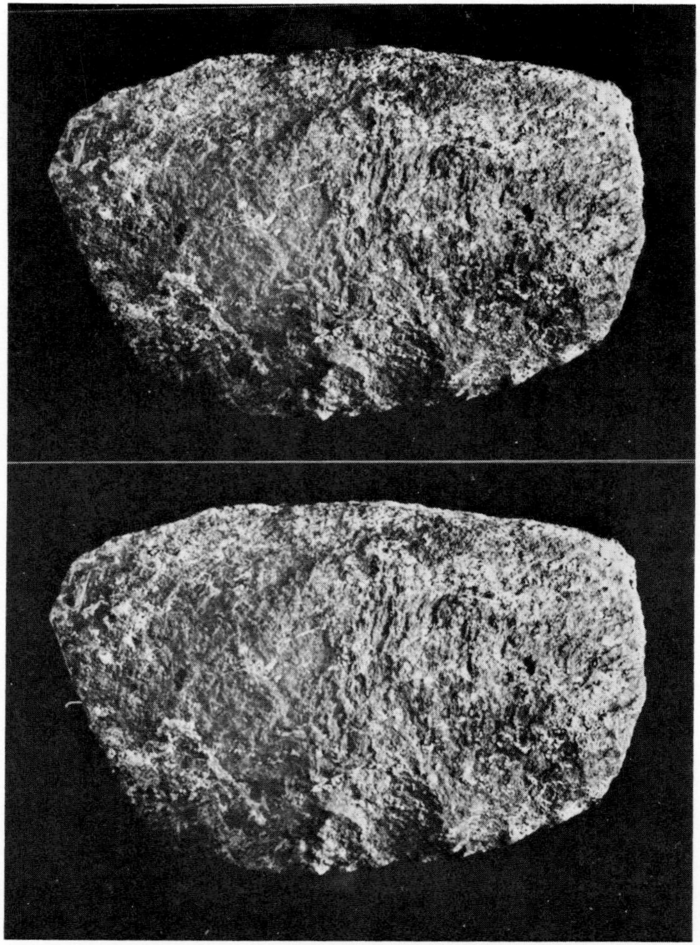

Plate 59. Tr. Tr., 140-150 floor

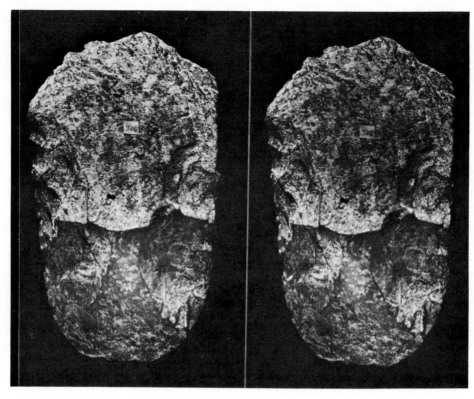

Plate 60. Tr. Tr.

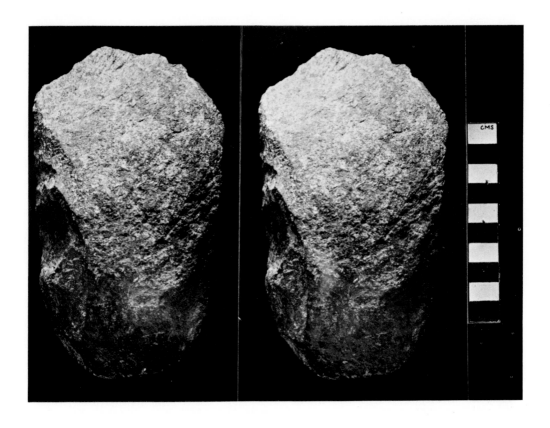

CAPTIONS

Plate 24. Typological designation: cleaver, atypical; Primary form: flake; material: lava; Length: 110 mm; B/L: 0.79; BA/BB: 1.31; BA/B 0.82; T/B 0.48; Site: Basal Bed A; Field Cat. No.: LSBL 583.

Plate 25. Typological designation: hand ax, subclassic; Primary form: corner-struck side flake; Material: trachyte; Length: 167 mm; B/L: 0.53; BA/BB: 0.61; BA/B: 0.48; T/B: 0.58; Sc.: 20; Scar bifac.: 0.8; Site: I 3; Field Cat. no.: I 3 94.

Plate 26. Typological designation: cleaver; Primary form: corner-struck side flake; Material: trachyandesite (1P); Length: 174 mm; B/L: 0.47; BA/BB: 0.85; BA/B: 0.72; T/B: 0.56; Sc.: 26; Scar bifac.: 0.9; Site: I 3; Field Cat. no.: I 3 302.

Plate 27. Typological designation: hand ax, subclassic/core; Primary form: indet.; Material: trachyandesite; Length: 114 mm; B/L: 0.70; BA/BB: 0.63; BA/B: 0.42; T/B: 0.47; Sc.: 16; Scar bifac.: 0.8; Site: I 3; Field Cat. no.: I 3 305.

Plate 28. Typological designation: knife; Primary form: indet.; Material: basalt; Length: 118 mm; B/L: 0.71; BA/BB: 0.94; BA/B: 0.71; T/B: 0.43; Sc.: 16; Scar bifac.: 0.3; Site: I 3; Field Cat. no.: I 3 352.

Plate 29. Typological designation: hand ax, classic, chisel-ended; Primary form: indet.; Material: trachyte; Site: DE/89 A; Field Cat. no.: Tr. Tr. B2 (LSBL) 441.

Plate 30. Typological designation: hand ax, subclassic, chisel-ended; Primary form: indet.; Material: trachyte; Length: 226 mm; B/L: 0.48; BA/BB: 0.58; BA/B: 0.5; T/B: 0.57; Sc.: 40; Scar bifac.: 0.8; Site: DE/89 A; Field Cat. no.: Tr. Tr. B2 (LSBL) 445.

Plate 31. Typological designation: hand ax, subclassic, with a notch-defined "nose"; Primary form: ? side-struck flake; Material: obsidian; Length: 176 mm; B/L: 0.64; BA/BB: 0.42; BA/B: 0.35; T/B: 0.58; Sc.: 23; Scar bifac.: 0.6; Site: DE/89 A; Field Cat. no.: Tr. Tr. B2 (LSBL) 447.

Plate 32. Typological designation: triedre (unifacial); Primary form: ? end-struck flake; Material: trachyte; Length: 171 mm; B/L: 0.63; BA/BB: 0.50; BA/B: 0.48; T/B: 0.39; Sc.: 20; Scar bifac.: 0; Site: DE/89 A; Field Cat. no.: Tr. Tr. B2 (LSBL) 451.

Plate 33. Typological designation: hand ax, classic; Primary form: indet.; Material: trachyandesite; Length: 156 mm; B/L: 0.52; BA/BB: 0.41; Scar bifac.:--; BA/B: 0.38; T/B: 0.59; Sc.: indet.; Site: DE/89 B; Field Cat. no.: Tr. Tr. B4 (LSBL) 149.

Plate 34. Typological designation: cleaver, convergent, oblique; Primary form: ? side flake; Length: 181 mm; B/L: 0.52; BA/BB: 0.93; BA/B: 0.80; T/B: 0.60; Sc.: 36; Scar bifac.: 0.8; Site: DE/89 B; Field Cat. no.: Tr. Tr. B4 (LSBL) 339.

Plate 35. Typological designation: hand ax, classic; Primary form: ? flake or tabular spall; Material: trachyte; Length: 164 mm; B/L: 0.71; BA/BB: 0.72; BA/B: 0.54; T/B: 0.33; Sc.: 30; Scar bifac.: 0.6; Site: DE/89 B; Field Cat. no.: Tr. Tr. (LSBL) B4 341.

Plate 36. Typological designation: hand ax, classic, chisel-ended; Primary form: ? flake or tabular spall; Material: trachyte; Length: 192 mm; B/L: 0.58; BA/BB: 0.96; BA/B: 0.73; T/B: 0.37; Sc.: 31; Scar bifac.: 0.7; Site: DE/89 B; Field Cat. no.: Tr. Tr. B4 (LSBL) 431.

Plate 37. Typological designation: cleaver; Primary form: side-struck flake; Material: trachyandesite; Length: 215 mm; B/L: 0.51; BA/BB: 0.78; BA/B: 0.69; T/B: 0.46; Sc.: 27; Scar bifac.: 0.7; Site: DE/89 B; Field Cat. no.: Tr. Tr. B4 (LSBL) 438.

Plate 38. Typological designation: cleaver, parallel; Primary form: indet.; Material: trachyte; Length: 210 mm; B/L: 0.62; BA/BB: 1.32; BA/B: 0.95; T/B: 0.40; Sc.: --; Scar bifac.: --; Site: DE/89 B; Field Cat. no.: MS 3111.

Plate 39. Typological designation: hand ax, subclassic/pick-like; Primary form: side-struck flake; Material: basalt; Length: 191 mm; B/L: 0.48; BA/BB: 0.42; BA/B: 0.40; T/B: 0.51; Sc.: 16; Scar bifac.: 0.5; Site: H/6; Field Cat. no.: MS 4166.

Plate 40. Typological designation: hand ax, subclassic, chisel-ended; Primary form: side-struck flake; Material: basalt; Length: 234 mm; B/L: 0.47; BA/BB: 0.51; BA/B: 0.44; T/B: 0.51; Sc.: 7; Scar bifac.: 0.2; Site: H/6; Field Cat. no.: MS 4188.

Plate 41. Typological designation: picklike hand ax; Primary form: corner-struck flake; Material: ? trachyandesite; Length: 196 mm; B/L: 0.56; BA/BB: 0.48; BA/B: 0.44; T/B: 0.66; Sc.: 20; Scar bifac.: 0.8; Site: H/6; Field Cat. no.: MS 4189.

Plate 42. Typological designation: hand ax, classic, chisel-ended; Primary form: indet.; Material: trachyandesite (1P); Length: 146 mm; B/L: 0.49; BA/BB: 0.56; BA/B: 0.47; T/B: 0.63; Sc.: 33; Scar bifac.: 0.8; Site: Mid; Field Cat. no.: LA 1.

Plate 43. Typological designation: hand ax, classic; Primary form: indet.; Material: trachyte; Length: 195 mm; B/L: 0.46; BA/BB: 0.68; BA/B: 0.54; T/B: 0.47; Sc.: 29; Scar bifac.: 0.7; Site: Mid; Field Cat. no.: 207.

Plate 44. Typological designation: cleaver, parallel, oblique; Primary form: side-struck flake; Material: trachyte; Length: 188 mm; B/L: 0.55; BA/BB: 0.98; BA/B: 0.87; T/B: 0.42; Sc.: 18; Scar bifac.: 0.5; Site: Mid; Field Cat. no.: 235.

Plate 45. Typological designation: cleaver, parallel; Primary form: corner-struck flake; Material: trachyte; Length: 165 mm; B/L: 0.59; BA/BB: 1.25; BA/B: 0.88; T/B: 0.37; Sc.: 14; Scar bifac.: 0.2; Site: H/9A; Field Cat. no.: MS 1556.

Plate 46. Typological designation: hand ax, classic, double-ended; Primary form: indet.; Material: trachyte; Length: 252 mm; B/L: 0.48; BA/BB: 0.85; BA/B: 0.67; T/B: 0.36; Sc.: 29; Scar bifac.: 0.8; Site: H/9 A; Field Cat. no.: MS 1286.

Plate 47. Typological designation: hand ax, classic; Primary form: indet.; Material: basalt; Length: 201 mm; B/L: 0.59; BA/BB: 0.90; BA/B: 0.75; T/B: 0.47; Sc.: 25; Scar bifac.: 0.8; Site: H/9 A; Field Cat. no.: MS 1586.

Plate 48. Typological designation: cleaver, parallel/convergent, barrel-shaped; Primary form: side-struck flake; Material: ? trachyandesite; Length: 197 mm; B/L: 0.56; BA/BB: 0.92; BA/B: 0.51; T/B: 0.43; Sc.: indet.; Scar bifac.: --; Site: H/9 A; Field Cat. no.: MS 2510.

Plate 49. Typological designation: hand ax, classical, chisel-ended; Primary form: cobble segment, or abraded slab; Material: trachyte; Length: 160 mm; B/L: 0.69; BA/BB: 0.72; BA/B: 0.64; T/B: 0.30; Sc.: 26; Scar bifac.: 0.6; Site: H/9 A; Field Cat. no: MS 1594.

Plate 50. Examples of elongate subfoliate biface forms from the surface scatter at LHS. Better examples of this form are known from Tr. Tr. M 10, and the Catwalk, but photographs are not available. Both of lava.

Plate 51. Typological designation: hand ax, classic, double-ended or limande; Primary form: ? corner-struck flake; Material: trachyte; Length: 254 mm; B/L: 0.48; BA/BB: 1.06; BA/B: 0.75; T/B: 0.31; Sc.: 41; Scar bifac.: 1.0; Field Cat. no.: MS 581.

Plate 52. Typological designation: hand ax, subclassic, chisel-ended; Primary form: ? corner-struck flake; Material: trachyte; Length: 246 mm; B/L: 0.45; BA/BB: 0.67; BA/B: 0.59; T/B: 0.57; Sc.: 14; Scar bifac.: 0.7; Site: H/9 AM; Field Cat. no.: MS 715.

Plate 53. Typological designation: hand ax, classic; Primary form: indet.; Material: trachyandesite (1P); Length: 182 mm; B/L: 0.48; BA/BB: 0.56; BA/B: 0.49; T/B: 0.53; Sc.: 32; Scar bifac.: 0.8; Site: Meng I, ext. 1; Field Cat. no.: 250.

Plate 54. Typological designation: hand ax, subclassic, chisel-ended; Primary form: indet. with cortical surface; Material: ? trachyandesite; Length: 146 mm; B/L: 0.55; BA/BB: 0.63; BA/B: 0.60; T/B: 0.60; Sc.: 21; Scar bifac.: 0.5; Site: Meng II; Field Cat. no.: 256.

Plate 55. Typological designation: hand ax, classic; Primary form: indet.; Material: trachyte; Length: 156 mm; B/L: 0.52; BA/BB: 0.55; BA/B: 0.52; T/B: 0.51; Sc.: 27; Scar bifac.: 0.8; Site: Meng I; Field Cat. no.: 271.

Plate 56. Typological designation: hand ax, subclassic, untrimmed butt; Primary form: indet. with cortical surface; Material: trachyandesite; Length: 138 mm; B/L: 0.61; BA/BB: 0.60; BA/B: 0.51; T/B: 0.54; Sc.: 27; Scar bifac.: 0.9; Site: Meng II; Field Cat. no.: 288.

Plate 57. Typological designation: cleaver, parallel; Primary form: flake; Material: trachyte; Length: 249 mm; B/L: 0.54; BA/BB: 1.10; BA/B: 0.93; T/B: 0.36; Sc.: 57; Scar bifac.: 0.5; Site: Tr. Tr. E surface; Field Cat. no.: LA 109.

Plate 58. Typological designation: cleaver, convergent/parallel, barrel-shaped; Primary form: indet., ? end flake with cortex on dorsal face; Material: fine-grained lava; Length: 154 mm; B/L: 0.68; BA/BB: 0.99; BA/B: 0.83; T/B: 0.34; Sc.: 29; Scar bifac.: 0.3; Site: Tr. Tr. 140-150 floor; Field Cat. no.: 135.

Plate 59. Typological designation: hand ax, classic, double-ended; Primary form: indet.; Material: fine-grained lava; Length: 204 mm; B/L: 0.47; BA/BB: 0.87; BA/B: 0.64; T/B: 0.36; Sc.: 40; Scar bifac.: 1.0; Site: Tr. Tr. 140-150 floor; Field Cat. no.: 385.

Plate 60. Typological designation: cleaver, divergent/parallel (? unifacial); Primary form: side-struck flake; Material: fine-grained lava; Length: 169 mm; B/L: 0.60; BA/BB: 1.15; BA/B: 0.98; T/B: 0.50; Sc.: 12*; Scar bifac.: 0.0*; Site: Tr. Tr.; Field Cat. no.: 426.

*Some of the apparent platform facets may be secondary platform reduction scars.